Documents of Modern Art. *Director: Robert Motherwell: Volume 12*

Contemporary Sculpture

An Evolution in Volume and Space

A Revised and Enlarged Edition

Carola Giedion-Welcker

Selective Bibliography by Bernard Karpel: Modern Art and Sculpture

George Wittenborn, Inc., New York 21, N.Y.

Acknowledgement:

The publisher takes this opportunity to thank a host of friends, both American and foreign, who have made it possible to realize this greatly enlarged and revised edition of *Modern Plastic Art,* which was published originally in Switzerland by H. Girsberger in 1937.

This is the third revised edition and the second enlarged edition (1955) of the twelfth volume in the series, "The Documents of Modern Art."

The text of the book is set in Garamond # 3 Light. The paper for the text and illustrations is Cameo dull coated 80 lb. Layout and format, including cover and jacket design, by Chermayeff & Geismar Associates. Typesetting by Haber Typographers, Offset by Connecticut Printers, Inc., Hartford, Connecticut. Binding by J. F. Tapley Co., Long Island City, New York.

Contents

In this third, revised edition of CONTEMPORARY SCULPTURE a number of works by younger artists have been added. Some of them are supplementary in character and others are by artists not represented in earlier editions. In the field of metal sculpture, the followers of Gonzalez and Pevsner, in stone, those of Brancusi, seem to me especially worthy of mention.

A new section, entitled "Totems and Stelae", deals with the contemporary form of the monumental, since this approach to sculpture is so frequently encountered to-day. In our age, the animistic concept of the "Totem" as an ancestral fusion of the animal and the human has slipped from its original form into the involvement of man with the machine, often with a satirical undertone. On the other hand the cult of legendary memorial "Stelae" is not primarily based on current trends, but rises out of the depths of primeval emotion projected into the present.

I should especially like to thank Georgine Oeri and Loly Rosset for their assistance in revising this book, Joyce Wittenborn for her translation of new material, as well as the various European and American museums and private collectors for their generous co-operation.

Zurich, 1960   *C. Giedion-Welcker*

I should like to take this opportunity of expressing my thanks to many of the sculptors and their relatives for their help in the biographical part of my work. The difference in the length of the biographical notes sometimes only reflects the amount of data available.

My gratitude for important help with documentary and photographic material is also due to the collectors, the directors and staffs of American and European galleries: Mr. Bernard Karpel, Museum of Modern Art, New York, Mr. James Johnson Sweeney, the Solomon Guggenheim Museum, New York, Mr. Marcel Duchamp, Yale University Art Gallery, Mme. Gabrielle Vienne, Musée d'Art Moderne, Paris, Mme. Roberta Gonzalez, Paris, Mme. Henri, Paris, Mme. Marthe Bois, Paris, Mr. André Bloc, Paris, Mr. Mario Brunetti, Galleria d'Arte Moderna, Venice, Dr. Palma Bucarelli, Galleria d'Arte Moderna, Rome, Mr. Francesco Rosso, Milan, Prof. Gino Ghiringhelli, Galleria del Milione, Milan, Dr. Georg Schmidt, Kunstmuseum Basel, Dr. R. Th. Stoll, Kunsthalle Basel, Dr. H. Keller, Kunstmuseum Winterthur, Dr. R. Wehrli, Kunsthaus Zurich, Mr. Arnold Ruedlinger, Kunsthalle Berne, the Curt Valentin and Willard Galleries, New York, the Galleries Jeanne Bucher, Louise Leiris, Louis Carré, René Drouin, Maeght and Denise René, Paris, the Tate Gallery, London.

My special thanks are due to the original translator of the text, Mrs. Mary Hottinger-Mackie, to Dr. Sonja Marjasch, who translated the biographical notes, to Mr. Hans Bolliger and to Mr. Bernard Karpel, whose accurate, illustrated bibliography has enlarged the scope of the book.

Zurich, 1954   *C. Giedion-Welcker*

Plastic art is visible and tangible. It is derived from the formation of actual bodies.

In periods of great religious activity this art was the vehicle of various cults that enshrined the memory of the departed or symbolized the conception of immortality. Plastic art, therefore, became an essential part of human culture almost from the outset. From the remotest times symbols, which were in no sense attempts at any portrayal, were employed as intermediaries for man's relations with the gods, the stars, the seasons, life and death. Their impersonal and spiritual function was part and parcel of a far wider complex of nature, religion and cult, the tribe or state, and its monuments. The emergence of individual at the expense of communal achievement, which began with the Renaissance, developed towards the end of the Nineteenth Century into a complete estrangement between art and life; for, once the former was debarred from its objective function, an artificial barrier was interposed. Simultaneously with this intellectual isolation, art became increasingly adulterated with elements that were alien to it, such as literature and psychology. The result of that infiltration is clearly evinced in late Nineteenth-Century memorials. These not only reflect a lack of contact with nature, religion and contemporary society, but actually embody historic reminiscences, literary associations, etc., which denote a fundamental negation of the basic principles of plastic art.

In order to understand the aesthetic goal of the Twentieth Century we must examine not only the reactions of our own age to these aberrations, but also its attempts to recreate a new plastic world for itself.

Concentration on legitimate means of plastic expression will not lead to an "art for art's sake" introversion so long as plastic art remains an intrinsic part of a much wider cosmic unity. In point of fact the very reverse of what happened at the end of the previous century is now taking place: there is a reintegration into the comprehensiveness of daily life, accompanied by the awakening of a new sincerity in means of expression which ruthlessly eliminates all that is extraneous or incidental.

Our life is divided between town and country, the technical and the natural worlds, and it is from our transitions between them that variety ensues. What is physical in us inevitably lives in a world of physical forms. From our impact with the reality of a tree growing in a wood, or the equal reality of a traffic-signal in the street, down to our daily associations with cups and saucers, apples and eggs, a continuous chain of impressions results which is obviously capable of influencing plastic design.

The problems of statics and dynamics, as of the disintegration of mass and the space-time interrelation of volumes, are bound to become a new plastic medium once their divorce from literary and psychological suggestion allows a return to first principles. What the artists who are preoccupied with these problems have to say can no longer be embodied in interesting or heroic motifs, but must rely exclusively on force of expression or the kind of symbols they choose. That these images are so simple is a direct reflection of our new attitude toward life. In contrast to that of the preceding age our own signifies the subordination of the individual, and his reacclimatization to nature and experience. This change is simply part of the psychological and social evolution of our age, and is in no sense due to esoteric little artistic *coteries*.

The examination of various recent movements in art which follows has been undertaken, not as an attempt to establish some sort of definitive classification, but solely in order to prove that, in spite of wide divergencies of idiom they have a common aim and a common basic language.

In the representation of the human body, whether clothed or naked, which has been the artist's principal medium ever since antiquity, the beginning of a fundamental change in outlook can be observed towards the opening of the present century.

With Maillol human figures begin to emanate a detached objectivity. His affinities with the antique are of secondary importance because we feel that the only significance of his robust limbs lies in the impersonality of their proportions, which transforms them into half-abstract elements of a new and more balanced sculptural vision. It is the discipline of his firmly handled neutral masses which alone matters to us. Maillol broke completely with the pretty-pretty ideals of a type of beauty that depends on detail, he substituted ponderous lumps of drastically simplified anatomical architecture. His Hellenism is peasant-archaic, not Olympian.

Maillol's contribution was to redress the balance of Rodin's superb one-sidedness. As we look back on Rodin to-day he seems to have been most significant as a precursor precisely where he was least affected by literary or psychological influences, as in those statues in which the human body is no longer primarily an instrument of our passions and emotions, but rather a medium for the expression of proportion and movement animated by light and informed by space. It is true Rodin once wrote: *"Le corps est un moulage où s'impriment les passions"*, but also that he said: *"Le pivot de l'art c'est l'équilibre : C'est-à-dire les oppositions des volumes, qui produisent le mouvement."*

By means of *"un rayonnement de formes"* Rodin dissolved the hard outline of contemporary Neo-Greek academicism, and thereby created a vital synthesis of opacity and transparency, volume and void.

As a wielder of volumes Maillol was static in the classic sense. The new plastic simplicity he achieved presents a marked contrast to the surface complexities of Rodin's liberation or sublimation of form. In the work of Daumier, Degas, and the later Rodin we see Impressionism unconsciously modernizing the baroque tradition through its emphasis on light and movement. The important point is that modern plastic art derives its technique from both baroque and classic sources. With Matisse we find a further development of the chiaroscuro rhythms of Impressionism, and a new feeling for freedom of proportion. The Futurist Umberto Boccioni proclaimed his adherence to Impressionism in his earlier manifestoes and proceeded to expand its theories.

To-day the baroque influence, transmitted through Daumier, Degas and Rodin to Matisse and Boccioni, may be said to have fused with the classic influence handed on by Maillol. Merged in turn with the forces of modern life, they have evoked a new optical vision. That vision can be expressed either by means of a deliberate simplification of volumes or in terms of the disintegration of mass through light. Behind each method there is the same belief in an elementary objectivity transcending purely human values.

The historic achievement of Cubism was the transformation of sentimental into abstract images. Picasso's (1909) and Modigliani's (1911-13) heads; Laurens' (1915), Lipchitz's (1915-19) and Juan Gris' (1917) compositions; the rhythmic discipline of Archipenko's (1909-20) voids and volumes; and the geometric construction of anatomy, which is characteristic of the work of Schlemmer (1918-21), show what revolutionary changes have been accomplished in spite of the retention of the human body as theme.

To Cubism we owe the introduction of "the object" and its optical analysis in terms of weight, density and volume. Fernand Léger, who was one of its pioneers, says: *"C'est le Cubisme qui a imposé l'objet au monde. La grande formule, c'est l'objet"* — that is to say, the complete elimination of any specifically human content. A human content remains, it is true, but is now sublimated and no longer in any sense recognizably naturalistic, since the theme has become a purely objective vehicle. When a Cubist painter like Juan Gris says: *"Du cylindre je fais une bouteille"* a change of approach is implied approximating to the architectonic standpoint. Out of the *"volume statique"* Cubism had in turn evolved the *"volume cinétique"*, which means the simultaneous coincidence of various spatial qualities.

Raymond Duchamp-Villon's *Horse* which is purely an embodiment of movement, presents an outstanding example of *"volume cinétique."*

"La spéculation pure voit les volumes prendre une vie spéciale et leur fait perdre toute consistance, d'ou le peu d'importance donnée — au début de la conception — à la matière qui sera choisie. On pourrait presque dire que le statuaire fait descendre peu à peu une création immatérielle jusqu' a la cristallisation dans la matière..." (1914.)

Laurens' early "constructions" show a much freer choice of material — corrugated cardboard, tin-plate, etc. — which is intended to assimilate everyday things to art and *vice versa*.

Futurism took much the same course in striving to dethrone art from its exalted pedestal, though as a *"concezione basate sulla sensazione dell' oggetto, e non sull' oggetto stesso. La transfigurazione della realtà". (Umberto Boccioni.)* These *"oggetti"* — for instance Boccioni's own ones — stand *"fuori dalla logica comune"* thanks to their fantastic permutations of the factors of time and space. The analytical sharpness of the French Cubists is renounced, and instead we have a combination of human emotion and mechanical dynamicism — for the artistic side of the latter needs to be postulated in a machine age such as ours. Exterior and interior, subject and object, become fused into what Boccioni calls a *"dinamismo umano"*.

The close affinity between this emotional dynamicism of the Futurists and the "kineticism" latent in the Cubists is clear enough; the only difference being that in Futurism, as in Surrealism, a psychological factor intervenes. Hence the emphasis which Futurist manifestoes lay on Futurism's derivation from Impressionism — meaning what Impressionism had achieved in the way of disintegrating mass and suggesting movement through the play of light.

Dadaism created a metaphysic of banality by discovering the plastic vitality that emanates from nameless or unnoticed things, and their unsuspected powers of self-expression. Its dethronement of the "masterpiece" as a snobbish value, like its anarchistic rejection of all outworn beauties or conventional forms, led art back to the humdrum, but none the less potentially significant, realities it had so long disdained. The first plastic applications of the Dadaist doctrines were produced by Marcel Duchamp and Man Ray in New York (1915-18)[1], Jean Arp and Max Ernst in Cologne (1918-19), Raoul Hausmann in Berlin (1919), and Kurt Schwitters ("Merz") in Hanover (1919). Besides being amusing squibs to *épater le bourgeois* they revealed a serious attempt to unveil humble plastic realities of our visible world that had remained ignored. The cardinal plastic principle seems far more evident in them than in what are called "choice" works of art. Like Picasso, Braque and Miro's original *collages,* the Dadaist examples just mentioned were primarily dependent on individual resourcefulness: "Material has no sentimental importance; invention is everything[2]". And just as the first *collages* had been a protest against the decadent refinement of pictorial sensuality, so these heralded a revolt against the cult of materialism in marble.

Surrealism dissolves the wall between our inner and outer life. It permeates dreams with reality and reality with dreams, confronting or fusing the psychical and the physical, the conscious and the subconscious, the individual and the community.

"Je crois à la résolution future de ces deux états, en apparence si contradictoires, que sont : le rêve et la réalité en une sorte de réalité absolue, de surréalité, si l'on peut ainsi dire." (André Breton, *Manifeste Surréaliste, 1925.*)

There is a continuously active process of metamorphosis in Surrealism which corresponds to the kinetic and dynamic qualities in Cubism and Futurism. All biological and psychical frontiers are blurred: men and beasts, animate and inanimate objects, converge and coalesce to proclaim the sovereign domination of transience.

"...des êtres-objets (ou objets-êtres?) caractérisés par le fait qu'ils sont en proie à une transformation continuent et expriment la perpétuité de la lutte entre les puissances agrégeantes, qui se disputent la véritable réalité

[1] Marcel Duchamp's topsy-turvy china water closet, exhibited in New York in 1917, and Max Ernst's madonna built up from a series of hat dummies, shown in Cologne in 1919, were still more startling anti-aesthetic and anti-conventional manifestations. (See also "The Dada Painters and Poets", New York, 1951.) They offer a parallel to Charlie Chaplain's systematic "debunking" of the hero in the films.

[2] *La Peinture au Défi* by Louis Aragon.

et la vie..." (André Breton, *Objets Surréalistes, Exposition Galerie Ratton, 1936.*) A positively magical aura emanates from the simple volumes Alberto Giacometti calls *"objets mobiles et muets"* : stones that merge into architectural forms, prisms into heads, organic into geometric shapes.

"Toutes choses...près, loin toutes celles qui sont passées et les autres par devant, qui bougent et mes amies, elles changent (on passe tout près, elles sont loin), d'autres approchent, montent, descendent...des canards sur l'eau, là et là, dans l'espace, montent, descendent...mais tout est passé..." (1932.)

The danger of literary associations to which Surrealism is often exposed seems unimportant in comparison with its vitalizing rehabilitation of forgotten things, its exaltation of what is banal into what is extraordinary, and its tenacious insistence on the unity of life and art. The Surrealists turn commonplaces into paradoxes to show us what the German Romantics called "the rare blue flower" growing, not at the back of beyond, but at our own doorsteps.

Jean Arp has exercised a stimulating influence on the evolution of modern plastic art. Though he has no direct affinity with the Surrealists he has certain points in common with them.

The originality of his work lies in its uncompromising elementalism. This leads him to prefer essential organic forms, identical beneath their mutations, which he uses as symbols of preexisting archetypes. He finds that common elemental prototype, either overt or concealed, ever-present in nature and the works of man. All Arp's work mirrors a state of cosmic flux. Movement is conveyed by the suggestion of growth into shape, or by the rhythms of ebb and flow. There is no attempt at mental or visual fixation; indefinite primordial shapes arise, serenely detached and self-sufficient, which yet somehow convince us that they belong to the natural world. We should be less surprised to encounter these supernaturally billowing forms in some quiet region of the earth than in a crowded art gallery, for they seem to have received their lineaments from the slow grinding of millenary glaciers rather than the pliant hand of man. Arp's apparently straightforward touch conceals an incessant industry and an alert responsiveness to proportion. With him, too, the feeling for nature, being direct instead of sentimental or intellectual, has ceased to be a conscious factor.

"When Dada revealed his deepest truths to man he laughed indulgently, and went on babbling. Now in art, too, men love what is vain or dead. They cannot understand that painting is anything more than a landscape with a dressing of vinegar and oil, or that sculpture can assume any other form than the faking of a woman's thighs in bronze or mable. All vital transformations in art seem to them just as detestable as life's own eternal transformations. Art is a fruit which is born of man himself; as a fruit grows on a tree or an embryo in its mother's womb. But whereas all fruits have forms intrinsically their own—forms which never resemble toy balloons or French Presidents in evening dress—the human fruit we call "Art" nearly always embodies a ridiculous resemblance to something else. It is reason that has inflated man's pride with the fond belief that he is lord over nature and an infallible criterion in himself; reason that has encompassed his divorce from nature; reason that has turned him into an at once hideous and tragic figure. I love nature, but not its substitutes. Illusory art is simply a bad substitute for nature." (From Jean Arp's Diary, 1931.)

It was thanks to Constantin Brancusi that modern plastic art was first able to explore entirely new ground. Brancusi's compact, exquisitely molded volumes were the earliest and purest expression of a still wider range of vision.

This Rumanian sculptor remained aloof from contemporary tendencies, yet touched the very core of the problem that was engaging all of them. As early as 1908 (that is to say even before the emergence of the first Cubist sculpture) he had begun to envisage a plastic revival from a wholly original standpoint.

With Brancusi the egg continually recurs in some guise or other as the symbol of all life[3], and the virtual key-form of a primeval monopsychic world. In his quest for absolute proportions he whittles away every detail until he has evolved a finite simplicity; or as he puts it:

"La simplicité n'est pas un but dans l'art, mais on arrive à la simplicité, malgré soi, en s'approchant du sens réel des choses."

After years of patient experiment he will evoke some unprecedented significance out of wood, marble or metal. Brancusi does every bit of his work himself and disdains preliminary models. He likes to keep his material under constant observation so as to study its "inner life" and be able to make rapid changes in his treatment of it. For him there is therefore no longer any dividing line between craftsmanship and creation.

"La taille directe, c'est le vrai chemin vers la sculpture, mais aussi le plus mauvais pour ceux qui ne savent pas marcher."

Every fibre, every vein, each fresh shade of polish is welded into an integral part of his composition. Under his hands inchoate material is developed out of itself and made to ring true to its own intrinsic nature; its dumbness becomes articulate, its urge for self-expression fights through stratum after stratum till it stands revealed.

To the achievement of this complete amalgam of mind and growth, material and spirit, geometrical and organic forms, Brancusi brings a peculiar gift for the humor latent in certain forms, much as Joyce discovers it in the sound of certain words. If he starts from the incoherence of the subconscious, it is because this alone offers him a way of coming to grips with the deeper meaning of life.

The years of almost monomaniac labor he will expend on a single work are inspired by the determination to restore the sovereign clarity of simplicity wherever meaningless complexity has been suffered to intervene, and to impart a new honesty to the idiom of sculpture by purifying it of all asso-

---

[3] The primordial egg is a mythical symbol among many peoples. "It embodies a sense of repose and an almost fluid balance," c. f. Greek myths, the Finnish Kalevala, American Indian legends, etc.

ciative corruptions. As he himself says, simplicity is only the means to an end, and that end is perfection. Brancusi lives in a world of forms as simply and intimately as St. Francis of Assisi dwelt among the birds.

Henry Moore and Barbara Hepworth have also succeeded in imparting plastic intensity to simple organic volumes.

The intersection of purely organic forms by sharp geometrical planes, which can sometimes be detected in Arp's and Giacometti's work as well, implies the introduction of a new element that is semi-architectural and, one might almost say, intentionally civilizing.

Both Neoplasticism and Constructivism have contributed to a clearer line of demarcation by a systematic separation between what is, and what is not, of fundamental importance to expression; though from a rather different angle. Both adopted an almost geometric morphology, the object of which was to dematerialize and volatize volume by the creation of light-conditioned spatial values.

The Dutch painter Piet Mondrian was one of the founders of an active group of artists known as "De Stijl" (1917-31), the leader of which was the architect Theo van Doesburg, who died in 1931. Mondrian summed up the ideology of this group rather later on as follows:

"Dans l'art nouveau les formes sont neutres. Elles le sont à mesure qu'elles s'approchent de l'état universel. L'effort de l'art nouveau supprime le sujet et la forme particulière ... La vie est une transformation continuelle et la nouvelle culture est celle des rapports purs ..." (Piet Mondrian, *L'Art Nouveau et la Vie Nouvelle,* 1931.)

The Belgian George Vantongerloo used solid rectangles to contrast their formal opposition and bring out their relation to one another in terms of space. The decisive factor in his evolution is the increasingly important role he began to give to spatial tension between elements grouped together as a composition.

"Nous avons besoin de l'espace pour situer les choses. L'espace, dont nous ne pouvons nous passer, sans toutefois le définir, est inséparable de la vie."—a phrase which aptly defines the interactions between space and volume. Space, in fact, becomes the imponderable element in all calculable factors. There is a close parallel between Neoplasticism and the New Architecture. This is no mere coincidence since it was in Holland that both first took root. In the Neoplastic theories the essential interdependence of architecture, painting and sculpture, and the basic identity of art and science, was always stressed. Thus a way was opened for establishing a fresh contact between life and art, and indeed every sphere of modern thought and activity. The outstanding importance of the pioneer work accomplished by the Bauhaus in Weimar and Dessau (1919-28) under Walter Gropius must be mentioned in this connection.

Suprematism has been an isolated though none the less stimulating influence. It aimed at the total elimination of the object by the substitution of a sign language of absolute forms and formal relations as the proper medium for the expression of our emotions. Though Kasimir Malevich's

"Dynamic Architecture" does not deal in any sense with actual buildings, it is surprising to what extent it assimilates architectonic to plastic values. The link between Suprematism and the New Architecture is consequently self-evident. Malevich has defined his perception of reality as follows:

"When sitting or lying our sensations are essentially plastic. These sensations have called into being the things we require for sitting, lying, etc. and govern their shapes. Chairs, beds, and tables are embodiments of purely plastic sensibilities[4]."

Constructivism likewise seeks to make art an integral part of the stuff of life by utilizing it to solve the problems of the modern world. Though it adopts the dynamic principles of Cubism and Futurism, it translates them into mechanistic terms. The Constructivist Movement started in 1920 in Moscow and appeared a little later in Berlin. All Constructivist exhibitions and manifestoes proclaim the sovereign virtue of *movement.* Constructivism goes further than any of the various tendencies that had preceeded it in its insistence on the sublimation of mass into "virtual volumes." This implies the optical disintegration of material solidity by light so as to enable movement to become a plastic element.

"Since space and time constitute the basis of life, art must realize human experience in terms of space and time." (N. Gabo and A. Pevsner, *Realist Manifesto,* Moscow, 1920.)

"We must substitute the dynamic principle of the universality of life for the static principle of classic art." (L. Moholy-Nagy and A. Kémèny in *Sturm,* published in Berlin, 1922[5].)

What is new and important in the work of the Constructivists is their whole-hearted acceptance of technique. Physics and mechanics provide the stimulus for their imagination. Since they regard the *Zeitgeist*—that is to say manifestations of our modern civilization like standardization, collective organization, etc.—as the decisive factor of our generation, it follows that their work is permeated by what might be called a specifically industrial content. It is for this reason that they usually confine their choice of materials to glass, aluminum, nickel, celluloid, casein, etc. The work of Tatlin, Rodchenko, Moholy-Nagy, Pevsner and Gabo—to mention only leading names—demonstrates how fantasy can be evoked from a deliberate use of the rationalizing elements of contemporary existence. It must not be imagined that the difference between their work and straight-forward engineering is the substitution of mechanically aesthetic for mechanistically functional motifs. This important difference can best be explained by reference to the Constructivists' belief that there is a general intellectual principle implicit in the use of a given material or technical process.

The clarification brought about by the logical design and structural discipline of the various abstract tendencies that have just been mentioned has helped to bring them into close touch with analogous objectives in the

[4] *Die gegenstandslose Welt,* Bauhausbücher, Langen-Verlag, München, 1927, and Chicago, 1960.
[5] See also L. Moholy-Nagy, *Von Material zu Architektur* (1929), *The New Vision and Abstract of an Artist,* re-print ed. 1955. George Wittenborn, Inc., New York.

New Architecture, and even rather dissimilar trends in other branches of plastic art.

Picasso's *Composition in Wire* and his *Project for a Monument,* 1928, offer us examples of a peculiar, and altogether original, crasis of geometric and organic expression.

"Un personnage, un objet, un cercle, sont des figures, elles agissent sur nous, plus ou moins intensément. Les unes sont plus près de nos sensations, produisent des émotions, qui touchent à nos facultés affectives, d'autres s'adressent plus particulièrement à l'intellect. Il faut les accepter toutes, car mon esprit a autant besoin d'émotion que mes sens." (P. Picasso, *Cahiers d'Art,* 1936.)

Julio Gonzalez and Max Bill—to name only two—follow much the same course, which may be summed up as a plastic fusion of apparently heterogeneous elements.

In this connection mention should be made of Alexander Calder's *"Mobiles"* —swaying or rotating bodies whose spatial ambiance is defined by wires— which are the fruit of an almost astronomical imagination.

Kurt Schwitters has developed his earlier manner into a much more lucid presentation in which Dadaist fantasy and mathematical precision are strangely combined[6]. The forms he now evokes from wood, plaster and stone demonstrate an elemental plastic principle achieved with very simple means that are quite free from incidental adjuncts.

"Plastic art," he wrote in 1933, "means the relation of form to form, surface to surface, line to line, regarded in a non-accumulative sense. It unites all of these by means of their continuous intersection."

If we probe deeper into the many different tendencies during the last thirty years, every one of them reveals the same constantly recurring phenomenon: a pronounced reaction from the sensual-sentimental individualist angle towards a wider and more objective human outlook, combined with a vigorous revolt against the use of art as an overflow-reservoir for our private emotions.

In direct contradiction to the pathos, heroics, or "inspiration of genius" of Art with a capital A, the first prerequisite for this kind of plastic exteriorization is an unbiased concentration on the most elementary aspects of expression. By delicately sacrificing what in the last analysis is only incidental, it becomes possible for the artist to confine himself to a very few, but all the more direct, means of expression which may be defined as the shaping of volumes perceived in terms of space.

The close accord between these deliberate abnegations and those of the New Architecture should bring about a final liberation from the specious ornamentalism or theatricality which has hitherto atrophied the vitality of plastic art. Once we discard imitation and illusion, and with them all literary encumbrances, a self-sufficient plastic reality is free to emerge, which is

[6] Thus he has transformed his house in Hanover into a sort of shelter for plastic forms, which he describes as a little world of branching and building where the imagination is free to climb at will.

just as real as the reality of nature and human life, all necessarily different to both.

The new freedom and independence of conception, which results from this transmutation of static into dynamic values through the sort of formal shorthand that has supplanted wealth of description, goes hand in hand with complete subordination to the specific nature and utilization of the medium chosen. The human scale, the human angle, has ceased to be the universal norm. Hence there is no longer any finite or "consecrated" ideal of beauty; no emphasis on detail, no senseless flamboyance or display of good material. This universal adoption of an elementary formal idiom and commonplace motifs seems to be in conformity with a far-reaching intellectual process that has been closely identified with the general cultural revolution of our age.

The underlying solidarity among the various aspects of plastic art that have already been referred to clearly points to a consensus of convictions common to all of them. This prompts a leading question: Is there a direct analogy between what is happening in modern sculpture and recent developments in other spheres of culture? To ask it is forthwith to envisage the evolution of plastic art from a much wider angle than the purely aesthetic. The really important consideration here is that these other spheres have already effected an equally drastic purge of alien influences. The rehabilitation of everyday themes and their reassimilation into the broad stream of life, which spells the progressive eclipse of the overweening pretensions of individual inspiration, has permeated not only the arts, but philosophy and science as well.

In much the same way the practical organization of the interior in terms of spatial design is the dominant note of the New Architecture[7]. The comprehensive planning of a city supersedes representational pomp and chaotic juxtaposition; and its master-plan is the carefully calculated result of a detailed technical study of all the relevant biological, sociological and climatic conditions.

With modern poetry[8] the immediate stimulus to the creation of new forms has been a rediscovery, a reanimation of the primal visual images and oral values latent in simple words. Slang has been enlisted for the excellent

[7] The open planning of the New Architecture, the lightening of its volumes, and its emphasis on transparent, almost imponderable, surfaces finds an echo in certain prominent tendencies in modern plastic art.

[8] To say that Rimbaud's *"poésie pure ... verbe accessible à tous les sens"* has begotten a decadent verbal mannerism is an unjustified assumption. To use language primarily as a sensitive tonal medium does not mean playing with words for the mere fun of the thing, any more than an absence of plot means an absence of content. The pioneers of the modern literary movement, Baudelaire, Rimbaud and Mallarmé, continually reaffirmed the spiritual purpose of poetry. The explosive, yet associative dynamicism of Arp, Ball, Schwitters, Eluard, and Tzara's writing evokes a continuous sequence of mental vistas. In James Joyce's last publication, *Work in Progress,* the logical time sequence of characters and events, human and natural history, is deliberately discarded. Instead we are given a vivid reconstruction of his subject-matter into something that is at once wholly new, yet by force of association virtually familiar. His projection of images on to a universal plane of time-space presents a close parallel to the emphasis on "simultaneity" in the plastic arts.

XVIII

reason that it provides the most direct and vivid form of verbal impact on the reader. Psychological reflections, anecdotage, and the more personal point of view, are studiously avoided. The rule is stressed, the exception ignored. There is a renunciation of the old structural development, sentence by sentence, in favor of a dynamic association of ideas, accomplished by a successively penetrative effect rather than a consecutive use of words; while the stylistic balance between the latter echoes emotion rather than logic.

The equivalent process in painting is the abandonment of illusory perspective and the recognition of surface, color and light as the true components of a picture.

In music[9] it is the direct, primal relation of tone picture to tone picture without intermediate psychological garnishing. Igor Stravinsky has said that his composition is architectonic, not an anecdote, "an objective, not a subjectively descriptive structure." Here the deliberate introduction of modern dance music, extraneous noises, once more implies a return to the soundtrack of daily life.

In certain branches of philosophy, too, there has been a return to those essentials which Rudolph Carnap deals with in his *"Scheinprobleme in der Philosophie[10]."* A notable instance of the similarity between the revolutions in artistic and scientific methods at the beginning of the present century can be found in the work of the English philosopher Bertrand Russell. Some thirty years ago Russell succeeded in formulating a series of basic axioms, uncolored by metaphysical speculation, that are common to logic and certain branches of mathematics. A group of Viennese philosophers known as the *Wiener Kreis* has developed this side of Russell's philosophy into a "system of axioms", for which, in part anyhow, mathematical formulæ were adopted—still another example of symbolical expression. The standpoint of the modern philosopher is no longer that of the poet, for he has to keep a close watch on mathematics and physics. His work must be severely to the point, severely scientific.

There is an even closer affinity between contemporary physics and modern plastic art. The fundamental transformation undergone by the former has radically modified our conceptions of space, time and motion and has likewise superseded the old ideal of mass, since the ponderosity of mass is now considered a factor conditioned by speed.

This necessarily rather sketchy outline of the parallelism between the methods now being adopted in the various fields of cultural activity at least provides sufficient evidence of the vitality of each. The community of spirit between science and art, which even today is often considered a far-fetched

[9] Thus the basis of Hindemith's musical idiom is "anti-individualistic counterpoint". Vide H. Curjel's *Triumph der Alltäglichkeit* (Hesse-Verlag, Berlin, 1929), and C. F. Ramuz's *Souvenir sur Igor Stravinsky* (1932), as also Igor Stravinsky's *Chroniques de ma Vie* (Denoël et Steele, Paris, 1935).
[10] Vide Carnap's *Der logische Aufbau der Welt* (Weltkreis-Verlag, Berlin, 1928), Schlick's *Raum und Zeit in der gegenwärtigen Physik* (Berlin, 1918), and Hans Reichenbach's *Wahrscheinlichkeitslehre* (A. Sijthoff, Leiden, 1935).

notion, was regarded as a self-evident platitude right up to the age of the baroque.

The evolution of modern art is not yet complete. But this much can already be discerned with some confidence: it is not a form of aesthetic self-indulgence, disdainfully remote from daily life, but a vital creative force intimately associated with the general cultural development of our age. The broad universality of its impersonal form and content, its close relation to nature and all the manifold problems of contemporary existence, predestines this art to public recognition and general acceptance. It is, of course, true enough that this art can as yet only be seen in private collections and studios, or a few score houses and gardens; and that its *clientèle* still remains severely limited. Those who acquire and those who produce its works are equally devoid of influential connections. But to deny a civilizing role to this art on that score seems premature; for, though all creative artistic production is necessarily compounded of past and present elements, its more essential significance belongs wholly to the future. Outstanding historic examples prove that it often requires much longer than a single generation before the artistic reorientation achieved by the pioneers of a given period has had time to permeate the consciousness of the community.

The fundamental assimilation of our new vision to the realities of life has already been conclusively demonstrated, if only in an anonymous sense. It is no longer possible to remain blind to the direct formal affinity between the purely utilitarian mechanism of modern industry, transport and publicity[11], and those so-called utopian experiments in art which, in part at least, had anticipated them. The priority of one or the other in point of date is far less important than their reciprocal stimulus.

Finally, still another remarkable similarity remains to be considered: that between modern and primitive art, whether savage, archaic or prehistoric. This is not inspired by any romantic or modish hankering after the barbaric, or a nostalgia for what is strange and distant. There is an absence of literary influences in both, and a common predilection for a clear structural formation and simple plastic transmutations. It is perhaps not without significance that a century as conscious of the highly-developed and complex civilization it has evolved as our own should manifest such a warm sympathy for the unsophisticated emotions and forthright plastic creations of mythical times[12]. The morphological synthesis of these chronologically and culturally opposite poles has resulted in the perfection of sculptural forms (that highly specialized modern tools have revealed to us) which in the simplicity of their line recall the first dawn of plastic art[13].

Zurich, 1937.

[11] E.g. Traffic-signals, various types of modern transport, shop-window-dressing, advertisement lay-outs, etc.

[12] As long ago as 1910 Umberto Boccioni wrote *"Siamo i primitivi di una nuova sensibilità"*.

[13] A peep into Brancusi's studio, with its extraordinary collection of tools and instruments, reveals certain points of contact between even work of so timeless a quality as his and the field of modern inventions. Brancusi's preference for showing his sculpture on revolving turn-tables, and his claim that films are the only adequate means of illustrating it, provide pertinent cases in point.

The present edition of this book is a revised and expanded version of the original which was first published in 1937; the lines on which it was then written, however, have remained essentially the same, though the viewpoint is that of today.

It is true that the situation of sculpture has grown more varied and complex owing to the appearance of new works by sculptors previously considered and the rise of a younger generation. There has also been a change in the nature of public response to sculpture and to painting; it is no longer possible to dismiss the kind of sculpture that has for forty years gone by the name of "modern" as sporadic, utopian efforts. The European museums, following the admirable initiative of the United States, and more recently, South America, have opened their doors to it. The vitality and expressiveness arising from the different regional sources and spiritual attitudes have been brought before the public in various ways: first of all in great open-air exhibitions such as those at Battersea Park, 1951, and South Bank, 1952, in London, the Venice Biennale, 1950, 1952 and 1954; and those at Hamburg, Antwerp, Varese, 1953. In the second place, there have been sculptures incorporated into public buildings, as, for instance, by Jacques Lipchitz for the Ministry of Education (1944), Rio de Janeiro; by Henry Moore for the Time, Life and Fortune Building (1953), London; and by Isamu Noguchi for Lever House, New York. Also the sculptures for the University of Caracas by Arp, Laurens, Lobo, and Pevsner (1954), as well as Gabo's design for the "Bijenkorf Warenhuis", a department store at Rotterdam (1955), are to be mentioned. Finally, there has been the competition for the *Monument to the Unknown Political Prisoner,* 1953, which united sculptors of all countries in work on a common theme. There are few countries, in Europe or elsewhere, where the right of "modern" sculpture to exist is now challenged. We have also witnessed the passing of the "isms" and manifestoes in which sculptors of the various groups presented their most profound ideas and aspirations to the public. Then, too, there has been a general improvement in the position of sculpture within the visual arts; it is steadily growing in importance and esteem. There are even grounds for believing that an "Age of Sculpture" is on the way; we can see this in the growing demand for more pageantry and emotional expression in public life. From that demand sculpture will receive an immense impetus. It has always been closely identified with public life, and its very essence is monumentality. The growing interest in murals and mosaics, and public art in general, to give life both to the public buildings and the open spaces which embody the corporate life of the municipality, will also increase the importance of sculpture.

The fundamental aim of this survey is to comprehend that complex unity called "modern sculpture" in its common development and general reorientation. The grouping does not aim at the greatest possible completeness, but rather at the demonstration of underlying ideas which can already be traced in the art of our time.

Thus there is no separation into hostile camps of figurative and non-figurative art. What ultimately matters is the intensity and freedom of the creative imagination as expressed in both types.

The first general tendency to be observed is the detachment from all illusionism, hence from all imitation of nature, and the inclination towards elementary forms freely created and closely dependent on the inherent properties of the material used.

Almost equally important seems the penetration and sublimation of matter, the extreme dematerialization of the once static and compact mass. Whether this result is achieved by means of polish and proportion, by a reduction of mass and emphasis on linear structure, by the translucency of the material itself, or by means of planes opened up to space, there can be felt throughout a depreciation of the compact, static volume. This began when the Cubists first shattered volume into its structural components, when Archipenko created his first counterpoint of solid mass and air volumes, and when Lipchitz, early in the third decade of the century, reduced the compact mass to a flowing pattern of lines. Even among the youngest of the present-day sculptors this airy pattern of lines persists, either as a language of signs in the manner of Gonzalez whose point of departure is usually a definite subject, or as the abstract, linear web of relationships. A world of shapes, bathed in space and creating space, seems to be in full process of evolution. We often find everything that is worth saying confined solely within the precise, sharply defined course of lines, a tendency already evident in Lehmbruck's insistence on the importance of the contour.

A momentous stage has been reached, not only in contemporary art, but in our entire picture of the universe, where the static is being transformed into the dynamic, and matter into energy. It is within this general trend that the epoch-making change in the outlook of the artist and his language of form has taken place since the early years of this century. Whatever we consider, whether it is the early Cubists or Futurists splintering, opening and disciplining volume; whether it is Brancusi, Arp, and their followers turning back to the archetypal in form; or whether it is the sculptor enclosing space in an architectural or transparent framework, what is obviously going on is a new conquest of space by radiation of volume or enclosure of the void. A new and fundamental sense of space seems to be manifesting itself. Figures and objects are no longer placed in self-contained isolation; the sculptor's aim is to animate the space surrounding the form and emanating from the form. He uses every possible means of bringing space to life as an emotional stimulus. Man is no longer the measure of all things; his microcosm has been absorbed into a much vaster macrocosm. It is obvious that this new conception of space is far closer to the baroque philosophy of life and creative principles than to the classical. The tradition descends, by way of Daumier and Rodin, to the sculptors of today, a tradition that began at the moment when light and shade first attacked the sculptured mass, causing it to stream out into its wider environment.

Just as Brancusi erects his mystic *Colonne sans Fin* like endless steps of prayer into the universe, or establishes a grand relationship with Heaven
in the soaring vertical of his *Bird, "pour remplir la vôute du ciel"*, Pevsner's
Developable Column of Victory and Gabo's *Construction in Space* are related to and enter into a kind of fierce possession of the space around them. This dynamic process occurs under our very eyes, and involves the most minute details of such constructions. The result is a many-faceted whole in full process of evolution which the spectator does not comprehend by summing up the views from successive angles; it is the very openness or transparency that enables him to grasp the whole simultaneously from within and without. This method of telescoping and communicating a whole complex of form is characteristic of our time. It appears in painting in the superimposed aspects of the object, and in architecture in the inter-penetration of rooms effected by transparent materials and spatial methods of construction.

It was significant in the competition for the *Monument to the Unknown Political Prisoner,* with its wide range of sculptural expression, that space and the mastery of space was the central problem for nearly all competitors. This emerges clearly when we compare entries with very different approaches to the subject, such as those of Minguzzi and Pevsner, Butler, Gabo and Mirko.

The Group

Both the double form *(forme jumelle)* and the group, whether they appear as a subdivision or an interplay of form, in a loose constellation or taut composition, are relevant here. They appear in all techniques of plastic art, in carving, modelling or spatial constructions. The principle itself of grouping, is carried out in many ways. In Arp's language of nature, shoots seem to sprout from the parent form; in Lipchitz, the parts of the whole are densely interwoven; in Giacometti, the group is an anonymous relationship, a scattered passage of skeleton figures which incorporate a commonplace and yet mysterious constellation in time and space.

Pure tensions of proportion and balance appear in architectural groupings. In the early work of Vantongerloo, Doesburg and Malevich, there is an interplay of solid rectangular forms within a compact or loose unity
arranged in accordance with the laws of proportion. Vantongerloo, however, has now completely sublimated the mass. In his later work the only active element remaining is energy which is expressed in soaring lines of force, generally in transparent material.

Interpretation

The subject matter of today's sculpture is often challenged by an uneasy or hostile public; it is neither the narration of an event, nor the description of the "beautiful" physical forms which still populate the public parks in every country. The language of the living sculpture of today is symbolic, not narrative; it communicates universal aspects of spiritual or natural events, but not banalities decked out in human form. It is a formal language which the mythologist J. J. Bachofen defined in relation to the art of the past as "touching all chords of the human spirit at once, suggestive of emotional awareness where rational language is merely explanatory". Henri

François Stahly, one of the younger generation of sculptors, moves in the same direction of thought when he writes: "The restriction to a single point of view made way for works whose meaning was shifting and multiple. This groping, without knowledge, for a possible meaning is our myth." In its emphasis on the irrational, emotional springs of life, the art of today is attracted by primitive magic, by folklore and the archaic, though the formal kinship is a growth from within and not an eclectic adoption of external aspects.

Spatial Construction

The surrender to the free play of the creative imagination is widespread and decisive. Even the spatial constructions which use purely geometrical means of expression are not rational statements; they are of the imaginative nature of poetry and detached from all that is functional and calculable. "There is no more mathematics in my work than there is anatomy in a figure by Michelangelo" says Gabo when his work is misinterpreted as a mathematical demonstration; and Pevsner emphasizes "the poetry of space, which can be felt, but not measured". Thus even in this kind of sculpture, which seems purely objective, it is the creation and evocation of an emotional experience that counts; this is part of the artist's intention.

Expressive Volume

This perceivable irruption of emotion into form, which signed the death warrant of the academic canons, appeared with considerable violence in Rodin whose human figures are dramatically agitated by inner feeling. This same force of feeling found, in the Italy of his day, a more lyrical, more reserved and gentler expression in the work of Medardo Rosso. But wherever we turn, the emphasis on psychological processes stands in sharp contrast to the emotional aridity, sentimentality and petrified formulas of neoclassicism. Both Rodin, the romantic realist, and Bourdelle, who was inspired by classic idealism and whose return to the strict architectural discipline of sculpture placed him in direct opposition to his master Rodin, emphasized this new content of inner life and feeling. Bourdelle's attitude closely resembles that of the Symbolist poets of his time with whom he was closely associated. The same climate of ideal humanity is found in the work 28, 29 of his younger German contemporary, Wilhelm Lehmbruck, who derived from another tradition than the Mediterranean and strove to impart to his figures a certain Gothic aura of devout contemplation. Brancusi, too, who 34-37 started with the human figure, created in his early work an inner reality, not an external, formal beauty. He surpasses Modigliani in making the human head a symbol of profound recollection and a focus of intense radiation from within. The spiritual translucency of his *Sleeping Muse* is one 124-127 of the earliest and purest examples of the abandonment of external reality in favor of illuminating the depths of inner life through the simplest of forms.

The abandonment of the naturalistic model, of the purely visual experience, and of all anatomical conventions in the representation of the human figure cannot be interpreted merely as a weariness of rationalism. New, hidden worlds of inner experience have come to the surface, requiring a new language of symbols that point from the visible world in which we live to another world of invisible powers. Thus, in works whose original impulse was the human figure, we find startling abbreviations. There is an impressive revival of the torso and the fragment in Rodin, Brancusi, Lehmbruck, Maillol, Archipenko and Schlemmer, culminating in the magic gesture of the solitary *Hand* of Giacometti. A tendency to abbreviate, to abstract, is manifest also in the fabulous, totem-like vertical forms of Max Ernst and Miro, as the human figure has now a supra-personal communication to make which far transcends its existential form. Brancusi evolved steadily in the direction of the pure, organic, primeval form which becomes a profound symbol of man's union with all creaturely life. This form, in its proportions, material, and concentration alone, displays the miraculous power of nature, man's brotherhood with all creations of life, and his free surrender to the infinite. "One thing I have sought for all my life is the essence of flight", said Brancusi. His symbolic bird verticals with their burnished surfaces and

132, 140, 141

freely soaring, inspiring forms have left far behind the original figure of the bird which was once his point of departure. They became more and more the pure expression of deliberation. In imparting multiple, transcendental meaning to anonymous volumes, in creating pluralistic symbols Brancusi has given an absolutely new life to sculptural creation.

Giacometti, too, seeks to do justice to a more complex vision and a deeper sense of reality and the fundamental mystery of life. Like Klee, he does so by "totalizing the object". Giacometti's figures are materially evanescent, but all the more concrete as expressions of the multiple experience of the human form. These utterly dematerialized beings, spiritualized and bathed in space, spring from the emotional life of their creator. "It was not the outer existence of the world which marked my life, but only what I felt", he once confessed. Here again is an example of the artist's detachment from purely visual experience applied not only to the purely-objective, spatial

96, 105, 107

fantasies of the Constructivists but also to the treatment of the human figure. What Jeans said of science may also hold true of art, that "in our time matter has been spiritualized and the spiritual materialized".

Structure and Material

We can also recognize this close interpenetration of substance and form, of spirit and matter, in the sculptor's concentration on the inherent properties and structure of the materials used, in order to elicit the utmost expression from their own microcosm, whether it be the veins in the marble of Brancusi's *Fish,* the scorched, lava-like crusts of Roszak's *Fire Bird,* the erupting surfaces of Giacometti's and Richier's figures where the stratification of the surface is so extreme that we can no longer interpret it merely as an enveloping skin. In Pevsner's and Gabo's spatial constructions, the structure of the curved plane evolves out of the linear pattern like the leaf

107, 133, 176-193, 256, 259

out of the vibrant life of its veins.

The World of Things

It is not only figures that are infused with psychological meaning and subordinated to an idea; the same happens in the world of things. When the human figure was discredited through long imitation of classical models and their banal smoothness, a new interest in the anonymous *objet* arose. It was in their depersonalization and geometrical treatment of the human figure and in their invention of non-human motifs that the Cubists found their own version of the contemporary idiom. Confrontation, proportion and spatial relations were illustrated with common objects. The Futurists not only mechanized the human organism; they aggressively stressed its spatial dynamics. Boccioni's "striding muscles", like the Cubist Duchamp-Villon's "motorized horse", are important milestones along this road, while the rotating, Futurist *Bottle* avoids the human element as a medium of expression, and again makes use of any everyday object to reflect the new kinetic view of the world.

87
77
89

The transformation of apparently harmless and insignificant objects into highly charged stimuli of definite ideas and associations was first carried out with greater emphasis on the psychological factor by the Dadaists in 1916. The Pre-Dada "ready-mades" of Marcel Duchamp, 1914, and the succeeding "found objects" of the Dadaists and Surrealists, were reinterpreted and combined into a new world of fantasy, irony, and poetry. The object was removed from its rational connections and given a new and unprecedented meaning. The intellectual aggression which that implied sprang in part from a critical outlook on the world. In this spiritual process, a new language of form was also discovered which persisted through later periods. Thus, Picasso's *Bull,* 1943, a late work in this series, is translated into an esthetically startling form by the slightest of deviations from its functional use. By a recombination of parts of a common object, here the seat and handlebars of a bicycle, the artist fans into life a miraculous expressiveness which springs equally from formal and utilitarian roots. There is good reason why the succeeding sculptors of all camps repeatedly turned back to this work, in which a "nothing" had become art, and which was actually created by the eyes, rather than the hands, of the sculptor.

91
93

The return to the human figure, a trend evident not only in Giacometti, but also in Laurens, Lipchitz, Moore, Hepworth, and, to a lesser degree, in Arp and a number of other sculptors of the last twenty years, does not imply a return to the static representation of the human form, or to the classical idea of beauty based on man as the isolated and sole center of the world. This new image of man is made from a totally new angle, incorporating the sculptor's spiritual and formal experience. It is man closely bound up with the life of all created things, man as one small point in the huge web of time and space, or, as Klee put it, "a creature on one star among other stars". The human figures of Lipchitz, and to a certain extent, those of Laurens, return to the mythical foundations of human history. In Arp's work, man seems to exist in his archetypal and primeval form, in a recollection of beginnings. This feeling also pervades the figures of Henry Moore and Barbara Hepworth, with their cavities hollowed out, as it were, by the elemental forces of time and nature. But the synthesis and simultaneity of outer and inner form is again entirely contemporary.

Return to the Human Figure

144-150, 153, 155

This recollection of a mysterious participation of man with nature and the world of creatures is also expressed in sculptures which embody a demoniac menace to man's existence and have a certain kinship of form with the masks and totems of primitive cults. From this irrational sphere, the eternally active past of man makes its way into the present, and so into present-day art.

The conscious and merciless domination of the present by technology, on the other hand, has left its mark on the sculpture of the younger generation. The predicament of modern man finds its paradoxical counterpoint in the precision of the machine. The humorous fables which flowed from Gonzalez' hand in his mastery of traditional Catalan wrought-iron work are matched by the current and rising generation of sculptors with technical harshness and cruelty. This is the language and vision of a generation which has again been taught by recent events to turn a critical eye on the world.

195-201

213, 215, 253-257

If we look back and ask whether, in the last generation or two, determinant new directions may be discerned whilst still retaining the great basic tendencies—, we may note in particular a process of transformation which may be of great significance for the future: where a form, originally purely geometrical, begins to approximate an organic form. We can, for instance, note a great divergence from the former purely mathematical and technical means of expression when organic forms and associations — echoes of shells and insects unfolding — suddenly emerge from a mathematical method. Even a comparison between the titles of today and yesterday shows the difference; Pevsner introduces such names as *Construction in the Egg, Germ,* and *World,* as contrasted with his former titles: *Projection into Space,* and *Developable Surface.* If we think of Kandinsky's late work, which is interspersed with organic forms, we can detect the same process of transformation as in Gabo, Pevsner, Moholy or Calder. Even in architecture, this symbiosis of biological growth and technological construction seems to be making increasing headway. In the domain of technology the hard angular frame of the aeroplane is developing more and more into the great simplified lines of a gigantic bird.

180-183

175, 180-183, 189, 205, 227

While on the one hand the pure constructions of today show a bias toward flexible, living form, on the other, the organic form, already referred to, displays a tightened structure and often a tendency toward the technical.

197, 213, 253-256

In this all-around expansion, this complex interpenetration of different domains, of the primitive and the contemporary, of the psychological, biological and technological, we can discern the complex and far-flung nature of our world, which is simultaneously symbolized in the burning-glass of art. This art, which encloses nature and civilization in pure forms of energy, mirrors our dynamic conception of the world, whether its shapes incorporate the basic principles of growth in nature, or express in constructions the mind of man again on the march into the future. Thus, the art of today has returned to the essential centers of life, nature and the spirit, and from them it draws its manifold impulses and directions towards basic themes expressed in the universal language of symbols. On the one hand it relates man to the organic world in organic forms; on the other it constructs symbols of the contemporary mind with specifically contemporary means in an abstract mathematical language.

What still remains to be said is that we are witnessing the shaping of a new, inward beauty. It seems to be evolving in multiple aspects. Its mutability and manifoldness were already proclaimed by Guillaume Apollinaire in crass contrast to all static and final aesthetic standards. "That monster beauty, is not eternal." No definition of this new conception of beauty can as yet be made. It can only be sensed in the intensity it draws from spiritual sources, encompassing the conscious and unconscious, emotion and thought. It is the symbol of the "world wideness" of the man of today, while on the other hand it springs from the deepest sources of his unchanging inner life. The most significant name which James Joyce gave to his many-armed river goddess in his modern myth, *Finnegan's Wake,* is the third and last, as it flows from the past through the present to the future. It sounds like a prophecy: *"Plurabelle* is to be."

Zurich, 1954

Illustrations

Single measurements refer to height. Where several measurements are given, height precedes.

Honoré Daumier's work as a sculptor is beginning to attract increased attention for its vital importance in the evolution of present-day sculpture. Through him the baroque tradition descends directly to Rodin. *Ratapoil,* 1850; the Caricature of Napoleon III; the *Self-Portrait,* 1855; and 36 clay busts of French deputies (Le Ventre Législatif), 1830-32, are the most outstanding examples of his manner. These busts were modeled from memory, not from life. Their most striking characteristics, like those of *Ratapoil,* are the fleeting quality of the poses, the freedom of the contours, and the intense quality of life which radiates from them. The material seems to have liquefied under the pressure of the physical and emotional atmosphere. These are more than rapid caricatures; they are prototypes of the great human comedy.

Honoré Daumier *Le Dégout Personnifié* Portrait Bust of Senator Fruchard 1830-32 Colored clay 5½" Louvre, Paris

Honoré Daumier *Ratapoil* 1850 Bronze 18½″ Louvre, Paris Plaster original Coll. Henry Bing, Paris

Edgar Degas *Girl Dancer of Fourteen* 1880 Bronze and fabric 40" Louvre, Paris

A shifting balance of space and light plays around *Degas'* Dancers. They are snapshots in the round, and the impression of a fleeting moment captured is enhanced by the improvised costumes in actual materials (tulle, silk). They perpetuate the realism and illusionism of the Baroque, and at the same time "debunk" the solemnities of academic sculpture by restoring three-dimensional art to everyday subjects. "...to express everything that can bedevil reality — that is the art which it is our duty to practice...to give reality the appearance of madness." (E. Degas, *Letters,* 1890.) In defense of this kind of sculpture, which seemed revolutionary to its time, Joris Karl Huysmans, Degas' friend and contemporary, made points which still hold good today: "...to catch a pose, a movement, on the wing — that is his great personal achievement, but the interest of his exhibition is entirely centered on a statuette called *Girl Dancer of Fourteen.* The public, startled, even uneasy, turns away. The terrible reality of this statuette clearly causes discomfort. All our notions of sculpture, of cold, immaculate whiteness, of solemn pomposities which have been copied for centuries, go by the board. The fact is that, from the outset, M. Degas has overthrown the tradition of sculpture just as he undermined the conventions of painting years ago. While returning to the methods of the old Spanish masters, he makes them both individual and modern through the originality of his talent. This statuette, both refined and barbaric, with its sophisticated costume and its palpitating, colored flesh, is the one real attempt to create a language for modern sculpture known to me today." (J. K. Huysmans, *L'Art Moderne, l'Exposition des Indépendants,* 1881.)

Edgar Degas *Variations on the Grande Arabesque* 1882-95 Bronze 15¾″ Musée de Paume, Paris

Degas' chief aim in these variations of movement is to express the extension of the body in space, its thrust and spread. This is akin in principle to the later Constructivist idea of space, but Degas is an Impressionist, and his point of departure is the human figure. His greatness in conceiving and shaping complex sculptural experience is also revealed in the suppression of all incidentals such as the individual features, and in the merging, here and there, of the feet with the surface of the pedestal.

Auguste Rodin *Balzac* 1893-98 Bronze 8′11″
Boulevard Raspail, Paris

Brancusi considered this statue of Balzac to mark the beginning of modern sculpture.

Auguste Rodin *Le Jongleur* 1909 Glazed clay 16″ Musée Rodin, Paris

Auguste Rodin broke away from the emotional rigidity and academic routine of his time by using light to break up masses and lend them movement. He abandoned classical composition based on the relief in favor of the "all-round" view. In our day the appeal of his work has suffered somewhat owing to its theatricality, yet its veracity and élan of pure feeling poured new life into sculpture. "I feel the cubic meaning of all things — the plane, the volume — come home to me as the law of all life and all beauty ... I believe I have always remained a realistic sculptor ... Beauty is not a starting point — it is a goal; a thing can only be beautiful if it is true." (Etude de Auguste Rodin, *Le Musée,* 1904.)

"... And then again the human body is conceived as an urn. Viewed from that standpoint, all that appears is the silhouette, tapering to the waist, widening at the hips, and forming a vase of exquisite shape with an outline of astounding perfection — the amphora, which holds in its flanks the life of the future." (Rodin, *L'Art,* Edition Mermod, p. 172.)

Auguste Rodin *Great Head of Iris* Bronze 24" x 14" Musée Rodin, Paris

Auguste Rodin *Torso* 1914 Bronze 21¼" x 24½" Tate Gallery, London

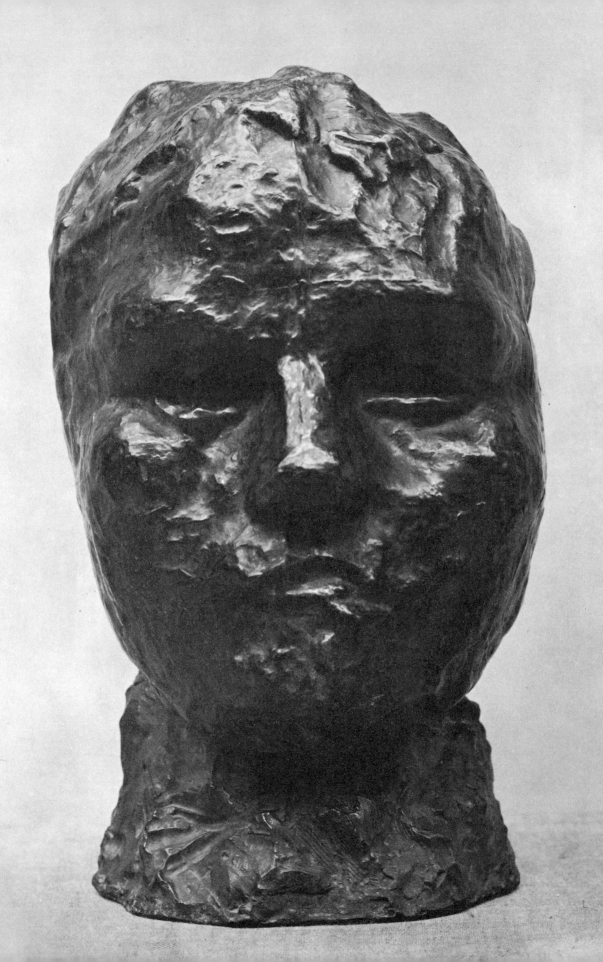

Medardo Rosso's great artistic achievement was the use of light to dematerialize volume. "It is all a question of light. There is no matter in space." He believed that sculpture could be made to vibrate in countless ruptures of the line, and come alive in the wing-beat of light and shade. He strove to rid vision of 19th century detail, to unite man with the cosmos, and to comprehend the figure in and through its surroundings. Rodin's effects are dramatic and dynamic, both in conception and form. Rosso worked in more lyrical fashion with delicate gradations of reflected light. And while Rodin's volumes are agitated by humps and hollows, Rosso preserves his surfaces, winning from them through softer handling a new translucency. His groups are born of merging vibrations of forms, of the movement of drapery, as in his *Conversazione in Giardino,* 1893, or in the flitting and fluttering of his *Paris at Night,* 1895. *Madame X* is one of the mature works of Rosso's Paris period. The features shimmer through a play of light and shade on the calm ovoid of the head. Only the essential elements of a head are alive; it is a head as stripped of all incidentals as Brancusi's later *Sleeping Muse.* A new language of symbols has evolved. These are real achievements of Impressionistic technique, while his heads are subtly differentiated statements of changing emotions and moods. That "human clockwork, that flashing trepidation of our state of mind, ever one yet ever changing," as he wrote to a friend, was what he wished to shape. He disliked intensely the academic blandness of isolated and limited "statuary" as deeply as he disliked all conventional notions of beauty. A new nobility and an equally challenging ugliness find mature expression in his work.

Medardo Rosso *Yvette Guilbert* 1894 Terracotta 16" Cà Pesaro, Galleria d'Arte Moderna, Venice

The portrait bust of the French chanteuse, which Rosso made in Paris, contains more than close and lively observation. It is a grandly conceived expression of the human soul.

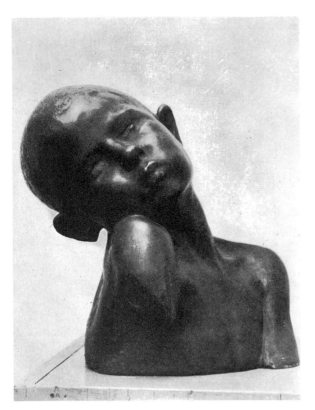

Constantin Brancusi *Supplice (Torment)* 1906
Bronze 8″ Coll. G. David Thompson, Pittsburgh, Pa.

Wilhelm Lehmbruck *Bust of Kneeling Girl* 1911
Cast stone 19¾″ Gift of
Robert Allerton, The Art Institute of Chicago

Medardo Rosso *Sick Child* 1895 Bronze 10¼″ x 7″ Coll. Gianni Matteoli, Milan

Rosso found the inspiration for this bronze in a Viennese hospital. The inclined head is characteristic of his work; the light makes it translucent and weightless, and seems to impart the sublime expression of vanishing life. "The human countenance is no longer a shell, a motionless form, for nothing is motionless; every object participates in the swift and multiple improvisation of the universe." (M. Rosso.)

14

Medardo Rosso *Conversazione in Giardino*
1893 Plaster original 12⅝" x 25¼"
Medardo Rosso Museo, Barzio/Lecco

Here is the fluid grouping of the Impressionists. In
the foreground, seen from behind, the superb figure of
the sculptor, which inspired Rodin's *Balzac*. As compared with the heroic compressions of the *Burghers
of Calais,* this group is remarkable for the fine inner
vitality of form which gives life to an impersonal
situation.

Medardo Rosso *Boulevard Impressions, Paris at Night* 1895
Wax 27" x 22¼" Cast of the original in the Noblet
Collection, Gesains sur Aube, destroyed in World War I

The later group was made in Paris. It captures the
movement of anonymous beings, flitting and fluttering
like great birds under the street lamps and vanishing
in the depths like spectres melting into the night.

Medardo Rosso *Madame X* 1913 Wax 11¾"
Cà Pesaro, Galleria d'Arte Moderna, Venice

As a sculptor, *Matisse* started to model in the style of the Impressionists. His work is marked by freedom in the distribution of masses and in the play of light and shade. We can see in it how the artist liberates himself from the subject by means of certain expressive deformations. "I wish to be judged by my work as a whole, by the general line it took." (Henri Matisse.)

Henri Matisse *Torso* 1906 Bronze
8⅝" Photo: Courtesy Curt Valentin Gallery, New York

Pablo Picasso *Statuette* 1945-47 Bronze
5¾" Coll. G. David Thompson, Pittsburgh, Pa.

Picasso's *Statuette* is an interesting example of the evolution of the small figures with which Matisse had begun early in the century. It carries the simplification of the form still farther in the direction of the ritualistic idol.

Henri Matisse *Serpentina* 1909 Bronze 22¼"
Museum of Modern Art, New York, Gift of Mrs. John D. Rockefeller, Jr.

The most impressive feature of this Fauve piece is the delicate outline of the figure, the "linea serpentinata." Matisse is expressing only the rhythm of a movement, without any shaping of detail.

19

Raymond Duchamp-Villon *Female Head (Maggy)* 1912
Bronze 28″ Galerie Louis Carré, Paris

Pablo Picasso *Female Head* 1932 Bronze 34½″
Coll. the artist

In their female heads of 1910 and 1912, Matisse and Duchamp-Villon had already introduced that grotesque emphasis on single forms which became, in Picasso's hands, the domination of the whole by great expressive volumes.

Henri Matisse *Jeannette V* (1910-11?) Bronze 22⅞″ Art Gallery, Toronto

Henri Matisse *Tiara (Le Tiaré)* 1930 Bronze 8½" Coll. Martin Becker, New York

Henri Matisse *Venus on a Shell* ca. 1930 Bronze 13" The Cone Collection, Baltimore Museum of Art

Archaic Torso of Apollo 6th century B.C. Marble Louvre, Paris

Aristide Maillol *Night* ca. 1902 Stone 38″ Kunstmuseum, Winterthur

Aristide Maillol *L'Action Enchainée (Fettered Action)* Torso Monument to Louis-Auguste Blanqui 1906 Bronze 49″
Tate Gallery, London

Maillol is one of the inaugurators of a new epoch in sculpture. He had no feeling for the disrupted forms of Rodin, and aimed at compression and compactness, building up the human figure in fundamental organic volumes. Since he championed the classical and static ideal of the human body, his figures are simple, self-contained structures. They radiate a feeling of natural animal strength and beauty. Maillol helped to revitalize sculpture by restating classical ideas, and by overcoming both the petrified formulas of Neo-Classicism and the subjective sentimentality of the late 19th century. He realized anew, in a radiant Mediterranean spirit, the clear, architectural representation of the human figure. "There is something to be learned from Rodin...yet I felt I must return to more stable and self-contained forms. Stripped of all psychological details, forms yield themselves up more readily to the sculptor's intentions." (A. Maillol.)

26

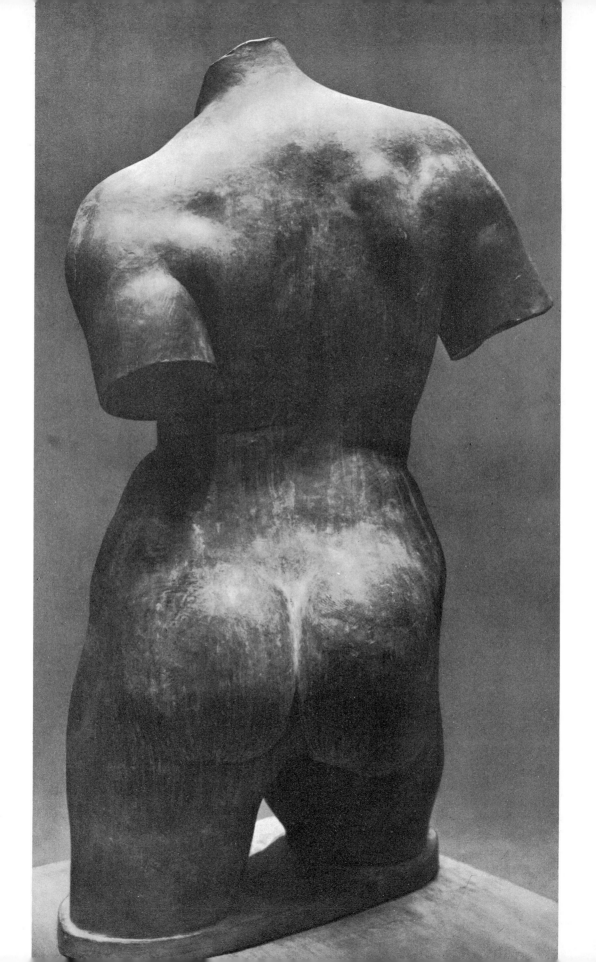

The fresh emphasis on clarity and self-sufficiency which *Bourdelle* inaugurated with his reaction against the tumultuous stress and strain of Rodin's work renewed the bond between sculpture and architecture. Bourdelle found much of his inspiration in early Greek art. "From the life in the human model the sculptor must pass on to the life in his work, and from that to its setting against an architectural background. That is the great law by which stone can achieve its august destiny in human gestures." Yet Bourdelle was closely in touch with his time. He might be called the symbolist of sculpture. For him, as for the symbolist poets of his time, music was the supreme art, "the great harmony of numbers." Like Mallarmé, he strove to achieve "the pure canticle of perfect balance."

Antoine Bourdelle *L'Eloquence* 1917 Bronze 19″ Musée Bourdelle, Paris

Antoine Bourdelle *Hercules* 1909 Bronze 8'3" x 4'11" x 5'5½" Musée d'Art Moderne, Paris

Antoine Bourdelle *Grand Masque Tragique de Beethoven*
(4 ième étude) 1901 Bronze 30¾" x 17¾" x 19¾"
Musée Bourdelle, Paris

The romantic expressiveness of Bourdelle's art is effectively displayed in this pathetic mask of Beethoven.

Antoine Bourdelle *Sélène* 1917 Bronze 34" Musée Bourdelle, Paris

The fine tension of this figure, the freedom of its proportions, and the expressiveness it gains through elongation show another aspect of Bourdelle's work which continues the French tradition of the 17th century and reappears also in the work of Henri Laurens.

Like Bourdelle, *Karl Burckhardt* was mainly inspired by early Greek art in his evolution towards the simplification and compression of sculptured form, which interested him chiefly as a "space-forming energy." In his conception sculpture was a pure source of elemental vitality, to be stripped of all naturalistic and psychological ballast. Liberated from the weight of detail, and from every intrusive individual shape, it was to become the embodiment of basic proportions. He regarded "distant form" (form as seen from a distance), extending into space and bathed in air, as the essential form of sculpture, the ultimate aim being the radiation of its inner structure.

Karl Burckhardt *In Memory of H. Dieterle* 1919 Bronze 26½" Kunsthaus, Zurich

This bust, as the sculptor makes clear in his title, is the vision of the inner man. This is not his outward aspect, but his spiritual being, from which all realism of anatomical detail has fallen away.

Karl Burckhardt *St. George* 1923 Bronze 6′2″ Am Kohlenberg, Basel

Owing to the height of its pedestal, this composition takes on something of the nature of a column. The figure mounts quite naturally towards the sky from out of its urban environment, the living background of a city hill with its rows of houses. The bold arch of the horse's legs outlines a space which is set in deliberate contrast to the massive parts of the body. This is the "sculpture of distance and daylight," (as the sculptor himself called it), rising to an ideal height above the workaday world, yet without breaking the bond between the real and the ideal.

Between the compact and solidly established forms of Maillol and the bold and sensuous "linea serpentinata" of Matisse, there stands the sensitive attitude of *Wilhelm Lehmbruck's* figures. A profound inwardness casts a Gothic light of contemplation over his line, which derives from Art Nouveau in its organic, sinuous movement. This deepening of the meditative element finds expression in the attenuation of the human figure and the delicacy of the silhouette. It is the same close interrelation of proportions as we find in Modigliani, though here in more tender and contemplative form. But it is not only the depth of feeling which saves Lehmbruck from mannerism. "All art is dimension — that is the whole of art. Dimension, or in figures, proportion, determines the impression, the effect, the bodily expression, the line, the contour, everything. A good sculpture must, therefore, be handled in the same way as a good composition, as a building in which dimension responds to dimension." (W. Lehmbruck, 1918.)

Wilhelm Lehmbruck *Kneeling Woman* 1911 Synthetic stone 69½"
Museum of Modern Art, New York Mrs. John D. Rockefeller, Jr., Purchase Fund

Ste. Radegonde 2nd half of 15th century Stone Castle Chapel, Châteaudun (Eure-et-Loire)

Wilhelm Lehmbruck *The Fallen* 1915-16 Synthetic stone 30″ x 96″ Coll. Lehmbruck, Tuebingen

This tragic tribute to those who fell in World War I was originally intended as a war memorial and stands in marked contrast to the official notions of heroism of its time. There is no monumental or artistic architecture without contour or silhouette." (W. Lehmbruck, 1918.)

A completely unheroic but very profound conception of a war memorial also finds expression in one of Lehmbruck's poems:

> Who remains?
> Who stands alive, a relic of the slaughter?
> Who has arisen from the sea of blood?
> I take my way across the stubble field
> And look about me where the crop lies spread,
> The aftermath of hideous murdering.
> Friends lie in peace all round me on my way,
> My brothers are no longer by my side.
> And faith and hope have far from me departed,
> For death has covered every path and flower.
> O fate! O thousandfold and cruel fate!
> Hast thou, who granted death to all these hosts,
> No death for me?
>   January, 1918.

Wilhelm Lehmbruck *Standing Youth* 1913 Synthetic stone 92″
Museum of Modern Art, New York Gift of Mrs. John D. Rockefeller, Jr.

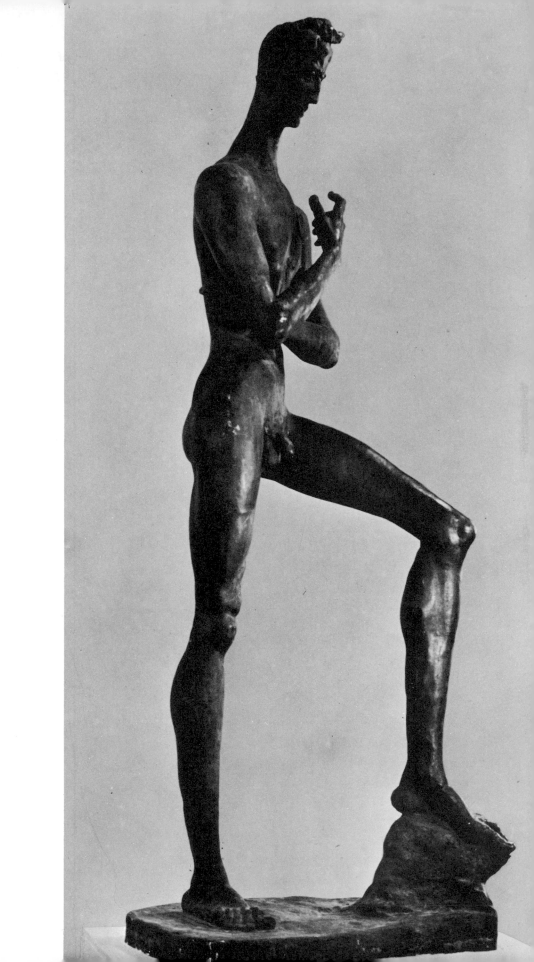

In *Modigliani,* the expressiveness of the proportions and the consolidation of organic form go hand in hand with spiritual intensity. The structure of his heads is formally akin in its austerity to primitive and archaic art. The kinship, however, is not to be sought in any borrowing of form, but rather in a similar method of stressing essential volumes. In this head we can see a close relationship between Modigliani and his friend Constantin Brancusi.

Prehistoric Effigy Persian alabaster 42" x 29½" x 20½" Museum of Fine Arts, Boston

Amedeo Modigliani *Head of a Woman* 1910-13 Stone 35" Tate Gallery, London

Constantin Brancusi *Head* 1907-08 Stone 11¾"

Amedeo Modigliani *Head of a Woman* 1912 Stone 23" x 5" Musée d'Art Moderne, Paris

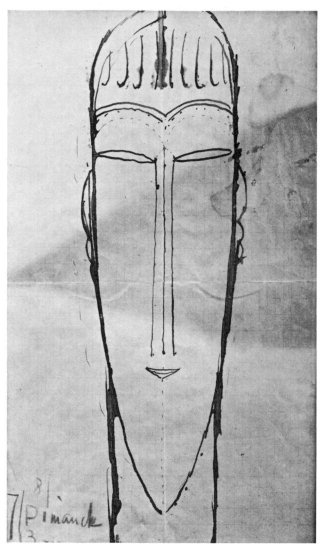

Amedeo Modigliani *Study of a Head for a Sculpture* Drawing 1913 10½″ x 5¾″ Collection Jesi, Milan

Amedeo Modigliani *Woman's Head* 1913 Wood 22″ Coll. M. & Mme. Deltcheff, Paris

The painter André Derain has created, in his only sculptural work of importance, a precubistic piece of sculpture of great force. Here is a monumental transformation of the human figure into an architectural structure. In contrast to the frontal view, the accentuation in the rear view is based on simple, organic forms. This work is permeated by a rustic strength, approaching the feeling of folk-lore.

André Derain *Crouching Man* 1907 Stone 13″ Coll. L. Leiris, Paris

45

Pablo Picasso *The Jester* 1905 Bronze 16¼″ Kunstmuseum, Winterthur

Picasso's origins in the French Impressionist tradition, which he shares with Matisse, emerge clearly in this example of his scultpure belonging to his "période rose" in painting.

Pablo Picasso *Female Head* 1910 Bronze 16¼″ Kunsthaus, Zurich

With *Picasso's* bronze head, cubist analysis of the object is inaugurated. The flickering light of Impressionism has yielded to a harder technique, though traces of it still remain. In this head, light is used as an active factor in composition, giving us the dynamics rather than the description of form. The volume of the head seems to have been shattered into many facets and reconstructed in a free rhythm. The relationship between positive and negative form is clearly brought out. "When we created cubism, our intention was not to create cubism, but to express what was in us." (Picasso, *Cahiers d' Art,* 1930-35.)

Otto Freundlich *Head* 1910 Bronze ca. 47″ Coll. Carl Jatho, Cologne

Otto Freundlich's Mask marks the mature stage in an evolution of heads which proceeded slowly from Impressionistic modeling with light to a grand and monumental condensation of rhythm and form. After his first abstract sculpture in 1916, Freundlich developed steadily in the direction of bold and dynamic balance, with an upward shift in the center of gravity. "The artist's work is a summary of constructive acts. Artistic culture is and has always been the same thing — preparation for the future." (O. Freundlich, Le Mur, Académie, 1938.)

Otto Freundlich *Mask* 1912 Bronze cast ca. 47″ Coll. Dr. Wissinger, Berlin

Otto Freundlich *Ascension* 1929 Plaster 60″ Coll. Mme. Freundlich, Paris

Juan Gris *Harlequin* 1917 Colored plaster 22″ Philadelphia Museum of Art

The only sculpture made by *Juan Gris,* the Cubist painter, again illustrates the architectural quality of his approach. It is the establishment of a relationship of clear, geometrical masses, of positive and negative volumes — a mathematical depersonalization of the human figure.

Alexander Archipenko *Boxing Match* Paris, 1914 Painted plaster 23¾″
The Solomon R. Guggenheim Museum, New York

Archipenko, the Russian, and *Schlemmer,* the South German, who are contemporaries, both regard the human figure simply and solely as the starting point of a fugue in three dimensions. Archipenko pioneered in this conception, taking up this line as early as 1911. His is another attempt to strike a mean between the antique attitude toward the human body and the modern formal dynamic. The work of both sculptors shows how great has been the development since Maillol's more natural forms; it marks the growth of a new freedom in the creation of independent form. Volumes, and above all, hollows, light and shade, air and mass, give Archipenko's figures a contrapuntal rhythm, while Schlemmer grasps the body in its functional aspect and shapes it into abstract form. Schlemmer's work is almost a grammar of fundamental sculptural values.

Oskar Schlemmer *Sculpture* 1921 Plaster 43″ x 27″ Coll. Frau Tut Schlemmer, Stuttgart

Alexander Archipenko *Standing Figure* 1920 Hydrostone 5½″ Coll. Museum Darmstadt

 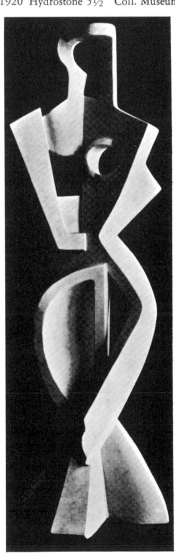

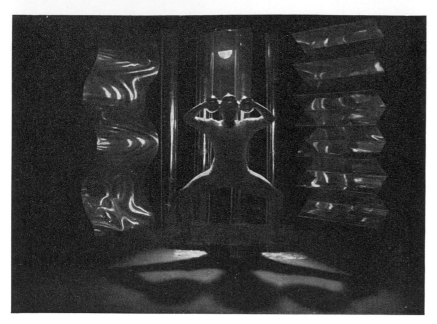

Oskar Schlemmer *Dance in Metal* 1926 Bauhaus stage

What Schlemmer expressed in *Mensch und Bühne* also holds true of his sculpture — it is the relationship of the organism "man" to space, a mutual understanding on the part of subject and object. "Man, the dancer, obeys both the law of the body and the law of space. He expresses both his own physical being and his sense of space." (O. Schlemmer, *Die Bühne im Bauhaus,* 1926.)

The montage of various materials (wood, metal, glass) in what *Archipenko* calls "Medranos" is an experiment in a new means of expression. Constructivism developed the method later, although from a different angle, making conscious use of the industrial materials of our time. The Dadaists ostentatiously stressed the common things of everyday life with the same means; Archipenko's work, however, is primarily based on a new conception of volume and concavity as an active element in the whole.

Alexander Archipenko *Medrano* Paris 1915
Painted tin, glass, wood, oilcloth 49½"
The Solomon R. Guggenheim Museum, New York

Jacques Lipchitz *Man with Guitar* 1917
Stone 29¾″ Yale University Art Gallery, New Haven

Jacques Lipchitz *Figure* 1926-30 Bronze 7′ 1¼″
Museum of Modern Art, New York.
Photographed at Exhibition in Varèse.

In his early work *Lipchitz* achieved a vertical, block-like orchestration of stone in a strictly cubist sense. The Cubist painters, too, set up their "unreal vertical" in opposition to "descriptive perspective". A new sense of space was struggling through to expression. Works such as *Man with Guitar*, 1917, retain of the "subject" only the original impulse to a free association of forms. Subsequently Lipchitz dissolved the mass of his early sculpture in stone into a mobile pattern of lines (1925-28), in which nothing remains but shapes of air bounded by ropy strands of bronze. This extreme disembodiment results in elasticity and rhythm.

56

Jacques Lipchitz *Song of the Vowels* 1931-32 Bronze 6' 6¾" without base Photographed at Le Pradet-Toulon, France
Gift of Mme. H. de Mandrot to Kunsthaus, Zurich

"For my part, I maintain that sculpture, being essentially an art of the crowd, should be conceived and executed with the people in mind. The great sculpture of all epochs was an art which brought some kind of satisfaction to everybody. But if the artist thinks of the crowd, the crowd, in turn, must think of the artist; art can only become great through this mutual comprehension." (J. Lipchitz, *Cahiers d'Art,* 1935.)

Jacques Lipchitz *Joie de Vivre* 1927 Bronze 78″ without base Coll. Comte de Noailles, Hyères

This sculpture, which stands in a southern garden, is related both to its natural setting and to the house beside it (G. Guevrekian, architect). It is this harmony which brings out its intrinsic beauty.

Jacques Lipchitz *Mother and Child* 1941-45 Bronze 50″ Coll. Edgar Kaufmann, Bear Run, Pa.
House by the Waterfall, Frank Lloyd Wright, architect

In this group a human emotion finds superb expression. It becomes a monumental gesture, revealing a natural relation-ship between free-standing sculpture and architecture. The same note sounds through the sculpture, the building, and the structure of the walls.

Jacques Lipchitz *Prometheus and the Eagle*
1943-44 Bronze 102″ Ministry of Education, Rio de Janeiro
(Photomontage in the proportions intended)

In this work, forms are compressed into cloudy shapes with fluttering baroque effects of light and shade. As the size of the sculpture was considerably reduced in the execution, the work is dwarfed by the expanse of the wall. The original proportions have been lost, along with the superb play of light and shade on the white surface.

Jacques Lipchitz *Woman with Guitar* 1927 Bronze 14″ Coll. the artist

Jacques Lipchitz *Barbara* 1942 Bronze 14⅝″ Smith College Museum, Northampton, Mass.

In his mature period, after he had transformed matter into a mobile play of lines, Lipchitz's characteristic development of the organic human form into "transparent sculpture" was fulfilled. This airy sculpture of his, created as early as 1925, belongs to the most important new directions in modern sculpture. It involves a hitherto unknown method of sublimation and graphic expression, one which is still being practiced by the generation of today. This development also involves the elaboration of a special manner of "portrait sculpture" in which the individuality of the head is treated in terms of the fantastic. Something similar occurs in Picasso's painting when, with an actual experience as his original impulse, he achieves an absolutely unprecedented transposition of the individual into the abstract by means of the bizarre quality of the picture's internal relationships.

Henri Laurens *Man with a Pipe* 1919 Stone 14½" x 9½" Fine Arts Associates, New York

In his early work, *Laurens*, like Lipchitz, starts out with a strictly architectural construction, which he transforms into an artistic creation by the methods of "collage" in painting, with its deliberate contrasts between different materials (wood, sand, tin, paper) drawn from the "elements of reality". In his *Compositions in Sheet Iron*, with their positive and negative volumes and basic forms, he anticipates the methods which were later systematically developed by the Constructivists. Later, Laurens became increasingly preoccupied with the female figure, which he shapes like a reclining Gaia Tellus in every possible variation, and in the fabulous forms of sirens and nereids as the incarnation of the forces of nature.

Henri Laurens *Composition* 1914 Black and red sheet iron
8″ x 11¾″ Coll. Maurice Raynal, Paris

Umberto Boccioni *Horse and Houses. Dynamic Construction of a Gallop*
1912-13 Wood, metal, cardboard 28″
Coll. Benedetta Marinetti, Rome (Courtesy Cahiers d'Art)

Constantin Brancusi *The Prodigal Son* 1914 Wood 29⅝" x 8½" x 8¾"
Arensberg Collection, Philadelphia Museum of Art

Henri Laurens *Crouching Woman* 1931 Wood Coll. Mme. H. Laurens

Constantin Brancusi *Three Penguins* 1914
Marble 26″ x 21″ x 12½″ Arensberg Collection, Philadelphia Museum of Art

Henri Laurens *The Water* 1937 Terracotta Paris World Exhibition, 1937

This monumental group embodies a superb interplay of welling forms reduced to their essence. They are not unlike those of Brancusi's *Three Penguins* although the latter seem more like archetypal shapes coming to life in the stone.

Henri Laurens *The Mother* 1935 Bronze
24″ Coll. S. and C. Giedion-Welcker, Zuri

Taddeo Landini *Fontana Delle Tartarug*
(The Tortoise Fountain) 1585 Rome
(Giacomo della Porta, architect)

The abstractness which Laurens achieved at one time through the strictly constructive quality of his work is now generated in the rhythm and expressive deformation of organic forms which are pure creations of the sculptor's imagination. The attenuated proportions recall the formal language of Italian mannerism towards the end of the Cinquecento. Even their allegorical significance seems recreated in a current language as he combines animal and human forms to express natural forces.

Henri Laurens *Siren* 1944 Bronze 48″ x 25″ x 26″ Musée d'Art Moderne, Paris

The *Siren* of 1944 is one of a long series of variations on the theme which Laurens began in 1937. With soaring grace a fabulous creature arises which seems to have its origin in the "linea serpentinata" of the late Cinquecento. For all its intense, space-creating vitality, the movement has great delicacy. It recalls the swiftness of Bourdelle's *Selene*.

71

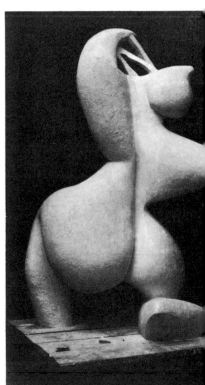

Henri Laurens *The Great Musician* 1938
Plaster 84″ x 48″
Musée d'Art Moderne, Paris

This figure was made during the dark days of the fall of France, and it is a powerfully dramatic symbol of the collapse. In contrast to the strictly structural quality of the *Crouching Woman,* 1931, the psychological content finds expression in a ponderous massing of organic volumes.

Henri Laurens *L'Adieu* 1941 Bronze 29″ x 34″ x 26″ Bronze cast in the Musée d'Art Moderne, Paris

Henri Laurens *Amphion* 1952 Bronze 13′3″ University of Caracas, Venezuela

Raymond Duchamp-Villon *The Little Horse* 1914 Lead 17⅓" Galerie Louis Carré, Paris

Raymond Duchamp-Villon, a cubist pioneer who died early, left behind in his work a premature but important foundation for future developments in sculpture. There is first the reduction to essentially plastic values, as in the *Head of Baudelaire,* 1911, and in the *Seated Woman,* 1914, where the upward spiral already prefigures the bold synthesis of different phases of movement which was to find supreme realization, in a completely new artistic language, in *The Horse,* 1914. This sculpture seems to have captured bodily function and rhythm alone, so that the natural creature, horse, vanishes entirely in the presentation of the principle of energy. "Movement was at all times the goal of Duchamp-Villon's art." (Guillaume Apollinaire, 1912.) The definition of this "ideographic writing" is provided by the humorous name applied to it by contemporaries, "machine horse — almost steam horse". The work is also linked with the dynamics of the Futurists and their synthesis of successive movements.

Raymond Duchamp-Villon *The Horse* 1914 Bronze 39" x 44" x 44" Musée d'Art Moderne, Paris

Raymond Duchamp-Villon *Seated Woman* 1914 Bronze 27″ x 9″ x 11″ Yale University Art Gallery, New Haven

Raymond Duchamp-Villon *Baudelaire* 1911 Bronze 15½″ x 8½″ x 10″ Musée d'Art Moderne, Paris

Duchamp-Villon's last work, *Head of Professor Gosset,* 1917, shows progressive simplification and concentration on a few large sculptural elements. "It is impossible to express the needs of art in our own day in the idiom of bygone times. We wish to comprehend in sculpture things with which sculpture has never yet been involved. Who is right, sculpture or we?" (Duchamp-Villon, Military Hospital, 1915.)

Raymond Duchamp-Villon *Head of Professor Gosset* 1917 Bronze 4″ x 2⅞″ Coll. Jacques Villon, Puteaux

Hermes Bicephalus (detail), Roquepertuse 3rd-2nd Century B.C. Musée Borély, Marseilles

Umberto Boccioni *Concave and Convex Abstraction of a Head*
1912 Plaster (Destroyed)

Alexander Archipenko *Head*
(Construction with Crossing Planes)
1913 Bronze 15″ Perls Galleries, New York

Both artists construct the human head by means of expressive concavities and intersecting planes.

Wilhelm Lehmbruck *Head of an Old Lady* 1913 Plaster 20½″
Städtisches Museum Duisburg, Germany

In *Boccioni's Antigrazioso (Head of the Artist's Mother),* the humorous vitality of the grotesque stands out in contrast to all academic notions of "bellezza". The sculptor is out to grasp the intensity, the dynamic quality of life. The intersection of the head by architectural details (a window) is characteristic; it is a means of expressing man's link with his surroundings. A comparison with Medardo Rosso's *Concierge,* 1883, shows that even Rosso, who was Boccioni's predecessor, and whom Boccioni always regarded as a pioneer, had made a stand against academic formulas by the direct and living relationship to his model and by his grasp of essential sculptural values. In this portrait, an unusual one for him, Wilhelm Lehmbruck achieves a similar forthrightness in form and interpretation.

84

Medardo Rosso *Concierge* 1883 Wax 15½" Cà Pesaro, Galleria d'Arte
Moderna, Venice

Umberto Boccioni *Antigrazioso (Head of the Artist's Mother)* 1911 Bronze
28" Coll. Benedetta Marinetti, Rome

The most important works by Umberto Boccioni, the Futurist, date back to 1910-13, before World War I. The titles themselves sound like the proclamation of a new departure — for instance, *Concave and Convex Abstraction of a Heád,* or *Forms which Exist only in the Continuity of Space.* Marinetti, the inaugurator of Futurism, speaks of a deliberate rejection of the notion that the human figure is the sole foundation of beauty in sculpture. The new sculpture, according to him, must unite a feeling for movement with a feeling for mass (as in Cubism). As in Duchamp-Villon's *Horse,* the function of stepping is the focus of interest — energy, not the static anatomy of the mass in the sculpture *Muscles in Motion.*

Pierre Puget *Perseus and Andromeda* 1684 Marble 126″ Louvre, Paris

Umberto Boccioni *Muscles in Motion (Muscoli in Velocità)* 1913 Bronze Private Collection, Milan

Pablo Picasso *Absinthe Glass* 1914 Bronze 8¾″ x 3″ Coll. Curt Burgauer, Zurich

Umberto Boccioni *Development of a Bottle in Space* 1912 Bronze 15″ Museum of Modern Art, New York Aristide Maillol Fund

This representation of the expansion and development of a simple object in space and time, the gyration of a life-sized bottle and plate, expresses in simplest form the relationship of mass to space. The newly-added dimension of time can be felt more clearly than in the slightly later compositions of the Cubist sculptures of Picasso. The commonplaceness of the object and its reduction to mathematical forms are as fundamental as in the Cubist conception.

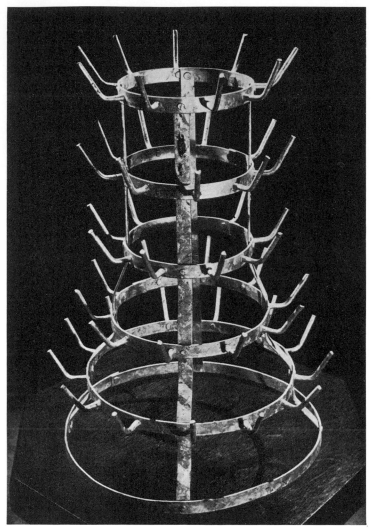

Marcel Duchamp *Ready Made (Bottle Rack)* 1914 Iron Coll. Man Ray, Paris

These specimens of Dada have primary importance as documents of their time, demonstrating its new anti-aesthetic feeling and technique, and its preoccupation with everyday life. The decisive factor is invention, the expressive quality that can be distilled from the most commonplace materials. *Kurt Schwitters' Merz Construction* and *Max Ernst's Objet Dad'Art,* which are of the same period, use the Dada method of combining "found objects" to create a new world of the imagination. *Raoul Hausmann's Mechanical Head* ridicules the shattered Greek ideal and the mechanized man of today who lives on "ready mades." This world had already been discovered in 1912 by *Marcel Duchamp,* and apart from the joke, it reveals the expressive power of simple forms. In this composition, the object, transferred from the utilitarian to the irrational sphere, acquires an entirely new force of expression. In being considered solely for its form it seems to take on a new and absurd intensity. "What we call Dada is a tomfoolery in the void in which all great questions are involved . . . a game with shabby remains." (Hugo Ball, Zurich, 1916)

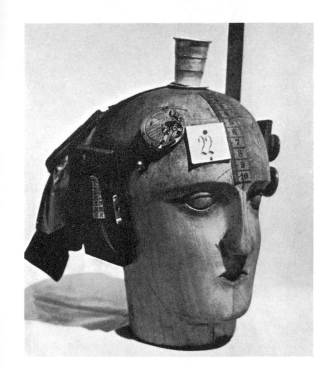

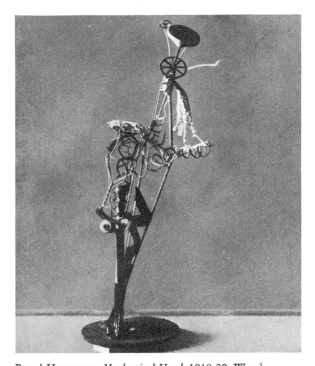

Raoul Hausmann *Mechanical Head* 1919-20 Wood
and various other materials 10″ Coll. the artist

Max Ernst *Objet Dad'Art* 1919-20 String, wood, fabric
and wire 31½″ (Destroyed)

Sophie Taeuber-Arp *Dada Head* 1920 Wood 13″
Coll. Jean Arp, Meudon

Kurt Schwitters *Merz Construction (Gallows of Lust)*
1919 Wood, iron and papier maché (Destroyed)

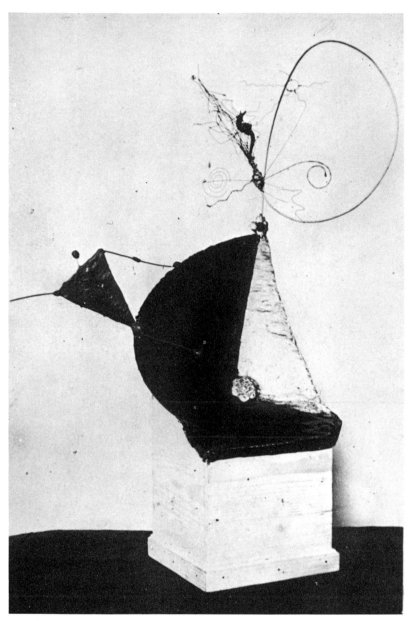

Marcel Janco *Construction 3* 1917 Wire and plaster

In this vibrating skeletal construction much is basically anticipated which later became pulsing movement in space (see Calder).

Pablo Picasso *The Bull (Metamorphosis)* 1943 Bronze 16½" Coll. the artist

Picasso's *Bull,* the last link in this chain, is composed of bicycle parts. As compared with Marcel Duchamp's "ready mades," this is not merely a reinterpretation of a real object; it is a transformation executed with a gesture of pure genius. The result is a strange fusion of purely expressive and purely utilitarian form.

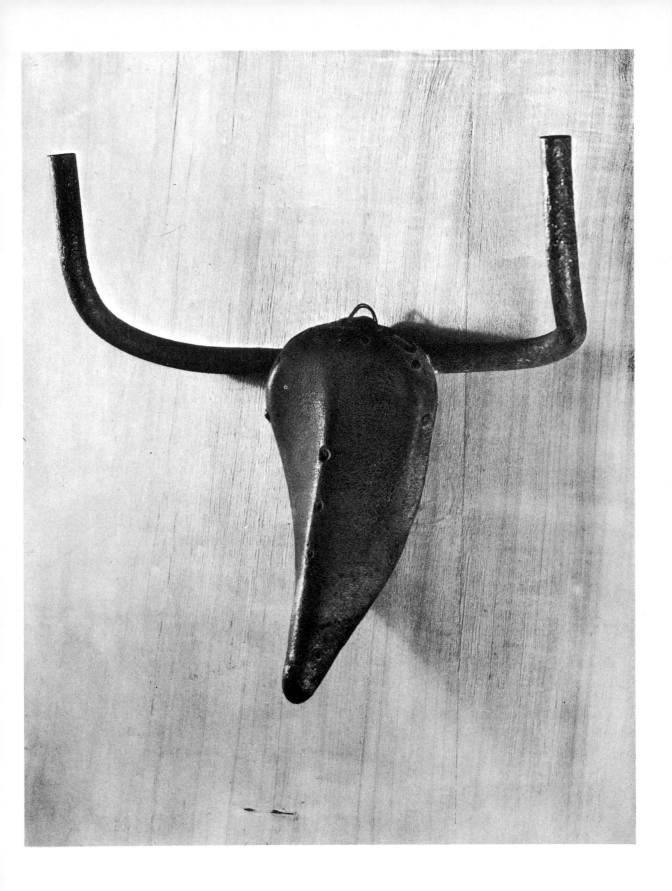

Men an Tol Prehistoric Monoliths Neolithic age Cornwall

95

Alberto Giacometti *Head* 1934 Plaster 7½" Coll. the artist

Everything *Alberto Giacometti* has ever created has been a fresh start in his progress toward a distant goal. His works are conscious experiments in capturing and keeping alive vitality and mobility. He prefers plaster as a medium, since its ductility lends itself most readily to the shaping of his nervous and sensitive vision.

Sartre realized Giacometti's central problem when he wrote: "In frontally opposing classicism, Giacometti restored an imaginary and inseparable space to his statues." (Catalogue, Matisse Gallery, New York, 1948.)

He began with "mobile, dumb objects," bodies which, floating or at rest, are primarily expressive as volumes. These "objects" possess a radiant vitality which is both natural and strange. There is at times a contrapuntal relationship between the organic and the geometrical in their subsequent integration in a single body. There are unexpected transformations, contrasts and connections, often recalling prehistoric sculpture in the manner of awakening form in the stone, and in the crescendo and diminuendo of volume. We find in Giacometti's work pure, basic form and a relentless search for a language to describe the relation of sculpture to space *(Projet pour une Place)*. Side by side with this are freely associated dream fantasies *(Palace at 4 A.M.)*. But, as in the contemporary work of Miro and Arp, even here the dominant factor is the basic form in its strange spatial relationships.

Alberto Giacometti *The Palace at 4 A.M.* 1932-33 Construction in wood, glass, wire, string 28¼" x 15¾" x 25"
Museum of Modern Art, New York Purchase Fund

"I whirl in the void. In broad daylight I contemplate space and the stars which traverse the liquid silver around me...
Again and again I am captivated by constructions which delight me, and which live in their surreality — a beautiful
palace, the tiled floor, black, white and red under my feet, the clustered columns, the smiling ceiling of air, and the
precise mechanisms which are of no use." (A. Giacometti, *Charbon d'Herbe,* Paris, 1933.)

Liver. Etruscan Votive Offering Hellenistic Bronze ca. 3⅛″ x 8″ Museum of Piacenza

Parts of entrails are loosely arranged as dwelling places for the gods. Their size, color and position predict good or evil fortune. Their flat surface is divided into regions, each named after a god and oriented toward the friendly sun and hostile moon. In this way the microcosm relates to the macrocosm.

There is no direct ritual reference in Giacometti's work. Yet it is filled with mysterious psychic energies seeking their own expression in symbols. At the same time it reveals a mysterious relationship to the peasant tradition of his own country.

"Once the object is constructed, I tend to see in it, transformed and displaced, facts which have profoundly moved me, often without my realizing it; forms which I feel quite close to me, yet often without being able to identify them, which makes them all the more disturbing." (Alberto Giacometti, *Minotaure,* 1933.)

Swiss Peasant Table (Muldentisch) 17th-18th Century Wood Schweizer Landesmuseum, Zurich

98

Alberto Giacometti *Projet Pour Une Place* 1930-31 Wood 4″ x 12″ x 9″ Coll. the artist, Paris

Giacometti's *Model for a Square* is an interplay of primitive forms which cast a powerful and mysterious spell, an interaction of hollow and mass on the most basic level.

Alberto Giacometti *The Hand* 1947 Bronze 16″ x 28″ x 8″ Coll. the artist

What we feel in this lonesome hand is the magic aura of the fragment, its solitude in space and, still more, the symbolic expressiveness of a detached form, lost and floating in the universe.

While Bourdelle's treatment of an isolated arm with its poetic attribute (the lyre) derives from the nostalgic era of *symbolisme,* Giacometti's expression is developed from the inexorable existentialist consciousness of his generation.

100

Antoine Bourdelle *Dying Centaur* 1914 Bronze 11
Bronze 113½" x 39¾" Musée Bourdelle, Paris

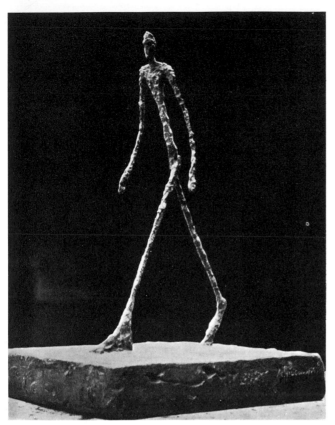

Alberto Giacometti *Man Walking Across a Square in Sunshine*
1948 Bronze 27½" Galerie Maeght, Paris

Venice The Piazza

Alberto Giacometti *City Square* 1948-49 Bronze figurines 5"-6" Coll. Peggy Guggenheim, Venice

Giacometti does not deal with the human group as it was understood by medieval artists and by Rodin in his *Burghers of Calais,* that is, as a whole, united from within through a common action and emotion. He is interested in the movement of the anonymous city-dweller, both in his individual isolation and his collective relationships. The mysteriousness of everyday life, and the relationships of amorphous bodies in space that marked Giacometti's early work are now transformed into a counterpoint of moving human figures composed of little more than armatures. Everything is tense with movement and ravaged by space, and in this space, the human figure moves like a disembodied cipher. This work could not suffer a tactile approach since that would rob it of its mysterious tension in time and space. Very often Giacometti withdraws his figures from possible intimacy by interposing a pedestal and raising them into a spatial and spiritual zone of unreality. Their presence is submerged in dreamy remembrance; their intensity is psychic. They are parables of life, and they embody no actual event. They stand in complete contrast to Rodin's heroics, and are spiritually and formally more related to Medardo Rosso's anonymous groups.

Alberto Giacometti *Female Figure* 1948 Bronze 5′8″ Coll. the artist

Statuette of a Youth
called *The Shadow of Evening* Etruscan idol
ca. 200 B.C. Bronze
22½″ Museo Guarnacci, Volterra

Alberto Giacometti *Man Pointing (L'Homme au Doigt)* 1947 Bronze 70″ Tate Gallery, London

"I have never regarded my figures as a compact mass, but as transparent constructions. It was not the outward form of human beings which interested me, but the effect they have had on my inner life." (Alberto Giacometti.)

In contrast to the fully developed, quiet vibration of Lehmbruck's contours, in Giacometti's work it is the erosion of the plastic substance by space that comes home to us as a dynamic form of energy. The point of similarity between the two artists is the subtlety of the psychic atmosphere emanating from their work.

Giacometti, who began with the *objet surréaliste,* has since 1940 devoted himself more and more to the human figure. His first work in this line was a portrait bust of his brother in many variations, some in minute dimensions. In the treatment of proportions he discovered an affinity between himself and the 17th century artist, Jacques Callot, who also sought to enclose a totality in the most minute dimensions. "Impossible to grasp the whole of a figure. We were too close to the model, and if we started on a detail — a heel or a nose — there was no hope of arriving at the whole. The distance between one nostril and the other is like a Sahara, boundless and elusive." (Alberto Giacometti, *Letter to Pierre Matisse,* 1947.)

Alberto Giacometti *Head of the Sculptor's Brother* 1950 Plaster 8″ Coll. the artist

Wilhelm Lehmbruck *Head of a Thinker with Hand* 1918
Synthetic stone 24½″ Coll. Lehmbruck, Tübingen

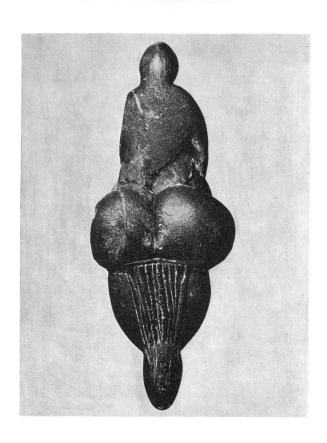

Prehistoric Statuette from the Cave of Lespugue, Aurignacian Mammoth Ivory ca. 6″ Musée St. Germain-en-Laye, (S.&O.)

Jean Arp arrived at sculpture in the round via the relief. In his early work, he sets basic geometrical and organic forms in contrast. His cylinders, bottles, and discs are arranged "acccording to the laws of chance." Intimate objects take on human form, human figures become things, all with the same undertone of humor that distinguished his reliefs. Later, he turns his attention almost exclusively to the great processes of nature. The spirit of growth and change, he says, must be felt in the organic form and fused with the human. His sculptures are signs, condensations of nature. They are related to trees, to stones and earth, yet they are transformed by the human and artistic substance in which they are embodied.

"Works of art should remain anonymous in nature's great studio — like the clouds, the ocean, the animals, man. Yes, man must re-enter nature." (Jean Arp.)

Snow Formations

Jean Arp *Configurations* 1932 Three Forms Movable on One Large Form Plaster 9″ x 13″ Coll. the artist

"When I exhibited my first 'concrete' reliefs, I issued a little manifesto declaring that bourgeois art was sanctioned lunacy. These naked men, women and children in stone or bronze, set up in public places, gardens and forest clearings, indefatigably dancing, chasing butterflies, shooting arrows, offering apples and playing flutes, are the perfect expression of a crazy world. These gibbering figures should no longer be allowed to sully nature. Like the early Christians, we must go back to essentials. The artist of today must let his work create itself directly. We are no longer concerned with subtleties. My reliefs and sculptures merge of themselves into nature. But if observed more closely, they reveal the work of a human hand. That is why I named a number of them *'Stone Shaped by Human Hand'*." (Jean Arp, *On My Way,* Documents of Modern Art, Vol. IV, New York, 1938, p. 97.)

Jean Arp *The Shepherd of the Clouds* 1949-53 Plaster 128″ Exhibition Yverdon, Switzerland Coll. the artist

The peaceful, slumbrous atmosphere of forms nestling together in nature, an essential gesture of animal creation, finds its artistic echo in Jean Arp's "Concrétions Humaines".

Young Swan Asleep

Jean Arp *Concrétion Humaine* 1936 Stone 19½″ Coll. Mrs. Maja Sacher Pratteln/Basel

Modulations in Snow

Jean Arp *Fruit of a Pagan Stone (Fruit D'Une Pierre Paienne)* 1942 Black granite 8″ x 13½″ Coll. Mrs. Mary Callery, New York

"Art is a fruit which is born of man, just as a fruit grows on a tree, or an embryo in the mother's womb. But whereas all fruits have forms intrinsically their own, the human fruit we call art nearly always embodies a ridiculous resemblance to something else...It is reason that has inflated man's pride with the fond belief that he is lord over nature and an infallible criterion in himself. Reason has turned him into a tragic and ridiculous figure...I love nature, but not its substitutes." (Jean Arp, *On My Way,* 1948, p. 93.)

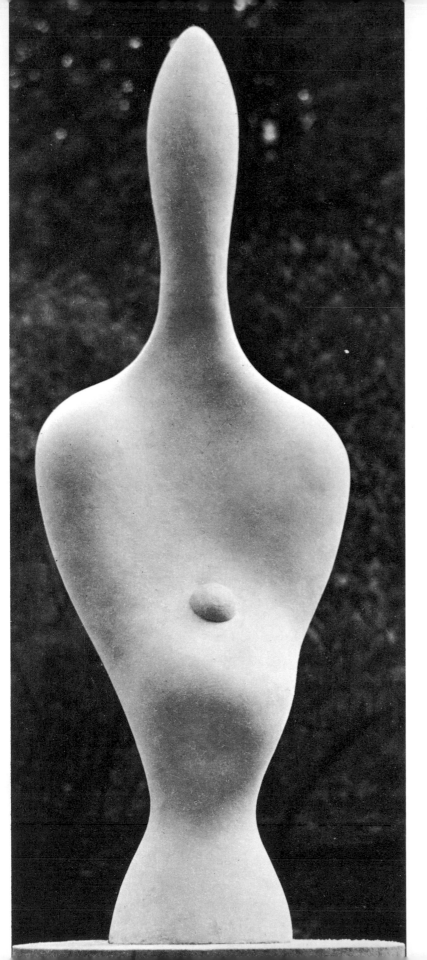

Jean Arp *Idol* 1950
Plaster 43½" Coll. S. and C.
Giedion-Welcker, Zurich

Jean Arp *Evocation of a Form
Human, Lunary, Spectral* 1950
Cast cement 33½" Museo d'Arte
Moderna, Rio de Janeiro

Jean Arp *Star* 1939 Gilded bronze 6¾" x 4⅝" x 1¾" base: 5⅛" x 4⅜" Coll. Baronne Lambert, Brussels

Jean Arp *Ptolemy (Ptolemaeus)* 1953 Limestone 40½″ Coll. Ambassador and Mrs. William A. M. Burden, New York

Constantin Brancusi's work points to a region where the contingent is reborn to become a comprehensive synthesis of the universal. It seems to have been born of a higher kind of consciousness, and communicates to the spectator that feeling of detachment and sublimity which is the distinguishing mark of Eastern philosophy and religion." *"Crime, Ordeal, Nirvana,"* the confessions of the Tibetan monk and poet Milarepa (11th century) became Brancusi's book of books. For the sculptor, however, the path trodden by the poet led to a final clarification of form, and the ultimate penetration of matter by the spirit. Thus the centuries were linked by a common spiritual atmosphere.

Brancusi's work unites the radiant formal beauty of the Mediterranean with an Oriental wisdom of form and symbolic power. It stands at the point of intersection of Eastern and Western civilization. No other sculptor of our day has achieved this fusion of sensuous understanding of all creaturely life with the supreme spiritualization of form. The essential shape, the universal significance of his forms resides in their ultimate simplicity. They have reached perfection through the unremitting labor of the master's hand. The products of this slow process of creation stand in almost startling contrast to the rapid sculptural improvisations of Picasso, having left behind them all that is personal and contingent, and expressing a devout submergence of the individual in the universal. While his works in stone and marble have a transcendental radiance, his wood carvings, as might be expected from the different material, are inhabited by another spirit. What they have to say is not primarily harmonious, relaxed, but very often grotesque and fantastic. Ancient bedevilments are coupled with a humor which brings relief. Brancusi works direct on his marble with the chisel, without any preliminary studies in clay; in the same way he goes straight to work on his tree trunks with the axe. His strange monsters, chimeras and witches, Adam and Eve, The Prodigal Son and Socrates, seem to rise in bizarre and burlesque form from trees, cottages and myths.

Constantin Brancusi *Sleeping Muse (La Muse Endormie)* 1906 Marble

Constantin Brancusi *Sleeping Muse (La Muse Endormie)* 1909-10 Marble 11″ x 12″ x 6½″ Coll. B. A. Davies

Sleeping Muse, Constantin Brancusi's female head of 1909-10, is stripped of all incidentals. The mere hint of eyebrows and eye sockets interrupts the surface of the ovoid. Since producing this work, Brancusi has become increasingly preoccupied with the ovoid and its simple, flowing outline as a primary element of sculptural form. It symbolizes the genesis of life in the widest sense, beyond all psychological analysis and detail. The distinctive feature of Brancusi's work, whether in wood, metal, or stone, is its floating poise, at times unbelievable from a strictly technical point of view. He calls his sculptures fish, bird, column, and head, but these names are mere tags for grandiose symbols of nature which have essential truths to express, and which arise from the depths of time immemorial.

Here again, Brancusi plucks from the marble the simplest of forms, the egg; it is poised on the faint movement of the neck, which is rendered in a few large curves. This rhythm of the human body was already intimated in the earlier *Pogany Busts* and in the model for the *Narcissus* spring.

Brancusi's works need freedom, space and light. He created them, as he says himself, "for everybody's recreation, and for large, open spaces." Their perfection of technique has raised them above the level of personal expression. "There is an aim in all things; to reach it we must detach ourselves from ourselves." (Brancusi.)

Constantin Brancusi *Mlle. Pogany* 1919 Marble 27½" x 8¾" x 11" Coll. Mr. Lee A. Ault, New Canaan, Conn

Constantin Brancusi *Study* Gouache Brancusi's Studio

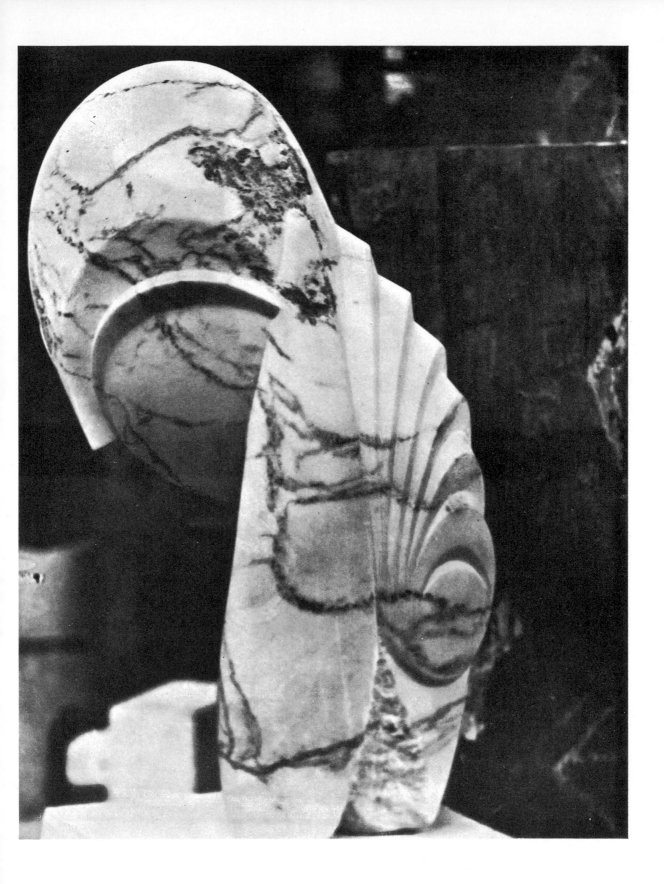

Constantin Brancusi *The Beginning of the World* 1924 Marble 6″ x 12″ x 7″ Coll. Mme. H. P. Roché, Sèvres, France

Here the purest form of ovoid volume — which originally began by making an abstract form of the human head — becomes the symbol of the mythical beginnings of the world. Its owner, the late Mr. Roché, called it "the stone that conveys the most forceful messages and is filled with immeasurable undertones."

Constantin Brancusi *Leda* 1923 Marble 26″ x 19″; height with base: 51⅛″ The Art Institute of Chicago, Catherine S. Dreier Estate

Constantin Brancusi *Leda* 1922-24 Burnished bronze 26¾″ Brancusi's Studio

Constantin Brancusi *Yellow Bird* 1925 Marble Arensberg Collection, Philadelphia Museum of Art

Constantin Brancusi *Fish* 1930 Blue-green marble 21″ x 71″ Museum of Modern Art, New York Acquired through the Lillie P. Bliss Bequest

The *Fish,* an elongated oval in polished marble, rotates on a stone drum. Created not for the confined studio or museum, but for the open spaces of nature, to respond to the wind and draw life from all growing things, this fish embodies the primeval form of all fish.

Constantin Brancusi *The Miracle (Le Miracle)* 1936 Marble 64″ x 44″ x 14½″
Photographed in Brancusi's studio The Solomon R. Guggenheim Museum, New York

Camel Ming Tombs North of Peking

134

Constantin Brancusi *The Kiss* 1908 Granite Cemetery of Montparnasse, Paris

The first important commission Brancusi received in Paris was for a tombstone. He executed it with superb simplicity as a double vertical, the coupling of two stelae, a symbol of union and love triumphant over death.

Constantin Brancusi *The Gate of the Kiss* 1935-38 Stone Targujiu, Carpathians, Rumania

In this work the double column of the early tombstone reappears, but in disembodied form, incised in the stone, and acting as a kind of leitmotif.
Brancusi's conception of architecture represents a principle totally different from that governing the all-round openness of contemporary architecture. An example is his design for a temple of meditation in India. Its primary aim is meditation and withdrawal from the world; it is the vessel of the contemplative life. Brancusi's architectural ideas recall the self-contained beauty of the massive peasant architecture of Europe's Mediterranean coast and Greek islands.

Pagoda on the shore of Lake Batur Central Bali

Constantin Brancusi *Endless Column* (Final Version) 1937 Gilt steel 97' 6" Targujiu, Carpathians, Rumania

Brancusi never abandoned the conception of prayer as a vertical on which every cathedral and every pagoda is based. In his *Colonnes sans Fin,* 1916-37, he repeatedly gave expression to that fervent ascent to heaven. The daring equipoise he achieves in his proportions defies belief; yet they are pure creations, not based on technical calculations.

Constantin Brancusi *Maiastra* 1912 Burnished bronze 30″ Coll. Peggy Guggenheim, Venice

In the Rumanian fairy tale, Maiastra, the fabulous bird, leads the wandering lover to his beloved. From 1912 on, Brancusi treated this bird subject repeatedly in marble and bronze as a symbol of the soaring spirit. It led him to impart an unprecedented elasticity and vitality to his material. As in the *Colonnes sans Fin,* the concept of verticality, of a great upward urge, is expressed in three-dimensional form. The first name he gave the sculpture was not only pregnantly poetic, but also descriptive of the problem he had set himself: *Bird, a Design Which Should Expand to Fill the Vault of Heaven.* All that is incidental and personal has fallen away, so that the form, pure and radiantly spatial, may take on a symbolic function. The vitality of Brancusi's work has increased steadily, hand in hand with the sublimation of his material. "All my life I have been seeking to capture the essence of flight." (Brancusi.)

Constantin Brancusi
Bird (L'Oiseau) 1940
Burnished bronze 59"
Coll. Peggy Guggenheim,
Venice

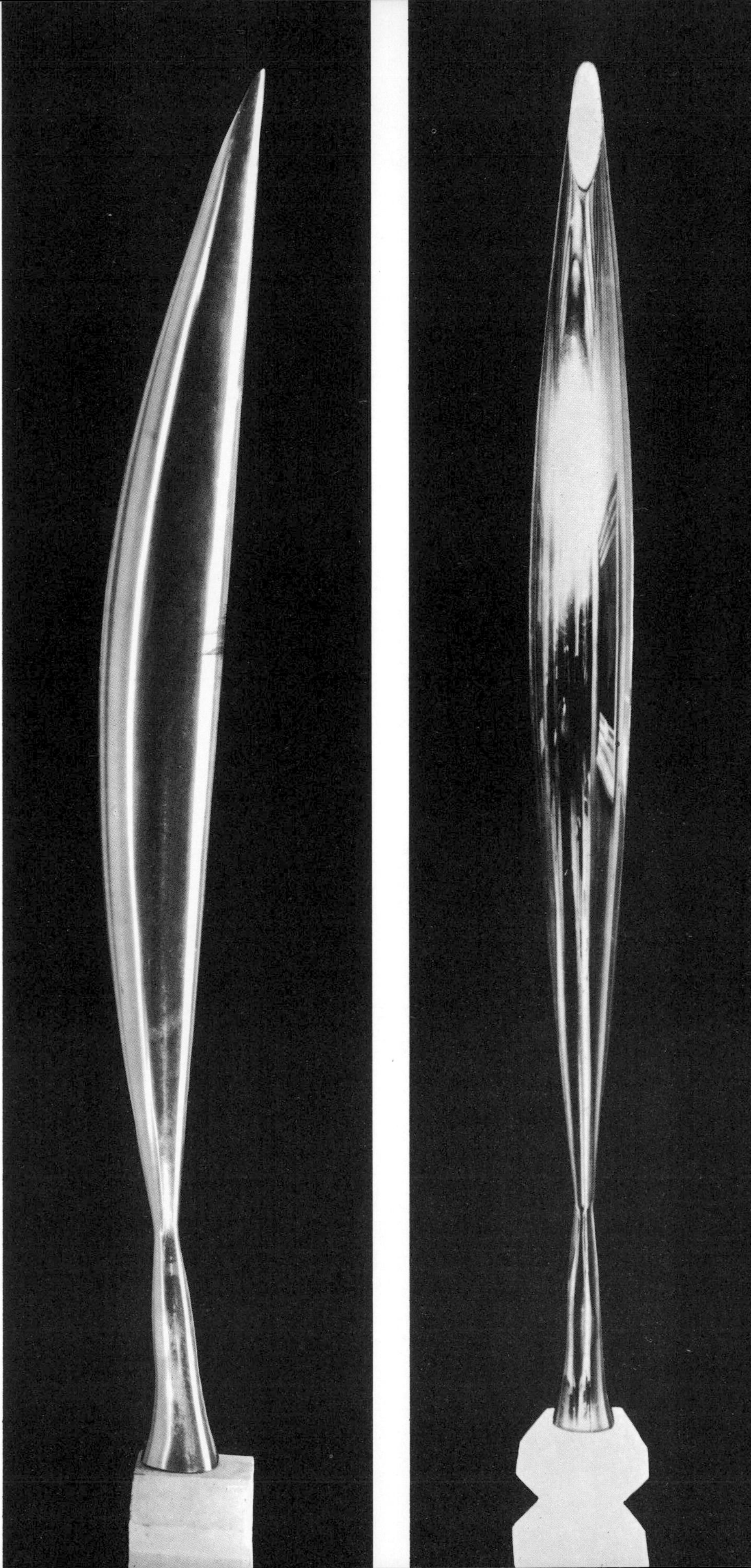

Constantin Brancusi *Chimera* 1918
Wood 36½"; base: 23⅛" Arensberg Collection
Philadelphia Museum of Art

Brancusi carves forms in wood which recall the gargoyles on medieval cathedrals. They are bizarre creatures with oval and round apertures; they have wings and talons; their heavy beaked heads are precariously poised. The underlying structure, however, is strictly architectural.

Constantin Brancusi *The Cock* 1924
Polished bronze 41″ x 8½″ x
4¼″ Musée d'Art Moderne, Paris

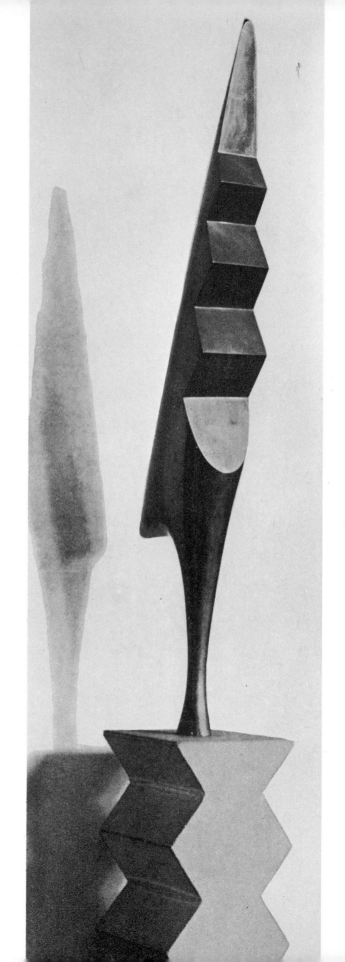

Brancusi has treated the cock in a number of variations since 1924. The teeth of the comb are also
intended to symbolize the rising tonal scale of the
cock's crow. Its shape is a synthesis of bird and scale.
(Pages 140 and 141).

Henry Moore *Two Forms* 1934 Pynkado wood 11″ Museum of Modern Art, New York Gift of Sir Michael Sadler

In the early work of *Henry Moore* we can trace a steady movement away from the naturalistic and personal towards the fundamental and symbolic form. In his intense preoccupation with the inherent properties of his material, he is concerned mainly with grasping an underlying biological concept. From time to time, mathematically sharp incisions in these symbols of natural growth seem to imply the introduction of an architectural, urban element. In his later work, Moore has shown an increased interest in the human figure. "The human figure is what interests me most deeply, but I have found principles of form and rhythm from the study of natural objects such as pebbles, rocks, bones, trees, plants, etc." *(Essays by Henry Moore,* edited by Herbert Read, 1934.)

Henry Moore *Sculpture* 1937 Stone 20″ Coll. the artist

144

Ara Head Toltec Basalt 23″ Xochicalco, Mexico

Henry Moore *Square Form* 1936 Brown Hornton stone 24" long Coll. the artist

"A hole can itself have as much shape — meaning — as a solid mass. The mystery of the hole — the mysterious fascination of caves in hillsides and cliffs." *(Essays by Henry Moore, 1934.)*

Henry Moore
Double Standing Figure
1950 Bronze 7' 3"
Coll. L. J. Salter,
New York

Henry Moore *Reclining Figure* 1945-46 Wood 76″ long Cranbrook Academy of Art, Michigan

Moore realizes the human figure in its static vitality as a grand rhythm of convex and concave, of dark cavities and brilliant protuberances. He has himself defined this transmutation and dissolution of the static as follows: "Masses being static in the sense that the center of gravity lies within the base (and does not seem to be falling over or moving off its base) — and yet having an alert dynamic tension between its parts." *(Essays by Henry Moore, 1934.)*

149

Henry Moore *Family Group* 1945-49 Bronze 59¼" Museum of Modern Art,
New York Acquired through the Lillie P. Bliss Bequest

The variations in the conception of the group may be touched on here in connection with Henry Moore's *Family Group.* In it we find the static coordination of large and small figures, differing from the natural human body only in the large deformations of detail and free treatment of the proportions. Contrasted with this is the free conception of Arp's *Mediterranean Group,* which retains as the symbol of the family the basic mass, and then thrusts out in all directions, stretching and contracting. It is intentionally ambiguous. The same interweaving and upward movement may be seen in Lipchitz's *Rescue,* where, however, it takes on a dramatic tension deriving from its particular subject.

150

Jacques Lipchitz *The Rescue* 1945 Gilt bronze 16″
Fine Arts Associates, New York

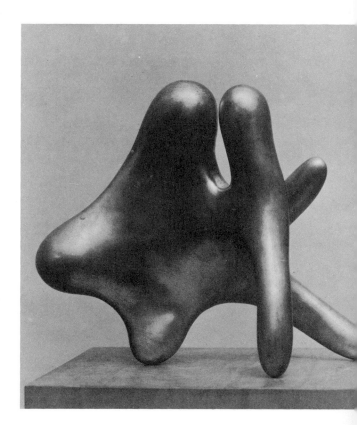

Jean Arp *Mediterranean Group* 1941-42 Bronze 10″ x 15″
Coll. the artist

151

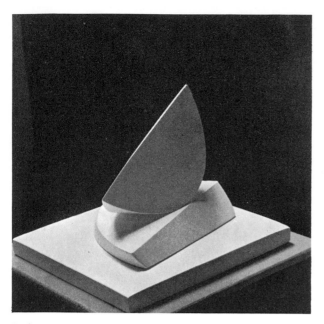

Barbara Hepworth *Carving in Marble* 1936 12" Coll. the artist

Barbara Hepworth has progressed from studies of the human body to an ever increasing and more expressive simplification of form. In her early work certain influences from Arp, Brancusi and Henry Moore can be traced. Since 1946 she has returned to the study of the human figure with an entirely new approach. She regards sculpture as a link between the human scale and the architectural. "Sculpture should act not only as a foil to architectural properties, but the sculpture itself should provide a link between human scale and sensibility and the greater volumes of space and mass in architecture." (Barbara Hepworth, *Carvings and Drawings,* 1952.)

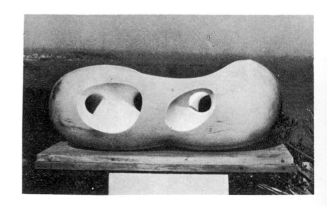

Barbara Hepworth *Pendour* 1947 Painted wood 28" long Coll. the artist

Pendour expresses the physical sensation of lying on a beach, the surge of the sea hollows out the form, creating a rhythm like a whorl in the grain of the wood. A fusion of cosmic and human experience is translated into organic and geometrical terms. However lively the movement may be in detail, the hollows and masses, the light and color, create an effect of calm and balance. "From the sculptor's point of view, one must either be the spectator of the object or the object itself. For a few years I became the object — I was the figure in the landscape and every sculpture contained to a greater or less degree the everchanging forms and contours embodying my own response to a given position in that landscape." (Barbara Hepworth, *Carvings and Drawings,* 1952.)

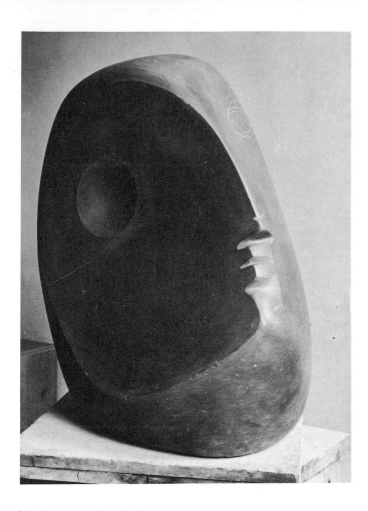

Barbara Hepworth *The Cosdon Head* 1949
Blue marble 24" City Art Gallery,
Birmingham, England

The impressive block of this head takes on an inner expressiveness as a result of a few simple accents.

Barbara Hepworth *Form Enclosed* 1951-52
Alabaster 17" Coll. the artist

Barbara Hepworth *Dyad* 1949
Rosewood 50" Coll. the artist

In *Dyad,* the dynamics of living growth flow naturally into a firm, yet soaring body.

Visual representation of an algebraic formula, $xyz = k^3 (x + y + z - 1)^3$ H. Henrici 1876 Science Museum, London

Georges Vantongerloo *Construction in a Sphere* 1917
Plaster 7″ x 7″ x 7″ Museum of Modern Art, New York Purchase Fund

While a faint trace of "subject" can still be discerned in the work of the Cubists, *Vantongerloo* eliminates it entirely. His impulse to create comes from the desire to express an objective law in art. The early work of Vantongerloo, the only sculptor member of the Stijl group until 1919, is based on elementary volumes and proportions.

Georges Vantongerloo *Construction in an Inscribed and Circumscribed Square of a Circle* 1924 Cement
10" x 10" x 14" Coll. Peggy Guggenheim, Venice

In Vantongerloo's work, geometric form plays a leading part in the clarification and purification of the structure as a whole. "The proportional relations between the volumes impart a sense of space, the distance between them a sense of time." (Georges Vantongerloo, *Abstraction, Création,* Paris, 1932.)

Georges Vantongerloo *Construction* 1931 Wood 26¾″ x 21½″ x 20½″ Coll. the artist

Georges Vantongerloo *Nucleus* 1946 Nickel wire 8″ x 8″ x 8″ Coll. the artist

Vantongerloo has abandoned his earlier, strictly architectural formations and the pure relationship of volumes. He is evolving toward a disembodied dynamic of space expressed, with supreme artistic asceticism, in transparent materials. Here is the artistic imagination working in the spirit of the modern scientist's conception of the universe, with the notion of energy as its starting point.

Theo van Doesburg *Design for a Monument for the City of Leeuwarden* 1916 Coll. Nelly van Doesburg, Meudon

H. P. Berlage, pioneer of modern Dutch architecture, awarded the prize to this design for a public monument, the work of the leader of the Stijl Group. The design reveals the clear interplay of slabs and rectangular solids in a great upward movement. Though it is constructed in an architectural spirit, it has no actual architectural aim.

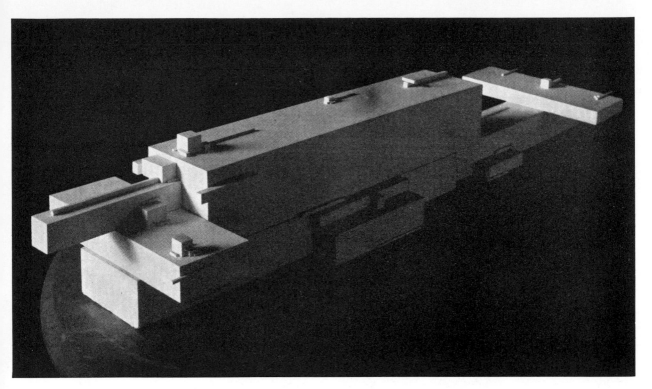

Kasimir Malevich *Dynamic Architecture* 1920-22 Wood

Kasimir Malevich *Suprematist Architecture*
1920-22 Wood Coll. H. and S. Syrcus, Warsaw

The work of the Suprematist painter, *Kasimir Malevich,* also shows, in these years, a close connection between sculpture and architecture. His constructions are not architectural models, but a general expression of the laws of proportion and of the interrelationships of simple geometrical solids.

163

Hermann Obrist *Design for a Monument* Before 1902 Plaster 36″ (Posthumous) Kunstgewerbemuseum, Zurich

"The fatal delusion that the human figure is the alpha and omega of sculpture has been a stumbling-block for genera-tions. True, the human figure contains wonderful potentialities for the sculptor. But look at the Tortoise Fountain in Rome. Its basins are a riot of sculptured forms, perhaps the most luxuriant in the world, but what has the shape of their contours to do with the human nude?" (Hermann Obrist, *Catalogue of the Exhibition "Um 1900"*, edited by H. Curjel, Zurich, 1952.)

Antonio Gaudi *Casa Mila* Sculptured Chimney 1905-07 Mosaic surface with fragments of crockery, Amigos de Gaudi, Barcelona

This outstanding modulation of a functional form shows, in full vigor, even as early as the "Art Nouveau" period, the interrelation of solid and perforated volumes with their interplay of lights and shadows. These methods of giving sculptural life to architecture and architectural details were later adapted by Le Corbusier in a more geometrical manner (see page 204).

Auguste Rodin *Project for a Monument to Labor* 1897 Plaster model Rodin Museum, Meudon

Rodin's project renews in the epoch of "Art Nouveau" the Gothic structure of a perforated tower (Pisa) moving upwards in a spiral curve.

Vladimir E. Tatlin *Design for a Monument to the Third International* 1920 Iron Moscow

Thus Rodin, Gaudi, Obrist and Tatlin illustrate how vigorously movement has overcome static form and how the vital, sinuous line of "Art Nouveau" has been ultimately transformed into the abstract language of today. In a fundamentally similar direction, Boccioni's *Development of a Bottle in Space* should also be mentioned here.

167

Vladimir E. Tatlin *Construction* 1919 Iron Moscow

This work is one of the earliest of purely abstract constructions. In its unprecedented use of a new and unusual material, it is related to Cubism and Dada, though the spiritual approach is quite different.

168

Kasimir Meduniezky *Construction* 1919 Iron and brass 17¾" Yale University Art Gallery, New Haven

In *Meduniezky* there is an interplay of air volumes circumscribed by iron bands. The massive cube of the pedestal enhances the freedom and buoyancy of the construction. The clarity and force of the whole is increased by the reduction of the medium to a minimum.

Alexander Rodchenko *Construction* 1921 Metal Moscow

Rodchenko, with supreme technical precision, dissolves the mass of a spherical body into compartments of air, achieving an effect of floating lightness.

Though primarily structural in intention, Picasso's design for a construction in wire is humanized by the addition of witty and paradoxical details like the head and hands.

170

Pablo Picasso
Design for a Construction in Iron Wire
1928 30″ Coll. the artist

Laszlo Moholy-Nagy *Construction* 1923 Opaque, ground and transparent glass, nickel and vulcanite fibre
Coll. Sybil Moholy-Nagy, New York

Moholy-Nagy was first chiefly preoccupied with the contrast of materials and the relationship of simple geometric forms. At the Bauhaus his teaching was along these lines. His work embodies the ideas of Constructivism, both in its mathematical precision and in the "newness" of the materials used. But the effects he achieves by these methods and media are purely artistic.

Laszlo Moholy-Nagy *Space Modulator* 1940 Plexiglass and wire 24″ Coll. Sybil Moholy-Nagy, New York

This composition was modeled by hand in plexiglas, a material more ductile than glass, and combining the advantages of transparency and airy lightness. Space modulators are constructions in the most contemporary of materials; but their form begins to show a closer approximation to organic spontaneity and mobility. The wires spread like veins, and the perforations create a free play of light and shade which informs the whole with vitality and poetry. Moholy-Nagy himself described the aesthetic effect of this material: "This composition demonstrates three types of transparent walls, circumscribed by the thick edges of the flexible glass or wire. One is moderately transparent (rhodoid), the second perfectly transparent (plexiglas), and the third super-transparent (air)." (*Vision in Motion,* 1947.)

In his *Light Requisite* of 1930, Moholy-Nagy's aim was to elicit a time-space effect from the interpenetration of separate phases of movement. In his later work he abandoned entirely these pure technical constructions in favor of spontaneous artistic utterance, bursting with kinetic energy — a perfect synthesis of rhythm and sensitivity expressed with modern means.

Interpenetrating forms bathed in light are immediately intelligible by virtue of their transparency. The totality of the composition is superbly fused with the shifting interplay of its parts. A similar suggestiveness, a similar rhythm and ghostly unreality are attained, but with a totally different means of expression, in Arp's *Human, Lunary, Spectral.*

"Since light is an element of the time-space continuum, by the mere fact of devoting fresh attention to the problem of light, we enter into the domain of a new feeling for space which it would be premature to analyze today. And yet it is a thing which can be summed up in a word — floating." (From a letter to C. G.-W. by Moholy-Nagy, 1937.)

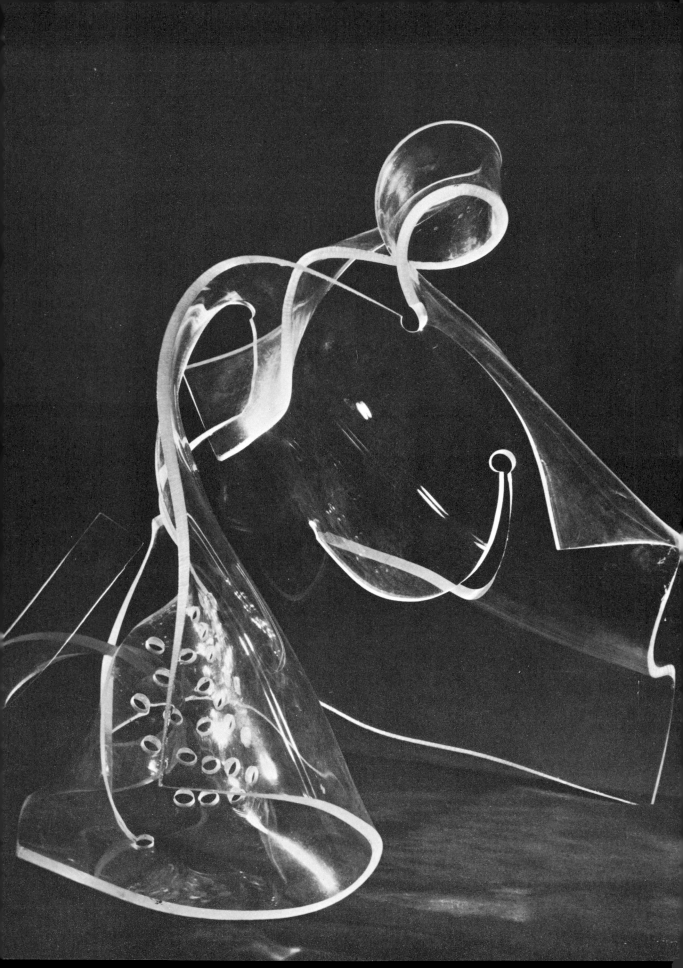

Naum Gabo *Head* 1916 Iron 17⅜" Gemeente Museum van Amsterdam, Holland

Naum Gabo's *Head,* 1916, shows a systematic refining away of material and a recombination with open spaces. Its mathematical sharpness stands out in comparison with the much softer transitions of Picasso's Cubist head and Boccioni's head of 1912, both of which already demonstrated the break-up of the volume. The predominance of expressive hollows demands a new kind of vision.

Naum Gabo, the founder, with his brother Antoine Pevsner, of the Constructivist movement, aspires to give expression to the new and expanded conception of the universe opened up by science. This new conception of the universe is, for him, constructive in character. ("The new image is a constructive image.") The determining factor in his view of things, as in that of the Stijl group and Moholy-Nagy, is the realization of a definite stage in a process of spiritual development — a stage absolutely of the present and pointing to the future. It is not, as with Arp, the idea of a biological cycle. "Those mentally constructed images are the very essence of the reality of the world which we are searching for." (Naum Gabo, *On Constructive Realism,* lecture, Yale University, 1948.) This is a testimony to his belief in the progress of *homo sapiens.* Gabo's choice of materials is fully consonant with his ideas. He began with constructions in iron and glass, later turning to combinations of light, synthetic substances. He does not use them exclusively toward certain aesthetic ends; their transparency is a means of capturing space and rendering it visible in an absolutely new way.

176

It is interesting to note that methods so different as shown in Brancusi's *Bird* and Gabo's *Kinetic Sculpture* attain very similar results: a fundamental similarity of vision and approach due simply to their being contemporaries. Brancusi achieves momentum precisely by retention of the solid mass, by proportion, and by his use of light to impart vitality and luminosity to his polished surfaces. In works created quite independently of each other, there is the same expression of disembodied flight into space.

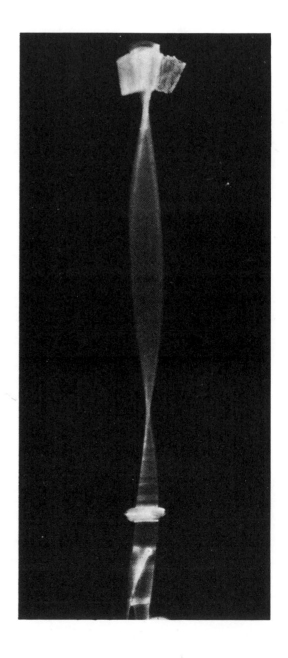

Naum Gabo *Kinetic Sculpture* 1920 Steel spring 30″ Coll. the artist

Naum Gabo *Construction for Chicago Swimming Pool* 1932 Model in metal and glass Maryland Club Gardens

"We call ourselves Constructivists because we no longer paint our pictures or carve our sculptures, and because both are 'constructed' in space and with the help of space. Thus we break down the old distinction between painting and sculpture. By way of the Constructivist principle the visual arts enter the domain of 'architecture;' by architecture I mean not only the building of houses, but the whole edifice of our everyday existence." (Naum Gabo, *Abstraction, Création,* Paris, 1932; *Circle,* London, 1937.)

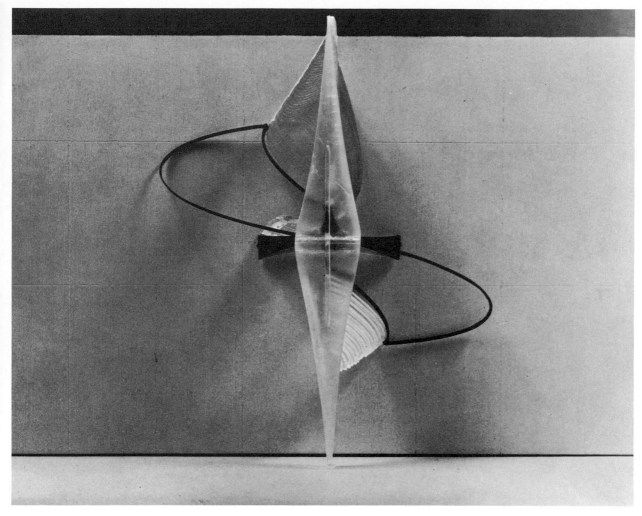

Naum Gabo *Model for the Entrance Hall of the Esso Building, Rockefeller Center, New York*
1949 Ironwire and plastic ca. 17' Museum of Modern Art, New York

Gabo regards a close collaboration between sculptor and architect as indispensable. He means no mere juxtaposition, but a close and intimate union of their work on the basis of a common idea. By their lightness and radiance, these fantastic "architectures," which are constructed with extreme mathematical precision, cast a veil of poetry and freedom over the commonplace architectural environment. In these works Gabo reveals himself as the lyric poet of space and light. "There is no more mathematics in my work than there is anatomy in a figure of Michelangelo." (Naum Gabo, *On Constructive Realism,* 1948.)

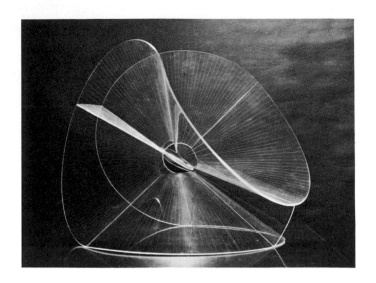

Naum Gabo *Translucent Variations on a Spheric Theme*
1937 Plastic and nylon 22¾"
The Solomon R. Guggenheim Museum, New York

Along with a penchant for monumental construction, which he was able to realize for Marcel Breuer's Bijenkorf Building in Rotterdam (1955-1957), Gabo has also conceived smaller works of sublime translucency and linear beauty in a more lyrical manner. These creations tend (since 1937) more and more toward a spontaneous, flexible organic form.

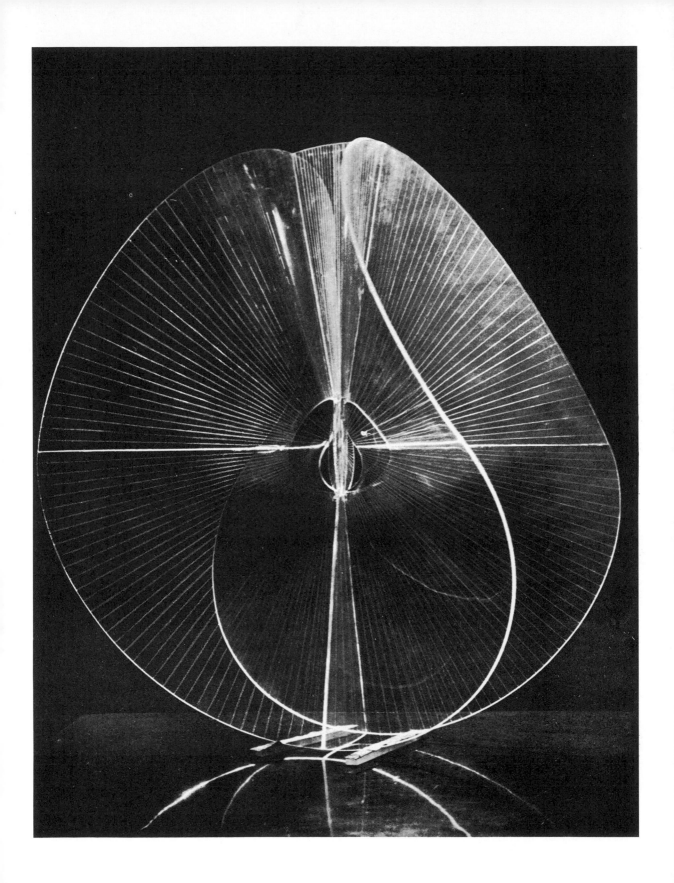

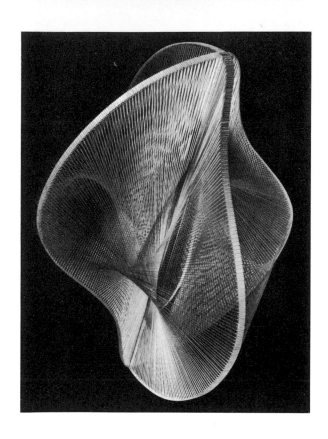

Naum Gabo *Linear Construction in Space* 1949 Plastic and nylon 3' Coll. the artist

Naum Gabo *Construction in Space* 1955-57
Steel covered with bronze; middle sculpture stainless steel; base covered
with Swedish granite 84′ 6″ Bijenkorf, Rotterdam, Holland

184

The interior view of this spatially activated construction (here seen from below) reveals the effect of interpenetrating forces which was first accepted esthetically in the Eiffel Tower and is here conveyed by means of today's intensified dynamics.

Antoine Pevsner *Composition in Space (Project for a Fountain)*
1929 Sheet-brass and glass 27″ Kunstmuseum Basel Emanuel Hoffmann Foundation

Pevsner's forms open up and leap into space like projectiles. There is no area of softness or yielding; all is dynamic, structural, and incisive. Under Pevsner's hand the mass disintegrates, weight is shed, and dimensions multiply. Like Gabo, he gives increasing emphasis and vitality to the spatial element.

In his later work, Pevsner's dynamic development in space progressively loses its mechanical character. Within a serried bundle of metal strands, a grand upward movement unfolds in a curved plane. Pevsner's artistic development is akin to that of his brother, Naum Gabo, in his steady approach to organic form. The rational and functional aspects of form vanish in the face of Pevsner's power to "energize" space and enclose it in the funnels and pockets created by light. Here color is not applied; it is produced by light that falls on prepared structures and is eternally renewed by the intersection of planes. While Gabo mainly uses transparent materials, Pevsner prefers bronze, which, disembodied by light, relates the construction to natural atmospheric happenings. Most of Pevsner's works are models for execution on a monumental scale, emblems for airports and fountains. They are free symbols of the movement of the universe, rapid in pace and animated by deep and genuine feeling. What these forms express is, in the main, space and energy, but their ultimate source is the depths of human emotion.

Antoine Pevsner *Projection into Space* 1938-39 Bronze 19¼″ Coll. Mrs. Maja Sacher, Pratteln/Basel

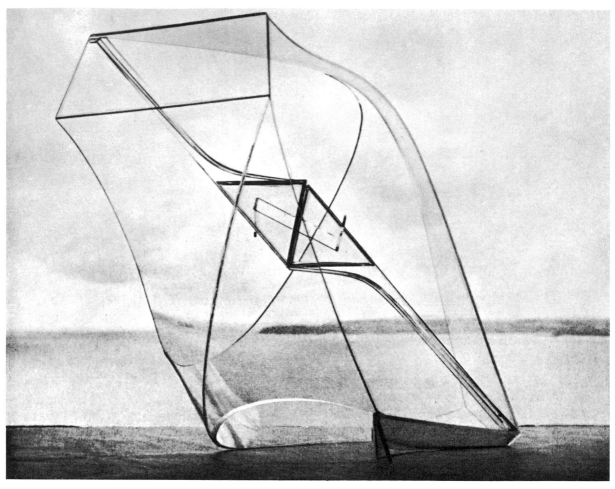

Naum Gabo *Construction in Space with Crystalline Center* 1938 Plastic and crystalloid 18½″ Coll. the artist

Antoine Pevsner *World Construction* 1947 Brass and oxidized tin 28″ Coll. the artist

These examples illustrate in various ways a dynamic event, the radiation of a cell into form. They express the dynamic relationship of microcosm and macrocosm and the genetic center of growth. (Refer also to the expressive methods of Barbara Hepworth in this direction. Page 154 and Vantongerloo page 161).

Antoine Pevsner *Developable Column of Victory* 1945-46 Brass and oxydized tin 41″ Coll. the artist

This V-sign is conceived as a universal symbol of liberation and victory. It is designed for our time, and replaces the obsolete, heroic triumphal arch. The flow of space can be felt at all points. The movement is accomplished before our eyes in a great, pulsating rhythm. This contemporary symbol is permeated by genuine, restrained emotion.

Antoine Pevsner *Dynamic Projection in the 30th Degree*
1950-51 Brass and oxydized bronze 8′ 4″ x 7′ 4″ University of Caracas, Venezuela

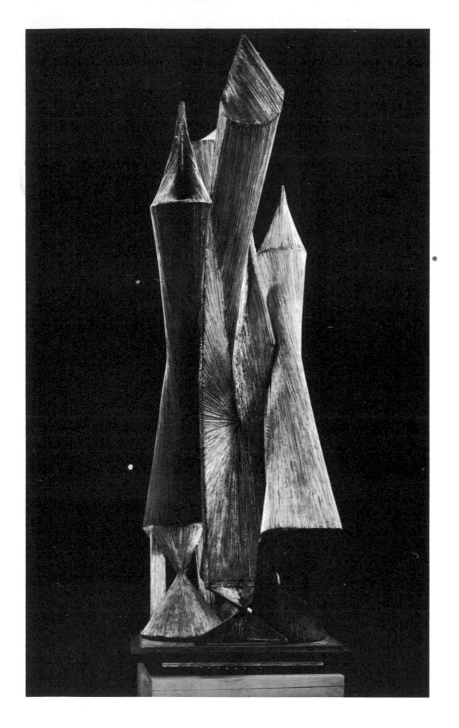

Antoine Pevsner *Column Symbolizing Peace (La Colonne Symbolisant La Paix)*
1954 Bronze 53" x 35½" x 19¾" Rijksmuseum, Kröller-Müller, Otterlo, Holland

Walking around this piece of sculpture one discovers one surprise after another. From each new viewpoint it seems to be a different composition. The rich and lively orchestration of this group of forms, with their centrifugally motivated rhythms, emerges in ever fresh variations. It is worked out to the minutest detail and filled with that "emotion" of poetic spatial dynamics which is peculiarly Pevsner's own and on which he has been working for the past forty years.

Julio Gonzalez, who abandoned painting for sculpture only late in life, carries on in modern form the old Catalonian tradition of wrought iron work. In Paris, under the influence of Cubism, he refines away more and more of the material — sheet iron and iron rods — of which his complex and space-enclosing constructions are made. Some are purely constructive in intention; others are humanized by gesticulation and achieve a kind of sparkling wit. Gonzalez executed a large number of pieces for Picasso, inspiring the latter's work in this medium. He is one of those who exert the strongest influence on the younger generation today, particularly in England and America.

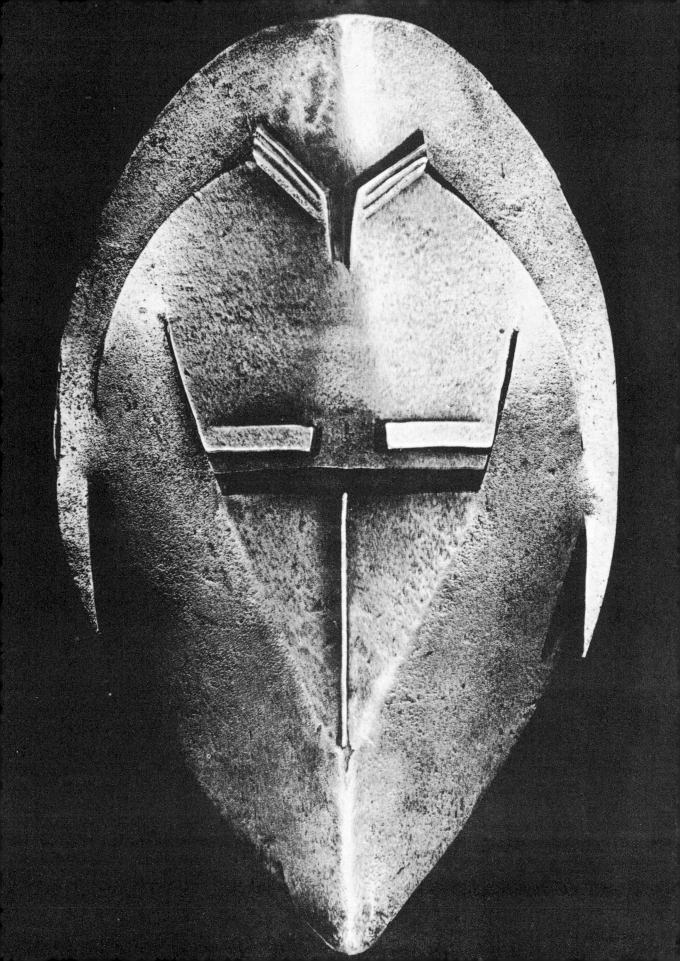

Julio Gonzalez *Venus* 1927 Wrought iron
Private Collection, Paris

Julio Gonzalez *Dancer* 1934 Wrought iron 25"
Coll. Roberta Gonzalez, Paris

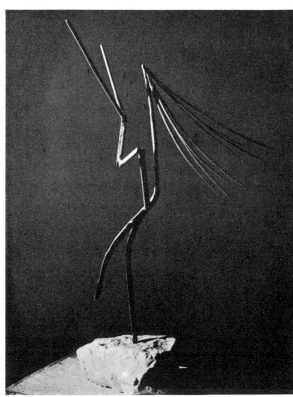

Julio Gonzalez *Reclining Figure* 1936 Wrought iron 12½" Coll. Roberta Gonzalez, Paris

"All true artists are of their time. It could not be otherwise, for if it is true that a period produces its artists, that is because the artists have left their mark on the period. If one generation has not succeeded in giving full expression to its aims, the next may succeed. Whether the public understands or not, the artist must not yield an inch." (Julio Gonzalez, *Cahiers d' Art,* 1935.)

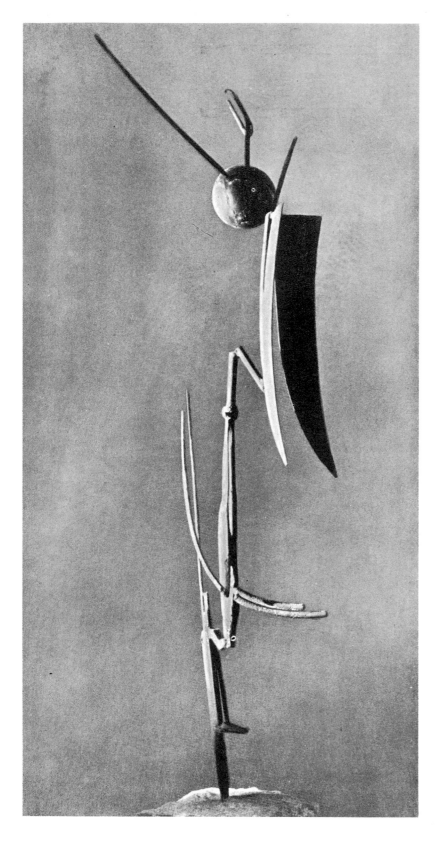

Julio Gonzalez *Angel* 1933
Wrought iron, 63"
Musée d'Art Moderne, Paris

Julio Gonzalez *Woman Combing Her Hair*
1936 Wrought iron 52"
Museum of Modern Art, New York

Julio Gonzalez *Woman and Mirror (Femme Au Mirroir)* 1936 Iron 82″ Coll. Roberta Gonzalez, Paris

Julio Gonzalez *Standing Figure (Personnage Debout)* 1937 Iron 22½″ Coll. Hans Hartung, Paris

Eduardo Chillida *Mute Music (La Musica Callada)* 1955 Iron width 61″ Private Collection, Basel, Switzerland

Himself a blacksmith, Chillida administers and transmutes the inheritance he received from his Catalan compatriot, Gonzalez. In his work we can plainly see the trend of the younger generation. The gently lyrical (and often humorous) half-tones of his forerunner, with their psychological allusions by means of bizarre details of form and highly contrasted combinations (including Ready-Mades), have been swallowed up in a sea of universal psychic vibrations. Here, too, the material is uniform and the work permeated by great waves of rhythm. We experience the flow of a dramatically exciting development and variations of themes expressed with unbroken but wonderfully disciplined vehemence. The emotional timbre and power of these forms, forged in fire, are richly orchestrated in space. Even their titles, *In Praise of Fire, In Praise of Iron, The Tremor of Iron, Mute Music, Articulated Reverie,* imply the different "degrees of heat" — and also the inner temperatures — involved. Expressive scansion, sudden retardation, aggressive thrusts and sharply silhouetted movements create a musical interplay of the component elements. The result is an intensive gesticulation in space, a passionate language conjured out of intransigeant material. This mysterious blend of passion and asceticism is grounded in the depths of Spanish tradition.

Eduardo Chillida *Murmur of Boundaries No. 3 (Rumor de Limites No. 3)* 1959 Steel width 51" Galerie Maeght, Paris

The progenitors of *Calder's* art are those airy constructions that revolve on roofs and church spires. Their movement is borrowed from the wind, their existence airy and playful. Calder's "mobiles", as children of their time, are made of plain sheet iron and tin, mounted on thin wires and rods. They belong to a mechanical age and a technological country, but both mechanics and technology are overcome by their human sensitivity and poetry. A master of delicate craftsmanship, Calder uses the simplest of elements, outlining, balancing, and combining them with the utmost precision in a spreading play of forms. The vivacity of this unprecedented fusion of the organic and the mechanical is revealed when these black or colored discs rise along their stems of wire, cutting into space like a knife and combining in ever-new constellations. A "fish", a metal oval, swims irrationally in air inside a flexible system of coordinates of points and lines; a black "morning star" quivers in the wind among the grass, set in a poised interplay of balls and lines. Calder's extremely sensitive art developed out of the humorous wire and wood toys with which he began. "Homo ludens" plays just as great a part in his work as it does in the poetic burlesques of William Saroyan. Against the background of the rationalized and overorganized life of our day, his art stands out in joyous detachment. It is just as true to the physical laws of its constructive principle (and hence to the industrial mind of America) as it is to capricious spontaneity. A kinetic energy is released in Calder's early work by mechanical means (motor power), and later by cosmic currents, by the faintest breath of wind. It is a dance of abstract forms in their simple, dynamic interrelationships in time and space.

Alexander Calder *A Universe* 1934 Wire, wicker
and wood 40½" Coll. Museum of Modern Art
Gift of Mrs. John D. Rockefeller, Jr.

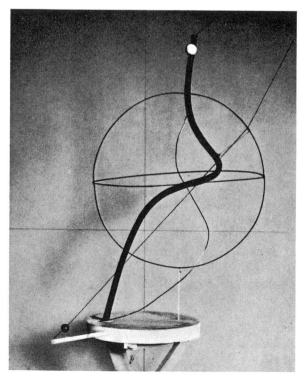

Alexander Calder *Steel Fish* Mobile 1934 Sheet metal, sheet aluminum and steel rods 10' Museum of Fine Arts, Richmond, Va.

Calder's *Steel Fish* is a montage of steel rods and sheet aluminum, set up in a natural background and translated into a free play of natural movement. Under the influence of the wind it indulges in fantastic dips and floppings. A shifting equipoise results like that which Brancusi achieves in his marble *Fish* by means of proportions and the play of light which sublimates the block of solid marble on the rotating stone drum.

Alexander Calder *Portrait of Shepard Vogelgesang* 1930 Wire 15″ Coll. Vogelgesang, New York

The living lines of this wire relief describe three-dimensional forms as it sways in space. A similar effect can be found in the drawings of Klee, Picasso and Braque, where the line moves of its own volition.

Alexander Calder *Morning Star* 1943 Sheet iron, wire and wood 6′ 7″ Coll. the artist

Alexander Calder *Le Plumeau Bleu* 1950 Sheet iron and wire 43½″ Galerie Maeght, Paris

"Any element that possesses motion, whether within itself or in space, that can oscillate, come and go, stands in a dynamic relationship to the other elements composing its world." (Alexander Calder, *Abstraction, Création,* 1932.)

Alexander Calder *Black Beast* Stabile 1940 Sheet iron 8′9″ Curt Valentin Gallery, New York

A fantastic construction comes stepping along on pointed feet, describing triangles and curves, and throwing its dainty elegance open to space. There is a free rhythm of plane and void, air and metal. Although the soberly technical character of the construction stands fully revealed, it never detracts from the poetic atmosphere of the whole.

Kenneth Armitage *Standing Group 2* (Large Version)
1952-54 Bronze 41¼"
Bertha Schaefer Gallery, New York

Here, construction of plane surfaces like walls, rhythmically activated and extending into space coalesces with the figuration to form a single unit.

Kenneth Armitage *Family Going for a Walk*
1951 Bronze 26" Museum of Modern Art, New York

A forward movement, streaming and gliding, is held in a grand, flat diagonal form. It is a subdivided unit, and not, like Giacometti's groups, a juxtaposition of separate spatial rhythms. The fluttering of the clothes, a rare motif in modern sculpture, had already been an outstanding feature of Medardo Rosso's *Boulevard.* Viewed from any angle, the work has its surprises, all of which lie within the sculptor's intention. The whole is dominated by the equipoise of a complex organism in a state of dynamic movement.

"In *Family Going for a Walk,* 1951, I desire to express a large volume with a minimum of material. The discovery of flatness has dominated my work for the time being. Hence a large, flat slab in the middle. Pleasure from wondering what is on the other side. Pleasure from the division. Pleasure from seeing washing hanging on a line." (Kenneth Armitage, Letter to C. G.-W., 1953.)

Reg Butler the English sculptor-engineer-architect, creates fragile constructions in iron and stainless steel. Some look like plants, others recall insects, and all are enclosed in delicate silhouettes. It is characteristic of Butler's work that it retains human gestures and rhythms. Though fundamentally constructive, its original impulse is obviously an encounter with nature. Bathed in light and air, it shares in the life of nature. The dominants are line and structure. The tendency is toward a rigid economy of material. This sculptor, who combines the mechanical with the poetic, the cruel with the tender, was influenced in his beginnings not only by Henry Moore, but also by Gonzalez and Calder.

The Oracle is a fusion of the archaic and technological. Mechanical (aircraft) and organic forms are combined in a new symbolic expression of traditional and present-day life. In the sculptor's own words: *"The Oracle* is a personage in the depths of the college."

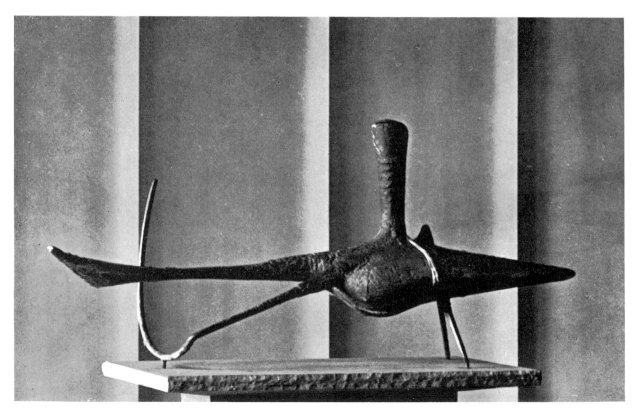

Reg Butler *The Oracle* 1952 Shell bronze on forged armature 6′ 6″ long Hatfield Technical College

Reg Butler *Boy and Girl* 1950 Iron 6'9" Arts Council of Great Britain, London

Pablo Picasso *Construction*
1930-31 Wrought iron 82¾"
Coll. the artist

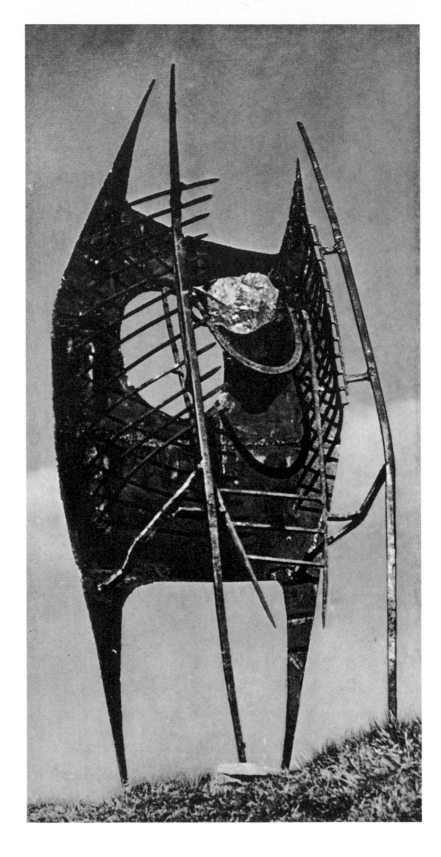

Lynn Chadwick *The Inner Eye*
1952 Iron, glass and wire 7'
Museum of Modern Art, New York

There is in this construction that
sensitivity of form which so many
young British sculptors so ably distill
from the hard and linear medium of
iron. Here again we find the dematerialization of mass and the vitality
of line which is also characteristic
of modern drawing. The austerity of
the construction is mitigated by the
variety of textures, colors and media.
Chadwick unites "stabile" and "mobile" in a single construction.

Through purely abstract means, lines and plane surfaces are stretched and curved in dynamic movement and interwoven into floating structures.

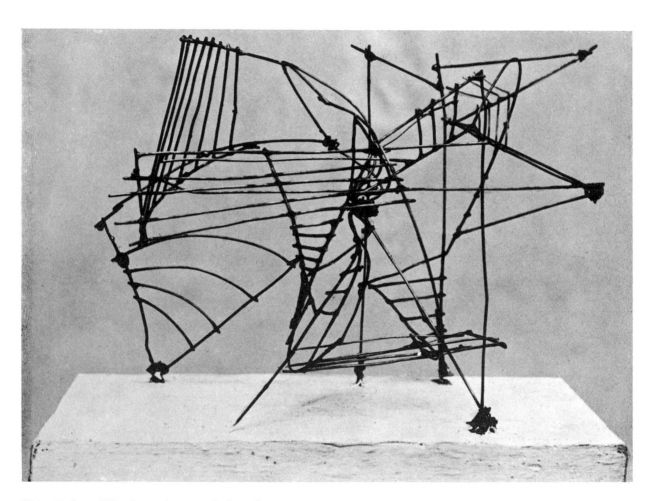

Walter Bodmer *Wire Composition* 1936 7″ x 11″ Coll. the artist

Walter Bodmer *Floating Sculpture* 1953
Wire and tin, painted in red 11″ Owned by the Federal Government, Berne, Switzerland

The wire compositions of *Walter Bodmer,* the Swiss sculptor and painter, unfold in space, delicate and fantastic as spider's webs. Uncontaminated by subject, they live in an atmosphere of their own. Rising and falling movement and swaying flight are expressed in many variations and rhythms. The thin lines create zones of tension which recall Klee's linear architectonics. In Bodmer a powerful imagination goes hand in hand with supreme precision of craftsmanship. The quivering balance of these subtle constructions seems to ignore the law of gravity.

216

217

William Turnbull *Mobile-Stabile* 1949 Bronze base: 26″ x 18″ Coll. the artist

The early work of *William Turnbull,* one of the youngest of the English group, shows an interpenetration of planes thrusting into space such as can be found in the early reliefs of Pevsner. His later tendency has been toward purely linear effects. With his fine sense of rhythm and proportion, he is able to create vital, space-enclosing compositions with elementary and fragile means.

Hans Uhlmann *Sculpture* 1954 Steel 31½" x 47" x 39" Coll. the artist

Mary Vieira *Tension-Expansion (Rythmes Dans L'Espace)* 1959 Aluminum 66¼" x 99¼" Middelheim Park, Antwerp, Holland

José de Rivera *Construction No. 48* 1957 Chrome-nickel-steel, forged rod 9″ Coll. Mr. & Mrs. George Staempfli, New York

Mary Vieira and Jose de Rivera, both of Latin origin, have in common an ascetic purity of spatial conception. While the connection with mathematical thought and proportional distinction is evident in Vieira's work, the floating swiftness of Rivera's airy constructions seem to be based, to a certain extent, on the impact of industrialism.

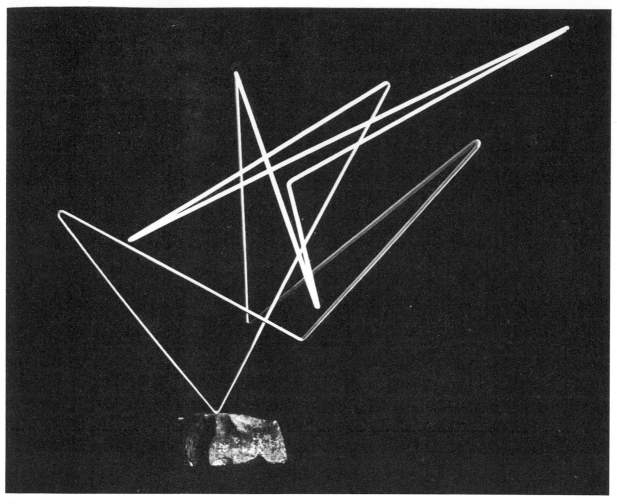

Norbert Kricke *Space-Time Sculpture. Red and White* 1954 Steel rod 23½" x 27½" x 15¾" Museum Wuppertal, Germany

Norbet Kricke *Space Sculpture* 1958
Stainless steel, Museum Schloss Morsbroich,
Leverkusen, Germany

Commencing with rigid geometric constructions, Kricke's art has gradually developed a more relaxed but dynamic linear expressiveness and use of space. The movement is richly orchestrated to attack space from all angles. "My problem is not concerned with mass and not with the figure but with space and motion, with space and time. I do not want to describe real space nor create real movement (mobiles), but I do want to suggest movement by developing a spatial activity from all directions. I want to express the unity of space and time." (Norbert Kricke.)

Richard Lippold *Variation No. 7, Full Moon* 1949-50 Nichrome and brass wire 10'
Museum of Modern Art, New York Mrs. Simon Guggenheim Fund

224

In his gossamer constructions in wire, *Richard Lippold* expresses "a mystical, boundless sense of space." His *Full Moon* makes the radiation of moonlight the symbolic expression of the structure of the world. If a single link in this closely woven chain breaks, the whole complex structure collapses.

"The world is learning to exist with all of matter in a most tentative state...The firmer the tensions within this construction *(Full Moon)* are established, the more placid is the effect." (Richard Lippold, 1952.)

Ibram Lassaw *Nebula in Orion* 1951 Bronze 35" Coll. John D. Rockefeller, III

This scaffolding, opened-up from all sides, shows the same complex interplay of spacial relationships that characterizes the free spatial fantasies of the younger generation of painters: Vieira da Silva, Mark Tobey or Bazaine. In this case, too, the subtle variation of tensions arises from the changing density of interweaving and the elastic interplay between the various compartments of air.

Max Bill *Construction of 30 Identical Elements* 1938-39 Gilt brass Coll. the artist

Max Bill carries the "mathematical way of thinking" into the domain of art, and attempts to overthrow the barriers between artistic intuition and scientific knowledge. He sees geometry, the mutual relationships of surfaces and lines, as the primary foundation of all form. Herein lies also the source of the aesthetic expression of mathematical figures. By giving concrete form to abstract thought — as in the mathematical models of space — he introduces an element of feeling into it. "Mathematical thought in our time is not mathematics itself. It is the creation of rhythms and relationships, of laws which have a personal origin, just as mathematics originates in the thought of pioneer mathematicians." Thus art is characterized as "thought in form," although, as he emphasizes, "thought which leads to the frontiers of the inexplicable."

226

Max Bill *Rhythm in Space* 1947-48 Plaster 60" x 20" x 58" Coll. the artist

Max Ernst *Lunar Asparagus (Mondspargel)*
(Les Asperges De La Lune) 1935 Plaster 65" high
Museum of Modern Art, New York Purchase Fund

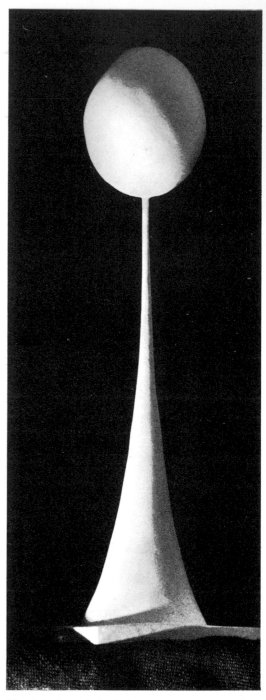

Kurt Schwitters *Spherical Form* 1932 Plaster and
stone, painted ca. 20" (Destroyed)

Compared with the fantastically tall and thin dream-growth of Max Ernst's *Lunar Asparagus,* the *Spherical Form* of
Kurt Schwitters is an elemental composition with "found" materials. An upward shift of the centre of gravity brings
out the precariousness of the balance.

With steady consistency, *Etienne Béothy* has evolved a sculptural language full of inner vitality and musicality to evoke the gesture of plant life. "The whole life of the plant is one great gesture, — an ever-welling spring, coming from the depths." (Etienne Béothy.)

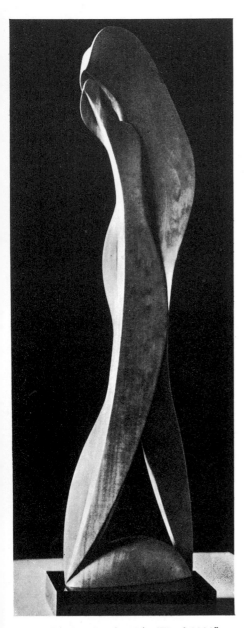

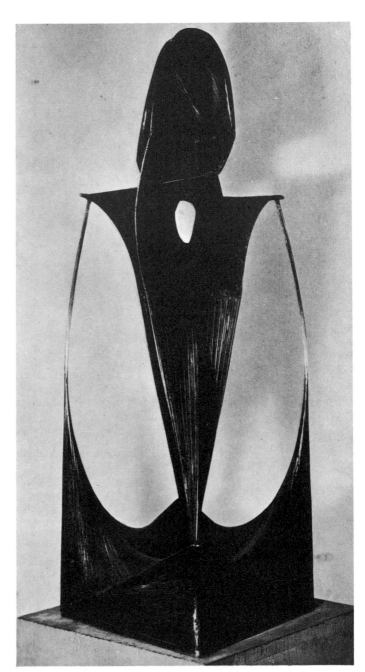

Etienne Béothy *Couple* 1947 Wood 23½"
Coll. Landau, Paris

Antoine Pevsner *Twinned Column* 1947 Bronze 42" x 20" x 17"
The Solomon R. Guggenheim Museum, New York

Pevsner's construction presents very subtly the familiar problem of top-weight and duplication of form which is frequent in modern sculpture and space constructions. (Brancusi, Béothy, Gabo, Hepworth, Moore, etc.)

Architecture with a sculptural approach

Le Corbusier *Chapel of Ronchamp* 1955 Ronchamp, France

Through the intensity of its plastic modelling the building also becomes a sculptural symbol dominating the landscape.

Le Corbusier *Ozon 2* (Recherches en faveur d'une plastique destinée à l'architecture)
1948 Painted wood 43½" Executed by J. Savina Coll. the artist

According to *Le Corbusier,* sculpture is the resonance and radiation of its architectural and natural environment. His aim is to insert it, as an organic construction, into a larger whole, the essence of which it incorporates and reflects poetically. The Cubist origins of Le Corbusier's sculpture are obvious in the interpenetration of planes, but it evolves in more organic shape towards a more general synthesis and symbol of life.

"Around the building, inside the building, there are definite places, mathematical points, which integrate the whole and which establish platforms from which the sound of speech would reverberate in all parts. These are the predestined sites for sculpture. And that sculpture would be neither a metope, a tympanum, nor a porch. It would be much more subtle and precise. The site would be a place which would be like the focus of a parabola or an ellipse, like the precise point of intersection of the different planes which compose the architecture. From there the word, the voice would issue. Such places would be focal points for sculpture, as they are focal points for acoustics. Take up your stand here, sculptor, if your speech is worth hearing." (Le Corbusier, *Les tendances de l'architecture avec la collaboration de la peinture et de la sculpture.* Rome, Typogi-Bardi, 1936.)

Here simple volumes achieve monumental effect, regardless of their technical function, through contrast and proportional relationships. Thus they pass out of the purely utilitarian into a poetic atmosphere where they come to life in a completely new significance.

Le Corbusier *Unité D'Habitation*
Terrace roof with ventilation
shafts 1952 Marseilles

The Open Hand is a monumental work, the crowning point of an urban situation; it is a visual and emotional synthesis linked to the great natural background of the Himalayas and to the architecture surrounding it. The sweeping symbolic gesture penetrating space has a human derivation. This sculpture is made of carved wood overlaid with wrought iron, the technique employed in India for water jars. It rotates on ball bearings and thus contains within itself a multiple kinetic energy. Uncontaminated by functional intention, it emphasizes the emotional origin and aim of what has been built by human hands for man.

Le Corbusier *The Open Hand* 1952
Sketch for Chandigar, India 54′ 8″

Gilioli has chosen a closed, crenelated form for his *Monument for the Unknown Political Prisoner,* one that well illustrates its title, *Prayer and Force.* This powerful sculpture diffuses at one and the same time a strong feeling of confinement and inner strength.

Day Schnabel *The Town* 1953 Stone 35″ x 78″ The Brooklyn Museum, New York

Here is the sculptured symbol of a city, growing out of tensions and proportions of volume and containing a strong rhythmical expression.

234

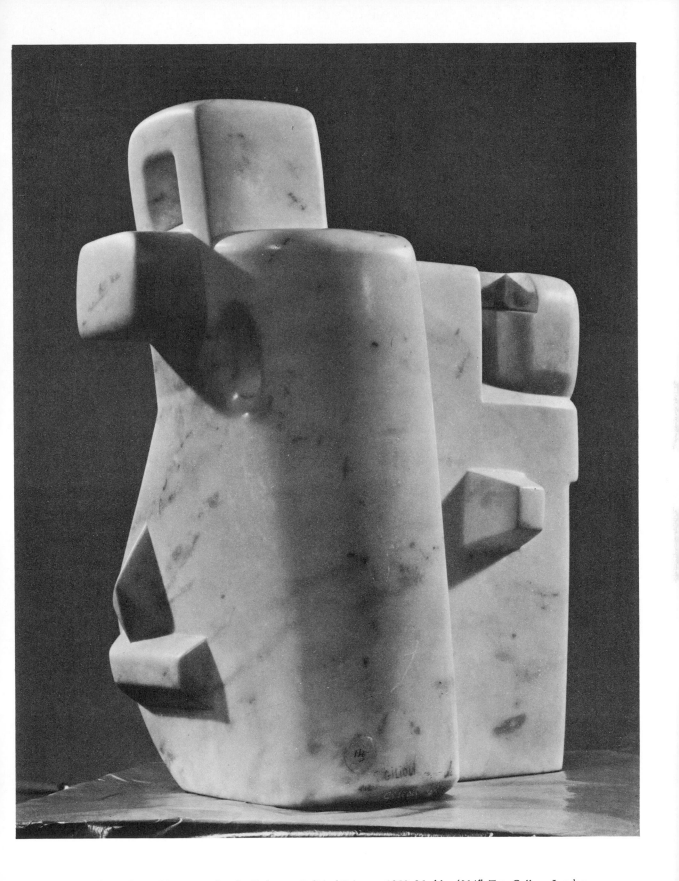

Emile Gilioli *Prière et Force. Monument for the Unknown Political Prisoner* 1953 Marble 43¼″ Tate Gallery, London

Paul Speck *Bread and Wine (Pane e Vino)* Architectural Composition 1957 Granite 49¼" Coll. the artist, Zurich

This horizontally elongated stone architecture, austerely rustic in form, is endowed with the meaning and visible symbols of the meal as a sacred rite.

Constantino Nivola *Vadiano* 1958 Cast stone 35′ Coll. the artist

"*Nivola* has made magnificent sculptures on sand. Where the devil did he go to look for the undeniable style which animates his work? He is a son of Sardinia, an island left, until now, happily sheltered from covetous machinations. There must be on this island traces of the oldest civilizations, and Nivola has unquestionably made a discovery at the right moment." (Le Corbusier.)

André Bloc *Construction* 1953 Plaster 24″ x 12″ Coll. the artist

André Bloc constructs an architectonic shell, enclosing space and displaying here a marked tendency to organic form. This is set, as a mass, in dynamic balance with the hollow.

Luciano Baldessari *Architectural Construction for the Entrance to the Breda Works Exhibition*
1952 Concrete 52′8″ Milan Industrial Fair

An expressive sculptural form, a huge spiral, encloses and articulates space, giving rhythm to the shifting life of an exhibition. The movement spreads ribbon-like out of a huge shell. The activity of an industrial concern, ramifying and concentrating, finds expression in a gigantic sculptural form, and the visitor's passage through the section is guided and enlightened.

Emile Gilioli *Paquier* 1951 Bronze 26½" Coll. the artist

Gilioli achieves that fusion of basic geometrical and organic forms out of which the expressive quality of volume emerges as a unity. "In sculpture we must break the absolute sphere, as the egg breaks it to give birth to life." (Emile Gilioli.)

George Henri Adam *Sculpture Monument for the Gardens of the Museum of Le Havre* 1959 Concrete 22′6″ x 72′11″

In its geometrical acuity, this monumental sculpture for the Museum at Le Havre is perfectly adjusted to the spirit of the building.

George Henri Adam *Sleeping Woman* 1945 Plaster 9′6″ long Garden of the Villa Mirabello, Varèse

Adam disrupts the anatomical continuity of a body in order to transmute it into fantastic architecture of convex and concave forms, and to express the changing aspects of rise and fall. Like his graphic work, his sculpture is markedly monumental in character.

241

Maurice Lipsi *Sculpture* 1958 Lava 17" x 18" x 7¾" Coll. the artist

Lipsi, too, allows the natural power of the rough lava full play and contrasts it contrapuntally, with a geometric precision of volume and contour. The central part relates to the oval form arching over it in a unifying spatial activity.

Hans Aeschbacher *Figure I* 1955 Lava 73" The City of Bienne, Switzerland

This austere architectural stela works on us through the sensitivity of its proportions, through the way its monolith quietly unfolds and fans out. The quality of the raw material out of which it is formed (lava) is strongly accented. It binds the organization and articulation of the condensed geometrical forms to their natural surroundings.

242

Gabriel Kohn *Pitcairn* 1959 Wood 36″ x 48″ x 33″ Albright Art Gallery, Buffalo

The artist has achieved a taut interpenetration of forms by the use of free construction within the confines of an architectural discipline. The texture of the wood plays thereby a decisive role through the rhythms of its variegated graining.

At first glance, just two simple, related forms. But slowly we become aware of the mysterious interplay of relationships created by the vision and hand of the artist. They have given a uniformly black hue to the wood and endowed the silhouettes and surfaces with the most delicate traces of incisions and knife-indentations. Despite this treatment, the material continues to exist in its natural graining, playing the role of animate "Nature" in the well-modulated realm of light and shadow created by the two basic forms. Impregnated with monumental traits quite independent of their actual size, fantastic leafy mountains become the bearers of a multiplicity of emotions. Architectural design and natural growth have been fused into a new unity.

"My total conscious search in life has been for a new seeing, a new image, a new insight. This search not only includes the object, but in-between places. The dawns and the dusks...." (L. Nevelson statement for *Nature in Abstraction* by J. H. Baur, 1958.)

Louise Nevelson *Lovers Leaves* 1955 Wood Haskell Collection, New York

Day Schnabel *Temple* New York 1957 Bronze 7″ Coll. the artist

Open and loosely composed organic forms dominate here, both in structure and in the interplay of interior and exterior space.

Vojin Bakic *Leaf Form No. I (Razlistana Forma I)* 1958-59 Plaster 31½"

Lynn Chadwick *Moon of Alabama* 1957 Iron composition 60" Coll. the artist

Ibram Lassaw *Zodiac House* 1958 Copper, nickel-silver and bronze 31″ x 14″ x 17″ George Staempfli Gallery, New York

In Lassaw's *Zodiac House,* as well as in Chadwick's *Moon of Alabama* fantastic architectural forms are balanced on light supports with the action on the main upper portion. (See also pages 228 and 229).

Robert Jacobsen *Hengist* 1953 Wrought iron 30″ x 17¾″ Musée de Liège, France

Jacobsen, whose artistic expressions exploit the utmost potentialities of his material, proceeds from a basis of rhythmically soaring, yet architecturally disciplined forms. "Material repays in inspiration what you have given it in your attempt to serve it." (Robert Jacobsen.)

Berto Lardera *Sculpture* 1950 Iron 6′ 6″ x 6′ 6″ Coll. F. Pensotti, Legnano

Here again, by building into space, the sculptor imparts rhythm to the fluctuating interplay of hollows and surfaces. This construction, floating in space, seems to capture and concentrate its natural environment and to reflect it in a multiplicity of different aspects.

The development of opened spatial composition.

Mary Callery *Fish in Reeds* 1948 Bronze 12¾" x 15½" Coll. the artist

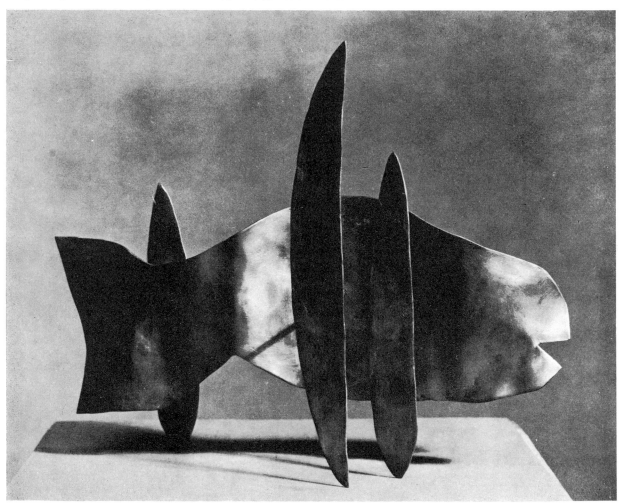

The undulating forward glide of the simplified, elongated fish form acts as a counterpoint to the verticals of the reeds. A delicately orchestrated harmony results from the economy of the forms.

David Smith *Arc-Wing* 1951 Steel 20¾" Willard Gallery, New York

Like Richard Lippold, and in keeping with the American situation, *David Smith* gained his first experiences of material in industry. Compared with the flexibility of the handicraft of Gonzalez, with whom he has many points in common, Smith shows a greater aggressiveness in conception and a crasser emphasis on the technical aspects of formulation. "Possibly steel is so beautiful because of all the movement associated with it, its strength, and functions. Yet it is also brutal, the rapist, the murderer and the death-dealing giants are also its offspring." (David Smith.)

David Smith *Cock Fight* Variation 1945 Steel 45¼" City Art Museum, St. Louis

The dynamics of a cockfight are given spatial expression by the mobility of a few basic forms and the shifting interplay between them. "A form going places," as the sculptor calls it.

Mirko's Bull is pure movement encased in an open scaffolding. The dynamic quality which an earlier generation (Duchamp-Villon in his *Horse*) first elicited from volume is here — as in David Smith's *Royal Bird* — rendered as a pure form of energy.

Mirko Basaldella *The Bull* 1948 Bronze

David Smith *The Royal Bird* 1948 Steel, bronze and stainless steel 23″ x 8½″ x 60″ Walker Art Center, Minneapolis

Roszak's fantastic bird unfolds in space through variations of structure and color. The gnarled and thorny lines and shapes symbolize the powers of nature, both creative and destructive. It is with the same idea in mind that the sculptor scorches and scratches his surfaces — to reach a final synthesis of instinct and discipline. "The rhythm between the discipline of the classic and the emotional stirring of the baroque may well establish a new synthesis toward the completeness of man and his hopes for the fullness of life." (Th. J. Roszak in: Andrew C. Ritchie, *Symposium on the New Sculpture*, 1952.)

Theodore J. Roszak *Fire-Bird* 1950-51 Welded and hammered steel 32" x 42" Coll. J. Z. Steinberg, Chicago

Luciano Minguzzi *Model for the Monument to the Unknown Political Prisoner* 1953 Bronze 22″ x 22″ Tate Gallery, London

Here again, in the symbolic expression of the deprivation of liberty, the crushed and enwebbed volume comes into an intense relationship with space. It is a sculptural parable of the menace to a personal sphere of life.

Maria Martins *Ritual of Rhythm*
1958 Bronze 23′ x 16′ 5″
Palace of the President, Brasilia

Germaine Richier *The Bat* 1952
Plaster 47"

Germaine Richier, who worked for many years in the studio of Bourdelle, has joined Giacometti — also once a pupil of the same master — in the disembodiment of the surface. The disintegration and fraying out of the compact mass give rise to new and expressive structural life with a demonic undertone. *The Bat* shows a strange transmutation of animal into vegetable life, of the animal's body and wings into a significant and ambiguous ramification.

Eduardo Paolozzi *The Cage* 1950-51 Bronze 6′ x 4′ Arts Council of Great Britain, London

Herbert Ferber *Spheroid 2* 1952 Copper and lead 42″ Kootz Gallery, New York

James Rosati *Bull* 1951 Bronze 30″ Coll. the artist

Carel Visser *Bird Lovers* 1954 Iron 19¾" Stedelijk Museum, Amsterdam

This twin bird form, an irregular, oval air-space, is flight-poised horizontally but, at the same time, seems to dart forward. The harsh, dark material from which they are formed delineates these floating shapes, conceived with architectural tautness. Positive and negative volumes are equilibrated. One is aware that here a younger generation is at work, converting the achievements of the De Stijl movement into new forms freer than those of the preceding period.

Richard Stankiewicz *My Bird* 1957 Iron and steel 45″ x 17″ x 16″ Coll. the artist

Robert Müller *Larva* 1957 Steel 21¼" long Private Collection, Paris

Both artists integrate odds and ends of "Ready-Mades" into the basic composition of their work. In Müller's method there is a perceptible tendency to transform these into basic fundamental forms that modulate space like curved armor, while Stankiewicz's final effect achieves a sensitive transparency of bizarre component parts.

The works of younger artists, who lean towards methods of expression initiated by Brancusi and Arp, show a new evolution through changes in proportion and shifts in accentuation. (Pages 266-275).

Alberto Viani *Sitting Nude (Nudo Seduto)* 1954 Marble 67″ x 63″ Coll. Willard Gidwitz, Chicago

Viani's figures are in a process of eternal metamorphosis. He does not, like Arp, start out from an archetypal vision, but from the transformed and abbreviated expression of human form.

Karl Hartung *Primeval Branchings* 1950 Plaster for execution in bronze 78½″ wide Coll. the artist

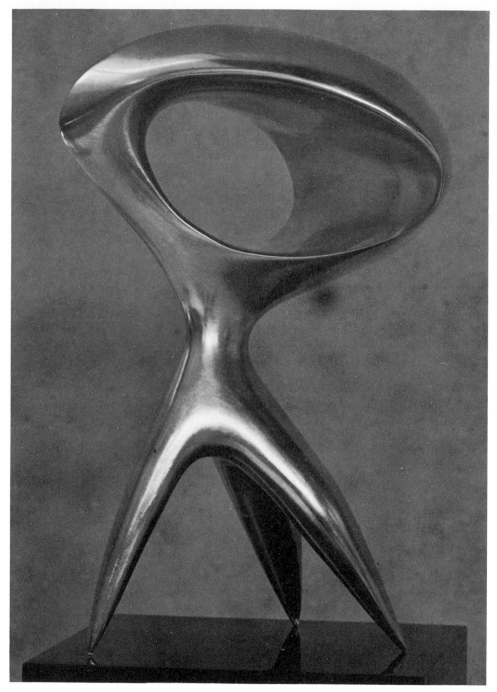

Antoine Poncet *Tripatte* 1958 Bronze 16¼" x 5⅛" x 4"

Wander Bertoni *Ikarus* 1953 Stainless steel 47¼" x 37⅞" x 19¾"

A special tendency towards rhythmical balance is elaborated in the sculptures of Antoine Poncet (Paris) and Wander Bertoni (Vienna), recalling similar tendencies in the realm of architecture, such as the gracefully floating columns of Oscar Niemeyer's presidential palace in Brasilia.

Etienne Hadju *Head* 1946 Marble 19¼" x 19¾" Coll. the artist

The most impressive features of this *Head* are the magnificently fluid simplifications of form and the extreme subtlety with which the surface and the structure of the relief are treated. Again in the double form of *Bird Lyre* it is a nearly archetypal shape that dominates. Its great dignity and serenity is due to its harmonious proportions and to the soft modulation of its large frontal planes. The beautifully veined marble of Paros seems to rise quietly by interior breathing. The silhouette is designed through simple cuts and curves showing perforation of the mass and contouring the outer and inner space that permeates the volume. In its noble simplicity this sculpture approaches the idol-like shaping of form which distinguishes Brancusi's work, and its patient and meditative treatment of the material also seems related to the methods of the Rumanian master. However, like many sculptors of his generation Hadju is interested in other problems as well and these he attacks especially in his reliefs.

Etienne Hadju *Bird Lyre* 1956 Marble 21″ x 13¾″ Coll. Baronne Lambert, Brussels

Isamu Noguchi *Capital* 1939 Marble 16″ Museum of Modern Art, New York Gift of Miss Jeanne Reynal

Isamu Noguchi *Cross Form Development* 1958 Marble 13″ Coll. the artist

The delicate power of this form glides gently into a torso-like expression of organic life. The inner animation of its stereometrical elements is of the same order as Brancusi's *Torso of a Young Man 1924*.

274

James Rosati *Phoenix and the Turtle* 1958 Marble 12″ x 10″ Fine Arts Associates, New York

The intensity of this work is not merely due to the precision of its craftsmanship; it also stems from a definite intellectual approach that is primarily concerned with essentials. A self-contained duality that melts into a whole is a motif often found in contemporary art, but here the wonder of transformation is achieved with calm assurance. The dignity which permeates the entire mass is enriched by the play of variations over its voluptuous surfaces.

By means of various contemporary techniques and ideas the image of the human head has been formed and transformed into new expressiveness. This is achieved not only by intensive structural articulation (bronze) but also by the high polishing and subtle modelling of integral volume (marble).

As far back as 1932, *Lipchitz* invented the form of a head dramatically broken open to show a mysterious inner spatial construction. Despite its small size, this piece of sculpture exerts a monumental effect and opens new areas.

Jacques Lipchitz *Head* 1932 Bronze 9¾″ Stedelijk Museum, Amsterdam

William Turnbull *Head-Object* 1955 Bronze 9″ Coll. D. Blinken, New York

Fritz Wotruba *Head* 1954-55 Bronze 18½″ Coll. Baronne Jeanne Lambert, Brussels

Carlo Sergio Signori *Black Portrait* 1958 Marble 17¾″ x 11½″ Coll. the artist

Vojin Bakic *Head* 1956 Marble 14¼" Coll. the artist

The modern expression of primeval forces.

The Mediterranean Mother from Senorbi ca. 1500 B.C. Marble 17¼″ Museo Nazionale, Cagliari, Sardinia

In wood carving, a younger generation too creates, like Brancusi, a magical simplicity in realizing the potentialities of the material, the total effect being determined entirely by the intensity of feeling uncontaminated by any decorative intention. The forms here suggest those dominating, irrational and primeval forces whose ritual sense has been lost in our time.

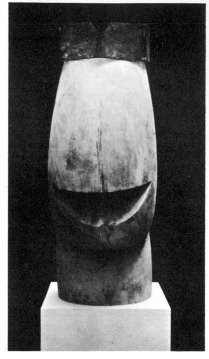

Constantin Brancusi *The Chief (Le Chef)*
1922 Wood 20″ without base
Coll. Mrs. B. Lambert, New York

Erik Thommesen *Head of a Child*
1951 Wood 12″ Coll. the artist

Helen Phillips *Genetrix*
1943 Grey marble 28″
Coll. Jeanne Reynal, New York

Erich Müller *Woman* 1951 Wood 26¾″ x 11¾″ Coll. the artist

Juana Müller *Head of a Child*
1950 Wood 6″ Galerie Mai, Paris

Marino Marini *Horse* 1957 Bronze 12½″ x 14½″ World House Galleries, New York

Since his beginnings in the Munich "Blauer Reiter" group, *Mataré* has been especially interested in the elementary forms and self-containedness of the recumbent animal. "I am not copying, I visualize the lying down. I construct the act anew and try to build the quality and sensation of lying." In spite of its compression, this variation of the theme is also charged with natural vitality. For Mataré, the essential appeal of sculpture is tactile. "A sculpture can exist in the dark, but not a painting." (Ewald Mataré.)

Ewald Mataré *Cow* 1948 Wood 6¼" Coll. the artist

Louise Bourgeois *Garden at Night*
1953 Wood 36"
Mr. & Mrs. Arnold Maremont, Chicago

Like Stahly, *Louise Bourgeois* combines single forms in a group which is balanced in its proportions, creating spatial tensions and awakening free associations through the elemental quality of its shape.

François Stahly *The Castle of Tears*
(Château des Larmes) 1952 Wood 51″
Coll. Miss Darthea Speyer, Paris

In *Stahly's* work, organic life lux-
uriates in a firmly built composition.
It has a poignant rhythm and poetry.
"In the work of art, the prejudice
of the single solution has been replaced by a multiplicity of changing
significances." (F. Stahly.)

François Stahly *Mountain Mothers (An-Di-Andi ou Les Mères Montagnes)*
1956-57 Cherry wood 51¼" x 23½" x 17¾" Coll. the artist, Paris

The abundance and density of volume to be found in Stahly's *Mountain Mothers* is reminiscent of prehistoric fertility symbols, but it is absolutely free of stylization or imitation of such forms.

Etienne Martin *D'Eux (From Them)* 1955-56 Wood 4' 8" Coll. Miss Darthea Speyer, Paris

These densely-crowded, gnarled forms seem to be struggling up from a mysterious root-world. They give an overwhelming impression of growth, of deeply rooted psychic forces. The transformation of a primordial aspect of nature at the hands of the artist, in the form of a triple-rhythmed sculpture, is superbly fused into a primeval caryatid structure upon which our world rests as on the roots of an ancestral tree.

Elementary simplification in archaic and surrealist modes of expression.

Group of Deer and Fawn From the Kabeirion at Thebes 8th-7th Century B.C. Bronze 2⅞" Museum of Fine Arts, Boston

Georges Braque *Ibis* 1940-45 Bronze 5" Galerie Maeght, Paris

Georges Braque *Horse's Head* 1943-46 Bronze 48½" Galerie Maeght, Paris

Braque's Horse's Head, which starts out from the shaping of surfaces, is mainly effective by reason of its structural contrasts and fluidity of line. The *Ibis,* whose vivid silhouette is reduced to an elementary linear pattern, possesses a powerful spatial energy. "The limitation of the means gives style, engenders form, and impels to creation." (Georges Braque, 1948.)

David Hare *Catch* 1947 Bronze 15″ Kootz Gallery, New York

In *David Hare's* work, the surrealist metamorphosis of form is marked by ironic accents. Later, the grotesque atmosphere is underlined not only by the adventurousness of the form, but also by a peculiarly fantastic use of material. Owing to its formal diversity, *Catch* is particularly stimulating to free associations, the wanderings of the mind's memory, as Hare puts it. "The universe of emotion has no space in the sense of distance, but it has memory, which is the **space of** time." (David Hare, *The Spaces of the Mind,* 1950.)

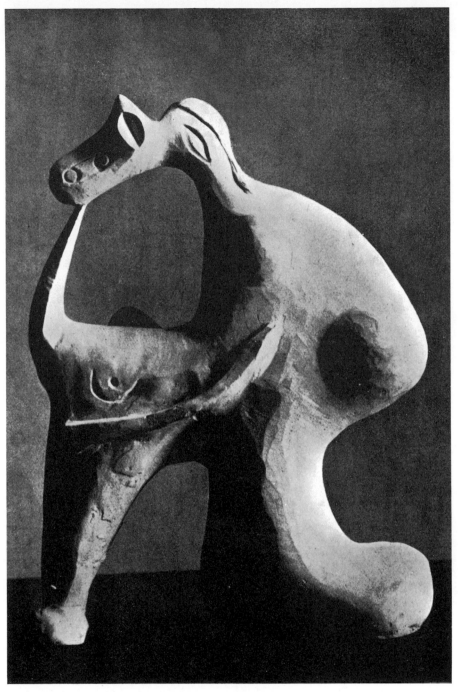

Pablo Picasso *Sculpture* 1929 Bronze 9" Coll. the artist

Picasso's fabulous creature, which belongs to his Dinard period, is a burlesque assemblage of organic fragments in an absolutely unprecedented sculptural form. There is a multiplicity of themes so that the whole becomes involved in a perpetual process of transformation.

Max Ernst *King Playing with the Queen*
1944 Bronze 3' x 2'9"
Museum of Modern Art, New York

This chimeric king belongs to the family of modern, anthropomorphic creations, where organic and mathematical forms are fused into a new fantastic unity.

Joan Miro *Bird* 1944-46 Bronze 7" Galerie Maeght, Paris

In *Miro's* bronzes, as in his painting, the spatial force resulting from the deployment of primal organic volumes is felt along with a certain burlesque bias on the part of the artist.

Max Ernst *Sculpture* 1935 Granite Giacometti Residence, Maloja, Switzerland

"Alberto Giacometti and I are afflicted with sculpture-fever. We work on granite blocks, large and small, from the moraine of the Forno Glacier. Wonderfully polished by time, frost and weather, they are in themselves fantastically beautiful. No human hand can achieve such results. Why not, therefore, leave the spadework to the elements and confine ourselves to scratching on them the runes of our own mystery." (Max Ernst, from a letter to C. G.-W., Maloja, 1935.)

Pablo Picasso *Design for a Monument* 1928 Pen and ink drawing

Picasso, who devoted himself almost exclusively to painting for ten years after 1918, began work for monumental sculpture in 1928 on a series of designs. His *Design for a Monument* shows a superb merging of simple biomorphical and geometrical forms. These monuments, designed in many variations as sculptural signs for the outermost coastline of the Riviera, stand in perfect and vital relationship to the surroundings and scenery.

300

Stelae and totem forms from the contemporary standpoint.

Le Corbusier *Totem* 1945 Wood 47½" Executed by J. Savina Private Collection, Paris

The expressive, mask-like head, extended open-mouthed into space is connected by its columnar base with the central rectangular part, discharging into softer curves. At play here is an exciting contrast of natural and contrived forms, both organic and geometrical, tautly and plastically expressed. Deep troughs of shadow, that seem to be listening, activate the empty spaces. Here the primitive and the contemporary are consciously welded into a single unity.

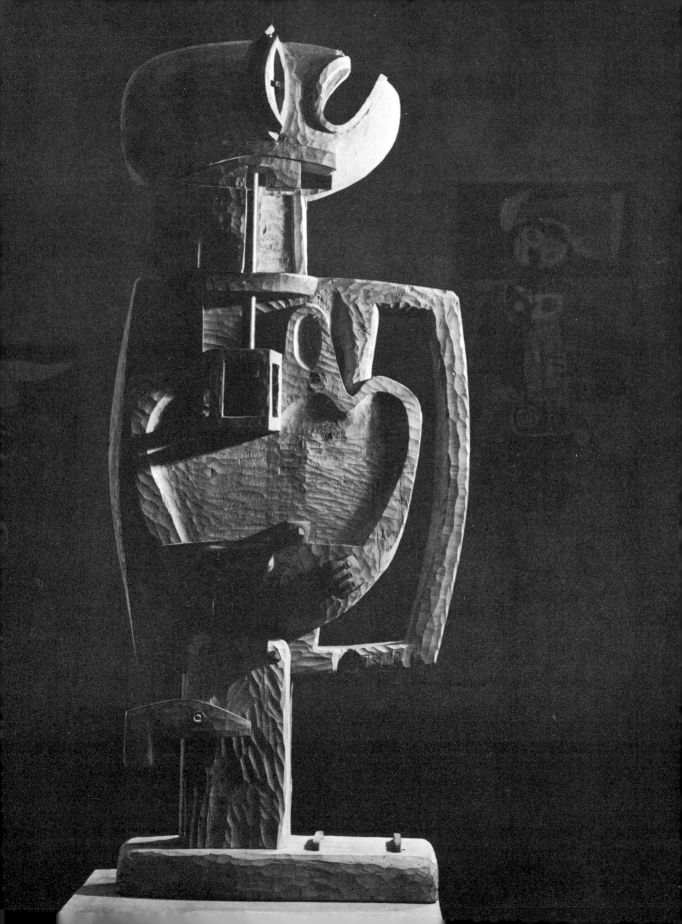

Pablo Picasso *Bather* 1958 Bronze 78″ x 69″ Galerie Leiris, Paris

Picasso has created a totemlike configuration of his *Bathers* with the most modern means. Gesticulating in a fantastic sign-language, mysterious yet whimsical forms have been contrived out of odds and ends of planking, from broom-handles and frame-corners to round and curved staves. The transformation of the wood texture into bronze produces a magical effect.

The *Tanktotem* consists of strongly contrasted spatial forms, convex-bellied and standing on a three-tiered base. It has a throat-like, elongated upper part which encircles the "head" in a horizontal movement that brings fresh spatial animation to the composition by a change of direction. This artistically balanced concept is enlivened by a humorous internal play on the tank "deus ex machina" of our time.

David Smith *Tanktotem III*
1953 Steel 87″ Coll. the artist

H. J. Gisiger *Totem* 1956-58
Steel 75″ Coll. the artist

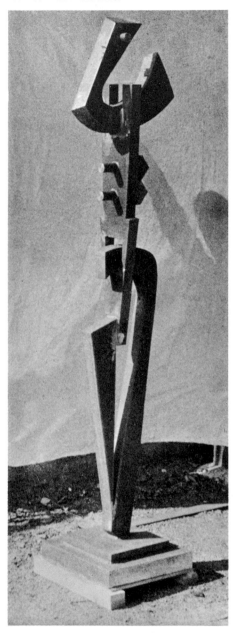

Gisiger's *Totem,* made of bent and elongated bars, stands out sharply in space. Despite its mechanical severity it has lyrical overtones and a rhythmically accentuated swing. Its various elements are precisely dovetailed so as to develop spatial activity. Here, too, one can feel a certain humorous attitude towards "Homo-Totem". The artist is not merely interested in solving an esthetic problem but is also concerned with expressing emotional content.

Rudolf Hoflehner *"Sysiphus" (Homage to Albert Camus)* 1959 Solid iron 7' 4½" Coll. the artist

This austere yet generously constructed *Sysiphus Figure*—a memorial to the poet Albert Camus—has a monumental character throughout. Its curved and rectangular iron components are cut from solid stock and welded together. With its tense verticality and spatially expanding planes of its upper part it embodies not a static but a dynamic attitude, making a completely new and original contribution to the theme of the transformed human statue.

Roël D'Haese *Legendary Personage (Personnage Légendaire)* 1956 Bronze 28¾" x 14" Coll. B. Goldschmidt, Brussels

In *Roël D'Haese's* work we find a highly animated plastic microcosm created out of both "Ready-Mades" and ingeniously new forms fused into an organic unity. Again, it is the vibrating texture with its fantastic details, the tensions generated by its varying proportions, the changing contrast of light and shadow, which define the strange, prickly character of this figure from the world of legend.

César Baldaccini *Homage*
1958 Iron 51¼″
Coll. Maillard, Paris

César's iron tree, entitled *Homage,* shoots up vertically in triple rhythm from a stem-like columnar base to branch out luxuriantly in richly contrived relief. The three vertical notes of the base are repeated in the horizontal bands of hollowed spaces that entrap deep shadows. The whole rises out of darkness into light in a play of strong contrasts. A sense of humor often evident in César's work (he was, by the way, born in Marseilles) and which first appeared in his amusingly grotesque sculptural "collages" of "Ready-Mades" is reminiscent of Flemish Roël D'Haese's weird methods of expression, but today the meridional French artist seems to be turning more and more to simpler and bolder forms.

Robert Müller *Aaron's Rod (Aaronstab)*
1958 Iron 56″ Private Collection, Paris

This vertical plant-like form, with
its upward thrust and the biblical
overtones of its botanical title, has
the character of a bizarre stele.
Arching masses are richly built up
in a rhythmical crescendo to culmi-
nate in a full display at the top. The
various elements grouped together
here are made up of odds and ends
(tubes and bars, bowls, scythes, etc.)
cut, hammered and welded into a
new sculptural existence. They rise,
linked together in steady equilib-
rium, to form a new, organic whole
filled with spatial vitality. Moreover,
this well-crafted, precisely handled
sculpture is imbued with inner
meaning beside the purely esthetic
perfection of its form.

Alicia Penalba *Plant Liturgy No. 1*
(Liturgie Vegetale No. 1) 1956 Bronze 26½"
Galerie Claude Bernard, Paris

    Alicia Penalba's *Plant Liturgy*
builds up its sacramental stele in
a series of concave forms whose
shadowed niches contribute to the
articulation of the organic structure.
Growth is built up, fused, combined
with architectural principles in such
a way that the horizontal and vertical accents give the impression of a
contrasting vertical whole.

Mirko Basaldella *The Great Initiated (Il Grande Initiato)* 1956 Bronze 110" Coll. the artist, Cambridge, Mass.

The Great Initiated is a hollowed, highly articulated construction. The human figure on which it is based has been architecturally transformed and the surface strewn with hieroglyph-like forms. Human proportions appear to be on a giant scale. The upward-surging detail, with its alternating play of convex curves and concave hollows, its heavily accented contrasts of light and shadow, achieves a strange transformation of the human into the superhuman. By elementary sculptural means it manages to suggest an aura of the magical. Thus, the sculpture in its entirety is endowed with the power of a ritual statue.

Bernard Rosenthal *Jericho II* 1957 Red brass 84" x 45" Catherine Viviano Gallery, New York

Here, the horizontal accents unfold like a flag fluttering above its vertical shaft. Thin, angular metal plates, made of reddish brass, are combined in rigid forms and endowed with an expressive rhythm through the contrast of proportion and direction, both in height and width. The patterns of light and shadow strike a fine lyrical note. If it can be said that Lipton's organic imagination continually reactivates his material, then one might also say, in the same sense, that Rosenthal's style is dominated by a geometric concept of form.

Seymour Lipton *Pioneer* 1957
Nickel-silver on monel metal 81"
Museum of Modern Art, New York

Lipton cuts, bends and hammers his thin sheets of metal; beats, rolls and elongates them into biomorphic forms. The elan with which he assembles them into a fulcrum is almost dramatic. The light that streams from their convex surfaces is contrasted with dark, shadowed shafts, creating strong interior movement. "Gradually the sense of the dark inside, the evil of things, the hidden areas of struggles became for me a part of the cyclic story of living things...." (S. Lipton.)

Isamu Noguchi *The Family. Three Columns* 1957 Stone
On the Grounds of the Connecticut General Life Insurance Company, Bloomfield, Conn.

Noguchi's three columns stand in front of a low, elongated building set in a large, park-like area. They bring a massive, primordial element into the highly technical atmosphere of this glassed-in building. These sonorous, sculptural organisms, with their spreading capitals, stand out like so many cyclops — mythical echoes from the past that still permeate the present. The balance of their spatial and formal interrelationship is as sensitively conceived as is their proportioning within a consciously archaic concept.

In contrast to Chillida's tautly intertwined stelae and Noguchi's massive rustic stone constructions, *Henry Moore* modulates his *Glenkiln Cross (1956)* from swelling organic forms, then stretches and compresses them into a vertical column, thereby accentuating the elastic vitality of their amorphous elemental parts.

314

Henry Moore *Glenkiln Cross*
1956 Bronze 120⅜"
Marlborough Fine Art, Ltd., London

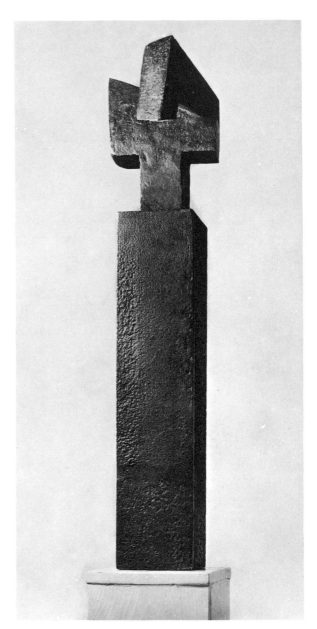

Eduardo Chillida *Ilarik, Sepulchral Stele*
1951 Iron 29" Coll. F. Meyer-Chagall, Berne

Two right-angled shapes in a powerful spatial embrace form the apex of this high plinth, expressed in the inexorable language of somber iron. This monumental memorial with its strong spatial tensions and controlled form belongs to the artist's early period.

Rows of Monoliths at Carnac, Brittany Neolithic Age

Monoliths grouped for ritualistic purposes in harmony with space, the cult, and the natural background

Constantin Brancusi *Endless Column* (Final Version) 1937 Gilt steel 97′6″ Targujiu, Carpathians, Rumania

"His gaze uplifted to the heights
Is farewell to the world of creatures.
His flight into the immensities of space
Is arrival on the shores of salvation."

Crime — Ordeal — Nirvana, by Milarepa,
Tibetan monk, 11th-12th century.

ADAM, GEORGES HENRI, sculptor, designer, painter, graphic artist and illustrator, was born in Paris, France, 1904, the descendant of a long line of goldsmiths. He began as a painter and designer, and had his first exhibition in 1935, at Billet Worms, where he was introduced by Cassou. In the same year he was awarded the Prix Blumenthal de Gravure, and came into contact with Picasso. He became a sculptor in 1939-40, executing the statue *Mouches (The Flies)* after a play of Sartre, for Dullin's Théâtre de l'Atelier, Paris. His *Grand Gisant (Recumbent Figure)*, 1943, exhibited at the Salon de la Libération, was followed by *Femme debout (Standing Woman)* and *Bête à cornes (Animal with Horns)*. In his graphic work he has abandoned etching and cold-needle technique for the burin with which he obtains striking effects of depth. In 1946-47 he designed tapestries, recreating the powerful rhythm of his graphic work on a monumental scale in black-and-white threads. In 1947-49 he designed the black-and-white illustrations to *Chimères*, by G. de Nerval, combining tense emotion with economy of form. His monumental sculpture, *Grand Eve (Nude)* was bought by the Musée d'Art Moderne, Paris. In 1949 a one-man show of his sculpture, graphic arts and tapestries took place at the Galerie Maeght, Paris. In 1952 his *burins sur cuivre,* exhibited at the Galerie La Hune, Paris, showed him achieving spatial effects by printing several plates on one sheet. In 1953 he exhibited at the São Paulo Biennial. A show of his entire work was given at the Stedelijk Museum, Amsterdam, in 1955, at Venice Biennale (graphic prize) 1956. He has contributed to the Biennial Liubliana and Tokyo, 1957; the Brussels World's Fair, 1958; and the "Documenta" exhibition in Kassel, Germany, 1959.

AESCHBACHER, HANS, sculptor, was born in Zurich, Switzerland, in 1906. Self-taught, he began his career as a sculptor in 1936, doing figurative work. He soon developed more and more purely abstract forms. He executed a monumental sculpture, *The Harp* (1946) for the Hospital Gardens in Zurich, and a stele-like *Figure I* (1955) for the town of Bienne, Switzerland. He participated in exhibition at Bienne, 1955 and 1958; Park Middleheim, Antwerp, 1957; the Venice Biennale, 1956; Basel, 1959; and the "Documenta," Kassel, 1959. His work is mentioned in the following publications: *Werk,* Winterthur, 1948, 1953, 1957; *Domus,* Milan, 1949, 1956; *Quadrum,* Brussels (U.S.A. Wittenborn), 1956; Du Griffon, ed., *La Sculpture Moderne en Suisse,* 1955; H. Schaefer Simmern, *Sculpture in Europe Today,* Berkeley, California, 1956. Lives in Zurich and near Toulon.

ARCHIPENKO, ALEXANDER, sculptor, painter, designer and teacher, was born, the son of an engineer, at Kiev, Russia, May 30, 1887. He attended the local art school, 1902-05, taking up sculpture in 1903. From 1905-08 he continued his studies in Moscow, where he also exhibited. In 1908 he attended the Ecole des Beaux Arts, Paris. He exhibited in Berlin and The Hague, 1910, and came into contact with the Cubists. A year later he introduced his first spatial sculptures. He opened his first school in Paris, 1912. His work was first exhibited in the U.S.A. at the Armory Show, 1913. In the same year he joined the Berlin Sturm Group and exhibited at the Herwarth Walden Gallery. Archipenko is one of the pioneers of modern sculpture. He simplified volume, inventing a large-scale rhythmical interplay of convex and concave forms. As early as 1912, in his "Medranos", he had introduced constructions of the greatest variety and had begun the use of transparent materials. In 1921 he opened his own school in Berlin, and two years later moved it to New York. He was appointed to the faculty of Washington State University, 1935. In 1937 he founded an art school in Chicago, and became an instructor in Moholy-Nagy's New Bauhaus. He reopened his school for sculptors in New York, 1939, and now lives in Woodstock, N. Y., where he has a summer school. *Exhibitions:* Section d'Or, Paris, 1912; Herbstsalon, Berlin, and Armory Show, New York, 1913; Société Anonyme, New York, 1921; Dresden, 1922; Kingore Galleries, New York, 1924; retrospective exhibition, Anderson Gallery, New York, 1928; Galerie Art Vivant, Brussels, and San Francisco Art Museum, 1931; Chicago World's Fair; Oakland Art Museum, and Los Angeles Art Museum, 1933; Museum of Fine Arts, Seattle, 1934; University of California at Los Angeles, 1935; Museum of Fine Arts, Seattle, 1936; Art Institute of Chicago, 1937; Kansas City Art Museum, Indianapolis Art Museum, 1938; Art Institute of Chicago, and Passadoit Gallery, New York, 1939; Art Alliance Gallery, Philadelphia, 1940; Art Institute of Chicago, 1942; La Plata, Argentina, 1946; Association of American Artists, New York, 1948; Witte Memorial Museum, San Antonio, Texas; University of Omaha; Syracuse Museum of Fine Arts, Museum of Fine Arts, Seattle, Santa Barbara Museum, all in 1949; Springfield, Mass., Art Museum, and Omaha University, 1950; Museum of Fine Arts, Kenosha, Wis., 1951; Museo d'Arte Moderna, São Paulo, Brazil, 1952; Exhibition, New York, 1954; Brussels World's Fair, 1958; Perls Galleries, New York, 1959.

ARMITAGE, KENNETH, sculptor, was born in Leeds, Yorkshire, England, 1916. He attended Leeds College of Art, 1934-37, and the Slade School of Art, 1937-39. From 1939-46 he was on active duty. His first exhibition was at the Institute of Contemporary Art, London, 1946. *Further Exhibitions:* "Young Sculptors", Institute of Contemporary Art, London; 26th Venice Biennale, British Pavilion; first one-man show Gimpel Fils, London, 1952; "Tendances de la Peinture et de la Sculpture Britannique Contemporaine", Galerie de France, Paris; 9th Salon de Mai, Paris; 2nd International Exhibition of Open-air Sculpture, Varese (Italy), and Antwerp; Industrial Design Exhibition, Zurich; Art Council Exhibition "Sculpture in the Home", London, 1953; first one-man show Bertha Schaefer Gallery, New York; London County Council, 3rd International Exhibition of Sculpture, Holland Park, London, 1954; "New Decade", Museum of Modern Art, New York, 1955; one-man shows at Bertha Schaefer and Rosenberg Galleries, New York; Brussels World's Fair, 1958; "Documenta" exhibition, Kassel, Germany, 1959. He lives in Corsham, Wilts., England.

ARP, JEAN, painter, sculptor, poet and graphic artist, was born in Strassburg, France, September 16, 1887. He studied first at the Weimar Academy, and in 1908 attended the Académie Julian in Paris. From 1909-12 he lived at Weggis, Switzerland, where he founded the Moderner Bund with

Georges Henri Adam   Hans Aeschbacher   Alexander Archipenko   Kenneth Armitage

Jean Arp   Vojin Bakic   Luciano Baldessari   Etienne Beothy

Max Bill   Andre Bloc   Umberto Boccioni   Walter Bodmer

Swiss artists whose exhibitions included the work of Paul Klee. He left Switzerland for Munich, 1911, where he joined the Blaue Reiter Group and was impressed by Kandinsky's art and personality. He participated in Blaue Reiter exhibitions and publications, 1912. He was a joint founder of the Dada movement with Hugo Ball and Tristan Tzara at Zurich, 1916, and with Max Ernst in Cologne, 1919. In 1921 he married Sophie Taeuber. From 1922-26 he lived mostly in Paris, occasionally in Zurich. With El Lissitzky he edited *Ismen* for the Rentsch Verlag, Zurich, 1925. He joined the Surrealist movement in Paris, and exhibited at the Galerie Surréaliste. Like Miro, he adhered to his own method of non-literary creation using simple, basic forms. In 1926 he settled at Meudon, near Paris. With Theo van Doesburg and Sophie Taeuber-Arp he decorated the interior of the Aubette Restaurant and Bar at Strassburg, 1927-28. These large mural decorations for the bar were painted over shortly before World War II. During the years 1930-40 he forsook relief for free sculpture. At the war's outbreak he fled to Grasse, Southern France, where his plan for collective artistic work, started with his wife, was carried out in collaboration with Magnelli and Sonja Delaunay. He returned to Switzerland in 1942. Sophie Taeuber-Arp died from an accident in Zurich, 1943. Arp visited the United States in 1949, and was commissioned a year later to do the mural reliefs for Walter Gropius' Graduate Center at Harvard University in Cambridge. In 1952 he traveled to Rome, Naples and Athens. Arp's *On My Way, Poetry and Essays, 1912-47,* was published, 1948, and his *Dreams and Projects,* 1952. In 1953-54 he was awarded an important commission for sculptures together with Calder, Pevsner and Laurens for the University of Caracas (Venezuela), built by the architect Villanueva. In 1954 he won the Biennale prize for sculpture at Venice. He lives at Meudon. *Exhibitions:* Moderner Bund, Lucerne and Zurich; Der Blaue Reiter, Munich, 1912; Erster Deutscher Herbstsalon, Berlin, 1913; Galerie Tanner, Zurich, 1915; Galerie Dada, Zurich, 1916; Galerie Montaigne, Paris, 1922; Galerie Goemans, Paris; Galerie Surréaliste, Paris, 1926; Société Anonyme, Brooklyn, 1926; Kunsthaus, Zurich; Galerie L'Epoque, Brussels, 1927; Galerie Le Centaure, Brussels, Kunsthalle, Berne; Kunsthalle, Basel, 1929; Kunsthaus, Zurich, 1929, 1932, 1934; Kunsthaus, Zurich; Museum of Modern Art, New York, 1936; Galerie Jeanne Bucher, Paris, 1939; Galerie des Eaux Vives, Zurich, 1945; Galerie d'Art Moderne, Basel, 1946; Exposition Surréaliste, Paris, 1947; Buchholz Gallery, New York; Galerie Maeght, Paris; Modern Art Society, Cincinnati, 1949; Sidney Janis Gallery, New York; Galerie Denise René, Paris; Galerie Maeght, Paris, 1950; Librairie La Hune, Paris, 1951; Bienal, Sao Paulo, 1952; A. P. I. A. W., Liège, Mons and Brussels, 1953; Curt Valentin Gallery, New York, and Walker Art Center, Minneapolis; Galerie Bing, Paris; Yverdon (Switzerland), and Zurich; Venice Biennale, 1954; Exhibition in Berne, Switzerland, 1956; Retrospective, Museum of Modern Art, New York, 1958; Brussels World's Fair, 1958; "Documenta", Kassel, Germany, 1959. A monumental sculpture for Bonn (garden of the university) and a relief for the Institute of Technology in Braunschweig, Germany, 1960.

BAKIC, VOJIN, sculptor, was born at Bjelovar, Croatia, in 1915. He studied at the Academy of Fine Arts in Zagreb with Mestrovic and Frank Krsinik. He had his first exhibition at Bjelovar in 1940. At that time he created a monument for the town of Bjelovar and, later, for other towns in his own country. He traveled in Italy, France and England. His works have been shown in numerous exhibitions, including the Venice Biennale, 1956; a show in Poland, 1956; the Brussels World's Fair, 1958; the Galerie Denise René, Paris, 1959; the "Documenta" exhibit, Kassel, Germany, 1959. Following

his early realistic and Neo-Cubist periods, he achieved an essential simplification in his choice and shaping of pure organic forms. He created compact volumes in marble, in the patient manner of Brancusi, and, in recent years, he has executed a number of open bronze sculptures which have a tendency to fold at the edges, as if to envelop space. His aim here is "the simultaneous composition of the concave and the convex," as he himself formulated it. He was awarded the 2nd Prize for sculpture at the First Mediterranean Biennial in Alexandria, and many prizes in his native country. He lives in Zagreb.

BALDESSARI, LUCIANO, architect, stage designer, was born at Rovereto, near Trento, Italy, December 10, 1896. He took his degree as an architect at the Institute of Technology, Milan, and worked in that profession in Berlin and Paris, 1922-26. He settled in Italy as an architect, 1927, and organized the Volta Exhibition of modern architecture at Como. In 1939 he lectured on modern Italian architecture at Zurich, Berne, and Basel. From 1939-48 he lived in the United States. In 1951, 1954 he was an executive member of the Milan Triennale. Baldessari has specialized in stage design and engineering problems connected with the theatre and cinema. He is responsible for the interior decoration of many apartments, commercial buildings, restaurants and yachts, among them the interiors for the Notari Bookshop, Milan. He lives in Milan.

BEOTHY, ETIENNE, sculptor, theorist, was born at Heves, Hungary, September 2, 1897. In 1915, upon graduation from high school, he volunteered for active service and was wounded. During his long convalescence he studied modern French and Russian literature and German philosophy. In 1918, after the dramatic end of the war in Hungary, he entered the Budapest School of Architecture, and began his mathematical studies on proportion a year later, working on his first concept of the *Série d'Or.* He was carving tombstones, 1919-21, and became friendly with Moholy-Nagy and the MA Group. From 1920-24, he studied sculpture at the Ecole des Beaux Arts, Paris, showing an increasing tendency toward simplification of form. In 1924-25 he toured Europe on a traveling scholarship, visiting Vienna, Munich, Paris, London, Florence, Rome, Naples and Venice. Returning to Paris, 1925, he settled down and attended the studios of Brancusi, Laurens, Maillol and Despiau. In the years 1928-31 exhibitions of his work were held at the Galerie Sacre du Printemps, Paris; Zak and Kovàcs Galleries, Budapest; Galerie Wolfensberg, Zurich (Exhibition: Production Paris, 1930). His work was on permanent exhibition at the Galerie Léonce Rosenberg, Paris, 1931-39. He was co-founder and vice-president, 1932-36, of the Abstraction-Création Group, exhibiting at the Galerie Abstraction-Création (Wagram), 1934. In 1938 he organized an exhibition of abstract French and Hungarian art in Budapest. His lecture, *The Problem of Form Creation* and his *Serie d'Or* were published by Chant, Paris, 1939. In 1939 he participated in the Réalités Nouvelles Exhibition, Galerie Charpentier, Paris. From 1941-43 he led an underground group of Hungarian artists and intellectuals living in Paris. After the war he participated in the Galerie René Drouin, Paris, 1945. In 1947 he was a committee-member of the Salon des Réalités Nouvelles and exhibited at the Galerie Denise René, Paris. He exhibited at the Galerie Maeght, Paris, 1948, the Galerie Blanche, Stockholm and in the Sculpture since Rodin Exhibition, Maison de la Pensée Française, Paris, 1949. He was co-editor of *Forme et Vie,* and a committee member of Groupe-Espace, 1951. In 1952 he collaborated with a group of architects on problems of form and proportion, and in 1953 was appointed instructor of color and proportion in the Department of Architecture of the Ecole des Beaux Arts, Paris.

BERTONI, WANDER, sculptor, was born in Codisotto, Reggio Emilia, Italy, in 1925 and came to Vienna in 1943, where he studied under Wotruba at the Academy. Still living in Vienna, he is a member of the Art Club and an artistic participant in city planning. He has exhibited in Vienna, Prague, Rome, Turin, Stockholm and at the Venice Biennale since 1950. He lives in Vienna. (see photo page 353)

BILL, MAX, architect, painter, sculptor, designer, typographer and theorist, was born at Winterthur, Switzerland, December 22, 1908. He studied at the Kunstgewerbeschule, Zurich, and the Bauhaus, Dessau. In 1931 he married Binia Spörri. Since 1930 he has practiced architecture in Zurich. In 1944-45 he lectured on formal design at the Kunstgewerbeschule, Zurich, and in 1948 was visiting professor at the Institute of Technology, Darmstadt. His publications include: *15 Variations on One Theme,* Paris, 1938; *Le Corbusier and Pierre Jeanneret, 1934-1938,* Zurich, 1938; *Robert Maillart,* Zurich-Erlenbach, 1949; *Modern Swiss Architecture, 1925-1945,* Basel, 1950; Co-editor of a book on *Kandinsky* with text by Hans Arp, Charles Estienne, Carola Giedion-Welcker, Will Grohmann, Ludwig Grote, A. Magnelli, Edition Maeght, Paris, 1951. His architectural work include the following buildings with prefabricated elements: Swiss Pavilion, Triennale, Milan, 1936; designs for the exhibition *Good Form,* Basel, 1949 (circulating exhibition shown at Cologne, Zurich, Constance, Ulm, Stuttgart, Darmstadt, Linz, Amsterdam and Vienna); Swiss Pavilion, Triennale, Milan, 1951; Hochschule für Gestaltung in Ulm, 1953-54. His sculpture includes: *Endless Loop,* 1935; *Continuity,* 1947; *Tripartite Unity,* 1948. One-man shows of his work have been held at: Bauhaus Dessau, 1928; Kunsthalle, Berne, 1930; Kunsthalle, Basel, 1944; Stuttgart, 1948; Galerie für Moderne Kunst, Basel, and Kunsthaus, Zurich, 1949; São Paulo, Art Museum, and Institute of Modern Art, Buenos Aires, 1951; Bienal, São Paulo, 1953. He was appointed director of the Hochschule für Gestaltung at Ulm which he built. In 1958, he contributed to the Brussels World's Fair; and, in 1959, to the "Documenta" in Kassel, Germany.

BLOC, ANDRE, sculptor, architect, painter, writer, was born in Algiers, 1896. Completed his engineering degree in Paris and pursued that profession until 1930. Returning from travels in Europe and South America, he founded the periodical, *Architecture d'Aujourd'hui,* 1930. In 1941-42 he produced his first sculptures in plaster, cement, and stone. In 1945-46 he abandoned sculpture with special subject content and showed his first abstract work at the Salon des Réalités Nouvelles and in the show, *Fifty Years of Sculpture,* at the Maison de la Pensée Française, 1949. In the same year he founded his review, *Art d'Aujourd'hui.* In 1950 he exhibited at the Institute of Contemporary Art, London, and at Denise René's "Espaces Nouveaux", Paris. In 1951 he showed at the Galerie Mai, Paris, in Nice, and in Copenhagen. In that year he founded the "Groupe Espace". He was given one-man shows at: Galerie Apollo, Brussels, 1952; Galerie Denise René, Paris, 1953 and 1958; Galleria del Fiore, Milan, 1954; A. P. I. A. W., Liège, 1955. He participated in the "Documenta" Kassel, Germany, and exhibited in the Museum of Modern Art in Rio and São Paulo, 1959. He is interested in spatial construction as well as in carving and tends towards a synthesis of architecture, painting and sculpture. In his *Rencontres de Plans* and *Volumes Complexes,* he achieves an interpenetration of organic and geometric forms. He lives at Boulogne-sur-Seine.

BOCCIONI, UMBERTO, painter, sculptor and theorist, was born at Reggio Calabria, Italy, October 19, 1882. From 1898-1902 he was in Rome, at the studio of Giacomo Balla whose pointillism influenced his paintings. Later, at Milan, Praeviati and Segantini impressed him with their use of light to dissolve mass. In 1902 he was in Paris, in 1903, St. Petersburg, and in 1906, Padua and Venice. He settled in Milan, 1907. In 1909 he came into contact with Marinetti and was a joint founder of the Futurist group with Carrà, Severini, Balla and Russolo, taking the lead in sculpture. In 1912 he wrote his *Manifesto tecnico della scultura futurista.* The theoretical conceptions of the movement had been summarized by Marinetti and published as the *Futurist Manifesto* in the Paris *Figaro,* February 20, 1909. As the leading sculptor of this movement, Boccioni was the first to introduce the concept of the dynamic, emotionally expressive *antigrazioso* as opposed to the static, petrified *bellezza.* He and his fellow Futurists were the first in Italy to draw attention to the work of the Piedmontese sculptor, Medardo Rosso, contrasting its direct expressiveness and spiritual radiance with the sterility and trite naturalism of officially recognized academic art. In 1913 he lectured and exhibited at the Galerie de la Boéthie, Paris. Shortly before the war he met Picasso and Braque. Boccioni volunteered for active service in 1914 and was killed two years later in an accident, August 16, 1916, at Verona. There is a striking resemblance between the short lives of Boccioni and the French sculptor, Raymond Duchamp-Villon. Both were convinced of the necessity of an artistic reorientation and renewal, and both gave their lives in the same war. *Exhibitions:* First futurist show, Milan, 1911; Galerie Bernheim Jeune, Paris; Galerie Thannhauser, Munich, 1912; Herbstsalon Sturm, Berlin; "Exhibition of Futurist Sculpture", Galerie de la Boéthie, Paris, 1913; Panama Pacific Exhibition, San Francisco, 1915; "Internationale Kunst", Düsseldorf, 1922; Société Anonyme, New York, 1923; retrospective exhibition Palazzo Sforza, Milan, 1933; "Twentieth Century Italian Art", Museum of Modern Art, New York, 1949; "L'Art Moderne Italien", Musée d'Art Moderne, Paris; Arts Council, London; Kunsthaus, Zurich, 1950; Rome, Winterthur, 1959; Venice Biennale, 1950, 1952, 1960.

BODMER, WALTER, painter, sculptor, teacher and graphic artist was born in Basel, Switzerland, August 12, 1903. He studied painting at the Kunstgewerbeschule, Basel. In 1928 he visited Paris, Southern France and Spain. His first exhibition was a joint one with his friends, Birrer, Otto Abt, and Walter Kurt Wiemken, at Basel, 1928. In 1933 he abandoned the impressionist technique for free use of form and color, first in painting and graphic art, then in wire sculptures, where the spatial problems attracted him. Since 1939 he has been an instructor in drawing at the Kunstgewerbeschule, Basel. He has exhibited in the larger Swiss cities and in Milan, Turin, Paris, Copenhagen, and Freiburg/Breisgau. Shortly after the war, a traveling exhibition of his work, sponsored by Pro Helvetia, visited Germany. He was represented at the First Bienal, São Paulo. Examples of his work are owned by the art museums of Basel, Zurich, and Berne.

BOURDELLE, ANTOINE, sculptor, painter, poet and teacher, was born at Montauban, France, October 30, 1861. He attended the Ecole des Beaux Arts, Toulouse, and from 1876-85, the Ecole des Beaux Arts, Paris, at first under Falguière, and then under Dalou, the pupil of Carpeaux. In 1896 he worked for Rodin. In later years Rodin often supported him in discussions with official authority. The classic idealism and structural discipline of early Greek sculpture gradually superseded the influence of Rodin and became the starting point for his own simplification of form and economy of expression. Unlike Rodin, whose aim was to capture spontaneity and movement, Bourdelle aspired to the monumental gesture. His favorite poets were Ronsard, Moréas (a Greek poet living in Paris) and Mallarmé. When serious illness forced him temporarily to abandon sculpture, he took up painting and drawing. In 1902 he completed his *Monument to the Dead of 1870* at Montauban. He had worked on the sculpture since 1893 when Rodin's influence was still strong. The same influence is apparent in his Beethoven bust. His personal style emerged clearly in the years 1900-09, for the first time in the *Head of Apollo*, which adds a modern sensitivity to a rigidly archaic form. 1905 marked his first exhibition at the Galerie Hébrard, Paris. In 1907 he made a statuette of Penelope, and a larger version of the same in 1912. His *Heracles, the Archer*, 1909, a monumental work of prime importance, caused a scandal when exhibited at the Salon in 1910. It was inspired by the archer on the Temple of Athena at Aegina. The work was re-exhibited at Toulouse, 1926, as the *Monument to Sport*. It is notable for its vitality of movement within the framework of strict structural principles. His *Pomona (Le fruit)*, 1911, is noted for its fine S-curve. Bourdelle lectured in Prague, on *Rodin et la sculpture*, 1909, describing him as the "poet of the human body" and his statue of Balzac as his most impressive work. ("One can hear the human spirit seething in this block of stone"). From 1909 until his death Bourdelle taught in his studio, La Grande Chaumière. His sculptural work for the Champs Elysées, 1912, gave him, for the first time, the opportunity of uniting sculpture with architecture, for him the fulfillment of all plastic creation. This new tendency, opposed to Rodin's, is expressed in the double meaning of Bourdelle's saying, "The time has come to build." His *Dying Centaur*, 1914, Buenos Aires, corresponds in spirit to symbolist poetry to which he was particularly attracted. In this statue the detachment of the arm with the lyra, nearly isolated from the whole composition, already foreshadows the lonely *Hand* of Giacometti in its tragic expressiveness. From 1920-22 he produced a series of portrait busts (Anatole France, Auguste Perret, etc.) and in 1922, his *Virgin of Alsace*, which is mounted on a rock at Niederbruck. In 1923 he finished his equestrian statue of Alvéar for Buenos Aires; preliminary sketches for this work date back to 1913. Bourdelle died in Paris, 1929. His teaching has had a lasting influence on the younger generation of sculptors. His theoretical work and lectures show that he approached the problem of sculpture from all directions, trying to relate it to the general perceptions of his time. His intimate knowledge of music and his love of symbolist poetry complement his plastic symbolism. He advised his pupils to be "mathematicians in form and musicians in proportion."

BOURGEOIS, LOUISE, painter, sculptor and graphic artist, was born in Paris, France, where she studied first at the Ecole des Beaux Arts, then with Fernand Léger. Since 1937 she has lived in New York, where she attended the Art Students League. She now works exclusively as a sculptor. Her one-man shows include: Bertha Schaefer Gallery, New York, 1945; Norlyst Gallery, New York, 1947; Peridot Gallery, New York, 1949, 1950, 1953; Galerie Mai, Paris, 1952; Allan Frumkin Gallery, Chicago, 1953; White Art Museum, Cornell University, 1959. Her work has been included in exhibitions at: the Museum of Modern Art, the Metropolitan Museum and Whitney Museum, New York; the San Francisco, Los Angeles, Rochester and Philadelphia Art Museums; the Walker Art Center, Minneapolis; the University of Illinois; the Allen Memorial Art Museum, Oberlin, Ohio; the Library of Congress, Washington, D. C. The Museum of Modern Art and the Whitney Museum own examples of her work.

BRANCUSI, CONSTANTIN, sculptor, architect and painter, was born at Pestisani, near Targujiu, Rumania, February 21,

1876. He attended the local carpentry school, where his talent was discovered. In 1902 he won a scholarship to the Bucharest Art Academy and received the Diploma on September 24, 1902. Setting out on a slow, frequently interrupted journey from East to West, he passed through Munich, Zurich and Basel, where he looked in vain for work in the building trades. In 1904 he arrived in Paris, where he settled for life. He worked at first with Mercié, an official academician of his time. In 1907, at an exhibition at the Grand Palais, where he was represented, he met Rodin who was struck by his genius and asked him to become his assistant. Brancusi refused, convinced that "nothing can grow under big trees", and continued to live in retirement and poverty. Since 1909 he was an intimate of Modigliani, later of Eric Satie, influencing Modigliani's first sculptures, and encouraging Satie to publish his opera (lost after the composer's death). Brancusi exhibited at the Grand Palais, 1920. His sculpture, *Princess*, 1916, was attacked by the critics on the grounds of obscenity. His first exhibition at the Brummer Gallery, New York, took place in 1926. From 1926-28 he was engaged in a lawsuit against the United States Customs Service which maintained that his sculpture, *Bird in Space*, was not a work of art and should be declared as "metal". With the help of American collectors and art critics, Brancusi won his case. He visited India, 1937, designing for the Maharajah of Indor a walled-in temple of meditation. It was to have been built in the form of a cross with a central pool reflecting his bird sculptures. The war and the changed political situation of India forced the abandonment of this project. Fragments of it still exist in Brancusi's studio in the form of sketches for mural paintings (white birds on a blue ground) and 3 bird-sculptures that were to have been welded into a spiritual and architectural unity. Brancusi's latest works are two turtles in wood and marble. His book of books is the Milarepa, the confessions of an 11th century Tibetan monk. The French translation, *Milarepa: Ses crimes, ses épreuves, son nirvana*, is for him an inexhaustible fountain of wisdom, spiritual beauty and simplicity. Until a few years ago the works of this great sculptor had found their way into only a few American, British, French, and Indian private collections. Today important museums own examples of his work: the Museum of Modern Art, New York; Musée d'Art Moderne, Paris; Solomon Guggenheim Museum, New York; Chicago Art Institute; Philadelphia Art Museum; Institute of Contemporary Art, London; Sociéte Anonyme Collection, Yale University, New Haven; Kunsthaus, Zurich, and Kunsthaus, Winterthur. He had a one-man show at the Solomon R. Guggenheim Museum, 1955-56, and at the Venice Biennale, 1960. Brancusi died March 16, 1957.

BRAQUE, GEORGES, painter, sculptor and illustrator, was born at Argenteuil, near Paris, France, May 13, 1882, the son of a house painter. He entered the Ecole des Beaux Arts, Le Havre, 1893. In 1900, after a year of apprenticeship to his father, he went to Paris and lived at Montmarte. He attended the Ecole des Beaux Arts (Studio Bonnat) for two months, then the Académie Humbert. In 1906 he exhibited at the Salon des Indépendants (Fauvism). In 1907 and 1908 he again contributed paintings to this salon, all of which were sold. His work done at La Ciotat and l'Estaque, 1907-08, showed the influence of Cézanne. At this time he met Picasso. At the Salon d'Automne, 1908, the jury rejected five of his pictures. In 1910 he adopted the style of analytical Cubism. He painted with Picasso in 1911 at Céret, and in 1912 at Sorgues, Provence, producing his first collage in 1912. He saw active military service, 1914-16, and was severely wounded in the head, 1916. In 1919 he had a one-man show at the Galerie

Léonce Rosenberg, Paris. His first sculpture in plaster was *Femme debout,* 1920, Collection Kahnweiler, Paris, Curt Valentin Gallery, New York. In 1923-24 he designed settings and costumes for *Les Facheux* for the Ballets Russes. He moved to his present address, 6 Rue du Douanier, Paris, in 1924. Braque was awarded first prize at the Carnegie International Exhibition, Pittsburgh, 1937. Since 1939 he has made small sculptures in limestone: *Pony,* 1939; *Fish,* 1942; *Ibis,* 1945; and several reliefs with incised patterns. In 1940 he fled to the Pyrenees, but returned to Paris in the autumn. In 1947 he published his *Cahier de Georges Braque;* it is an extract of sketchbooks kept for 30 years, a sort of diary with running illustrations, and the inspiration for many of his works. He was awarded the international prize at the Venice Biennale, 1948. In 1949 he had a large one-man show at the Museum of Modern Art, New York. In 1950 he designed the settings for *Tartuffe,* a Louis Jouvet production at the Théâtre de l'Athénée, Paris. In the same year his illustrations to *Milarepa* were shown at the Galerie Maeght, Paris. In 1953 Braque was commissioned to paint ceiling decorations for the Louvre. His sculpture was exhibited at the Venice Biennale, 1948, 1958, and at the Brussels World's Fair, 1958.

BURCKHARDT, KARL, painter, sculptor and theorist, was born at Lindau, near Zurich, Switzerland, January 13, 1878, the son of a clergyman. His first encounter with classic art was a liberation from his strict Pietist background. In 1900 he made his first journey to Italy, visiting Rome, Capo Circeo and Capri. Under the influence of Hans von Marees his painting became monumental and severely structural. In 1901 he took up sculpture in Rome. Disregarding the variety of natural shapes, he concentrated on elementary form and rigid structure, surpassing Maillol, who was his inspiring teacher. He exhibited in Florence and Forte dei Marmi, 1905-07. During the period 1909-14 he did reliefs, commissioned by the architect Karl Moser, for the Kunsthaus, Zurich. In 1918 he opened the Rodin exhibition at Basel. His book, *Rodin and the Problem of Sculpture,* is not only a brilliant study of Rodin, but also the illuminating confession of a modern sculptor in search of new plastic values. From 1914-21, in collaboration with other young Swiss artists, he executed fountain figures for the Badischer Bahnhof (Railway Station) in Basel, another commission from Karl Moser. His later works include: *In Memory of H. Dieterle,* 1919, Kunsthaus, Zurich; *Dancer,* 1921, Kunsthaus, Winterthur; *St. George,* 1923, Kohlenberg, Basel; and *Amazon,* 1923, now standing near the Rhine Bridge, Basel. Burckhardt died December 24, 1923, at Ligornetto, Ticino, Switzerland. His sculpture still ranks among the best and most advanced of Switzerland. His work has been shown at the Kunsthalle, Berne, 1952, and the Venice Biennale, 1954.

BUTLER, REGINALD, COTTERELL, sculptor, engineer, architect, teacher and editor, was born in Buntingford, Hertfordshire, England, 1913. He made his first sculptures at the age of seven, but trained as an architect, qualifying in 1937. From 1937-39 he taught at the Architectural Association School, and from 1939-50 practiced as an engineer. During the war years he worked as a blacksmith in a Sussex village. From 1946-50 he was technical editor of *The Architects Journal.* His first one-man show was at the Hanover Gallery, London, 1949. Since 1950 he has been Gregory Fellow in sculpture at Leeds University, and in 1952 began to teach at Hatfield, Hertfordshire, then at the Slade School, London University. In 1952 he entered in the Venice Biennale, and in 1953 took first prize in the competition for the Monument to the Unknown Political Prisoner. In 1954 he finished a commissioned sculpture for the entrance of the Hatfield Training

College; called *The Oracle,* it is a fusion of archaic and modern (technological) form. This subject is also in the collection of the Museum of Modern Art, New York. Exhibits of his work include: the Venice Biennale, 1954; a one-man show, New York, 1955; "New Decade", Museum of Modern Art, New York, 1955; "Documenta", Kassel, Germany, 1959. He lives in Berkhamsted, Herts.

CALDER, ALEXANDER, sculptor, graphic artist, engineer and illustrator, was born in Philadelphia, U.S.A., July 22, 1898, of a family of painters and sculptors. From 1915-19 he studied engineering at Stevens Institute of Technology, Philadelphia, while designing and painting in New York. In 1926, while an illustrator for the *National Police Gazette,* he had his first exhibition of animal sketches and started wood carving and wire sculpture. In 1926-27 he visited Paris. Regular attendance at circus performances stimulated him to create a miniature circus which he peopled with amusing figures in wood and wire. It was in this period that he developed his technique of suggesting three-dimensional form through linear movement. Back in Paris, 1929-32, he was in close contact with Mondrian, Miro, Léger and Arp, and his work became increasingly abstract. Calder's mobiles were at first based on mechanical, motorized movement, reminiscent of the important role technology has played in early Constructivist sculpture. He then progressed towards free organic movement, set in motion by natural means and obeying the laws and hazards of rhythmical vibration. In 1931 he married Louisa James and returned to Paris, joining the Abstraction-Création Group. In the same year he produced his illustrations for the *Fables of Aesop.* His mobiles were exhibited for the first time in Paris at the Galerie Vignon, and in New York at the Julien Levy Gallery, 1932. Since 1933 he has lived on his farm in Roxbury, Connecticut, and has made frequent trips to Paris. In 1936 he designed settings for Eric Satie's *Socrate.* In 1937 he executed the *Mercury Fountain* for the Spanish Pavilion at the Paris Exposition, and in 1939, a water ballet for the New York World's Fair. In 1944 he had a large one-man show at the Buchholz Gallery, New York. In the same year he illustrated *Three Young Rats,* and in 1946, the *Fables of La Fontaine.* He was commissioned to design a mobile for the Terrace-Plaza Hotel, Cincinnati (where Miro painted a large mural) in 1946. In 1947 he exhibited with Fernand Léger in Berne and Amsterdam. Visiting Mexico and Brazil, 1948, he exhibited at São Paulo and Rio de Janeiro. In 1950 he had a retrospective exhibition at the Galerie Maeght, Paris, and traveled through the prehistoric regions of Southern France (Lascaux), Brittany, Sweden and Finland. In 1953 he was included in the exhibition, "American Painters and Sculptors" at the Kunsthaus, Zurich. His works have been exhibited at the Brussels World's Fair, 1958; the "Documenta" in Kassel, Germany, 1959; at Amsterdam, Zurich and Perls Gallery, New York, 1960. Retrospective, Venice Biennale, 1952.

CALLERY, MARY, sculptor, was born in New York City, U.S.A., 1903. She grew up in Pittsburgh, and was educated in New York, attending the sculpture class of Edward McCartan at the Art Students League; later she studied under the sculptor Jacques Loutchansky in Paris. After working eight years in Paris she exhibited at the Salon des Tuileries. Her first one-man show was at the Buchholz Gallery, New York, 1944; she has since exhibited there regularly. Other exhibitions of her work include: Chicago Arts Club, 1945; Galerie Mai, 1949; Margaret Brown Gallery, Boston, 1951; Salon de la Sculpture en Plein Air, Musee Rodin, Paris, 1956; a one-man show, Knoedler Galleries, New York, 1957. She contributed a Mobile Fountain of Bronze to the Brussels World's Fair, 1958. Examples of her work are owned by the

Antoine Bourdelle	Louise Bourgeois	Constantin Brancusi	Georges Braque

Karl Burckhardt	Reginald Cotterell Butler	Alexander Calder	Mary Callery

Cesar	Lynn Chadwick	Eduardo Chillida	Honore Daumier

Edgar Degas

Andre Derain

Jose De Rivera

Roel D'Haese

Theo van Doesburg

Marcel Duchamp

Raymond Duchamp-Villon

Max Ernst

Herbert Ferber

Otto Freundlich

Naum Gabo

Antonio Gaudi

Museum of Modern Art, New York; Museum of Fine Art, Toledo; San Francisco and Cincinnati Art Museums.

CESAR, (César Baldaccini) sculptor, was born in Marseilles, France, in 1921. He began his studies at the Ecole des Beaux-Arts in Marseilles and, in 1943, went to Paris for further studies at the Ecole des Beaux-Arts. His works have been exhibited at: Galerie Durand, Paris, 1954; Galerie Rive Droite, Paris, 1955; Salon de Mai, Paris; Venice Biennale, 1956; Galerie Creuzevault, Paris, 1957; São Paulo Biennial, 1957; Biennale di Carrara, Italy, 1957; Hanover Gallery, London, 1957; "International du Bronzetto", Musée Rodin, Paris, 1957. He was awarded the Sculpture Prize for Foreign Participants at the Biennale di Carrara. Three of his works are owned by the Musée d'Art Moderne, Paris, and many are in private collections in New York, London, Paris, Venice, Brussels, Zurich and Amsterdam. He resides in Paris.

CHADWICK, LYNN, sculptor, designer, was born in London, England, 1914. In 1933 he took his degree in architecture. His first independent work, designs for exhibitions and textiles, was done in 1946. In 1947 he produced his first mobiles and constructions, exhibiting them at Gimpel Fils Gallery, London, 1949. His work shows the influence of Calder and Gonzalez. His "balanced sculptures" can be set in motion in various ways. These were exhibited at the Venice Biennale, 1952. He works in iron, bronze, copper, and glass. In recent years he has taken up stable constructions in iron, which he expands and develops as space-enclosing forms. In 1952 he was represented at the Venice Biennale. Chadwick lives in Pinswell, Gloucestershire, and in London. The Tate Gallery, London, the Museum of Modern Art, New York, the Salon de Mai, Paris, own examples of his work. *Exhibitions:* "The Unknown Political Prisoner," Tate Gallery, London; Salon de Mai, Paris, 1953; Park Middelheim, Antwerp, 1953; Whitechapel Gallery, Holland Park, London, 1954; Venice Biennale, 1956; "New Decade," Museum of Modern Art, New York, 1956; "Sculpture In Iron," Kunsthalle, Berne, 1956; Palace of Fine Arts, Brussels, 1957; Stedelijk Museum, Amsterdam, 1957; Brussels World's Fair, 1958; "Documenta," Kassel, Germany, Galerie Lienhard, Zurich, 1959. He won the Venice Biennale prize for sculpture, 1956.

CHILLIDA, EDUARDO, sculptor, was born in San Sebastian, Spain on January 10, 1924. He first studied architecture in Madrid, 1943-1947, then turned to sculpture in 1947. He first exhibited in the group show, "Les Mains Eblouies," Galerie Maeght, Paris, 1950. The Galerie Clan, Madrid, gave him his first one-man show. He received an honorable mention at the 1954 Triennale, Milan. In the same year he created four iron doors for the Basilica of Aranzazu. In 1955 he built a monument to Sir Alexander Fleming in San Sebastian and participated in the "Eisen Plastik" exhibition at the Kunsthalle, Berne. He was given his most important one-man show in 1956 at the Galerie Maeght, Paris, to which he contributed twenty-seven sculptures. He also contributed to the exhibition, "Architecture Contemporaine, Intégration des Arts," in 1957. He had a show of sculptures, drawings and collages at the Solomon R. Guggenheim Museum, New York, in 1958. Winner of the Biennale Prize, Venice and fellowship of the Graham Foundation, Chicago, 1958. His work is represented in countless private collections in Paris, New York, Zurich, Berne, Basel, La Chaux de Fonds, São Paulo and other cities.

DAUMIER, HONORE, painter, lithographer and sculptor, was born in Marseilles, France, February 26, 1810. He published his first lithographs in 1829, and in 1831 became a contributor to *Caricature,* a Paris journal opposed to the Third Empire. For the next 40 years he was unflagging in his activity as a satirical cartoonist of politics and society. From 1830-32 he modeled 36 polychrome clay busts of French deputies. His emphasis in sculpture on the grotesque element which transcends individual likeness and expresses a fundamental human experience, plus the tendency toward dissolution of volume in his work, make him a forerunner of modern sculpture. In 1850 he completed *Ratapoil,* a lampoon of Napoleon III. His *Emigrants,* 1871, a bas-relief in terracotta, expresses the elegiac mood of the subject in the slow, floating movement of the bodies. In 1878 a collective exhibition of his paintings and sketches was inaugurated by Victor Hugo, but proved a commercial failure. It was only after the Centennial Exposition, Paris, 1900, that his art was universally recognized. Daumier died at Valmondois, February 10, 1879. His principal sculptural work comprises: the 36 clay busts of the French deputies, now in the Philipon Collection, Paris; the *Ratapoil* statuette, (originally owned by the Galerie Bing, Paris; a bronze cast is in the Louvre); and the *Emigrants,* now in the Geoffroy-Dechaune Collection, Paris. Many hitherto unknown sculptures of Daumier have recently been found and today the artist is esteemed almost as highly for his sculptures as for his paintings and graphic art.

DEGAS, EDGAR, painter and sculptor, was born in Paris, France, July 19, 1834, of mixed Italian and Creole descent. From 1845-53 he attended a Paris lycée; among his classmates were the brothers Rouart, later famous as collectors. In 1853-54, while training as a lawyer, he studied with Ingres' pupil, Lamothe. His earliest extant paintings date from 1854. From 1854-60 he made frequent journeys to Italy with long visits in Florence, Rome and Venice. He was impressed by the work of Donatello and Benvenuto Cellini. His growing interest in sculpture made him hesitate between painting and sculpture. In 1855 he entered the Ecole des Beaux Arts together with Fantin-Latour and Bonnat. In the next year he was strongly impressed by Japanese woodcuts. In 1861 he first began to use horses as subjects for his painting. He came into contact in 1866 with the group of painters who formed the Impressionist movement: Bazille, Renoir, Cézanne, Sisley, Monet and Pissarro; and, at the Café Guerbois, with the writers, Zola and Duret. In the same year he produced his first sculptures— horses, then dancers—in wax. Working mainly in wax and clay, his technique was to build up volume out of bits of material, approximating the Impressionist technique of painting. Degas saw active service in the Franco-Prussian War, 1870-71. His first exhibition was held at the Durand-Ruel Gallery, London, 1871. In 1872 he began to paint dancers. In 1872-73 he was in New Orleans. From 1874-86 he exhibited at every Impressionist exhibition except that of 1882. In 1881 he exhibited his dancer in colored clay with a real tulle dress and real hair (*Danseuse de 14 ans de la petite classe de l'Opéra, modelée aux trois quarts de la nature*) at the Salon des Indépendants. It attracted general attention but the press and the public were hostile because he had dared to defy the academic tradition of heroic classicism by employing "grotesque" themes and "vulgar" materials. As a result of this reception Degas ceased to exhibit his sculptures publicly, and showed them only to his intimate friends. In 1886 he was included in the Impressionist exhibition in New York. He traveled to Spain, 1889; the impressions received on this journey may have inspired his sculpture, *Danseuse Espagnole.* In 1893, his eyesight, already impaired, deteriorated. Degas died in Paris, 1917. In his studio were found over 150 wax models of sculpture that he had never shown publicly. In 1919-21, 73 pieces were cast in bronze, each in 22 copies. All originals, including those not cast in bronze, were destroyed.

DERAIN, ANDRE, painter, graphic artist and sculptor, was born in Chatou, France, in 1880, but lived most of his life in Paris. Although he had intended to become an engineer, he began painting seriously at the age of fifteen. In 1904, he studied at the Académie Julian. He exhibited with Vlaminck and Matisse at the "Salon des Indépendants," in 1907, and again at the "Salon d'Automne," in 1907. In that same year, he became affiliated with Kahnweiler and produced some sculptures and woodcuts. *Crouching Man* was executed in 1909. In 1910, he did the woodcut illustrations for Apollinaire's *L'Enchanteur Pourrissant.* He joined Picasso in Spain and later visited the "Bateau Lavoir" in the rue Ravignan. During the first world war, he made masks from empty shells found on the battle fields. In his *Anecdotiques,* Apollinaire refers to the "transparency of his painting during the war years." In 1919, Derain designed scenery for the Ballets Russes. In 1928, he was awarded the Carnegie Prize. He had a one-man show at Paul Guillaume in 1931. He died in complete seclusion near Versailles, in 1954.

DE RIVERA, JOSE, sculptor, was born in Louisiana in 1904. For eight years he worked in various industrial plants, where he acquired foundry and machine shop practice. He studied drawing with John W. Norton in Chicago, then studied sculpture on his travels through Europe and North Africa. His work was first shown at the 1930 Annual of the Chicago Art Institute and has since been seen at all major American exhibitions, including the Whitney Museum, New York, 1934-1958; the Museum of Modern Art, New York, 1938, '39, '40, '42, '56; the New York and San Francisco World's Fairs; the School of Design at Harvard University, 1945; the Metropolitan Museum of Art, New York, 1951; and many others. He has also exhibited at the Willard Gallery, 1942, the Buchholz Gallery, 1942, and has had five one-man shows at the Grace Borgenicht Gallery, New York, between 1952 and 1958. He was included in group shows at the Galerie Denise René, Paris, 1956, and at the American National Exhibit in Moscow, 1959. Examples of his sculpture are owned by many museums and private collectors.

D'HAESE, ROEL, sculptor, was born in Grammont, Belgium, on October 26, 1921. While still very young, he worked for a blacksmith and later as a wood carver in a workshop where religious figures were made. He studied at the Académie d'Alost, and from 1938 through 1942 he worked with the sculptor, Oscar Jespers. After carving for a time directly in stone, he returned to iron forging, finally choosing bronze as his medium. Since the ordinary casting process did not meet his precise demands, he adopted the lost-wax technique. He works unassisted in his own studio, which explains the dimensions of his recent works. He had his first one-man show in April, 1949. He has since contributed to the Bienal in São Paulo, 1953, and won the Prix de la Jeune Sculpture in Belgium, 1954. Twenty-five of his works were exhibited at the XXIX Biennale in Venice, 1958. He was given a one-man show at the Palais des Beaux-Arts in Brussels, 1958, and has participated in numerous exhibitions both in Belgium and abroad. He now lives in Bierenberg near Brussels.

DOESBURG, THEO VAN, painter, sculptor, architect, typographer, poet and theorist was born in Utrecht, Holland, August 30, 1883. His first ambition was to become an actor. In 1899 he began to paint, and in 1902, to write plays and fables. His first exhibition was at The Hague, 1908. In 1912 his poems were published under the title *Volle Maan (Full Moon).* In 1914, the year he was called up for active service, he wrote the poem, *De Stem Uit de Diepte (The Voice from the Depths).* In 1917 he worked with the architect, J. J. P.

Oud. In the same year he and Mondrian founded the review, *De Stijl.* After touring Europe, 1920-21, he settled in Weimar and Berlin. He edited (with Arp, Schwitters, Tzara and Hausmann) the literary review, *Mécano,* in 1922, and arranged a Dada tour through Holland. In 1923 he exhibited at the Galerie Rosenberg, Paris, where a model of De Stijl house, constructed with the architect C. van Eesteren, was shown. In 1923-24 he lectured on modern architecture and produced his first neo-plastic paintings. During 1926-28 he worked on the interior decoration of the Aubette Restaurant and Bar in collaboration with Arp and Sophie Taeuber-Arp. In 1929-30 he built his house at Meudon and lectured on architecture in Barcelona and Madrid. Van Doesburg died at Davos, March 7, 1931. Examples of his work are in the collections of the art museums of The Hague and Amsterdam, the Kröller Museum, Otterlo, the Kunstmuseum, Basel, the Philadelphia Art Museum and Yale University Art Gallery, and in Swiss and French private collections.

DUCHAMP, MARCEL, painter, poet and writer, was born in Blainville, France, 1887, the youngest brother of the painter, Jacques Villon, and the sculptor, Raymond Duchamp-Villon. Their father was a lawyer in Rouen. Duchamp attended the Académie Julian in Paris, 1904, training also as a librarian. In 1911 he joined the Cubist movement. His painting, *Nude Descending a Staircase,* 1912, is a pioneer work of modern art. In it, Duchamp was not concerned as much with painting, as with the invention of a new optical language that would express motion in time and space. From 1913-15 he traveled in the U.S.A. on the occasion of the Armory show in New York. He was a co-founder and spiritual leader of the Dada movement in New York along with Man Ray and Francis Picabia. His "ready-mades", a protest against lifeless aestheticism, demonstrates how an artist's personality, his choice and interpretation of accidental and hackneyed forms, can endow dead objects with new vitality and expressive power. From 1915-23 he worked on his most original painting, the fantastic *La mariée mise a nu par ses célibataires, même (The Bride Stripped Bare by her Bachelors, Even).* Painted on glass, it is an interplay of abstract forms expressed in symbolic language. Its formal arrangement may, by shock, confer on the spectator its philosophical essence. In 1918 he visited Argentina, and a year later, returned to Paris. He was co-founder of the Société Anonyme with Katherine Dreier and Man Ray, 1920. In 1921 he produced his first abstract film composed of circles and spirals. He joined the Paris Surrealist movement in 1925, and wrote under the pen name Rose Sélavy. He has completely abandoned any form of artistic creation in favor of chess. The spiritual independence and intellectual vitality of the artist are paramount to him. This attitude is confirmed by his influence on the younger generation. Examples of his work were shown at the Brussels World's Fair, 1958. Duchamp now lives in New York.

DUCHAMP-VILLON, RAYMOND, sculptor, architect and physician, was born at Damville, Eure, France, November 5, 1876, the brother of Jacques Villon and Marcel Duchamp. Abandoning his medical studies, he took up sculpture in 1898. Early influences on his work were Rodin and Art Nouveau. In 1912 he joined the Cubists and produced his *Project for a Cubist House.* From 1912-14 he worked on numerous variations of his *Horse,* which became the manifesto of Cubist sculpture. In those years he also worked on his *Seated Woman* which is composed of simple, basic shapes, and on his *Head of a Woman (Maggy),* the prototype of Picasso's grotesque heads. During this period he was friendly with the poet Apollinaire. In 1914 he enlisted as a medical officer; he died at Cannes, 1918, of an infection incurred while carrying out his professional duties. "One might almost say that the sculptor gradually persuades an immaterial vision to descend to earth till it finally crystallizes into matter" (Duchamp-Villon). His exhibitions include: Société Naturelle des Beaux Arts, Paris, 1910; Salon d'Automne, Paris, 1905-13; Armory Show, New York, 1913; Salon d'Automne, retrospective exhibition, 1919; Société Anonyme, Brooklyn, N. Y., 1921; Brummer Gallery, New York, 1929; Galerie Pierre, Paris, 1931; Galerie de France, Paris (with Villon and Duchamp), 1942; Yale University Art Gallery (with Villon and Duchamp), 1945. "Le Cubisme", Musée d'Art Moderne, Paris, 1953; "Sept Pionniers de la Sculpture Moderne", Yverdon and Zurich, 1954.

ERNST, MAX, painter, illustrator, sculptor, poet, was born at Bruehl, near Cologne, Germany, April 2, 1891. In 1910 he entered Bonn University. From 1914-18 he was on active duty. In 1919, with Baargeld, he launched the Dada movement in Cologne and was editor of *Die Schammade* and *Der Ventilator,* 1919-21. He first met with Arp, Eluard, Tzara and Breton in the Tyrol, 1921. In the next year he met again with Eluard, whose *Répétitions* and *Malheurs des Immortelles* he illustrated in that year. In 1924 he was one of the founders of the Surrealist movement in Paris. His *Histoire Naturelle* was published by Jeanne Bucher, Paris, 1925. From 1925-30 he worked with the Révolution Surréaliste. In 1925-26 he collaborated with Miro on settings and costumes for Diaghilev's ballet, *Romeo and Juliet* at Monte Carlo. During the years 1926-39 he had one-man shows in Paris, Düsseldorf, Brussels, London, Zurich, Madrid, Berlin, New York and Los Angeles. In 1929 he wrote and illustrated *La Femme 100 Têtes* which was published by Carrefour, Paris. The same firm published his *Rêve d'une petite fille qui voulutentrer au Carmel,* 1930. In 1933 Ernst was branded a decadent artist by the Nazis. In 1934 his *Semaine de Bonté* was published by Jeanne Bucher, Paris. In that year he carved stones for Giacometti's garden at Maloja and painted a mural for the Corso Bar, Zurich. In 1937 he designed settings for Jarry's *Ubu Enchaîné,* a Comédie des Champs Elysées production. In that same year *Cahiers d'Art* devoted a special issue to Ernst. In 1938-39 he executed grotesque sculptures and reliefs for his country house at St. Martin d'Ardèche. From 1941-45 he lived in New York. During those years he had one-man shows in New York, Chicago, New Orleans and Washington, and was co-editor of *VVV* magazine. In 1942 a special number of *View* magazine was devoted to his work. His sculpture was exhibited at the Julien Levy Gallery, New York, 1944. In the same year he designed chess figures in boxwood. A retrospective exhibition was held at the Galerie Denise René, Paris, 1945. At this time Ernst collaborated with Hans Richter on the film *Dreams that money can buy* (New York). In 1946 he settled in Arizona. In 1948 his *Beyond Painting* was published by Wittenborn Inc., New York. He exhibited at the Galerie René Drouin, Paris, 1950, and the following year at Bruehl, Hamburg, Karlsruhe and other German cities. In 1951 he lectured at the University of Honolulu on the relation between primitive and modern art. In 1953, he exhibited at the Galerie Spiegel, Cologne, and in the same year his book *Das Schnabelpaar,* 8 colored etchings and 1 poem, was published by E. Beyeler, Basel, Switzerland. At the 1954 Venice Biennial he received the international prize for painting. He was given a show at the Galerie Creuzevault, Paris, in 1958; a Retrospective at the Musée D'Art Moderne, Paris, 1959 and there will be one at the Museum of Modern Art, New York, in 1961. He lives in Paris and Huismes (Loire).

FERBER, HERBERT, sculptor, was born in New York, U.S.A., 1906. He studied dentistry and oral surgery, then entered the Beaux-Arts Institute of Design, New York. His sculpture, exhibited in New York in 1937, 1943, 1947, and 1950, combines various metals, such as brass, tin, lead and copper, through soldering. His work was included in the exhibition, "Abstract Painting and Sculpture in America", Museum of Modern Art, New York, 1951. In 1951-52, he executed a large sculpture for the facade of the Millburn (New Jersey) synagogue. In 1952 he was selected for the "15 Americans" show at the Museum of Modern Art, New York. He was given a one-man show by the Kootz Gallery, New York, in 1955 and in 1957. In 1959 he was a contributor to the "Documenta", in Kassel, Germany. He lives in New York.

FREUNDLICH, OTTO, painter, sculptor, graphic artist and teacher, was born at Stoll, Pomerania, Germany, July 10, 1878. After studying art history with Woelfflin in Berlin he began to work as an artist, attending Kunowski and Corinth's school. In 1909 he left Berlin for Paris where he developed his art without reference to Cubism. "I brought the conception of purely flat painting with me, therefore, I could not join the Cubists" (Letter to S. Giedion). From 1909-15 he had his studio at Montmartre. In 1909 he produced his first sculptures, and the bronzes, *Female Bust,* 1910, and *Great Mask,* 1912. His first Paris exhibition was at the Galerie Saguet, 1910. He was included in the Kunstring exhibition, Amsterdam, 1911, and the Cologne Sonderbund exhibition, 1912. In 1918-19 he did a mosaic for the house of Feinhals, Cologne. In 1919 he participated in the November Group exhibition, Berlin. One of his sculptured heads was reproduced in *Genius* in the same year. In 1924 he returned to Paris where he designed a stained-glass window. He began to exhibit regularly at the Indépendants, Salles des Tuilleries, Surindépendants and Musicalistes. His first monumental abstract sculpture was done in 1928. In 1932 he exhibited with Group 1940 at the Galerie Renaissance, Paris. From 1932-35 he took part in Abstraction-Création exhibitions and was represented in that group's publications. On his 60th birthday in 1938 a retrospective exhibition of his work opened at the Galerie Jeanne Bucher. In that year he founded the Académie de Peinture, Dessin, Sculpture, Gravure, *Le Mur,* where he taught. In 1939-40 his sculpture *Homme Nouveau* was used by the Nazis as the cover illustration for the catalog of their Decadent Art Exhibition; it was also reproduced in the Nazi journal, *Der Stürmer.* He was twice interned and compelled to interrupt his lecture courses. From 1940-43 he lived with his wife in the Pyrenees area. On February 21, 1943, he was arrested and on March 4 deported to Lublin where he died. The last news of him was contained in a letter written by a nurse to his wife: "We are face to face with such unspeakable misery that our spirit is numbed. But the composure of your husband, Madam, is so magnificent that I must write to you about it." Exhibitions of his work were held at the Galerie Drouin, Paris, 1945; Museé d'Art Moderne, (Peintures et sculptures); Salon des Réalités Nouvelles, Paris, 1946; Salon des Artists Indépendants, Paris, 1947; Galerie Maeght; Museé de Grenoble; Museum of Modern Art, São Paulo, 1949; since 1945 every year in his atelier, 38 Rue Henri Barbusse, "Les expositions du souvenir" are held. Exhibitions at Galerie Colette Allendy, Paris, 1952; Galerie Rive Droite, Paris, 1954.

GABO, NAUM, sculptor, painter, architect, designer, theorist and teacher, was born in Bryansk, Russia, 1890. He attended high-school in Kursk. From 1910-14 he studied in Munich, at first medicine and natural sciences, then, under Woelfflin's influence, art history. After a journey to Italy he returned to Moscow where he became thoroughly familiar with the Stchukine and Morosow collections. His wide range of interests also included mathematics and technology. From 1914-17 he was in Oslo with his brother, Antoine Pevsner.

From 1917-20 he was again in Russia, teaching with Kandinsky, Malevich and Tatlin (who had been making reliefs out of everyday objects since 1913) at Vchutema, the Moscow school of art. The growing influence of Social Realism caused him to leave this school and led to a breach with Tatlin and Rodchenko. "Art is not a political instrument" (Gabo). 1920 saw the publication of the *Realist Manifesto,* the proclamation of free art, by Gabo and Pevsner. In the *Realist Manifesto* time and space are explained as fundamental elements of art and life; static mass is replaced by dynamic form. Underlying the whole is the new concept of space. As early as 1918-19 Gabo had opposed mechanical naturalism, calling it a "pseudo-constructive" art. "Either build functional houses and bridges or create pure art, but do not mix the two. That simply means imitating a machine." To Gabo movement is an integral part of construction. Starting from the demonstration of a physical movement, as in *Kinetic Sculpture,* 1920, where a steel spring vibrated in space, he moved gradually away from Calder's realm of actual movement to that of virtual movement. From the outset, Gabo has shown a marked interest in architecture, designing in 1919-20 a project for radio stations at Serpuchow, and in 1931 a project for a theatre auditorium. His first sculpture dates from 1916, busts in sheet iron, and heads in celluloid and metal. In 1922 he was represented in the Constructivist exhibition at the Galerie Van Dieman, Berlin. In 1923 he went into exile with Pevsner, remaining for the next ten years in Berlin. In 1924 he exhibited with his brother at the Galerie Percier, Paris, and joined the Berlin November Group (Klee, Kandinsky, Barlach, Mies van der Rohe and Belling), founded under the Weimar Republic, 1918. In 1926, Gabo, Pevsner and Doesburg exhibited at the Little Review Gallery, New York. In 1927 Gabo was included in the Société Anonyme Exhibition at the Brooklyn (N. Y.) Museum. In the same year he collaborated with Pevsner on settings and costumes for the Diaghilev ballet, *La Chatte,* produced in Paris, Monte Carlo, London and Berlin. In 1928 Gabo lectured at the Bauhaus, and in Hanover, Cologne, Amsterdam, Rotterdam, Utrecht, and met Mondrian and Rietveld. In 1930 he exhibited at the Kestner Gesellschaft, Hanover. From 1932-35 he was in Paris, and became a member of the Abstraction-Création Group. In 1936 he left Paris for London, exhibiting at the Lefèvre Gallery. In that year he exhibited at the Arts Club of Chicago with Pevsner and Mondrian. In 1936 his work was included in the Cubism and Abstract Art show at the Museum of Modern Art, New York. Also in that year he edited the magazine *Circle* in London with Ben Nicholson and J. L. Martin. After a visit to the U.S. he retired to St. Ives, Cornwall from 1939-45. There he became head of a group of young English artists. In 1946 he left England for the U.S.A., settling in Woodbury, Conn. Since 1948 he has lectured during the summer at the Graduate School of Design at Harvard University. He shared an exhibition with Pevsner at the Museum of Modern Art, New York, 1948. In 1952 he had a one-man show at the Pierre Matisse Gallery, New York. In 1953, he won a second prize in the Unknown Political Prisoner Competition. He completed *Construction in Space,* a monument in Rotterdam, in 1957. He participated in the Brussels International Exposition, 1958, and in the "Documenta", Kassel, Germany, 1959.

GAUDI, ANTONIO, architect, sculptor and ceramic artist, was born in Reus, Tarragona, Spain, in 1852. The spacial freedom and organic unity of Gaudi's work has remained of stimulating interest. Valued at the beginning of the 20th Century primarily for his "bizarre" imagination, he later became appreciated as an architectural innovator, a constructor and a sculptor of the organic. A graduate of the Barcelona School of Architecture, he developed an expressive "Art Nouveau" by giving new vitality to line, space and volume and creating original constructions, such as sloping pillars to take diagonal pressure. Gaudi was a deeply religious man and an uncompromising artist. Barcelona was the center of his life and work, and there, for his patron, Count Güell, he built a town house (1889), the Güell Chapel (1898-1914) and Güell Park (1900-1914). Here, he created an imposing children's play-terrace on high ground, it is shaped in swinging curves and inlaid with colored tile mosaics, which anticipated the Cubist principle of "collage." The Cathedral of Sagrada Familia, begun in 1883 and not completed at the time of his death, was his most ambitious project. Based on a plan which indicates a departure from Neo-Gothic concepts and an embracing of new theories of construction, it is noteworthy for its magnificent tower and its ornamental figures. His apartment houses and office buildings in the Paseo Gracia, Casa Batillo (1905-1907), and Casa Mila (1905-1910) illustrate his style which simultaneously exploits façade and spacial values. Here, his sculptural imagination reaches its highest expression in the fluid lines of chimneys and ventilators, as well as in the wave-like trellis-work of iron gates and balconies. Gaudi died June 10, 1926.

GIACOMETTI, ALBERTO, sculptor, painter, designer and poet, was born, 1901, at Stampa in the Italian-speaking area of Switzerland. His father was Giovanni Giacometti, the well-known Impressionist landscape painter. He produced his first sculpture in 1914. In 1919 he attended the Ecole des Arts et Métiers, Geneva. In Italy, 1921-22, he studied Tintoretto in Venice, and early Christian mosaics and Baroque art in Rome. From 1922-25 he was in Paris, working in Bourdelle's studio, La Grande Chaumière. His first "idolic" sculptures were produced in the years 1925-28. He joined the Surrealists, 1929, becoming their leading representative sculptor with his "objets" and cage-like constructions—emanations of subconscious psychic powers of a strange and dreamlike intensity. He also wrote poetry in these years. Since 1935 he has shown increasing interest in the human figure. Starting with portrait busts of his brother, he progressed to minute works of art expressing his painstaking investigation into new laws of proportion and their psychological and spatial effects. In the course of these experiments he encountered the work of Jacques Callot (1592-1635). "Our eye can absorb an object only if its measure is reduced" (G). In accordance with this conviction, Giacometti believes that he can convey the essence of reality only by representing it on an abnormal scale. He has adopted the method of reducing the normal size and density of an object in order to express its essential qualities. His unflinching self-criticism leads him to destroy his sculptures again and again. In 1938 Giacometti was a patient in Bichat Hospital, Geneva, for him a period of rich personal experience. From 1940-45 he was in Geneva, experimenting with increasing intensity on his "long-distance" sculpture; completely renouncing all tactile effects, he concentrates instead on rendering the impression of movement in space by means of a synthetic approach. After the war he returned to Paris where, in addition to sculpture, he has resumed painting with increased intensity. His exhibitions include: representation in all Surrealist exhibitions, 1930-47; a one-man show at the Pierre Matisse Gallery, New York, 1948 (with a catalog introduction, *The Search for the Absolute,* by J. P. Sartre); Stedelijk Museum, Amsterdam, 1949 (13 Paris Sculptors); Kunsthalle, Basel, 1949 (with André Masson); and a one-man show at the Galerie Maeght, Paris, (sculpture), 1951 and (paintings) 1954; Venice Biennale and Kunsthalle Bern (with sculptures and paintings), 1956; a one-man show,

Pierre Matisse Gallery, New York, 1958; Brussels World's Fair, 1958; "Documenta", Kassel, Germany, 1959.

GILIOLI, EMILE, sculptor, designer, painter, was born in Paris, France, June 10, 1911. In 1928 he attended the Ecole des Arts Décoratifs, Nice and in 1931 the Ecole des Beaux Arts, Paris. He first exhibited at the Galerie Bretau, Paris, 1945. In 1947 he joined the Abstract Group, exhibiting at the Denise René, Colette Allendy, and de Beaume galleries. In 1941 he designed a figure of Christ for the church of Sacré Coeur, Grenoble. He has designed several monuments: at Voreppe, 1946; Grenoble *(Monument to the Deported)*, 1950; Chapelle-en-Vercors, 1951; Vassieux, 1951. He won an award in the Unknown Political Prisoner Monument competition, 1953, in which he received a special distinction. He lives in Paris. Examples of his work are owned by the Musée d'Art Moderne, Paris, the art museums of Grenoble and Nice, and the Tate Gallery, London. *Exhibitions:* "Les Français Contemporains", Vienna, 1949; Galerie Exlibris (Sculptures, Tapisseries), Brussels, 1952; Parc Soonsbeek, Antwerp, 1953; Palais des Beaux Arts, Luttich, 1953 (with painter Poliakoff); "Tendances actuelles de l'Art Français", Ostende, 1954; Triennale, Milan, 1954; Bienal, São Paulo, 1954; Salon de Mai, Paris, each year; Galerie Denise René, Paris, 1955 (Dessins, Sculptures, Tapisseries). Regular participation at the Salon de la Jeune Sculpture. One-man show at the Galerie Carré, Paris, 1958; Documenta, Kassel, Germany, 1959; Galerie Craven, Paris, Svensk Franska, Stockholm, 1960.

GISIGER, HANSJORG, sculptor and graphic artist, was born in Basel, Switzerland, in 1919. He studied medicine for several years then decided to devote himself to sculpture (stone). For a period of two years he worked as an apprentice with a former student of Rodin. From 1945 to 1948 he lived in the French section of Switzerland, working independently and searching for a contemporary plastic language to express essential human values. At this time he was inspired by Maillol, Laurens and Arp. Although trained as a stonecutter, he has more recently preferred iron and steel to stone and developed a personal style somewhat reminiscent of Gonzalez. His graphic work is remarkable for its austerity and precision. He had his first show in 1948, and he has subsequently exhibited in Basel, Paris, Lausanne, Geneva, Bienne, Zurich and Düsseldorf. Examples of his work are owned by museums in Switzerland and France, as well as by private collectors in France, Germany, Spain, England and the United States. During the summer he lives in Epalinges, near Lausanne, and during the winter months in Paris.

GONZALEZ, JULIO, sculptor, designer, was born in Barcelona, Spain, September 21, 1876. His father was a Catalan blacksmith, a craft in which his family had excelled for generations. While apprenticed to his father he decided to become a painter and attended evening classes at the Barcelona Art Academy. In 1900 he left Barcelona for Paris. Though attracted at first by the work of Degas and Puvis de Chavannes, he soon joined the group led by Picasso, Manolo, Max Jacob, all closely linked by friendship and common artistic interests. From 1908 on he devoted himself almost exclusively to sculpture in wrought iron, leading a lonely existence made bearable only by the friendship of Picasso and Brancusi, who offered material and moral support. In 1927 he produced his first wrought-and-cut-iron sculptures, a series of masks and still-lifes; with these he overcame cubist influence which had still been noticeable in his *Venus*, 1927, and earlier work. His sculpture, although starting from a given theme, often wittily interpreted, tends at the same time towards absolute form.

His chief concern was always the problem of space. Gonzalez worked with Picasso, 1929-32, teaching him technical improvement of his then strictly Constructivist work. Material difficulties during the war forced him to leave several of his works unfinished. He died at Arceuil, March 27, 1942. Gonzalez has had a vital and fundamental influence on the younger generation of American and English sculptors. In 1952, the Musée d'Art Moderne, Paris, held a retrospective exhibition of his work, buying a considerable part for its permanent collection. *Exhibitions:* Yverdon and Zurich, 1954; Berne, Amsterdam, Brussels, 1955; Museum of Modern Art, New York and Institute of Arts, Minneapolis, 1956; Kestner Gesellschaft, Hanover and Galerie Berggruen, Paris, 1957; Galerie de France, Paris, 1959.

GRIS, JUAN (JOSE GONZALEZ), painter, illustrator and sculptor, was born in Madrid, Spain, March 23, 1887, where he attended the school of Arts and Crafts up to 1906. Thereafter he moved to Paris and witnessed the birth of Cubism. He was closely associated with the Rue Ravignan 13 Group, where he rented his first atelier in Paris. In 1912 he exhibited for the first time at the Salon des Indépendants. During World War I he lived in Paris and the Touraine. Besides his *Arlequin*, 1917, there exists an expressive *Masque* (paper), which he made for the Swedish ballet, 1923. His lecture "On the possibilities of Painting" at the Sorbonne, May 15, 1924, contains the basic idea of Cubism. Juan Gris died at Boulogne-sur-Seine, 1927.

HAJDU, ETIENNE, sculptor, designer, painter, was born in Turda, Transylvania, August 12, 1907, of Hungarian descent. Coming to Paris in 1927, he worked with Niclausse and Bourdelle. His first encounter with modern art, at the Fernand Léger exhibition, 1930, made a lasting impression on his artistic development. A naturalized French citizen, he saw active service in 1930. The years following again brought him into contact with modern art. On a visit to Greece and Crete he gained a special interest in early Greek art and antique relief. He made a cathedral tour through France, and traveled in Holland, where the work of Mondrian was a revelation in the use of fundamental forms. Vieira da Silva introduced him to Jeanne Bucher in whose gallery he first exhibited his sculptures. In 1940, after demobilization, he worked as a stone grinder at Bagnères, Pyrenees, becoming intimately acquainted with the potentialities of stone. Returning to Paris, he began to make full use of this experience, as shown by his delicate handling of stone surfaces and simple, direct treatment of bronze volumes. *Exhibitions:* Galerie Jeanne Bucher, Paris (1939-1958); Salon de Mai, Paris (since 1947); Group Exhibition, Lausanne, 1955; "The New Decade", Museum of Modern Art, New York, 1955; Galerie Suzanne Feigel, Basel, 1956; Galerie La Roue, Paris, 1956; Bienal at São Paulo, 1956; Cité Radieuse, Marseilles, 1956; Kunstgewerbemuseum, Zurich, 1957; Galerie Claude Bernard, Paris, 1958; Guggenheim Museum, New York, 1958; Knoedler Art Galleries, New York, 1958; Musée Rodin, Paris, 1958; "The 1958 Pittsburgh International Exhibition"; Park Middelheim, Antwerp, 1959; "Documenta", Kassel, Germany, 1959; Musée d'Art et d'Industrie, Saint Etienne, 1960. He lives in Bagneux near Paris.

HARE, DAVID, sculptor and writer, was born in New York, U.S.A., 1917. He attended school in New York, California and Colorado. He began his career as a commercial artist, portraitist and color photographer. He has published an album on the Indians of New Mexico and Arizona. During the war he worked with André Breton, Max Ernst and Marcel Duchamp on the New York review, *VVV*. His first sculpture, done in 1942, showed the influence of Giacometti's magic objects. In developing his style he has moved in the direction of Picasso's Surrealist metamorphoses. His latest work is characterized by an increasing dematerialization into transparent cobweb-like structures. At present he is the leading exponent of Surrealist sculpture in America. He participated in the "New Decade" exhibit, at the Museum of Modern Art, New York, 1955, and in the São Paulo Bienal, 1957. Since 1952 he has lived mostly in France.

HARTUNG, KARL, sculptor, was born in Hamburg, Germany, May 2, 1908. He studied with Bossert at the Landeskunstschule, Hamburg. From 1929-32 he was in Paris, coming under the influence of Maillol and Despiau. In 1932-33, working in Florence, he was impressed by Donatello and Etruscan art. Returning to Hamburg in 1933, he took up abstract sculpture. In 1936 he moved to Berlin. On active service, 1941-45, he was taken prisoner. Upon his release in 1945 he returned to Berlin where, in 1951, he was made an instructor at the Akademie für Bildende Künste. Since 1945 he has had exhibitions in all major German cities, in the U.S.A., Brazil, Switzerland, Sweden, Paris, Madrid, Antwerp, London and Amsterdam. His works were exhibited at the Biennale Venice, 1956; in Munich, Germany, 1958; at the Brussels World's Fair, 1958; the "Documenta", Kassel, Germany, 1959. He lives in Berlin.

HAUSMANN, RAOUL, painter, sculptor, photographer, poet and writer, was born in Vienna, Austria, July 12, 1886. With Huelsenbeck he founded in 1919 the Dada movement in Berlin; he is the author of Dada manifestoes, pamphlets, poetic grotesques and abstract drawings. His sculpture includes *Ready Made Sculpture (Head)*, 1920; one year later his *Optophonetic Poem*, inspired Schwitters to compose his *Ursonata Optophonetic Construction* followed, 1922. In 1933, in the Balearic Islands, he made studies and photographs of ancient architecture. He lives in Limoges, France.

HEPWORTH, BARBARA, sculptor, graphic artist and theorist, was born in Wakefield, Yorkshire, England, January 10, 1903. She started to model portraits in clay at the age of sixteen. In 1920 she attended the Leeds Art School, and from 1921-24, the Royal Art College, London. There she held a scholarship in drawing, but was soon attending only the sculpture classes. It was at this time that she met Henry Moore. In Italy, 1924-25, the master carver, Ardini, instructed her in the technique of carving in marble. In 1930 she married the English painter, Ben Nicholson. In 1932 she met Arp and Brancusi in Paris. In her art the emphasis on craftsmanship is fundamental. Her trained sensitivity and technical skill are almost exclusively devoted to the material itself, revealing its essential beauty by emphasizing its inherent qualities. She prefers hard woods for their great variety of color and surface finish. During the wartime shortage of wood she enriched her work with color, using it effectively to emphasize concave surfaces. From 1931-36 she belonged to Group 7 & 8, 1933-34 to Unit One, and from 1933-35 to the Paris Abstraction-Création Group. Since 1936 she has lived in St. Ives, Cornwall, an area whose light and color remind her of the Mediterranean seaside. There, living close to nature, she may observe with unflagging interest the interrelation between the human figure and its natural surroundings. In recent years her interest in the human figure has steadily increased. She had a retrospective at the Venice Biennale, 1950 and won the São Paulo prize of 1959, was awarded the Leeds Gold Medal for her *Biolith,* and in 1953, she won a second prize for her entry in

the Unknown Political Prisoner Monument Competition. She was given a retrospective at the Walker Art Center, Minneapolis, in 1955. Since 1956 she has exhibited at Gimpel Fils, London, at the Martha Jackson Gallery, New York, 1956. She was a participant in the Brussels World's Fair exhibition, 1958, the "Documenta" in Kassel, Germany, in Park Middelheim, Antwerp, 1959. She has exihibted in all the major cities of Europe and the U.S. Her works are in the collection of the Tate Gallery, London; the Museum of Modern Art, New York; the Kröller-Müller Museum, Holland; the Walker Art Center, Minneapolis.

HOFLEHNER, RUDOLF, sculptor, was born in Linz, Austria, in 1916. He completed his studies at the School of Engineering and at the Academy of Fine Arts in Vienna. From 1945 to 1951 he taught at the Institute of Applied Arts in Linz, and in 1947 he received a prize for artistic achievement from the Austrian Government. Since 1952 he has lived and worked in Vienna as an independent artist. He participated in exhibits in Munich, Basel and Vienna. In 1953 he was awarded a prize for his contribution to the Unknown Political Prisoner International Competition. In 1954 he spent six months in Greece on a UNESCO grant. His work has been included in group shows at the "Art-Club," Vienna, as well as in Rome, Turin, Linz and Salzburg. He has also contributed to the Carnegie Institute exhibit, 1952; the 2nd São Paulo Bienal, 1953-54; the Venice Biennale, 1954, 1960. Examples of his work are owned by private collectors in Austria, Italy and the U.S., and by museums in Austria and Germany. He created a number of "architectural sculptures" for bars, cafes, and espresso houses in Vienna. Bibl.: "Magazine of Art," 1953; "Das Werk IX," 1953; "Die Plastik des XX. Jahrhunderts," by W. Hofmann (Fischer Verlag 1959).

JACOBSEN, ROBERT, sculptor, was born in Copenhagen, Denmark, 1912. His first sculptures in wood were done in 1930; he began carving directly in stone in 1940. His first work was abstract. During the war he was impressed by Viking folk sculpture of his country. His first exhibitions were held in Denmark, 1940-41. In 1944-45 he was a member of the Salon d'Automne jury in Copenhagen. Since 1946 he has lived in Paris, closely linked with the Danish painter Mortensen and the Galerie Denise René. He has worked in iron since 1949, creating spatial compositions in which he achieves a harmonious balance between the open spaces and the metal strands enclosing them. He also works in stone and marble. His work is distinguished by an almost classical sensitivity to harmony and balance of form. He has had exhibitions in Ireland, Holland, Finland, Norway, Sweden, Denmark, Austria and France. His Paris exhibitions include: Salon des Réalités Nouvelles, 1948; Sculpture since Rodin Exhibition, Maison de la Pensée Française, 1949; Salon de Mai, 1949; Salon de la Jeune Sculpture, 1950, and one-man shows at the Galerie Denise René, 1947-50; Galerie de France, 1957, at the Basel Kunsthalle, 1958. His works have also been shown at the Palais des Beaux-Arts, Brussels, 1954; the Brussels World's Fair, 1958; and the "Documenta," Kassel, Germany, 1959.

JANCO, MARCEL, sculptor, painter and architect, was born in 1895, in Bucharest, Rumania. He was one of the founders of the Dada Group in Zurich and a co-founder, in 1919, of the "artistes radicaux" group in Switzerland. In that same year, he was editor of a Rumanian avant-garde art periodical: "Contimporanul." He contributed to many Dada exhibitions and made posters, decorations and masks for performances at the *"Cabaret Voltaire"* in Zurich. He did woodcut illustrations for the first *"Collection Dada,"* and he also created architectural reliefs in plaster and sculptures in wire. Founder of the Israeli artists' village, *Ein Hod,* he now lives in Tel-Aviv.

KOHN, GABRIEL, sculptor, was born in Philadelphia in 1910. He studied at Cooper Union and the Beaux-Arts Institute of Design in New York and at the Atelier Zadkine in Paris. From 1930 to 1934, he worked as an assistant sculptor on various architectural commissions, doing preparatory sketches. He assisted C. P. Jennewein with the relief façade of the British Empire Bldg. in Rockefeller Center, N. Y. From 1934 until he enlisted in the U.S. Army in 1942, he worked independently. After 1946, he lived for seven years in Europe, experimenting primarily in terra cotta. After a year in Paris, he went to work at Beaulieu-sur-Mer, by arrangement with the Ecole des Arts Décoratifs at Nice. He continued his terra cotta experiments in Rome, 1948-49, then in Paris and later in the U.S. at Cranbrook Academy, in Michigan. His works have been shown at: Galleria d'Arte Moderna, Rome, 1949; Salon de la Jeune Sculpture, Paris, 1950; Whitney Museum; "New Talent" show, Museum of Modern Art, N. Y., 1957; São Paulo Bienal, 1959; one-man show, Leo Castelli Gallery, N. Y., 1959. He won First Prize in the American entries to the Unknown Political Prisoner International Competition, 1953. He is represented in the collections of: Museum of Modern Art, N. Y.; Albright Art Gallery, Buffalo; Cranbrook Museum, as well as in many private collections.

KRICKE, NORBERT, sculptor, was born in Düsseldorf, Germany, November 30, 1922. He was educated in Berlin where he graduated from high-school. In World War II he took part as German flyer. He visited the academy in Berlin when Professor R. Scheibe was director. In 1947 he returned to Düsseldorf to develop his sculptural work independently. In the next years he traveled in France, Spain, Holland, and Italy. *Exhibitions:* In Holland, Belgium, and Germany. First one-man show at Orphir Gallery, Munich, and again at the Parnass Gallery, Wuppertal, 1954. Contributed to German pavilion of International Exhibition at Liège (The Beauty of Steel) with a colored sculpture, 1954. He was given a one-man show at Kunstverein, Freiburg, Germany, in 1957. Exhibits of his works include, Galerie Iris Clert, Paris, 1957; "Documenta," Kassel, Germany, 1959; Staempfli Gallery, New York, 1959. He designed a "Water Forest" of Plexiglass columns, nine feet in height, to adjoin the Opera at Gelsenkirchen, Germany, 1957, and a moumental composition in wire for the theater of Münster, Germany, 1959. He is greatly interested in a new way of "forming water." He wants "to endow water, itself a silent and shapeless element, with a voice and a form of its own." He will collaborate with Walter Gropius on a fountain design for the University of Bagdad. His works are to be found in many private collections in Germany, England, Switzerland and America. He is represented in some of Germany's museums and in the Huntington Art Gallery, U.S.A. He lives in Düsseldorf, Germany.

LARDERA, BERTO, sculptor and graphic artists, was born in La Spezia, Italy, 1911. He studied the classics at the University of Florence, also attending art schools. He is self-taught in sculpture and creates space constructions, "employing the materials which my age offers me and using the techniques that these materials demand." In 1945 he designed a monument to the partisans of Pian d'Albero, Florence. He has exhibited at Milan; Paris (Galerie Denise René); the Venice Biennale, 1948, 1952, 1960; and the São Paulo Bienal, 1951; Palais des Beaux Arts, Brussels, 1954; Haus Lange, Krefeld, 1956; Knoedler Gallery, New York, 1957; Venice Biennale, 1960. He lives in Paris.

LASSAW, IBRAM, sculptor, was born in Alexandria, Egypt, May 4, 1913. He came in his early youth to New York, where he studied at the Clay Club, Beaux-Arts Institute of Design and at the Art School of Amédée Ozenfant. He has created several constructions in bronze and cast iron for the Temple of Beth El, Providence, Rhode Island. He was given a one-man show at the Kootz Gallery, New York, in 1952, 1954 and 1958. He participated in the Venice Biennale, 1954, and the "Documenta," Kassel, Germany, 1959. He lives in New York.

LAURENS, HENRI, sculptor, painter, illustrator and graphic artist, was born in Paris, France, February 18, 1885. Like Braque, he began to work for a decorator. Starting with realistic sculpture in clay, he came under the influence of Rodin's drawing and sculpture, notably works like the *Danaids, Eve* and *La Source.* Laurens' lyrical temperament attracted him to Paul Reverdy, who belonged to the group of poets around Apollinaire, Max Jacob and André Salmon. In 1911, as a result of meeting Braque, he joined the Cubists and became, with Lipchitz, their foremost sculptor. The Cubist movement began with the painters who laid great stress on the structural austerity of their paintings and collages. Translated into sculpture this meant an almost exclusive concentration on the interplay of geometrical forms. The subjects were the same as the painters', chiefly still-lifes. Some of Laurens' Cubist constructions still retain something of the relief, but some may be regarded as true sculpture in the round. They correspond very closely to collages in their stress on fundamental contrasts of materials and forms. Laurens' polychrome sculptures in sheet iron, 1914, now in the M. Raynal collection, Paris, were a daring anticipation of Constructivist ideas in their deliberate use of voids and curved planes. Since 1930 he has shown a strong tendency toward humanization. The human figure, particularly the female, whose lyrical quality is achieved entirely apart from any literary associations, emerges in stone and bronze, the product of proportions, the rhythm of light and shadow, and broad modelling of form. The severely geometrical discipline of the Cubists can still be discerned in the clear definition of his organic shapes. Like Braque and Picasso, Laurens strives to re-embody Greek mythology (sirens, nymphs, Luna, Aurora, the elements and seasons). At the Paris World Fair, 1937, he exhibited in front of the Pavillon de Sèvres a monumental group, *L'Eau.* But he also aims at the symbolic expression of the present time, as in his cowering female figure, *Adieu,* 1940, which expresses the tragic hour of France. In his graphic work Laurens is also intent on reviving ancient mythology; he obtains striking effects by elongating slender bodies in the style of the 16th century Mannerists, a tendency that can sometimes be seen in his sculptures as well. His illustrations for the *Idylls of Theocritus,* 1945, and of Lucian's *Golden Ass,* 1947, bear witness to a revival and new interpretation of classical themes. In 1953 Laurens was awarded the sculpture prize of São Paulo and in the following year he contributed a monumental sculpture to the University of Caracas, Venezuela. In 1954 he illustrated *Three stories* by W. Saroyan. He died of a heart attack in Paris, May 18, 1954. His last confession as an artist is included in a few lines, which he wrote down for his friends two years before his death: « . . . une nouvelle assimilation de l'architecture: ce sera le travail des jeunes sculpteurs. Nous autres, qui venant de l'époque cubiste, livrés tout entiers aux recherches, aux essais, à leur lente mise au point, ne pouvions nous occuper de leurs applications. Le temps n'était pas encore venue, et les architectes ne cherchaient qu'à obtenir un parfait dépouillement, revanche des surcharges à la mode au XIXième siècle. Ils n'étaient pas disposés à une collaboration trop décriée. Mais je pense que, dans l'avenir, à la faveur du travail accompli par leur aînés, sculpteurs et architectes établiront les conditions d'une nouvelle alliance.» (*XXième Siècle,* 1952.)

Exhibitions: First exhibition Salon des Indépendants, Paris, 1913; Léonce Rosenberg, Section d'Or, Salon des Indépendants, Paris, 1920; Museum of Modern Art (Cubism and Abstract Art), New York, 1936; Salon des Indépendants, Paris, 1937; Petit Palais, Paris, 1937; Brummer Gallery, New York, 1938; Oslo, Copenhagen, Stockholm (with Picasso, Braque, Matisse), 1938; Galerie Pierre Loeb, Paris, 1939; Galerie Jeanne Bucher, Paris, 1942; Galerie Louis Carré, Paris, 1945; Curt Valentin Gallery, New York, 1947; Biennale, Venice, 1948, 1950; Kunsthalle, Berne (Sculpteurs Contemporains de l'Ecole de Paris); Stedelijk Museum, Amsterdam, 1949; Musée d'Art Moderne, Paris, 1951; Bienal, São Paulo prize; Musée d'Art Moderne, Paris (Le Cubisme), 1953; Yverdon and Zurich (Sept Pionniers de la Sculpture Moderne), 1954; Curt Valentin Gallery, New York, 1952; Galerie Spiegel, Cologne, Galerie Stevenson, Hamburg, Galerie Springer, Berlin, Galerie Berggruen (Collages), Paris, Galerie Creuzevault, Paris, 1955; Haus am Waldsee, Berlin, Kunsthalle Bale, Hamburg, 1956; Fine Arts Associates, New York, Galerie Louise Leiris, Paris, 1958; Documenta, Kassel, Germany, 1959; Galerie Claude Bernard, Paris, 1960. Laurens died in Paris, May 8th, 1954.

LE CORBUSIER (JEANNERET), CHARLES EDOUARD, architect, painter, sculptor, writer, was born in La Chaux-de-Fonds, France, October 6, 1887, the son of Georges-Edouard Jeanneret and Marie-Charlotte-Amélie Jeanneret-Perret. From 1901-03 he gained technical experience as an engraver. In 1908 he went to Paris to work with Auguste Perret. In 1910 he took a trip to Germany, stopping at Munich, Berlin, and Hellerau. He settled down in Paris, 1917, and started to build on his own since 1922. He constructed his first building at age of seventeen, then built numerous private houses in France and in foreign countries, planned cities of Buenos-Aires, Stockholm, Antwerp, Algiers, Nemours (Africa), Bogota, Chandigarh (India). Since 1921 he has been invited by governments and professional centres to lecture on architecture and town planning (Paris, Brussels, Madrid, Barcelona, Amsterdam, Rotterdam, Stockholm, Moscow, Rio de Janeiro etc.). In 1925 he constructed the *Pavillon de l'Esprit Nouveau,* International Exhibition of Decorative Arts, and in 1929-32 the *Camp of Salvation Army* and the *Swiss pavilion,* university city, in Paris. He was invited by the Russian Government to make report for urbanization of the city of Moscow, 1931, and planned the construction of the *Soviet Palace,* 1932. Then followed the plan for the university city of Ministry of Education and Public Health in Rio de Janeiro, 1937, the *Pavillon Des Temps Nouveaux* for the International Exhibition in Paris, 1937, and the construction of the *Unité d'Habitation* of Marseilles, 1948-52. He was chief of the architectural mission to U.S.A., 1945. He is consultant for town and country planning to numerous governments in Europe, Africa, America and Asia. Le Corbusier has always been directed towards the pure poetical side of creative work which he realized in his paintings and sculptures. He lives in Paris. *Publications: Après le Cubisme,* 1918; Founder and director of *L'Esprit Nouveau* (review), 1919-25; *Vers une Architecture,* 1923; *Urbanisme,* 1925; *La Peinture Moderne,* 1925; *Une Maison, un Palais,* 1928; *La Ville Radieuse,* 1933; *Quand les Cathédrales étaient blanches,* 1937; *Destin de Paris,* 1941; *Sur les quatre routes,* 1941; *La Maison des Hommes,* 1942; *Entretien avec les Etudiants des Ecoles d'Architecture,* 1943; *La Charte d'Athènes,* 1943; *Les 3 Etablissements Ilumains,* 1945; *Manière de Penser l'Urbanisme,* 1945; *Propos d'Urbanisme,* 1946; *United Nations Headquarters,* 1947; *L'Espace indicible,*

1947; *Le Modulor, Poesie sur Alger,* 1950; *Une Petite Maison,* 1954; *Oeuvre Complète,* 1910-1957, 6 Vols.; One Vol. Ed. (Condensed) 1960, Editions H. Girsberger, Zurich. *Exhibitions:* Galerie Gabriel Thomas, Paris, 1918; Galerie Drouet, Paris, 1921; Salon des Indépendants, Paris, 1922-23; Galerie Léonce Rosenberg (Effort Moderne), Paris, 1923; first great exhibition of his paintings: Kunsthaus, Zurich, 1938 (paintings from 1921-1937); Galerie Louis Carré, Paris, 1939; Walker Art Center, Minneapolis, 1946; Stedelijk Museum, Amsterdam, 1947; first exhibition of his sculpture: Musée d'Art Moderne, Paris, 1953, and Kunsthalle, Berne, 1954, (including paintings and carpets).

LEHMBRUCK, WILHELM, sculptor, painter, graphic artist and poet, was born in Duisburg-Meiderich, Germany, January 4, 1881, the son of a miner. He attended the Kunstgewerbeschule of Düsseldorf, 1895-99, and the art academy there, 1901-07. In 1905 he traveled to Italy on the proceeds of first prizes in sculpture. A second Italian tour followed in 1912. In 1910 he settled in Paris where his own style developed rapidly, culminating in his *Kneeling Woman,* 1911. This statue was first shown publicly the following year at the Cologne Sonderbund Exhibition, a survey of the decisive cultural trends of the time. Meier-Graefe was the first to acclaim Lehmbruck as the great German sculptor. He lived then in the Avenue du Maine. After an important exhibition in Paris, 1914, he returned to Berlin when war broke out. In Paris he had tried uncompromisingly to realize his artistic vision despite the most harrowing poverty. His artistic development had been greatly stimulated in the company of the international group of artists living and exhibiting in Paris: Maillol, Archipenko, Modigliani and others. When his work was attacked by reactionary critics, Meier-Graefe, Paul Westheim, Hans Bethge and Theodor Däubler rallied behind him. His *Dying Warrior,* later renamed *The Fallen,* was singled out for the most violent attacks when it was exhibited at the Berlin Secession, 1916. In 1917-18 he was in Zurich, working in a studio on the Zurichberg. In 1919 he returned to Berlin, where on March 25 he committed suicide. Lehmbruck left etchings on zinc plates that rank with his sculptures. These include illustrations to the Bible and Shakespeare. Important exhibitions of Lehmbruck's work include that at the Galerie Levesque, Paris, 1914 (catalog introduction by André Salmon); Kunsthaus, Zurich, 1917; Paul Cassirer Gallery, Berlin, 1920; Goltz Gallery, Munich, 1921; Städtisches Museum, Duisburg, 1925; Museum of Modern Art, New York, 1930; Kunsthalle, Berne, 1945; "Deutsche Kunst, Meisterwerke des 20. Jahrhunderts," Kunstmuseum, Lucerne, 1953; "German Art of the Twentieth Century," Museum of Modern Art, New York, 1957; Brussels World's Fair, 1958.

LIPCHITZ, JACQUES, painter and sculptor, was born in Druskieniki, Lithuania, August 22, 1891. Visited the commercial school at Bialystok 1902-06 and the high school at Vilna till 1909. Living since 1909 in Paris, he studied at the Ecole des Beaux Arts and the Académie Julian. In 1913 he met Picasso and collaborated in the Cubist movement. In 1913-14 he was strongly interested in Achipenko's sculptures. Since 1916 close friendship with Juan Gris. His encounter with Negro sculpture had also a certain influence on his work in the following years. Since these early times he developed also a special interest and faculty in collecting exotic and early art. Among his friends were Matisse, Modigliani, Picasso, and Max Jacob. In 1922 Lipchitz was a member of the Esprit Nouveau Group, with its tendencies to unite art with architecture (Le Corbusier, Ozenfant). In the years 1925-27 he began to alter the strictly structural spirit of his earlier work,

Alberto Giacometti Emile Gilioli Hansjorg Gisiger Julio Gonzalez

an (Jose Gonzalez) Gris Etienne Hajdu David Hare Karl Hartung

Raoul Hausmann Barbara Hepworth Rudolf Hoflehner Robert Jacobsen

337

Marcel Janco

Norbert Kricke

Gabriel Kohn

Berto Lardera

Ibram Lassaw

Henri Laurens

Le Corbusier

Wilhelm Lehmbruck

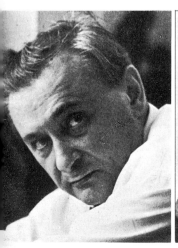

Jacques Lipchitz

Richard Lippold

Maurice Lipsi

Seymour Lipton

338

Aristide Maillol	Kasimir Malevich	Marino Marini	Etienne Martin

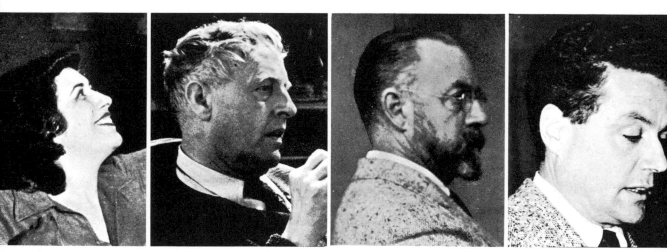

Maria Martins	Ewald Matare	Henri Matisse	Luciano Minguzzi

(Mirko Basaldella) Mirko	Joan Miro	Amedeo Modigliani	Laszlo Moholy-Nagy

Henry Moore

Erich Muller

Juana Muller

Robert Muller

Louise Nevelson

Costantino Nivola

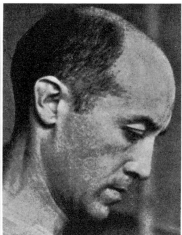

Isamu Noguchi

Hermann Obrist

Eduardo Paolozzi

Alicia Penalba

Antoine Pevsner

Helen Phillips

relieving it with linear movements, in which he disintegrated volume by a skilful interweaving of mass and void. He called these bronze sculptures *transparents*. In his later development he abandoned purely abstract construction, but retained the powerful tension between intricate forms and movements, using these methods to suggest dramatic scenes from the Bible or mythology, now more in a baroque manner of modelling expressive lights and shadows. In 1927 his sculpture *Joie de Vivre* was acquired by Vicomte Charles de Noailles for Hyères, 1928, the *Femme à la Guitare* by Madame Hélène de Mandrot for her garden in Le Pradet, Toulon. One of his most famous statues *Chant des Voyelles* was executed in 1931 also for her garden (today Kunsthaus, Zurich). In 1939-40 he temporarily lived in Toulouse. In 1941 he left Paris for New York, where he has carried out important commissions in connection with architecture: for the facade of the Ministry of Education (architects Le Corbusier and Oscar Niemeyer), Rio de Janeiro, a sculpture of *Prometheus and the Eagle,* 1936-44; for the Edgar Kaufmann House by Frank Lloyd Wright in Bear Run, Pa., *Mother and Child,* 1945. Short stay in Paris, 1946, connected with his one-man show at the Galerie Maeght. Chosen for the collaboration at the church of Assy (Savoye), 1950, he began working at the group *Birth of Muses* acquired by Mrs. Th. Rockefeller, New York. He settled down in his own house at Hastings-on-the-Hudson, N. Y., 1953. His exhibitions include: representation at the Salon des Indépendants from 1919 on; first one-man show at the Galerie Léonce Rosenberg, Paris, 1920 (Effort Moderne); Salon des Tuileries, Paris, from 1920 on; Galerie La Renaissance, Paris, 1930 (retrospective); Art Vivant, Brussels, 1931; Brummer Gallery, New York, 1935 (first one-man show in U. S. A.), 1942; Museum of Modern Art, New York, 1936 (Cubism and Abstract Art); Petit Palais, Paris, 1937; Curt Valentin Gallery, New York, since 1942; Galerie Maeght, Paris, 1946; Biennale, Venice, 1952, 1954; Museum of Modern Art, New York, 1954 (one-man show); one-man show at Fine Arts Associates, New York, 1957 and 1959; at Amsterdam and Zurich, 1958; Brussels World's Fair, 1958; *"Documenta,"* Kassel, Germany, and Fine Arts Associates, New York, 1959.

LIPPOLD, RICHARD, constructivist and industrial designer, was born in Milwaukee, Wisconsin, U.S.A., 1915. In 1933-34 he attended the Art Institute of Chicago and the University of Chicago. After a career as an industrial designer, 1937-41, he gave up that profession and became a self-taught sculptor, working in fine wire of every type. The spatial nature of his constructions is achieved through tense elaboration of the finest elements. He has taught at the Layton School of Art, Milwaukee, 1940-41; the University of Michigan, 1941-44; Goddard College, Plainfield, Vermont, 1945-47; and since 1947 at Trenton Junior College, where he heads the Art Department. His first one-man show at the Willard Gallery, New York, included his *Variation No. 7: Full Moon,* now owned by the Museum of Modern Art, New York. His work was included in the "15 Americans" show at the Museum of Modern Art, New York, 1952, and in "Fifty Years of Art in the U. S.," at the Musée d'Art Moderne, Paris, 1955. From 1953 to 1956, he worked on a sculpture, *The Sun,* commissioned by the Metropolitan Museum, New York, and now on exhibit there.

LIPSI, MAURICE, sculptor, was born in Lodz, Poland in 1898. He went to the Ecole des Beaux-Arts in 1916, where he studied with Coutan, Mercié and Injalbert. The Place de la Concorde with its Obelisk and the Chartres Cathedral were his first major spatial impressions. He had his first one-man show of ivory sculpture at the Galerie A. A. Hébrard (Rue Royale),

Paris, in 1922. He was given his second show by the Galerie de l'Art Contemporain (Boulevard Raspail), in 1927. In 1930 he married Hildegard Weber, a Swiss painter. He participated in the International Sculpture Exhibition in Zurich, 1931. A third one-man show was given him by the Galerie Druet, Paris, 1935. He became a French citizen and joined the French Army in 1940. From 1942 to 1943 he was forced to hide in Southern France and in Savoy. He finally made his way to Switzerland, where he created his series of Masks and Leaves (Geneva). It was during this period that he turned to abstract sculpture. Before returning to France, he exhibited at Kunsthalle, Berne, 1945. He had a one-man show at the Galerie Pierre Maurs (Avenue Matignon), Paris, in the same year that he created a large stone group for the Parc Montsouris. An impressive list of exhibitions includes: Maison de la Pensée Française, 1949; Galerie Palette, Zurich, 1951; "Three Artists from Paris" at Recklinghausen, Germany, 1952; Galerie Art Vivant, 1953; "Groupe Espace," Biot, 1954; Galerie Benno 1954; Biennial Park, Middelheim, Antwerp, 1955; Citadella, Ascona, 1956; French Plastic Art Exhibition, Berlin; Galerie de Coninck, Paris, 1957; the Galeries Arnaud and Claude Bernard, Paris, 1958; Museum of Nantes; Galerie Denise René, 1959. His works are represented in the Petit Palais, Paris; Musée National d'Art Moderne, Paris, and the Museum of Jerusalem. He lives in Chevilly-Larne, near Paris.

LIPTON, SEYMOUR, sculptor, was born November 6, 1903, in New York City. A graduate of Columbia University, he is self-taught as an artist. The ACA Gallery, N. Y., gave him his first one-man show in 1938. Since then he has had shows at the Galerie St. Etienne and the Betty Parsons Gallery, both in New York. He was included in the "12 Americans" show at the Museum of Modern Art, 1956, and in the Venice Biennale of 1958. His works have been exhibited in all the major museums both in the U. S. and abroad, including: Museum of Modern Art and Whitney Museum, N. Y.; Art Institute of Chicago; San Francisco Museum; Baltimore Museum of Fine Art; Brooklyn Museum; Albright Museum, Buffalo; Jewish Museum, New York; Musée d'Art Moderne, Paris; Tate Gallery, London; as well as in museums in Barcelona, Belgrade, the Venice Biennale, Frankfurt, and in Japan and Australia. He is represented in the permanent collections of many museums, as well as in important private collections. In 1957, he was awarded both the First Prize at the Chicago Institute Annual and the Top Acquisition Prize at the São Paulo Bienal. Examples of his work were shown at the Brussels World's Fair, 1958. "Sculpture by Lipton," a 15-minute sound film, demonstrates his technique and recent work.

MAILLOL, ARISTIDE, sculptor, painter, illustrator and designer, was born in Banyuls-sur-Mer, France, 1861. He started as a painter and carpet designer and studied first at the Ecole des Beaux Arts in Paris with Alexander Cabanel (1882-86). Impressed by Gauguin's paintings and the "Nabis," he abandoned impressionism for a more flat formation of colored planes. To realize this tapestry method his designs seemed most appropriate. He built majolica vases in the tradition of his country in these early years. His friendship with Maurice Denis was also important for his artistic development. Only at 40 he became a sculptor. In 1906 he lived in Greece, studied Greek art and was especially interested in the early sculpture of the 6th and 5th century. Maillol spent most of his life in Banyuls cultivating wine and olives in the traditional way of his ancestors. Some months each year he spent at Marly-Le-Roy, near Paris. He was killed in an accident near Banyuls, September 24, 1944. His main works are: in the Museum of Modern Art, New York; in the Tate Gallery, London; in the

Wallraff-Richartz-Museum, Cologne; in the Art Galleries of Düsseldorf; in the Musée d'Art Moderne, Paris; in the Kunsthaus, Zurich; in the Kunstmuseum, Winterthur, Basel, Berne; in the collections of Oscar Reinhardt and Hahnloser, Winterthur; in the Rijksmuseum, Kroeller-Mueller, Otterlo (Netherlands); and in the Stedelijk Museum, Amsterdam. His first one-man show was at the Galerie Vollard, 1905, and from 1905 onwards mostly at the Galerie Druet, Paris.

MALEVICH, KASIMIR, painter, sculptor, art critic, theorist and teacher, was born at Kiev, Russia, February 11, 1878. In 1908 he was influenced by Post-Impressionist and Fauve paintings seen in Moscow private collections. By 1910 his work showed marked Cubist tendencies. He founded the Suprematist movement in Moscow, 1913. In 1918 he exhibited his painting *White on White*. In 1919 he became a teacher at the Moscow Art Academy. In 1926 he met Kandinsky at the Bauhaus, Dessau. A year later, his treatise, *The Non-Objective World*, was published in the Bauhaus Books series. In 1935 he died in complete retirement in Leningrad. His exhibitions include: individual works shown in Moscow, 1913-19; Constructivist Exhibition, Berlin, 1922; Société Anonyme Exhibition, New York, 1924; Philadelphia, 1926; Museum of Modern Art, New York, 1936 (Cubism and Abstract Art); Yale University Art Gallery, 1948.

MARINI, MARINO, sculptor, was born in Pistoia, Italy, February 27, 1901. He studied at the Florence Academy with Trentacoste, and began as a painter. In 1928 he studied sculpture in Paris and traveled to Greece and other European countries. In 1929 he worked in Milan. From 1930-40 he concentrated on sculptured and painted portraits of acrobats and performers. From 1942-46 he lived in the Ticino, Switzerland. Since 1946 he has lived in Milan and Forte dei Marmi. He has exhibited in Milan, Basel, Zurich, Berne and at the Venice Biennale of 1950, 1952 and 1954. He was represented at the Brussels World's Fair, 1958, and at the "Documenta," Kassel, Germany, 1959.

MARTIN, ETIENNE, sculptor, was born in 1913, in Loriol, France. He entered the Ecole des Beaux-Arts, Lyon, in 1929, getting his diploma in 1933. Awarded a scholarship toward further studies in Paris, he worked from 1934 to 1937 at the Académie Ranson, under Malfray and Maillol. He won the Prix de Paris, 1933; Prix Paris-Lyon, 1938; Prix Blumenthal, 1948; Prix Jeune Sculpture, 1949; Honorable Mention, the Unknown Political Prisoner International Competition, 1952; Award, Milan Triennale, 1954. In 1952 the Salon de la Jeune Sculpture made him a member of their committee. His works have been shown at: Galerie René Drouin, 1945; Luxembourg Museum, 1946; Maison de la Pensée Française, 1950; Galerie Mai, 1948, 1950; Galerie Jeanne Bucher, 1948, 1949, 1950, 1952; Galerie Rive Droite, 1955-1957; exhibits in Angers and Dijon; Park Middelheim, Antwerp, 1953; Arnheim Biennial, 1954; Festival of Marseilles (Cité Radieuse), 1956; Galerie Claude Bernard 1957; Musée de Tours, 1957; Galerie Breteau, 1954, 1958; Musée Rodin, 1956, 1957. His work has also been exhibited regularly at the Salon de la Jeune Sculpture and the Salon de Mai, as well as in Japan, 1950-1951; the Tate Gallery, London, 1953; and subsequently in Germany, Norway, Sweden, Finland, Italy and Switzerland (1958). He participated in exhibitions at the Biennale, Venice, 1956; the Guggenheim Museum, New York, 1959; the Carnegie Institute, Pittsburgh, 1959. The French government has commissioned several works, and he is represented in numerous private collections. He has also executed a variety of works for churches in France: reliefs for Baccarat (1955); the bap-

tismal font for the church at Audaincourt (1956); the steeple for the church at Vaize (1957; and the ceiling for the Vatican Pavilion, Brussels, 1958.

MARTINS, MARIA, Brazilian sculptor, born in 1900, studied painting and music. Her first sculpture, in Ecuador, 1926, was inspired by the Baroque style surviving in native art. From 1936-39, in Japan, she worked mainly in terracotta. In Brussels, 1939, she was inspired by the sculptor Oskar Jespers. In the same year she settled in Washington, D. C., where she met the art dealer Brummer who encouraged her work. Her first exhibition was held in Washington, 1940. In 1943 her book, *Amazonia by Maria* published by Valentine Gallery appeared. In 1946, at the Museum of Modern Art, New York, she exhibited sculptures inspired by legends of the Amazon region. In 1949 she exhibited at the Galerie René Drouin, Paris. A poetical appreciation of her sculpture by André Breton appeared in 1949. She executed sculptural work for the French Embassy in Rio de Janeiro, 1957, and a garden sculpture for the president's palace in Brasilia, 1958-1959.

MATARE, EWALD, sculptor, painter and graphic artist, was born in Aachen, Germany, February 25, 1887. He studied painting and graphic art at the Berlin Academy under Kampf and Corinth, from 1907-14, later (1918) taking up sculpture in which he is self-taught. In 1911-12 he was in contact with the Blaue Reiter Group of Munich, and traveled in France, Italy and Finland. In 1932 he was appointed professor at the Düsseldorf Academy along with Klee. In the following year both were dismissed. Mataré was reinstated at the Academy in 1945. In 1947 he designed new doors for the Cologne Cathedral. His exhibitions include: November Group, Berlin, 1925; Berlin, 1928, 1930 (one-man show); Galerie Möller, Cologne, 1931; Société Anonyme, Brooklyn, N. Y., 1931. Exhibition of his works, Galerie Möller, Cologne, 1947. (see H. T. Fleming, *E. Mataré,* Prestel Verlag, 1955).

MATISSE, HENRI, painter, sculptor, graphic artist, illustrator and writer, was born at Le Cateau, Dpt. Nord, France, December 31, 1869. In Paris, 1892 he attended the Académie Julian, working with Bouguereau and Ferrier; in 1893 he was at the Ecole des Beaux Arts, under the intelligent guidance of Gustave Moreau. Visiting Provence in that year, he came under the influence of Cézanne. In 1900 he and his friend Marquet did decorative work for the Paris Exposition. His first figure sculpture, *Slave,* 1900-03, is reminiscent of Rodin's *Striding Torso.* In 1901 he modelled his first female figure, *La Madeleine,* already using the *linea serpentinata.* Turned down as a pupil by Rodin, he worked with Bourdelle at La Grande Chaumière. In 1904, after a short preoccupation with pointillism in painting, he returned to pure, flat colors. In 1905 he showed his painting, *Luxe, Calme et Volupté* in a joint exhibition with Derain, Vlaminck, and Rouault at the Salon d'Automne, Paris—the beginning of Fauvism. In 1906 he organized his own school in the Rue de Sèvres, later moving to the Boulevard des Invalides. Gertrude and Leo Stein introduced him to Picasso. Matisse bought Negro sculpture in 1906 which he showed to Picasso and other young artists. In 1908 he published *Notes d'un Peintre (A Painter's Notebook)* in which he stressed the expressive power of line and color. In 1908-09 he completed his sculpture, *La Serpentine;* the entire freedom of its proportions make it one of his most impressive works. In 1910-11 his five studies of heads for *Jeannette* with their broad treatment of volume prepared the way for the later heads of Picasso, and are similar to those of Duchamp-Villon. From 1911-13 he made two visits to Morocco. In those years contact with the Cubists reawakened his interest in sculpture. In 1915, his *Head of Marguerite* again stressed the theme of movement. In a certain sense he anticipates the heads done much later by Alberto Giacometti. Matisse settled in Nice in 1917. In 1920 he designed the settings for the ballet, *Le Chant du Rossignol*. In 1930 he traveled in Europe, Russia, Oceania (spending three months in Tahiti) and in the U.S.A., where he painted murals for Dr. Albert C. Barnes in Philadelphia. The influence of these travels could be traced in his sculpture which became more elemental in conception, freer in the handling of volumes, more polished and compact in form. Under the spell of Oceania he created *Tiara* and *Venus in the Shell*. In 1936 he had large, retrospective exhibitions in Paris, New York and Stockholm. In 1939 he settled in Vence. At that time he made numerous compositions of colored, cut paper. In 1943-44 he illustrated works by Ronsard, Montherlant and Baudelaire. In 1949 he began the decoration of the Dominican Chapel at Vence. Matisse died in Nice, November 3, 1954. His exhibitions include: four paintings at the Salon de la Société Nationale, Paris, 1896; Salon des Indépendants, Paris, 1901, 1907, 1909; Galerie Berthe Weill, Paris, 1902; Salon d'Automne, Paris, 1903, 1906, 1909; his first retrospective exhibition, Galerie Bernheim Jeune, Paris, 1910; representation at the Carnegie International Exhibition, Pittsburgh, 1929; Galerie Thannhauser, Berlin, 1930; Museum of Modern Art, New York, 1931 and 1951; Petit Palais, Paris, 1934; Salon d'Automne (Les Fauves), Paris, 1944; Victoria and Albert Museum, London, 1945; Palais des Papes, Avignon, 1947; Philadelphia Art Museum, 1948; Kunsthalle, Berne, 1950; Biennale, Venice, 1950; Curt Valentin Gallery (sculpture), New York, 1953; Tate Gallery, London; Kunstmuseum, Freiburg/Breisgau (Germany), 1953; Fine Arts Associates and Pierre Matisse Gallery, New York, Galerie Berggruen, Paris, 1958; Kunsthaus Zurich, Kunsthalle Berne (Collages and sculpture), 1959.

MEDUNIEZKY, KASIMIR, constructivist, was born in Russia, 1899. He studied at Vchutema, the Moscow art school, and was a leader of Obmochu, a group of young artists. In 1920 he was represented at the first Constructivist exhibition in Moscow, and in 1922 at the Constructivist exhibition in Berlin. In 1924 the Société Anonyme introduced his work to the U.S.A. He later worked in Russia as a designer for industry and the theatre.

MINGUZZI, LUCIANO, sculptor, was born in Bologna, Italy, May 24, 1911. He attended the Art Academies at Bologna and Milan. From 1940-45 he worked on reliefs which he entered for the Milan Cathedral Doors Competition. He lives in Milan. He was represented at the Venice Biennale, 1948, 1950, 1952, 1954, and the São Paulo Bienal, 1951; Varese, 1953. In 1953 he won a third prize in the Unknown Political Prisoner Competition. He was a contributor to the "New Decade" show, at the Museum of Modern Art, New York, 1955, to the "Documenta," Kassel, Germany, 1959, and to the Venice Biennale, 1960.

MIRKO (MIRKO BASALDELLA) sculptor and painter, was born at Udine, Italy, September 28, 1910. He studied in Venice, Florence and Monza. Since 1934 he has lived in Rome. His exhibitions include one-man shows in Rome, 1935, at the Galleria della Cometa, Turin, 1936, at New York, 1937, and in 1940 at the Galleria Nazionale d'Arte Moderna and the Galleria Roma at Rome. In 1938 he was represented in numerous Italian exhibitions shown in Paris, Brussels, Vienna, Budapest, London, San Francisco, and New York. His paintings were first shown at the Galleria dell'Obelisco, Rome, 1947. Both his paintings and sculptures were exhibited at the Knoedler Gallery, New York, 1947 and 1948, at the Viviano

Gallery, New York, 1950, at the Galleria del Milione, Milan, and at the Galleria San Marco, Rome, 1951. His work includes: bronze balustrades in the Mausoleo delle Fosse Ardeatine, Rome, 1950; reliefs, murals, mosaics and balustrades for the Food and Agriculture Organization Building, Rome, 1951. In 1953 he was awarded a second prize in the international competition for the Monument to the Unknown Political Prisoner. He participated in the Brussels World's Fair 1958, and in the "Documenta," Kassel, Germany, 1959, and in the Venice Biennale, 1960. For the last three years he has been professor at the Graduate School of Design, at Harvard University.

MIRO, JOAN, painter, graphic artist and sculptor, was born in Montroig, near Tarragona, Spain, April 20, 1893. In 1907 he entered the Barcelona Art Academy, and from 1910-15 attended the Gali Academy in the same city. In 1915 he produced his first original work. In Barcelona, 1917, he met the art dealer, Dalmau, a supporter of modern Catalan art, in whose gallery in 1918 Miro showed 64 paintings and drawings, his output of the previous four years. He first visited Paris in 1919, and settled there the following year, making the acquaintance of the Paris Dada group. In 1921 his exhibit at the Galerie Licorne was introduced by Maurice Raynal. In 1922 he finished his large painting, *La Ferme (The Farmhouse)*. In 1925 he exhibited with the Surrealists at the Galerie Pierre, Paris, and with Max Ernst designed costumes for the Diaghilev ballet, *Romeo and Juliet*. His work was included in the first exhibition of the Galerie Surréaliste, Paris, 1926. In 1928 he was mentioned in André Breton's *Le Surréalisme et la Peinture* as one of the leaders of the movement. In the same year he had his first American exhibition at the Valentine Gallery, New York. In 1930 he exhibited at the Galerie Pierre and was included in the collage exhibition at the Galerie Goemans, Paris, referred to by Louis Aragon in *La peinture au Defi*, 1930. At this time he made Surréalist sculptures called "objects" which are a combination of ready-mades and fantastic forms. In 1932 he designed costumes for the Monte Carlo ballet, *Jeux d'Enfants*. In 1937 he painted a mural for the Spanish Pavilion at the Paris Exposition, and in 1938 murals for the summer house of the American architect, Paul Nelson, at Varengeville, Normandy, where he was a frequent guest. In 1940-41 he returned to Barcelona, then to Palma di Majorca. In 1942 he decorated ceramics for Artigas. In 1946 he resumed sculpture which he had first attempted in 1943. In contrast to his earlier combined objects he now created fundamental forms. In 1947 he made his first visit to the U.S.A. where he was commissioned to paint a mural for the Terrace-Plaza Hotel in Cincinnati. In 1948 he returned to Europe. He lives in Montroig, Spain, making frequent visits to Paris. In 1948, 1950, 1953 he exhibited paintings, sculptures and ceramics at the Galerie Maeght, Paris. His mural for Walter Gropius' Graduate Center at Harvard University, Cambridge, was completed in 1950. In 1952 he completed a series of constructions recalling primitive fetishes, for his estate at Montroig. He received the International Prize for Graphic Art at the Venice Biennale of 1954. List of exhibitions to 1959 in the Mirko monograph by James Thrall Soby, p. 151.

MODIGLIANI, AMEDEO, painter and sculptor, was born at Livorno, Italy, July 12, 1884, the son of a banker. In 1898 he abandoned classical studies for painting. From 1901-05 he was convalescing in Naples after several illnesses. He attended variously the art schools at Naples, Rome and Florence, and the Venice Academy of Art. In 1906 he left for Paris where he set up his studio in Montmartre, 1907-08. In 1908 he was represented for the first time at the Indépendents. In 1909 he met Brancusi, beginning a life-long friendship. Brancusi initiated and encouraged Modigliani's interest in sculpture. His painting, *The Cellist,* one of the first to be characteristic of his artistic intentions was shown to the public at large at the Salon des Indépendents, 1910. From 1910-14 he concentrated almost exclusively on sculpture, shaping heads and caryatids for which many preliminary sketches still exist. He worked under the influence of Brancusi and was impressed, to a slighter degree, by the strange work of the Polish sculptor, Ellie Nadelmann, who was exhibiting in Paris, 1913-14. In 1914-15 he met the Polish poet Leopold Zborowski who at once realized Modigliani's extraordinary genius, bought some of his paintings and recommended him to the art dealer, Paul Guillaume. In 1917 Modigliani married Jeanne Hébuterne who committed suicide after his death. His first one-man show was held at the Galerie Berthe Weill, Paris, and was unfavorably received by the public. This was his most intense period of artistic creation. In 1918-19 he was in Nice, recuperating from a serious illness. He exhibited at the Salon l'Automne, Paris, and at the Hill Gallery, London, 1919. On January 25, 1920, Modigliani died of tuberculosis in dire poverty at the Charité, Paris. Shortly after his death the full importance of his art became universally known.

MOHOLY-NAGY, LASZLO, painter, sculptor, photographer, filmwriter and teacher, was born at Bacsbarsod, Hungary, July 20, 1895, the son of a farmer. During World War I he was wounded and began to sketch while convalescing in a field hospital. Portraits in watercolor and oil soon followed. After his discharge from the army he showed increasing interest in the modern movement, Malevich, Lissitzky, and the Russian School. In 1919, the year he obtained his law degree, he founded the MA Group and published an art quarterly. In Berlin, 1920, he progressed from representational Cubist painting to the pure abstraction of his collages and photograms. In 1921 he joined the Constructivists. His work was first shown at the Sturm Gallery of Herwarth Walden, Berlin, in 1922. In 1922 he became a member of the Stijl Group. In the following year Gropius appointed him head of the metal workshop at the Bauhaus, where he worked with Schlemmer and other members on murals, stage and ballet designs, experiments in light and color and typography. The focus of his interest was the conquest of space, an aim to which he devoted all his creative energy. From 1925-28 he and Gropius edited the Bauhaus Books which included Moholy's *Malerei, Photographie, Film,* 1925, and his *Von Material zu Architektur,* 1928 (published in English as *The New Vision,* 1938, 1946). He and Gropius resigned from the Bauhaus in 1928. Moholy went to Berlin working as a stage designer for Piscator's Theatre and for the State Opera. He designed settings and costumes for *Tales of Hoffmann, Madame Butterfly,* and *The Merchant of Berlin.* In 1930 he constructed his *Lichtrequisit,* a light-display machine which is also a rotating sculpture providing innumerable variations and degrees of light. From 1932-36 he was a member of the Paris Abstraction-Création Group, visiting Paris frequently, traveling in France, Finland, Norway, Italy, and Greece, an experimenting with color film in Holland. From 1935-37 he was in London. In 1938 he settled in Chicago where he was appointed director of the New Bauhaus, founded by the Association of Arts and Industries. After a year financial difficulties closed the New Bauhaus, but it was reopened 1939 by Moholy and his staff as the School of Design. Moholy died of leukemia, November 24, 1946, in Chicago. His last book, *Vision in Motion,* appeared in 1947. His exhibitions include: Berlin, 1926; Société Anonyme, Brooklyn, 1926; Museum of Modern Art, New York (Cubism and Abstract Art), 1936; Museum of Non-Objective Painting, New York (Memorial Exhibition),

1947; Chicago Art Institute, 1947; Institute of Design, Chicago, 1947; Yale University Art Gallery, New Haven, 1947; Kunsthaus, Zurich, 1953; Galerie Lutz & Meyer, Stuttgart, 1953.

MOORE, HENRY, sculptor, painter, draftsman and writer, was born at Castleford, Yorkshire, England, 1898, like Lehmbruck, the son of a miner. His first training was for the teaching profession. In 1917 he was gassed at the Battle of Cambrai. In 1919 he entered the Leeds School of Art, and in 1921 won a scholarship at the Royal College of Art, London, for study in Paris, Florence, Venice and Ravenna. The aim behind his early sculptural work is the release of the expressive force inherent in natural stone. Later he created human figures and simple forms with a pulsating rhythm obtained through an intense interplay of mass and void. During World War II Moore displayed his extraordinary talent as a draftsman by translating contemporary events into artistic visions. Here again, his attention was focused on the human figure and the space surrounding it as in his drawings of the underground air-raid shelters. Moore lives at Hadham, north of London. His exhibitions include: Warren Gallery, 1928; Leicester Galleries, London, 1931, 1935, 1936, 1940; Temple Newsham, Leeds, 1941 (retrospective); Museum of Modern Art, New York, 1946; Venice Biennale, 1948, 1952, 1954; Paris, 1949; Berne, 1950. The following institutions own examples of his work: Victoria and Albert Museum, London; Whiteworth Institute, Manchester; Museum für Kunst und Gewerbe, Hamburg; City Art Gallery, Wakefield; Tate Gallery, London; City Art Gallery, Leeds; Albright Art Gallery, Buffalo; Museum of Modern Art, New York. A partial list of his works includes: Relief, on Time-Life Building, London, 1953; Brick relief for the Bouw Centrum, Rotterdam, 1955; Several versions of *Glenkiln Cross,* 1955-56; *Reclining Figure,* for UNESCO Building, Paris, 1957. His works were exhibited at the Brussels World's Fair, 1958, and at the "Documenta," Kassel, Germany, 1959, where the following sculptures were shown: *Glenkiln Cross,* 1956; *Fallen Warrior,* 1957; *Draped Reclining Woman,* 1957, as well as other works. List of his exhibitions since 1928 in W. Grohmann's monograph, Rembrandt Verlag, Berlin, 1960.

MULLER, ERICH, sculptor and graphic artist, was born at Berne, Switzerland, 1927. There he went to school only up to the age of sixteen, as his one wish was to become a sculptor. For one year he worked as taxidermist at the Museum of Natural History, Berne. After several unsuccessful attempts to undergo a regular apprenticeship as a sculptor, he started on his own at Berne in 1947. He exhibited here in the following years and received an art prize of the town of Berne in 1949 and a state scholarship in 1951. Since 1951 he visited Paris, Brittany and Southern France. His latest sculptural works correspond in a certain degree to the painting of Jean Dubuffet (Art Brut). *Exhibitions:* Winterthur (Sculpture and graphic works), Solothurn, Thun, Galerie Chichio Haller, Zurich, Galerie Reveil, St. Moritz, 1952; Lucerne and Biel, 1953.

MULLER, JUANA, sculptor, was born in Santiago, Chile, 1911. In France after 1917, she became a citizen and lived in Paris. She worked mostly in wood, embodying human subjects in simple, basic forms. There is a noticeable influence of Brancusi in her work. « J'ai toujours cherché la même chose dans toutes mes sculptures, une résonance d'une état intérieur très différent de l'ordinaire dans lequel le conflit est dépassé et qui nous laisse le gout d'avoir touché à quelque chose qui nous dépasse infiniment. Elle devait apparaitre dans mes sculptures sous des jours différents seule la forme extérieure était changée, tel un vêtement. » (Juana Müller, *La jeune*

Sculpture, 4ième Salon, Edition Gizard, Paris.) This promising artist died in Paris, 1952. Her exhibitions include two at the Galerie Mai, Paris, where her *Head for a Tomb* and *Caryatide Enigmatique* were shown in 1950, and *Head of a Child* in 1951.

MULLER, ROBERT, sculptor, was born in Zurich, Switzerland, in 1920. From 1939 to 1944, he studied with Germaine Richier. In 1947 he went to live in Italy, and in 1950 he moved to Paris. Since 1953 he has exhibited at the Salon de Mai. His work has been shown at the Galerie Craven in Paris, 1954; the "Eisenplastik" exhibition in Berne, Switzerland; the Swiss Pavilion at the Venice Biennale, 1956; the Brussels World Fair, 1958; the Kunsthalle, Basel, and Helmhaus, Zurich, Switzerland, 1959; the "Documenta" exhibit, Kassel, Germany, 1959; the Galerie de France, Paris, 1960. Bibl.: René de Solier, Introduction, "Catalogue Galerie Craven," Paris, 1954; François Stahly, "Werk VIII," Winterthur, 1955; "Quadrum I," Brussels, 1956; "XX Siècle VIII," Paris, 1956/57. In 1956 he was awarded the Prize at the São Paulo Bienal and in 1957 the Regina Feijel Prize at the São Paulo Bienal.

NEVELSON, LOUISE, sculptor, came to Maine at the age of four and now lives and works in New York. She received her training in art both in America and in Europe and owes much of the quality of her work to her archaeological studies in Central America. An artist of varied skills, her first sculptures were shown at the Nierendorf Gallery in 1940, and that gallery represented her until 1947. Her works are included in the permanent collection of the Museum of Fine Arts, Texas; the Farnworth Museum of Art, Maine; Brandeis University, Massachusetts; the Birmingham Museum, Alabama; the Whitney Museum, New York; the Carnegie Institute, Pittsburgh; Newark Art Museum, New Jersey; the Brooklyn Museum, New York; and the Sara Robi Foundation as well as in many private collections. In 1958, she had a one-man show at the Grand Central Moderns, her fourth yearly show; and in 1959, she was included in the "16 Americans" exhibit at the Museum of Modern Art, New York. She is now represented by the Martha Jackson Gallery, New York, where she had a one-man show in 1959.

NIVOLA, COSTANTINO, sculptor, painter, draughtsman, was born in Sardinia, Italy, 1914, of artisan-parents. In 1922 he began to work in the family trade as a mason. He left his native village in 1926 to become assistant to a local painter-decorator, using plaster-stucco and other techniques. In 1930 he won a scholarship to the Art Institute, Monza (Milan). He executed in 1933, along with S. R. Francello, a ceramic mural for the Triennale, Milan. He graduated in 1935 from the Istituto Superiore d'Arte, Milan, and in the same year he visited Paris for the first time. In 1936 he joined the Olivetti Corporation as Art Director. He painted murals in the rural Arch. Pavilion for the VI Triennale and participated in the "Exhibition of the Mountain," Turin. He did murals for the Fiat Pavilion, Milan, and executed sculpture and display panels for the Textile Exhibition, Rome. In 1937, he did some murals for the Italian Pavilion at the World's Fair in Paris. In Milan he produced murals for the Olivetti Store, and in 1939 settled in New York, where he met Saul Steinberg. In the following years they exhibited together at the Betty Parsons Gallery. In 1937 he met Le Corbusier, who shared his painting studio with Nivola in U.S.A. and was an important influence on his further development. In 1947 he took a European trip, including France and Italy. In 1948 he exhibited in "American Abstract Art Show," Riverside Museum. By 1950 he had developed a new technique: sandcasting. In

1951 he had a one-man show at the Tibor de Nagy Gallery, New York, and also presented some of his sculptures at a group show, Kootz Gallery, New York. In 1953 (-54) he was commissioned to do a mural (70′ by 15′) employing a new technique (polychrome, bas-relief) for the Olivetti store, New York, in collaboration with the architects Peressutti, Rogers and Belgiojoso. In 1954 the Graduate School of Design, Harvard University, Cambridge, Mass. gave him an appointment to their staff and he became director of the design workshop (1956-57). Nivola exhibited in New York at the Tibor de Nagy Gallery, 1950, Kootz Gallery, 1951, and Peridot Gallery, May 1954. He executed monumental works for a memorial fountain near Washington, 1956 and murals for the Metropolitan Fair Exposition Center, Chicago, 1957, and a monument in cast stone *(Seneca)* for the garden of H. Bayer (Aspen).

NOGUCHI, ISAMU, sculptor, designer, photographer, writer, was born in Los Angeles, U.S.A., November 17, 1904, of Japanese-American parentage. He lived in Japan until the age of 14, attending school in Yokohama. In 1918 he was apprenticed to a cabinet maker. Returning to the U.S.A., he attended school in Indiana. He was apprenticed to Gutzon Borglum while tutoring the latter's son. In 1923 he took a pre-medical course at Columbia University, New York. In 1924, his interest in sculpture increasing, he studied at the Leonardo da Vinci Art School and East Side Art School, New York. In Paris, 1927-28, on a Guggenheim Fellowship, he worked for two years with Brancusi, but was also influenced by Calder and Giacometti. In 1929 he was back in New York, and from 1929-31, in China and Japan. He studied drawing in Peking and worked as a potter in Kyoto. He returned to the U.S.A. in 1931. In Mexico, 1936, he constructed a relief 65 feet long in colored concrete. In 1938 he won a competition for a relief for the Associated Press Building in Rockefeller Center, New York, and the following year was commissioned to design a fountain for the Ford Motor Co. pavilion at the New York World's Fair. In 1941 he voluntarily entered a Japanese segregation center in Arizona. In 1949-50 he traveled in France, Italy, Spain and the Far East. In 1953 he designed sculpture for Lever House in New York City. He now lives in New York and near Tokyo. His one-man shows include: Schoen Gallery, New York, 1929; Marie Sterner Gallery, New York, 1930; Harvard Society for Contemporary Art, Cambridge, 1930; Mellon Gallery, Philadelphia, 1933; Sidney Burnay Gallery, London, 1934; Museum of Modern Art, New York, and San Francisco Art Museum, 1942. Examples of his work are owned by the Albright Gallery, Buffalo, the Metropolitan Museum of Art, the Museum of Modern Art, New York, and the Toronto Art Gallery. In 1959, he was among the exhibitors at the "Documenta," Kassel, Germany.

OBRIST, HERMANN, sculptor, designer and theorist, was born at Kilchberg, near Zurich, Switzerland, 1863, the son of a Swiss country doctor and a Scottish aristocrat. He spent his youth at Weimar, at first in the study of medicine, but turning in 1888 to pottery. He then attended the Kunstgewerbeschule, Karlsruhe. In 1890 he studied sculpture in Paris and opened an artistic embroidery workshop in Florence. His lively designs were forerunners of abstract art. In 1894 he settled in Munich and became a leading figure in the rising Art Nouveau movement. Around 1900 and later he produced pre-abstract sculptures of daring design. His best-known writing is *New Possibilities in Art, Critical Essays, 1896-1900,* Leipzig, 1903. In 1902 he opened a training and experimental workshop for applied art in Munich, together with the painter Wilhelm von Debschitz who succeeded him as head of the school. He died in Munich, February 26, 1927.

PAOLOZZI, EDUARDO, was born in Edinburgh, Scotland, March 7, 1924; he studied at the Academy of Art there, and later in London. His early work showed the influence of Henry Moore (*Bird,* 1950); his subsequent work has tended more and more towards the skeletal in form. His sensitive treatment of relief recalls that of Hajdu. In 1951 he made a temporary fountain for the South Bank Exhibition, London. He has been associated with the Arts Council Commission in London since 1953. He has designed several fountains for a public park in Hamburg and reliefs for the flats of Maxwell Fry and Jane Drew, London. His exhibitions include the Venice Biennale, 1952, 1954; group show, Solomon R. Guggenheim Museum, New York, 1958; the "Documenta," Kassel, Germany, 1959; the Venice Biennale, 1960. He lives in London.

PENALBA, ALICIA, sculptor, was born in 1918, in Buenos Aires. After winning the "Prix de Peinture" at the National Salon of Buenos Aires in 1947, she went to France on a grant from the French Government, and there devoted herself to sculpture. Her works have been shown at the Salon de Mai, 1952; the Salon de la Jeune Sculpture, for six consecutive years, 1952-57; the "15 Sculptors" exhibit at Galerie Suzanne de Coninck, 1955, 1957; Park Middelheim, Antwerp, 1953, 1955; the Galerie Breteau; the Rodin Museum; the Tours Museum, 1957; the Galerie Claude Bernard, 1957-59. She was represented in "l'Ecole de Paris," at Angers, 1956, in a show in Japan, 1956; at the Biennale Triveneta, Padova, 1959, as well as in the "Documenta" exhibit, in Kassel, 1959. She has had one-man shows at the Galerie du Dragon, 1957; at the Otto Gerson Gallery, New York, 1960, and at the Galerie Claude Bernard, 1960. Her work is in various museums and private collections in South America, the U.S. and Europe.

PEVSNER, ANTOINE, constructivist, painter and theorist, was born in Orel, Russia, 1886. He studied at the Kiev Art Academy, 1902-09, visited Paris in 1910, and continued his studies at the St. Petersburg Art Academy. In 1913, in Paris, he became friendly with Modigliani and Archipenko. He spent the years 1914-17 in Oslo with his brother Naum Gabo. In 1917 he was appointed professor at the Moscow Art Academy with Gabo, Tatlin and Malevich. He abandoned the Cubist approach for abstract construction. In 1920, with Gabo, he wrote the *Realist Manifesto,* the theoretical and definitive foundations of Constructivism. He exhibited with his brother in Moscow in open opposition to the official use of art as political propaganda, publicly proclaiming the spiritual independence of the artist. In January 1923 he left Moscow for Berlin where he had participated in the Constructivist Exhibition and now devoted himself entirely to sculpture. In October he left Berlin for Paris. In 1924 he exhibited with Gabo at the Galerie Percier, Paris. In 1926 his work was exhibited at the Little Review Gallery and at the Société Anonyme, New York. In 1927 he collaborated with Gabo on settings and costumes for the Diaghilev ballet, *La Chatte.* In 1931 he was a co-founder of the Paris Abstraction-Création Group. He renewed his friendship with Kandinsky when the latter settled in Paris in 1933. In 1934 he exhibited at the Kunsthalle, Basel. From 1946-52 he was an active member of the Salon des Réalités Nouvelles. Recent exhibitions include: Galerie René Drouin, Paris, 1947; Museum of Modern Art, New York, 1948; Kunsthaus, Zurich, 1949; Battersea Park Exhibition, London, 1952; Musée d'Art Moderne, Paris, 1952; Tate Gallery, London, 1952; "Seven Pioneers of Modern Sculpture," Yverdon, Switzerland, 1954; Retrospective, Musée d'Art Modern, Paris, 1957; Venice Biennale, Brussels World's Fair, 1958, "Documenta," Kassel, Germany, 1959. In 1953 he became vice-president of the Salon des Réalités Nouvelles and won a second prize in the Unknown Political Prisoner

Competition. In 1950-1951 he executed a monumental sculpture for Carracas (Venezuela); in 1955 one for Detroit (General Motors building). He lives in Paris.

PHILLIPS, HELEN, sculptor, graphic artist, was born in Fresno, California, 1913. She was educated at the California School of Fine Arts, 1932-35. She is the wife of the painter and graphic artist, Stanley William Hayter. Her first commission came in 1936, to design a crucifix for St. Joseph's Church, Sacramento. In the same year she won the Purchase Prize at the San Francisco Art Association and a Phelan Traveling Scholarship. From 1937-39 she lived in Paris. In 1938 she was represented at the International Exhibition in San Francisco. She has won the Edgar Walter Sculpture Prize, 1947, the Timothy Pflueger Sculpture Prize, 1948, and a prize in the competition for the Monument to the Unknown Political Prisoner, 1953. She has exhibited at the San Francisco Museum of Art, 1940; New School for Social Research, New York, 1942; Art of This Century Gallery, New York, 1944; Hugo Gallery, New York, 1947; Whitney Museum, New York; Chicago Art Institute, 1948; American Abstract Group, 1949; Man and Wife Exhibition, Sidney Janis Gallery, New York, 1949; Petit Palais, Paris, 1950; Galerie Pierre, Galerie La Hune, and Salon de Mai, Paris, 1951; American Embassy, Paris, 1952; Salon de la Jeune Sculpture, Paris, 1952; Biennale, Antwerp; Galerie Martinet, Amsterdam, 1953; Copenhagen; Galerie Numero, Florence, 1954; "4 Artistes Américains de Paris," American Cultural Center, Paris. Since the war she has lived in Paris.

PICASSO, PABLO, painter, sculptor, graphic artist, stage and ballet designer, potter and poet, was born in Malaga, Spain, October 25, 1881. In 1895 he studied painting in Barcelona, and in 1897 in Madrid. He first went to Paris in 1900, returned there in 1901 and 1902, and settled down in 1904. Picasso's sculpture has developed in the same direction as his painting. The first sculptures, *Seated Woman* and *Harlequin* of 1899-1905 showed a marked Impressionist influence, but his *Head of a Woman,* 1909, already showed the beginnings of a free treatment and interplay of tectonic forms, paralleling his painting, *The Demoiselles d'Avignon,* which was influenced by Negro sculpture. From 1912-14 he executed collage reliefs and freestanding objects representing a new stage of development, a skilful interplay between areas of mass and interspersed voids. This stressed the structural contrast, breaking up mass and making it transparent. This tendency culminated in his *Absinthe Glass,* 1914, first modelled in wax and later cast in six bronze copies. After an interval of ten years Picasso again concentrated on sculpture. From 1928-30 his Surrealist period of Dinard found equivalent expression in fabulous sculptural metamorphoses. Later these were succeeded by austere iron constructions reminiscent of his abstract illustrations for the *Chef-d'Oeuvre Inconnue,* 1931. He also designed monumental compositions in 1928-29, destined for a site on the Riviera, looking out to sea. With these designs, which were never executed, Picasso rose to a new peak of powerful spatial expression, welding both the constructive and organic element into a telling symbolic synthesis. From 1929-32, with the technical assistance of his friend Julio Gonzalez he constructed several sculptures in cast iron, which, standing in the garden of his Boideloup studio, look like fusions of vegetable and constructive forms. In later years his attention again turned to the human figure as he modelled small "figurines batons", carved from cylindrical pieces of wood and then cast in bronze. Their proportioning recalls both Etruscan statuettes and although differing in structure the work of Alberto Giacometti. During the war years Picasso applied himself to turning "found objects" (in the Dada sense,

Pablo Picasso   Antoine Poncet   Germaine Richier   Auguste Rodin

James Rosati   Bernard Rosenthal   Medardo Rosso   Theodore J. Roszak

Oskar Schlemmer   Day Schnabel   Kurt Schwitters   Carlo Sergio Signori

347

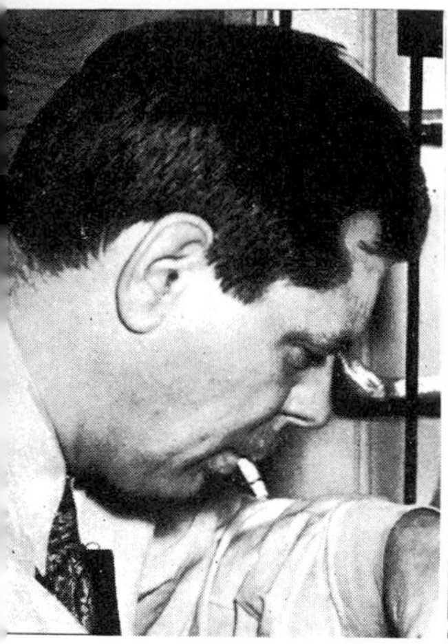

David Smith

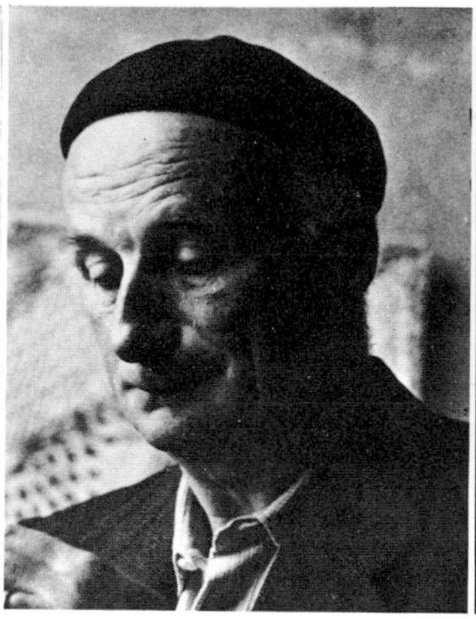

Paul Speck

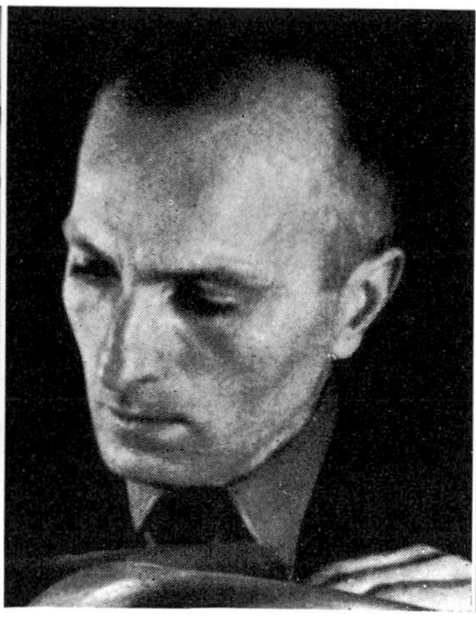

Henri Francois Stahly

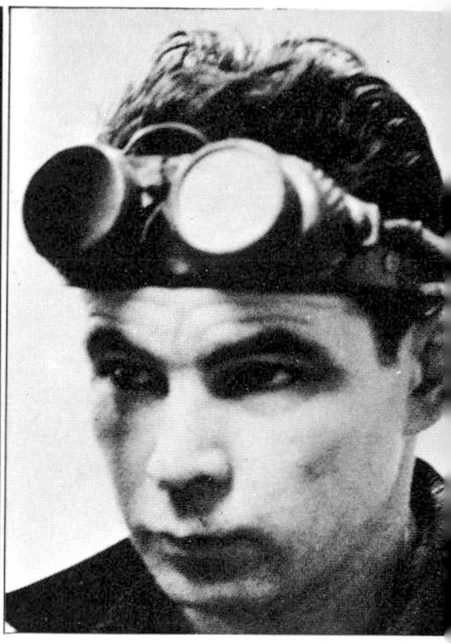

Richard Stankiewicz

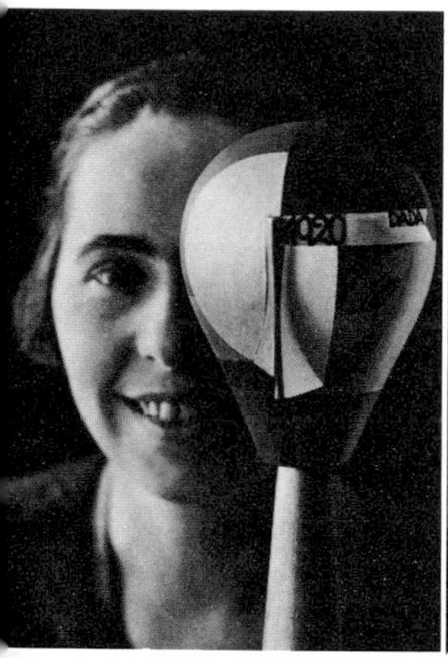

Sophie Taeuber-Arp

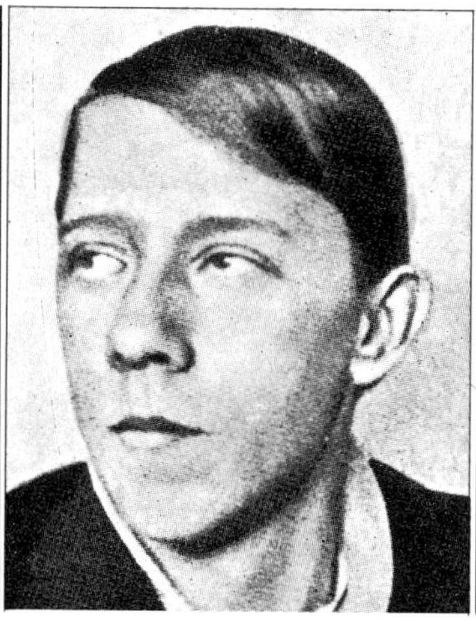

Vladimir E. Tatlin

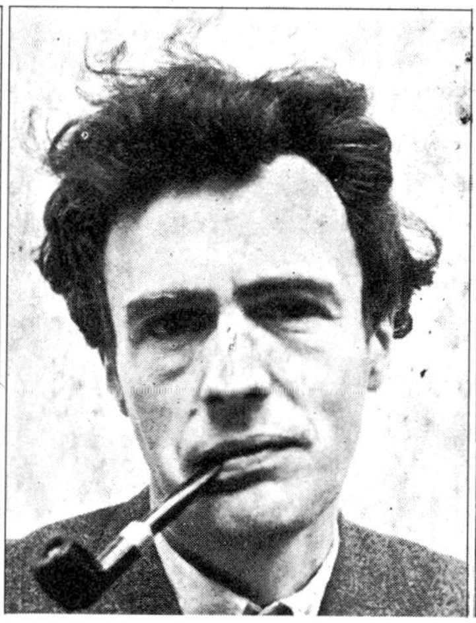

Erik Thommesen

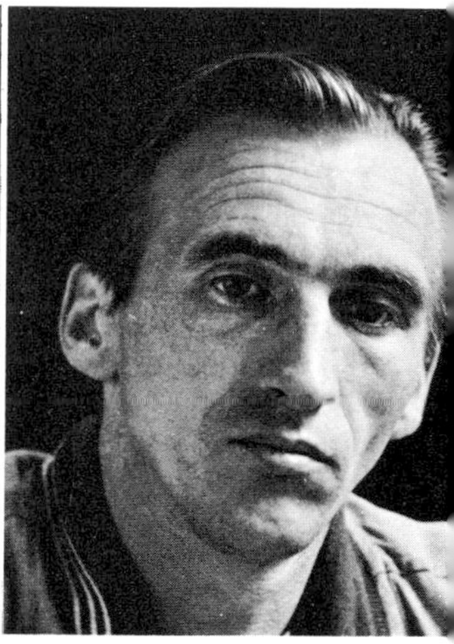

William Turnbull

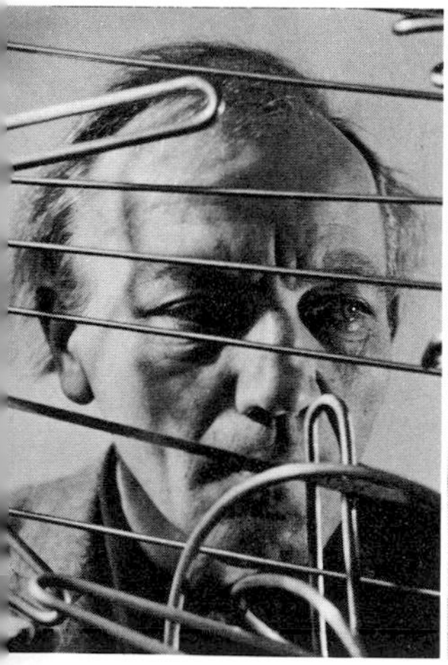

Hans Uhlmann

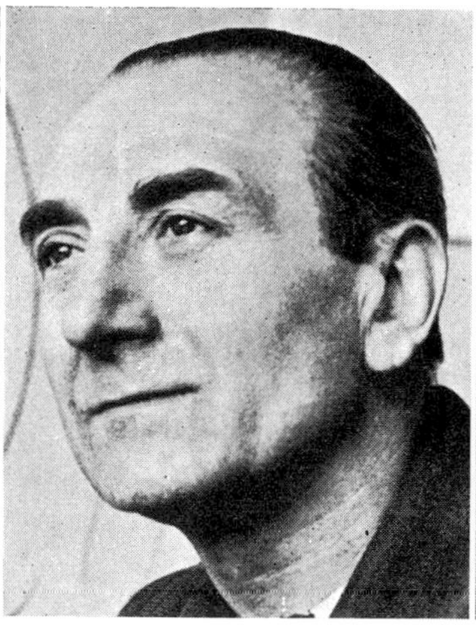

Georges Vantongerloo

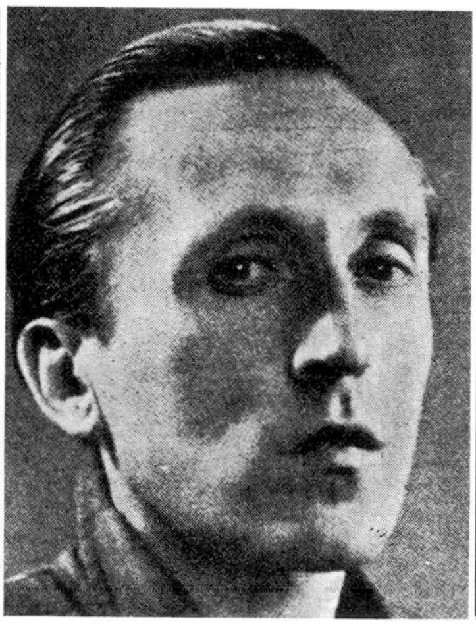

Alberto Viani

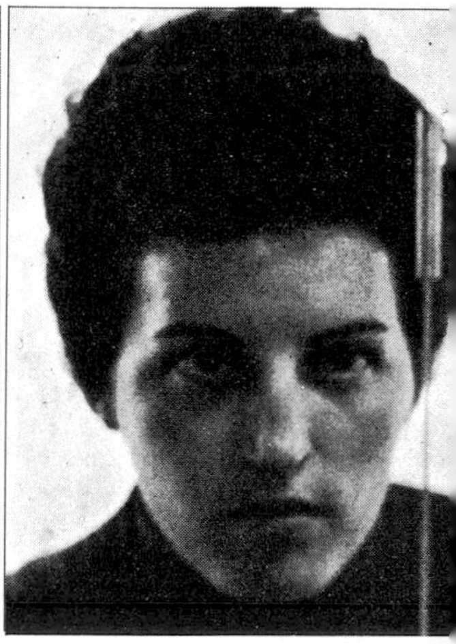

Mary Vieira

but without stressing the ironic overtones) into expressive sculpture. Thus, he transformed a saddle into a "prehistoric" head of a bull, or a hollowed-out stone into a macabre *Death's Head* (1943). With these experiments, however, he moved to the borderline of art. They represent the playful outburst of artistic vitality rather than fully developed works of art. In this quick attitude Picasso is the complete opposite of Brancusi, whose slow, painstaking labor is inspired by an unflinching desire for absolute perfection. Picasso's statue, *L'homme au Mouton,* executed, after some preliminary sketches, in a single day in 1944, and his *Cock,* 1943, constructed in an apparently friable material, may well be counted among his "vivacités sculpturales". The statue of *L'homme au Mouton* now stands in the town square of Vallauris. His *Bathers* (1958), originally constructed in wood in the collage manner and then cast in bronze, achieve a structural and proportional expressiveness with a minimum of means. For major exhibitions, see: Catalog by Alfred H. Barr, Jr.; Museum of Modern Art, New York, 1946. Further exhibitions of his sculpture: Maison de la Pensée Française, Paris, 1951; Musée de Lyon; Palazzo Reale, Milan; Galleria dell'Obelisco, Rome, 1953. Picasso now lives in the Château de Vauvenargues, Aix-en-Provence.

PONCET, ANTOINE, sculptor, was born in Paris in 1928. Son of the Swiss painter, Marcel Poncet, grandson of Maurice Denis, he assisted his father in the latter's stained glass and mosaic workshop. In 1942 he turned from painting to sculpture. Encouraged by Germaine Richier, who then lived in Switzerland, he studied at the Ecole des Beaux-Arts in Lausanne, 1943-46. After the war he settled in Paris and worked with Jean Arp on several sculptures. Since 1951 he has exhibited in group shows at the Salon de la Jeune Sculpture, the Salon des Réalités Nouvelles, as well as in Bienne, Winterthur, Yverdon and Paris. He was given a one-man show at the Galerie Iris Clerc, Paris, in 1959-60. He now lives in St. Germain-en-Laye, near Paris.

RICHIER, GERMAINE, sculptor, painter and graphic artist, was born in Grans, Southern France, 1904. She attended the Ecole des Beaux Arts, Montpellier. From 1925-29 she was a pupil and assistant of Bourdelle, and exhibited at the Salon d'Automne and Tuileries. In 1934 she won the Blumenthal Prize for Sculpture, and in 1937 was honored for her sculpture at the Paris Exposition. She spent the years 1939-45 in Switzerland. In 1952 she won the Sculpture Prize at the São Paulo Bienal. She was a committee member of the Salon de Mai. Her recent work has included collaboration with the painter Vieira da Silva. Since 1946 she has lived in Paris. Her exhibitions include one-man shows at: Petit Palais, Paris; Galerie Kaganovitch, Paris; Kunsthalle, Basel; Kunsthalle, Berne; Kunsthaus, Zurich; Kunsthaus, Winterthur; Anglo-French Art Center, London, 1947; and Galerie Maeght, Paris, 1948. She has also been represented at the following exhibitions since 1934: Blumenthal Foundation, New York, 1934; Exposition International, Paris, 1937; Kunsthaus, Winterthur, 1942 (with Auberjonois); Kunsthalle, Basel, 1943 (with Marini and Wotruba); Art français contemporain, Ottawa, 1947; La Sculpture française, Berlin, 1948; Sculpteurs contemporains de l'Ecole de Paris, Berne and Amsterdam, 1948; Frank Konst, Stockholm, 1949; Institute of Contemporary Art, London, 1950; Bienal, São Paulo, 1951; Biennale, Venice, 1952; Plastik im Freien, Hamburg, 1953; Venice Biennale, Kunsthalle, Basel, with Vieira da Silva, 1954. Musée d'Art Moderne, Paris, and the museums of Montpellier, Winterthur, Zurich, Basel, Curaçao, São Paulo, Stockholm and Rome own examples of her work. More recently, she has had one-man shows at: Stedelijk Museum, Amsterdam, 1955; Musée d'Art Moderne, Paris, 1956; Martha Jackson Gallery, New York,

1957. She was represented at the Brussels World's Fair and Kunsthalle Berne, 1958. She has illustrated the following works: Arthur Rimbaud's *Les Illuminations;* René de Solier's *Contre Terre;* and Pliny's *Natural History.* Germaine Richier died in Montpellier, France, in 1959.

RODCHENKO, ALEXANDER, painter, constructivist, typographer and photographer, was born in St. Petersburg, Russia, 1891. He attended art school in Kazan. His first abstract work was done in 1914. From 1915-20, in Moscow, he worked with the Suprematists, exhibiting with Malevich in 1919. From 1920-22 he took part in Russian Constructivist exhibitions, and in 1922, the Berlin Constructivist Exhibition. In 1925 he exhibited in Paris. He lives in Moscow, working in the applied arts field, designing furniture, type faces, posters, and stage and cinema decor. He was a member of the Lyev Group.

RODIN, AUGUSTE, sculptor, painter, designer, writer, was born in Paris, France, 1840. At fourteen he attended drawing classes at the Rue de l'Ecole de Médecine, Paris. From 1864-70 he worked in the studio of Carrier-Belleuse. In 1864 his *Man with a Broken Nose* was rejected by the Salon. His entry for a competition at the Ecole des Beaux Arts was also rejected. In Brussels, 1870-77, he worked in the studio of the painter Lecoq de Boisbaudran, studying Flemish primitive masters, Gothic art and Rubens. At this time he allied himself with the Impressionists in their fight against the Academy. In the years 1877-80 his statues, *Man with a Broken Nose, The Bronze Age,* and *St. John the Baptist,* were accepted by the Salon. In 1884 he began the *Burghers of Calais,* which was erected in 1895. In 1886 he made his first study for the Victor Hugo monument and in 1887, Project for the *Monument au Travail.* Along with paintings by Monet, his sketches for the *Burghers of Calais* were shown at the Galerie Georges Petit, Paris, 1889. He worked on *The Gate of Hell,* and on *The Thinker* which was finished in 1904. His international fame was established when, in 1900, he was given a special pavilion at the Paris Exposition. From 1895-98 he concentrated his labors on the Balzac statue which was rejected by the Société des Gens de Lettres. In 1903 he completed his bust of Victor Hugo. From 1906-10 he worked on a monument to Puvis de Chavannes, from 1911-14 on a bust of Clemenceau, and in 1915, a bust of Pope Benedict XV. Rodin died in Meudon, 1917. The bulk of his works are exhibited at the Musée Rodin, Paris, the Musée Rodin, Meudon, the Rodin Museum, Philadelphia. From the judgment of Brancusi—as well as from that of Bourdelle—one can conceive, what new directions and impulses Rodin gave the further development of sculpture and to the following generation: «Au XIXième siècle la situation de la sculpture était désespérée. Rodin arrive et transforme tout. Grâce à lui, l'homme redevient la mesure, le module d'après lequel s'organise la statue. Grâce à lui, la sculpture redevient humaine dans ses dimensions et dans la signification de son contenu. L'influence de Rodin fut et reste immense...» (Constantin Brancusi, *La jeune Sculpture,* 4ième Salon, Edition Gizard, Paris.)

ROSATI, JAMES, sculptor, was born in Washington, Pennsylvania, in 1912. He studied with the sculptor, Frank Vittor, in Pittsburgh and, in 1943, came to New York City, where he has lived ever since. His work was first exhibited at the Ninth Street show, 1952, and he was given his first one-man show by the Peridot Gallery in 1954. He has participated in the Whitney National exhibits of 1952, 1953 and 1954, and in all of the Stable Gallery Annuals. His work has also been shown at: Ohio State University; "Collectors' Show," Leo Castelli Gallery, 1957; Tanager Gallery, 1956, 1957; Rutgers University, 1958; Carnegie International of Pittsburgh, 1959.

He was given a one-man show by the Fine Arts Associates in 1959. He teaches at Cooper Union Art School and at Pratt Institute.

ROSENTHAL, BERNARD, sculptor, was born in Illinois, in 1914. A graduate of the University of Michigan, he studied with Carl Milles at Cranbrook Academy, in 1939. He has exhibited extensively in the U.S. and has had twelve one-man shows since 1947, several of them in public museums. His works were shown at the Catherine Viviano Gallery, N.Y.C., and at the Brussels' World Fair, in 1958. In 1950 he won prizes at both the San Francisco Museum and the Los Angeles County Museum, and, in 1957, the Los Angeles County Museum awarded him its Sculpture Prize. His many architectural commissions include bronze reliefs, thirty feet in height, for 1000 Lake Shore Drive, Chicago, and reliefs three stories in height for 260 Beverly Drive, Beverly Hills, California, (1950). He has also executed bronze fountains and other works for the Museum of Science and Industry, Chicago, 1941, and a ballet group for R.K.O. Studios, in 1952. His works are to be seen in numerous private collections, as well as at the Los Angeles County Museum; the Illinois State Museum of Natural History and Art; and the University of Arizona. He lives in Malibu, California.

ROSSO, MEDARDO, sculptor, painter, designer, writer, was born in Turin, Italy, 1858, the son of a railway official. From 1881-83 he attended Brera Academy, Milan, revolted against the sterile curriculum of the School and was expelled. In 1881-82 he produced his first sculpture comprising groups and individual figures taken from everyday life and a "bozzetto" for the Garibaldi monument. There followed various impressionist portraits and figures still reflecting 19th century naturalism. In *El Cantant a Spass*, 1882, the first sculpture modelled in his studio on the Via Appia, Milan, he found his personal style, characterizing the desperation of his own Bohemian existence in the resigned gesture of the starving street singer. This kind of social criticism in sculpture had started around 1850 with Daumier's *Ratapoil*. Rosso's *Impressione d'Omnibus*, 1883-84, a group of figures, and a truly remarkable work was unfortunately destroyed. It marked the first use of Rosso's original method of combining a series of impressionist snapshots of everyday life within the framework of a structural group. In 1884 he exhibited in Milan, Paris and Rome. Leaving Milan for Paris, he worked in Dalou's studio. In 1886 he had an exhibition at the Salon de Paris. From 1886-89, in Milan again, he executed several commissions for tombstones. Examples of his work, including *La Portinaia* and *Lo Scaccino,* were shown at Venice. In 1893 his sculptural group, *Conversazione in Giardino,* 1893, with the great figure turning its back, inspired Rodin in his Balzac statue, 1898. In 1896 several of his works were shown in London. In 1900 he was represented at the Paris Exposition with his *Sick Child,* 1893, *Laughing Woman,* 1891, *Head of a Child,* 1893, *Head of a Youth,* and *Portrait of M. Rouart,* 1890, and gained public recognition. His personal relations with Degas, Rodin and the collector Rouart brought him into contact with the center of artistic life in France. The diagonal, replacing immobility with expressive movement, is a predominant element in his compositions. It was the note of social realism that made Zola purchase Rosso's *Portinaia* (1883), while Rodin bought his *Laughing Woman* (1891), purely for its great artistic quality. During the Paris Exposition, 1900, the art critic, Charles Morice, devoted a lecture at the Rodin Pavilion to the work of Rosso which had been by-passed by the judging Art Committee. In 1904 he exhibited with Rodin at the Salon d'Automne, and in 1905 he had an exhibition of

22 sculptures in Vienna. Italy, his native land, was late to acclaim him. Only the Futurists, Boccioni, Carrà, and Soffici, from 1909 on began increasingly to praise him in their pamphlets, manifestoes and lectures as a pioneer of modern Italian art. They admired Rosso's attempt to replace the academic concept of sculpture as the representation of isolated objects with a new approach that stressed its relation to space. In 1910, at the suggestion of the painter, Ardengo Soffici and the writer Giovanni Papini, he took part in the Florence exhibition, Prima Mostra dell'Impressionismo, which finally brought him fame in his own country. In 1920 examples of his work were acquired by the art galleries of Florence, Rome, Venice, Turin and Piacenza. From 1923-28 he had several exhibitions in Milan. He died in that city, March 31, 1928. In 1929 the first retrospective exhibition of his work was held at the Salon d'Automne, Paris. In 1946 the first posthumous exhibition in Italy was arranged by the Galleria Santo Spirito, Milan. In 1950 a retrospective exhibition providing a general survey of his work and development formed part of the Venice Biennale. The Museo Barzio, Valsassina (a church transformed and provided with special light sources arranged by Rosso's son Francesco) houses most of the sculptor's works.

ROSZAK, THEODORE J., sculptor and painter, was born in Poznan, Poland, May 1, 1907. In 1909 he emigrated to the U.S.A. In 1928-29 he studied at Columbia University and at the Chicago Art Institute where he received a teaching appointment. From 1929-31 he visited Europe. In 1935 he took up abstract composition in the manner of the early Constructivists and was influenced by Moholy-Nagy. Since 1945 his style has undergone a fundamental change; he has replaced geometric order with organic growth, dynamic in movement, but structural in composition. "The work that I am doing now constitutes an almost complete reversal in idea and feeling of my former work (constructivist sculpture done before 1945) Instead of looking at densely-populated, man-made cities, it now begins by contemplating the clearing. The only reminder of my earlier experiences that I have retained is the overruling structure and concept of space..." From 1937-39 he was an instructor for the W.P.A. Art Project in New York. In 1940 he became an instructor at Sarah Lawrence College, Bronxville, N.Y. He lives in New York. His exhibitions include: Alberton Gallery, Chicago, 1928; Roerich Museum, New York, 1935; Albany Institute of History and Art, 1936; Julian Levy Gallery, New York, 1940; Museum of Modern Art, New York, 1946; Musée d'Art Moderne, Paris and Kunsthaus Zurich, 1953; "Documenta," Kassel, Germany, 1959; Venice Biennale 1960. He is represented in the permanent collections of the Whitney Museum of Art and the Museum of Modern Art, New York, and the Smith College, Northampton, Mass.

SCHLEMMER, OSKAR, painter, sculptor, stage designer and teacher, was born in Stuttgart, Germany, September 4, 1888. He attended the Stuttgart School of Arts and Crafts after a short apprenticeship at designing patterns for inlaid wood furniture. On a scholarship at the Stuttgart Academy he studied under Adolf Hoelzel, the avant-garde leader of the prewar period. There he met the painters Otto Meyer-Amden and Willi Baumeister who became his life-long friends. In 1911 he went to Berlin. In 1914 he designed murals for the German Werkbund Exhibition in Cologne. During his military service, 1915, he was seriously wounded. Like Paul Klee, Schlemmer showed a very mystic temperament in his early years; his diary contained entries like "the mystic of pictorial means", "the inner vision granted by the intercourse with nature..." He aimed at extreme simplification of figure composition and symbolic expression (as in his paintings *K,* and *Homo,* 1915).

In 1917-18 he was cartographer in the military headquarters at Colmar. In 1919 he exhibited at the Sturm Galerie of Herwarth Walden, Berlin. In the same year he produced his first abstract relief, a human figure reduced to ovoid and amphora shapes in a combination of organic and geometrical forms. From 1919-24 his sculpture stressed the rhythmical interplay of concave and convex forms. In 1920 Gropius appointed him to teach stone-carving at the Bauhaus. In 1921 he was producing free-standing sculpture of abstract figures. He designed the *Triadic Ballet* in 1922, and a year later, murals and reliefs for the Bauhaus workshop. In 1925-26 he produced *Hamlet* and *Don Juan* in Berlin, and Manuel de Falla's *A Short Life* in Magdeburg. In 1929 he was made a professor at the Breslau Art Academy. In 1929-30 he painted murals for the Hall of Fountains at the Folkwang Museum, Essen. These were destroyed in 1933. In 1931 he executed a metal figure for the hall of Dr. Raabe's house in Zwenckau and worked on wire constructions based on reliefs. In 1934 he settled at Eichberg, near the Swiss border and wrote a monograph on Meyer-Ámden. In 1937 he moved to Sehringen, near Badenweiler. His works were shown at the Munich exhibition of Decadent Art in the same year. In 1940 he painted murals for Dieter Keller of Stuttgart. Schlemmer died in Baden-Baden, April 13, 1943.

SCHNABEL, DAY, sculptor, painter, American of Austrian origin. She had a humanist education and studied painting at the Vienna Academy of Fine Arts, followed by architectural studies and sculpture in Holland, Italy and Paris. World War II she spent in New York. Since 1947 she works and exhibits both in U.S.A. and Europe. *Exhibitions:* One-man show Betty Parsons Gallery, New York, 1947, 1951; Group shows: Denise René, 1948; Salon des Réalités Nouvelles, Paris, 1948, 1949; "Vry Beelden", Stedelijk Museum, Amsterdam, 1949; Whitney Museum Annual, New York, 1949, 1950, 1952, 1953; "La jeune Sculpture", Jardin du Musée Rodin, Paris, 1948, 1951, 1952, 1953; Salon de Mai, Paris, 1949, 1950, 1951, 1952, 1953; Maison de la Pensée Française, (La Sculpture en France de Rodin à nos Jours), Galerie Colette Allendy, (Group of Abstract Painters and Sculptors presented by Charles Estienne), Paris, 1949; Third Open Air Biennale, Brussels, 1950; Traveling shows in U.S.A., 1953; Exposition Particulière, Galerie Exlibris, Brussels, 1953; one-man show Palais des Beaux Arts, Brussels, 1953; Open Air Show, Middelheim, Antwerp, 1953; Santander (Spain), 1953; Open Air Show, Ministry of Reconstruction, Paris, 1954; Betty Parson Gallery, New York, 1957. Her works are represented in Museums and private collection in both hemispheres.

SCHWITTERS, KURT, painter, sculptor, designer, typographer, illustrator and poet, was born in Hanover, Germany, June 20, 1887. From 1909-13 he studied at the academy in Dresden under Bantzer, Hegenbarth and Kühl, and later in Munich. He married Helma Fischer 1915 and settled in Hanover at 5 Waldhausenstrasse. In 1917 he did active duty and worked as machine designer in the steel Wülfel plants. At that time his artistic work was expressionistic; his first abstract painting dates from 1918. In that year he exhibited at the Sturm Galerie, Herwarth Walden, Berlin. In 1919, in opposition to the semi-political nature of the Berlin Dada movement, he founded Merz, a German variant of the Zurich Dada. His first Merz picture dates from 1919, and his poems, prose and sculptures, 1919-27, bear witness to his spiritual independence. His artistic work shows the influence of De Stijl. He was an active member of the Berlin avant-garde and worked

with the Sturm Group. He exhibited again, with Klee and Molzahn, at the Sturm Galerie, 1919, and the review *Der Sturm* published his poem *Anna Blume*. In 1921 he composed *Ursonata*, a highly fantastic work in basic sound tones, stimulated by a phonetic poem of Raoul Hausmann. From 1921-23 he contributed to *Mécano*, the Dutch Dada review edited by van Doesburg *(De Stijl)*. In 1921 he also exhibited at the Galerie Goltz, Munich and lectured in Prague with Raoul Hausmann and Hanna Höch. At that time he was constructing sculpture out of pieces of wood and other "found" materials. From 1924-35 this modern Till Eulenspiegel was fashioning in his Hanover home a Merz-Bau, a monumental example of ironic Merz art, a "colonne sans fin" of wit, poetic and picturesque ideas to which he constantly made fantastic additions, though always careful to preserve its architectonic vigor and unity. It was destroyed in an air raid in 1943. In 1925 his *Sonate in Urlauten* was recorded. He took part in the great exhibition "Surrealistische und abstrakte Malerei", Kunsthaus Zurich, 1929. In 1930 he collaborated with the Paris review *Cercle et Carré*, edited by Michel Seuphor. His *Merz 21, Erstes Veilchenheft* with a description of the Merz-Bau KDeE (Cathedral of Erotic Misery, 13,5" x 6,8" x 3,3") was published in 1931. The following year he joined the Abstraction-Création Group. In 1935 Schwitters went into voluntary exile in Norway, lived at Lysaken near Oslo. He was represented at the exhibitions Cubism and Abstract Art, and Fantastic Art, Dada and Surrealism, New York, 1936. In 1937 his art was defamed by his countrymen, four examples of his work were shown at the Decadent Art Exhibition, and 13 were confiscated in German museums. Schwitters was represented at the English "Counter-Exhibition" Modern German Art at the Tate Gallery, London, in the following year. After the German invasion of Norway, 1940, he fled to London on board an English ship. He lived in London, and later in Ambleside. There he was given an old tower surrounded by an organized wilderness of weeds, where he planned and started a new Merz column. In 1946 he exhibited his paintings in London and recited *Ursonata* and *Eve Flower*. He died at Ambleside, January 8, 1948.

SIGNORI, CARLO SERGIO, sculptor, was born in Milan in 1906. At the age of eighteen he came to Paris. Starting off as a painter, he worked under Bissière and André Lhote. He then studied sculpture at the Académie Ranson under the direction of Malfray. After the Liberation he was commissioned to design a monument in memory of the brothers Roselli, who were assassinated by the fascists at Bagnoles de l'Orne. This monument, carved out of a single piece of white Carrara marble weighing 24 tons, was one of the first abstract monuments in Europe. The potentiality of marble determined the goal of Signori as a sculptor of hard materials. His works are almost exclusively carved out of white and black marble, onyx and other stones. He taught at the Lycée Artistique in Venice in 1940, then he was made professor at the Académie des Beaux-Arts and assistant to Arturo Martini. He had a one-man show in Milan in 1946 and group shows in Milan, Venice, Trieste, Palermo, Rome and in all the major national and international exhibitions in Italy, as well as those sponsored by Italy abroad. Signori received the Prix de la Jeune Sculpture at the XXIV Biennale in Venice and the Premier Prix de la Ville de Varèse at the first outdoor international exhibition in 1949. His one-man shows include exhibitions at the Galleria del Fiore, Milan, 1954; Galerie Rive Droite, 1957; a room at the Biennale in Venice, 1958; Galerie Creuzevault, 1958; Hanover Gallery, London, 1959. He won the Prix d'Honneur de la Ville de Paris in 1950 and the Prix de Florence in 1953. He lives in Paris and in Carrara.

SMITH, DAVID, sculptor, was born in Decatur, Indiana, U.S.A., 1906. He attended Notre Dame and George Washington Universities. Working for a year at the Studebaker automobile factory in South Bend, Indiana, riveting and casting, he gained first-hand technical experience. He studied painting at the Art Students League, New York. His early sculpture was influenced by Calder and Gonzalez' cast-iron constructions. Where Gonzalez, however, is still rooted in the old European craft tradition, Smith is a genuine product of the American industrial background in his choice of materials and formal expression. "The change from one machine to another means no more than changing brushes to a painter or chisels to a carver..." In 1934 he made his first sculpture in steel. He carves directly in steel, bronze, and iron, rarely casting, but frequently cutting and welding. His work shows a strong sense of humor. In 1941 he set up his own workshop at the Terminal Iron Works, Bolton Landing, Lake George, N.Y. In 1950 he was awarded a Guggenheim Fellowship. Since 1937 he has exhibited at the Willard Gallery, New York. He was represented in a group exhibition of American artists shown in Paris, at the Kunsthaus, Zurich, 1953, at the Bienal at São Paulo and "Documenta," Kassel, Germany, 1959. His one-man shows include: Museum of Modern Art, N.Y., 1957; French & Co., N.Y. 1960. Bibl.: special David Smith number, "Arts," New York, February, 1960.

SPECK, PAUL, painter, sculptor and ceramic artist, was born in Hombrechtikon, Switzerland in 1896. A self-taught craftsman, he worked and taught in Munich and Karlsruhe, Germany, from 1914 to 1934. In 1934 he took up residence in Zurich, where he created fountains and garden sculptures, both figurative and abstract. His work has been exhibited at the Venice Biennale, 1954, and at the Swiss Exhibition of Sculpture at Bienne, 1955 and 1958. He lives in Zurich.

STAHLY, HENRI FRANCOIS, sculptor, graphic artist and writer, was born in Constance, Germany, March 8, 1911. Up to the age of 20 he lived in Switzerland, at Lugano, Winterthur and Zurich. He began his career as a graphic artist. In Paris, 1931, he attended the Académie Ranson under Malfray, and studied in Maillol's studio. In 1937 he was represented at the Paris Exposition and worked with the Témoignage Group. His first abstract work was done in 1938. In 1939 he enlisted in the French Army, thus becoming in French citizen. In 1945 he was represented in a collective exhibition of young artists at the Galerie René Drouin, Paris. After the war he exhibited at the Salon de Mai, Réalités Nouvelles, and the Salon de la Jeune Sculpture, Paris. Examples of his work were shown in group exhibitions in Germany, Sweden, Italy and Japan, at the opening exhibition of the Museum of São Paulo, at the exhibition of contemporary French sculptors, Berne (1949), and at the Antwerp Biennale (1951). Since 1949 he has lived at Bellevue-Meudon near Paris. In 1952 he had his first one-man show at Studio Facchetti, Paris. In the same year he collaborated with the architects Herbé, Le Couteur and Pinsard on a church at Bizerte, Tunis, and later worked with Kazis on a church at Baccarat. His most recent exhibits include: Park Middelheim, Antwerp, 1953, 1954; Biennial Arnheim and Bienal Sao Paulo, 1954; Milan Triennale (Gold Medal), 1954; Contemporary Sculpture exhibit, Rodin Museum, Paris, 1956; São Paulo Bienal (Grand Prix de Matarazzo), 1957; "Documenta," Kassel, Germany, 1959; Sculpture exhibition, Arnheim, 1959; Open-air exhibits, London and Amsterdam, 1960; one-man show, Bertha Schaefer Gallery, N.Y., 1960. In 1958, Stahly founded an art school in Meudon. His works include: window reliefs for the church of Baccarat, in collaboration with Poncet, Etienne Martin and Delahaye, 1955; transparent wall for the General Motors Ex-

hibition, Paris, 1956; religious sculptures for the Vatican Pavilion, Brussels World's Fair, and collaborated on the ceiling with Etienne Martin, 1958; worked on the belfry of the new cathedral at Algiers with the architects Herbé and Le Couteur, 1959; created a sculpture and fountain for a park near Paris, 1960.

STANKIEWICZ, RICHARD, sculptor, was born in Philadelphia, in 1922. He lived in Detroit from 1929 until 1941, then served in the U.S. Navy until 1947. Self-taught, he has worked both at painting and sculpture. In 1948, he came to New York and studied at the Hans Hoffmann School of Fine Arts. In 1949, he went to Paris, where for three months he studied at the Atelier Fernand Léger before going on to work at the Atelier Ossip Zadkine. Returning to New York in 1951, he set up his own studio and, in 1952, helped to found the Hansa Gallery, to which he belonged until 1958. He has had one-man shows each year at the Hansa Gallery through 1958, and, subsequently, at the Stable Gallery. His works have been exhibited in a number of shows, among them: the Biennial, at the Pennsylvania Academy of Fine Arts, 1954; the Whitney Museum Annual, 1956; the American Federation of Artists' traveling exhibit, 1956; "Sculpture U.S.A.," at the Museum of Modern Art, 1958, the International Exhibition, at the Carnegie Institute, 1958; the Venice Biennale, 1958; "16 American Artists," at the Museum of Modern Art, 1959. He is represented in numerous private collections, as well as in the Whitney Museum, the Museum of Modern Art and the Albright Museum.

TAEUBER-ARP, SOPHIE, painter, sculptor, weaver and teacher was born at Davos, Switzerland, 1889. Her mother was of Polish descent. From 1908-10 she studied at the Kunstgewerbeschule, St. Gall, and from 1911-13 at the Debschitz School, Munich. She taught at the Kunstgewerbeschule, Zurich, 1916-29. In 1916 she met Jean Arp and became an active member of the Zurich Dada Group until 1920. At that time she attended the Laban dancing school and performed at Dada evenings. In 1921 she and Arp married. In 1926 they settled in Meudon, in a house of her own construction. With Arp and van Doesburg she decorated the Aubette Restaurant and Bar at Strasbourg, 1927-28. She belonged to the Paris Abstraction-Création Group, 1931-36, and to the Swiss Allianz Group, 1937-43. In 1937 she edited the review *Plastique*. From 1941-43 she lived at Grasse in Southern France, sharing an artistic communal life with Arp, Magnelli and Sonja Delaunay. She died through an accident in Zurich, 1943. Her exhibitions include: Museum of Modern Art, New York, 1936 (Fantastic Art, Dada and Surrealism); Kunsthalle, Basel, 1936, 1944; Galerie Jeanne Bucher, Paris, 1939; Galerie des Eaux Vives, Zurich, 1945; Sidney Janis Gallery, New York; Galerie Denise René, Paris, 1950; Kunstmuseum, Berne; Galerie Bing, Paris, 1954.

TATLIN, VLADIMIR E., constructivist, painter and designer, was born in Moscow, Russia, 1885. He studied there at the Academy till 1910, then he worked at the school of Larionov's till 1912; cooperated with the Moscow "Primitives" and Cubists. His first constructions belong to the period 1913-15. He was a teacher at the Moscow Academy up to 1919. His project for a *Monument to the III International* dates from 1920. "The town itself must live in the monument of today" (Tatlin). He lived in Moscow.

THOMMESEN, ERIK, sculptor, was born in Copenhagen, Denmark, February 15, 1916. He is a self-taught sculptor who began with clay and has progressed to carving in wood and stone. His aim is to express in sculpture the organic movement of life. "Sculpture should grow into space as naturally

Carel Visser   Wander Bertoni   Fritz Wotruba

as a plant." He has exhibited in Copenhagen, Stockholm, Amsterdam, Liège, and at the Salon de Mai, Paris. He lives at Blistrup near Graested, Denmark.

TURNBULL, WILLIAM, sculptor, was born in Dundee, Scotland, 1922. He grew up in Edinburgh and now lives in London. He is now more interested in the human figure. In 1950 he had his first exhibition at the Hanover Gallery, London. In 1952 he was represented at the Venice Biennale. Examples of his work are in private collections in London and Paris. His exhibitions include: Venice Biennale, 1952; exhibition of British Sculptors, Sweden, 1956; São Paulo Bienal, 1957; and a one-man show at the Institute of Contemporary Arts, London, 1957.

UHLMANN, HANS, sculptor, designer, teacher, was born in Berlin, Germany, November 27, 1900. Up to 1933 he was at the Institute of Technology, in Berlin, first as a student, then as a teacher. His sculptural work dates back to 1925. His first exhibition was at the Galerie Gurlitt, Berlin, 1930. From 1933-1945 he did not show his work to the public; he was then working on sculpture constructed of metal sheets, wires and rods. This was exhibited for the first time in 1945 at the Galerie Rosen, Berlin. Since then he has often exhibited in Berlin and other cities (Galerie Günther Francke, Munich, 1950; Galerie Ferd. Möller, Cologne, 1952; Kestner-Gesellschaft, Hanover, 1953). In 1950 he was awarded the "Kunstpreis der Stadt Berlin" and, in 1954, the German Critics' Award. *Exhibitions:* Sao Paulo Bienal (where he was awarded a prize for his drawings), 1952; Lucerne, 1953; Hamburg, 1953; Amsterdam, 1954; "New Decade," Museum of Modern Art, New York, 1955; Kleeman Galleries, New York, 1957; "German Art of the Twentieth Century," Museum of Modern Art, N.Y., 1957; Brussels World's Fair, 1958; "Documenta," Kassel, Germany, 1959. In 1954, he created a sculpture for the new Berlin Music Hall and in 1957, a metal sculpture for "Innenbau-Ausstelung," Berlin-Hansaviertel, and, in 1958, he was commissioned to create several monuments and sculptures for the towns of Munich, Frankfurt/Main, Leverkusen, Freiburg/Breisgau University. Since 1959 he has been a professor at the Academy of Fine Arts, Berlin.

VANTONGERLOO, GEORGES, sculptor, painter, architect and theorist, was born in Antwerp, Belgium, November 24, 1886. He attended the academies at Antwerp and Brussels, studying sculpture and architecture. After moving to Holland he met Mondrian and Doesburg and joined the Stijl movement. Vantongerloo, the youngest member of the group represented the movement in the field of sculpture, and contributed stimulating suggestions to the development of the group. Today he is the sole survivor. From 1914-17, on active service, he designed airports and bridges and worked on city planning. From 1919-21 he lived on the Riviera and in Brussels, writing a series of essays on modern formal design in its relation to the contemporary cultural situation. His approach combines scientific knowledge, artistic invention, the mysteries of creative power, in one all-embracing unity. He expounded this theory for the first time in his critical study, *Art and Its Future*, Antwerp, Sikkel, 1924, and later in *Paintings, Sculptures, Reflections*, New York 1948. Although his art is based on measure and proportion, he moves poetically within newly discovered spatial dimensions that are both universal and unlimited. From 1932-35 he was an active member of the Paris Abstraction-Création Group. He lives in Paris. His exhibitions include: Geneva, 1922; Art d'Aujourd'hui, Paris, 1926; Brooklyn Museum, 1926; Kunsthaus, Zurich, 1929; Galerie Bonaparte, Paris, 1929; Stockholm, 1930; Wolfensberg Gallery, Zurich, 1930; Palais des Beaux Arts, Brussels,

1931; Aero-Nautique Exhibition, Paris, 1931; Abstraction-Création, Paris, 1934; Museum of Modern Art, New York, 1936; Mural Art Exhibition, Paris, 1936; Kunsthalle, Basel, 1937-39; Galerie L'Equipe, Paris, 1937-39; Galerie de Berri, Paris, 1943; Kunsthalle, Basel, 1944; Réalités Nouvelles, Paris, 1946; Kunsthaus, Zurich, 1949; Rose Fried Gallery, New York, 1953. Lives in Paris.

VIANI, ALBERTO, sculptor, was born at Quistello, near Mantua, Italy, March 26, 1906. From 1944-47 he studied at the Venice Art Academy under the sculptor Arturo Martini. He is a member of the Fronte Nuovo delle Arti, a postwar group. There is strong influence of Arp in his designs. In 1949 he won the Prize for Sculpture in Varese. His *Torso feminile* was bought by the Museum of Modern Art, New York. At present he is teaching at the Academia delle Belle Arte, Venice. His exhibitions include the Venice Biennale, 1950, 1952, 1954, 1956, 1958; "Documenta," Kassel, Germany, and the exhibitions at Varèse, Antwerp, São Paulo Bienal, 1953.

VIEIRA, MARY, sculptor, was born in São Paulo, Brazil, July 30, 1927. First she joined a group of young Brazilian sculptors, turning towards elementary forms of expression in 1950. She was impressed by an exhibition of the complete work of Max Bill at São Paulo and decided to become one of his pupils. Therefore she went to Zurich, 1952, and has been living there ever since. From Switzerland she took various trips to Germany, Italy and France. *Exhibitions:* II Bienal, São Paulo, 1953, (where she was awarded the "National Prize for Young Sculptors"); III Bienal, São Paulo, 1955; Kunstgewerbemuseum, Zurich (Brazil Builds), 1954; Brazilian Plastic Arts Exhibition at the Morsbroich museum, Leverkusen, Germany, 1956; "Interbau," Berlin, 1957; Gallery of Modern Art, Basel, 1958; Brussels World's Fair, 1958; Musée des Beaux Arts, Yxelles, Belgium, 1960, and Kunstmuseum St. Gallen, Switzerland, 1960.

VISSER, CAREL, sculptor, was born in Papendrecht, Holland, May 3, 1928. He first studied at the University of Delft, 1948-49, then at the Academy of The Hague, 1949-51. He traveled through England and France in 1951, then settled in Amsterdam. He created sculptures for the waterworks of Leerdam, 1954; the Netherland's Pavilion at the 1955 exhibition; the Police Station in Amsterdam West, 1957; the Netherland's Pavilion at the Brussels World's Fair, 1958. In 1957, he was awarded a grant by the Italian Government. His works have been shown at the Venice Biennal of 1958; Park Middelheim, Antwerp, 1958; in Sonsbeek, 1954, 1956, 1958. He was given a one-man show at the Stedelijk Museum, Amsterdam, in 1960.

WOTRUBA, FRITZ, sculptor, was born in Vienna in 1907. In 1938, he went to live in Switzerland and remained there until 1945, when he was recalled to Vienna to assume the directorship of the sculptor's school at the Academy of Arts. Trained as a stonecutter, Wotruba has been sculpting in stone since 1926. His work has been represented in numerous exhibits, among these: Werkbund Exhibition, Vienna, 1930; Folkwangmuseum, Essen, 1931; Kunsthaus, Zurich, 1931; Basel Museum, 1942; Kunsthalle, Berne, 1943; Venice Biennale, 1932, '34, '48, '50, '52; Musée d'Art Moderne, Paris, 1948; Institut Français d'Innsbruck, 1950; Salzburg, 1952; Gallery Würthle, Vienna, 1954; traveling exhibit to North and South America, arranged by the Institute of Art, Boston, 1955-56; Brussels World's Fair, 1958, "Documenta," 1959. His work is in private collections as well as in numerous museums, including the City Museum and the Austrian Gallery, Vienna; the Winterthur Museum; the Kunsthaus, Zurich; the Tate Gallery, London.

Modern art and sculpture

A Selective Bibliography by Bernard Karpel

The Librarian, Museum of Modern Art, New York

Within the framework established by the preceding text, this bibliography attempts to encompass the relevant literature. Consideration has been given to the need for: (1) general and individual references to books, catalogs and periodicals; (2) comparable materials in several languages when available; (3) divergent views on developments and artists of significant accomplishments; (4) bibliographical listings which indicate readings beyond the present survey of sculpture and sculptors; (5) incorporation into this record of all references noted in the first edition (1937), but under appropriate sections. Illustrations in the bibliography have been selected from material actually cited.

Of course, there remain matters of detail which are best answered by consulting the known magazine indexes, a point to be particularly observed in the instance of younger talents who lie just outside or inside the periphery of art publications. Too often, the "authoritative" study in the contemporary area seeks to revive a past already dead, or ignore the present which insistently eludes it. Only in recent years, dating approximately from the conception of Giedion-Welcker's text, has there been a sense of modernity among historians and critics able to escape the orbit of sculptural academism. In no small measure, that strength has been imparted by the artists themselves, whose insights have been not only plastic but verbal. Granted, as Reg Butler says, that "finding active verbal equivalents for plastic manifestations is the writer's excitement, not the working artist's," it is none the less true that creator and critic are jointly dedicated to a search for clarity in form and meaning. Perhaps it has never been more so than today, which itself is part of the contemporary esthetic.

The 1960 edition of *Contemporary Sculpture* has undergone numerous revisions, except for the scholarly bibliography by Bernard Karpel, which has been taken over without any corrections and changes from the 1955 edition. Readers of this new edition should consult other recent publications for additional information.

Abbreviations

bibl.	*item so numbered in the bibliography*
ch.	*chapter*
ed.	*editor(s), edited by ; edition(s)*
ill.	*illustrated ; illustration(s)*
incl.	*including*
no., nr.	*number, numéro, nummer, heft*
n. s.	*new series*
p.	*page(s)*
pl.	*plate(s)*
[ ]	*data supplied*
*	*noted in bibliography, 1937 edition*

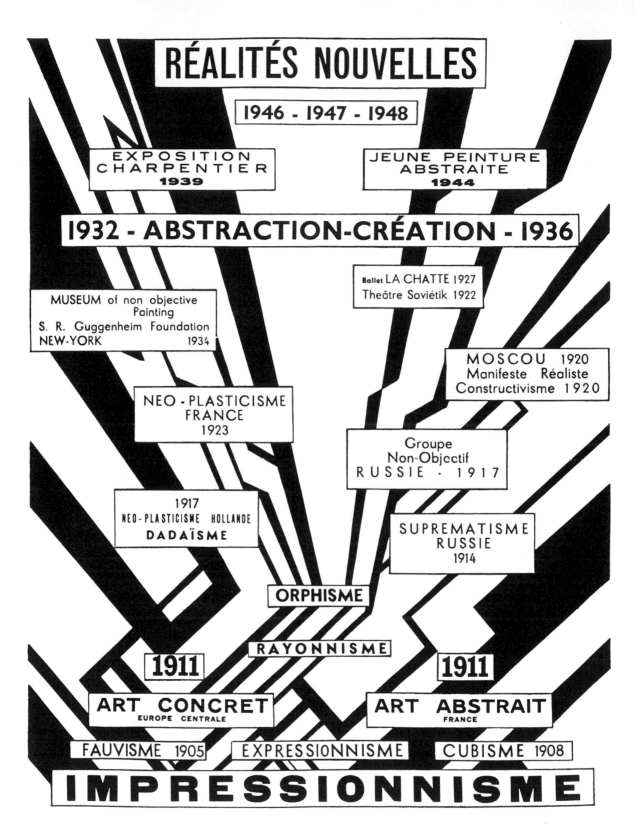

RÉALITÉS NOUVELLES

1946 - 1947 - 1948

EXPOSITION CHARPENTIER 1939

JEUNE PEINTURE ABSTRAITE 1944

1932 - ABSTRACTION-CRÉATION - 1936

Ballet LA CHATTE 1927
Theâtre Soviétik 1922

MUSEUM of non objective Painting
S. R. Guggenheim Foundation
NEW-YORK 1934

MOSCOU 1920
Manifeste Réaliste
Constructivisme 1920

NEO - PLASTICISME FRANCE 1923

Groupe Non-Objectif
RUSSIE - 1917

1917
NEO-PLASTICISME HOLLANDE
DADAÏSME

SUPREMATISME RUSSIE 1914

ORPHISME

RAYONNISME

1911

1911

ART CONCRET EUROPE CENTRALE

ART ABSTRAIT FRANCE

FAUVISME 1905

EXPRESSIONNISME

CUBISME 1908

IMPRESSIONNISME

Chart of Stylistic Evolution. From bibl. K 20, no. 2, 1948.

Arts of Today:
Art History and Theory

*A 1 BALL, HUGO. Die Flucht aus der Zeit. München und Leipzig, Duncker & Humblot, 1927. *New edition: Luzern, Stocker, 1946.*

*A 2 BENDIEN, J. Richtingen in de hedendaagsche Schilderkunst. Rotterdam, Brusse, 1935.

A 3 BILL, MAX. Form: a Balance Sheet of Mid — Twentieth Century Trends in Design. 168 p. ill. Basel, Werner, 1952. *Text in French, English, German.*

A 4 BILLE, EJLER. Picasso, Surréalisme, Abstrakt Kunst. 286 p. ill. Copenhagen, Helios, 1945. *Bibliography.*

A 5 BITTERMANN, ELEANOR. Art in Modern Architecture. p. 77–149. New York, Reinhold, 1952.

*A 6 BURGER, FRITZ. Einführung in die moderne Kunst. Berlin-Neubabelsberg, Athenaion, 1917.

*A 7 CARNAP, RUDOLF. Der logische Aufbau der Welt. Berlin, Weltkreisverlag, 1928.

*A 8 CARNAP, RUDOLF. Scheinprobleme in der Philosophie. Berlin, Weltkreisverlag, 1928.

A 9 COSTANTINI, VINCENZO. Architettura, Scultura, Pittura Contemporanea Europea in un Secolo di Materialismo. 350 p. ill. Milano, Ceschina, 1951.

*A 10 CURJEL, HANS. Triumph der Alltäglichkeit. Berlin, Hesseverlag, 1929.

A 11 DOCUMENTS OF MODERN ART. Edited by Robert Motherwell. New York, Wittenborn, Schultz, 1944, in progress. *Includes texts by Arp, Ernst, Kandinsky, Mondrian, Moholy-Nagy. Also Apollinaire, Duthuit, Kahnweiler, Raymond on major movementes and personalities.*

*A 12 EINSTEIN, CARL. Die Kunst des 20. Jahrhunderts. 3. Aufl. 656 p. ill. incl. pl. Berlin, Propyläen, 1931. *Zur Plastik, p. 218–229. Second edition, 1928 (576 p.). First edition, 1926.*

A 13 EVANS, MYFANWY, ed. The Painter's Object. 147 p. ill. London, Howe, 1937. *"Notes on Sculpture" by Moore, p. 21–29; "Mobiles" by Calder, p. 63–67. Also statements and essays by Kandinsky, Ernst, Picasso, Moholy-Nagy, etc.*

A 13 a FOCILLON, HENRI. The Life of Forms in Art. 94 p. ill. New York, Wittenborn, Schultz, 1948. *Second English edition, enlarged. French editions: Vie des Formes. (Paris, 1934, 1947).*

*A 14 FREUD, SIGMUND. Neue Vorlesungen über Psychoanalyse. Wien, 1933.

A 15 GHISELIN, BREWSTER. The Creative Process, a Symposium. 259 p. Berkeley and Los Angeles, University of California Press, 1952.

A 16 GIEDION, SIEGFRIED. Space, Time and Architecture. 3. ed. 736 p. ill. Cambridge, Mass., Harvard University Press, 1953. *The Charles Eliot Norton lectures (1938-1939) first published 1941; also 1949.*

A 17 GIEDION-WELCKER, CAROLA. Poètes à l'Ecart; Anthologie der Abseitigen. 272 p. ill. Bern-Bümpliz, Benteli, 1946. *Includes Arp, van Doesburg, Picasso, Schwitters and others. Biographical notes.*

A 18 GOLDWATER, ROBERT & TREVES, MARCO. Artists on Art, from the XV to the XX Century. p. 403 seq. New York, Pantheon, 1945. *Includes Bourdelle, Maillol, Picasso, Braque, Boccioni, Malevich, Gabo and Pevsner, etc.*

*A 19 HAUSENSTEIN, WILHELM. Die bildende Kunst der Gegenwart. Stuttgart und Berlin, Deutsche Verlags-Anstalt, 1914.

A 20 HILDEBRANDT, HANS. Die Kunst des 19. und 20. Jahrhunderts. p. 279–452 ill. Potsdam, Athenaion, 1924 (postscript 1931).

A 21 JAKOVSKI, ANATOLE. Six Essais. 47 p. ill. Paris, Povolozky [1933]. *Includes Arp, Calder, Pevsner. Subsequently enlarged to 20 Essais (1935), including Ernst, Giacometti, Gonzalez, Lipchitz, Picasso, Taeuber-Arp etc.*

*A 22 KANDINSKY, WASSILY. Über das Geistige in der Kunst. München, Piper, 1912. *Several language editions and translations, e. g. London, 1914, New York, 1946. Recent authorized edition:* Concerning the Spiritual in Art and Painting in Particular. 93 p. ill. *Wittenborn, Schultz, New York, 1947, reprint 1955.*

A 22 a KARPEL, BERNARD. Arts of the Twentieth Century: a Bibliography. [1000 pp.] ill. New York, Wittenborn, (scheduled for 1956). *Includes major section on Sculpture illustrating the polar concepts of realism and abstraction in contemporary practice.*

A 23 KASSAK, LUDWIG & MOHOLY-NAGY, LADISLAS, ed. Buch neuer Künstler. [94]p. ill. Wien, Zeitschrift "MA", 1922.

A 24 LEBEL, ROBERT, ed. Premier Bilan de l'Art Actuel, 1937–1953. 330 p. ill. Paris, Le Soleil Noir, 1953. *At head of title: Le Soleil Noir. Positions. No. 3 & 4, 1953. Max Clarac-Sérou: "Voies et impasses de la sculpture contemporaine", p. 123–127. Plates, p. 128–143. "Notices biographiques", p. 276–328.*

*A 25 LE ROUZIC, ZACHARIE. Corpus des Signes gravés des Monuments mégalithiques. Paris, Picard, 1927.

A 26 MALRAUX, ANDRÉ. Le Musée Imaginaire de la Sculpture Mondiale. 66 p. plus 704 pl. Paris, Galerie de la Pléiade (Gallimard), 1952.

A 27 MEIER-GRAEFE, JULIUS. Entwicklungsgeschichte der modernen Kunst. 2. Aufl. 3 vol. ill. Stuttgart, Hoffmann, 1914–15. *First edition, 1904. Partial contents, vol. 2 (1915): Europäische Plastik – Rodin – Impressionismus in der Plastik – Maillol – Von Maillol zu Lehmbruck (p. 435–555). Supplemented by his Die Kunst unserer Tage von Cézanne bis heute, 2. ed. (München, Piper, 1927).*

*A 28 MOHOLY-NAGY, LÁSZLÓ. Malerei, Photographie, Film. 133 p. ill. München, Langen, 1925. *Bauhausbücher 8. Second edition 1927.*

A 29 MOHOLY-NAGY, LÁSZLÓ. Von Material zu Architektur. 241 p. ill. München, Langen, 1929. *Bauhausbücher 14. "Der weitere Weg des Materials: das Volumen (Plastik)", p. 93–192. Translation:* The New Vision, from Material to Architecture. 191 p. ill. *New York, Brewer, Warren & Putnam [1930]. Issued in second edition by W. W. Norton (New York, 1938). Third revised edition by Wittenborn, Schultz, (New York, 1946, 5th printing 1955).*

A 30 OZENFANT, AMÉDÉE. Foundations of Modern Art. 348 p. ill. New York, Dover, 1952. *Translated from *Art (Paris, Budry, 1928). Revised French edition 1929 followed by 1931 editions: German (Leben und Gestaltung, Potsdam), English and American editions, (New York, Brewer, Warren & Putnam, 323 p.).*

359

*A 31   OZENFANT, AMÉDÉE & JEANNERET. La Peinture moderne. 172 p. ill. Paris, Crès, 1925. *Includes essays from* L'Esprit Nouveau *(1920–1925).*

*A 32   RAMUZ, C. F. Souvenir sur Igor Strawinsky. 1932.

*A 33   READ, HERBERT. Art Now: an Introduction to the Theory of Modern Painting and Sculpture. 3. enl. ed. 144 p. ill. London, Faber & Faber, 1948; New York, Putnam, 1949. *First edition issued 1936, "Epilogue 1947" surveys American art.*

*A 34   READ, HERBERT. The Meaning of Art. Rev. ed. 191 p. ill. Bungay, Suffolk (England), Penguin & Faber, 1949. *First edition 1931, also New York 1932.*

A 35   READ, HERBERT. The Philosophy of Modern Art; Collected Essays. 278 p. London, Faber & Faber, 1952.

*A 36   REICHENBACH, HANS. Wahrscheinlichkeitslehre. Leiden, Sijthoff, 1935.

A 36 a RITCHIE, ANDREW C., ed. The New Decade: 22 European Painters and Sculptors. 111 p. ill. New York, Museum of Modern Art, 1955. *Includes Armitage, Butler, Chadwick, Minguzzi, Mirko, Richier.*

A 37   SALVINI, ROBERTO. Guida all'Arte moderna. 307 p. ill. Firenze, L'Arco, 1949. *"Repertorio degli Artisti", p. 231–295.*

*A 38   SCHLICK, MORITZ. Raum und Zeit in der gegenwärtigen Physik. Berlin, 1918.

*A 39   SCHULZE-MAIZIER, FRIEDRICH. Die Osterinsel. Leipzig, 1931.

*A 40   SPEISER, ANDREAS. Die mathematische Denkweise. Zürich, Rascher, 1932.

*A 41   SWEENEY, JAMES J. Plastic Redirections in 20th Century Painting. 103 p. ill. Chicago, University of Chicago, 1934.

*A 42   SYDOW, ECKART von. Kunst der Naturvölker (Sammlung E. von der Heydt). Berlin, Cassirer, 1932.

A 43   TAPIÉ, MICHEL. Un Art autre, ou Il s'agit de nouveaux Dévidages du Réel. [122] p. ill. Paris, Gabriel-Giraud, 1952. *Includes plates by Richier, Butler and other sculptors.*

A 44   THIEME, ULRICH & BECKER, FELIX, ed. Allgemeines Lexikon der bildenden Künstler. 36 vol. Leipzig, Seemann, 1908–1947. *Includes biographical and bibliographical notes, with meagre coverage of modern artists in the early years, more satisfactory in the 30's and 40's, e. g. Rodin. To be brought up-to-date by three vol. edition entirely devoted to contemporary figures, edited by Hans Vollmer (1953–1955).*

A 45   THREE LECTURES ON MODERN ART. By Katherine Dreier, James Johnson Sweeney, Naum Gabo. 91 p. ill. New York, Philosophical, Library, 1949.

*A 46   WEYL, HERMANN. Raum, Zeit, Materie. 4. Aufl. 1921.

A 47   WHYTHE, LANCELOT L., ed. Aspects of Form: a Symposium on Form in Nature and in Art. 249 p. ill. London, Lund Humphries, 1951.

A 48   ZERVOS, CHRISTIAN. Histoire de l'Art contemporain. 447 p. incl. pl. Paris, Cahiers d'Art, 1938. *Partial contents: Influences de l'Art nègre — La Sculpture cubiste — Constantin Brancusi — Le Futurisme — L'Art abstrait en Russie — Dada.*

Movements

A 49   BÈRES, PIERRE, INC. Cubism, Futurism, Dadaism, Expressionism and the Surrealist Movement in Literature and Art. 33 p. New York, 1948. *Book catalog no. 15, issued for a sales exhibition, with annotations by Dr. Lucien Goldschmidt.*

A 50   CIRLOT, JUAN EDUARDO. Diccionnario de los Ismos. 414 p. ill. Barcelona, Buenos Aires, Argos, 1949.

A 51   FARNER, KONRAD. Bibliographie. In LUCERNE. KUNSTMUSEUM. Thèse, Antithèse, Synthèse. p. 18–38 1935. *Catalog for exhibition held Feb. 24– Mar. 31. Pt. I. Ideologische Situation der Gesellschaft — II. Periodica — III. Theorie — IV. Mathematik — V. Psychologie-Psychoanalyse — VI. Monografie.*

A 52   GUGGENHEIM, PEGGY, ed. Art of This Century. 156 p. ill. New York, Art of This Century, 1942. *Texts: Genesis and perspective of surrealism (André Bréton) — Abstract art, concrete art (Hans Arp) — Abstract art (Piet Mondrian) — Manifesto of the futurist painters, 1910 — Realistic manifesto, 1920 (Gabo and Pevsner) — Inspiration to order (Max Ernst) — Notes on abstract art (Ben Nicholson) — Quotations from artists represented in the collection.*

A 53   HUNGERLAND, HELMUT, ed. Selective current bibliography for aesthetics and related fields. *Journal of Aesthetics and Art Criticism,* 1945 — current. *An international selection, compiled annually, covering all the arts, with emphasis on theoretical articles on art, literature, philosophy and psychology.*

A 54   LEMAITRE, GEORGES. From Cubism to Surrealism in French literature. 2. ed. 256 p. ill. Cambridge, Mass., Harvard Univ. Press; London, Oxford Univ. Press, 1947. *On cubism, dada and surrealism. First edition, 1941. Bibliography, p. 225–248.*

*A 55   LISSITZKY, EL. & ARP, HANS. Die Kunstismen. 11 p. plus pl. Erlenbach-Zürich, München und Leipzig, Rentsch, 1925. *Cover-title: Kunstism 1914–1924. Text also in French and English.*

A 55 a MESENS, E. L. T., ed. 75 Oeuvres du demi-siècle, 14 juillet — 9 septembre. 64 p. ill. Bruxelles, La Connaissance, 1951. *"Knokke-Le Zoute — Albert Plage. Grand salle des expositions de la 'Reserve'."*

A 56   NEWHALL, BEAUMONT. Bibliography [of Abstract Art]. In NEW YORK. MUSEUM OF MODERN ART. Cubism and Abstract Art. p. 234–249, 1936. *Contents: Abstract art — Modern art — Painting — Sculpture — Photography and films — Movements: Abstract expressionism, Bauhaus Group, Constructivism, Cubism, Dada and surrealism, Futurism, Orphism, Purism, Suprematism, Synchronism, Vorticism — Monographs.*

Abstract Art and Cubism

*B 1   APOLLINAIRE, GUILLAUME. The Cubist Painters, Aesthetic Meditations 1913. 2. ed. 65 p. ill. New York, Wittenborn, Schultz, 1949. *French editions: 1913 (Paris, Figuiere), 1922 (Éditions Athena), etc. "Biographical notes on Apollinaire and Cubism", by B. Karpel, p. 54–64.*

B 2 ALVARD, JULIEN & GINDERTAEL, R. V., ed. Témoignages pour l'Art abstrait. 292 p. ill. Paris, Art d'Aujourd'hui, 1952.

B 3 AZCOAGA, ENRIQUE. El Cubismo. 33 p. plus 51 pl. Barcelona, Omega, 1949.

B 4 BONFANTE, EGIDIO & RAVENNA, JUTI. Arte cubista, con le Méditations esthétiques sur la peinture di Guillaume Apollinaire. 225 p. incl. 67 pl. Venezia, Ateneo, 1945.

B 5 FORNARI, ANTONIO. Quarant 'anni di Cubismo: Cronache, Documenti, Polemiche. 190 p. ill. Roma, Capriotti, 1948.

B 6 LA GAZETTE DES BEAUX-ARTS. Les Créateurs du Cubisme. Préface de Maurice Raynal, Catalogue par Raymond Cogniat. 2. éd. 32 p. ill. Paris, 1935. "*Exposition . . . no. 13 . . . mars-avril.*"

*B 7 GLEIZES, ALBERT & METZINGER, JEAN. Du "Cubisme". 44 p. plus 24 ill. Paris, Figuière, 1912.

B 8 GLEIZES, ALBERT & METZINGER, JEAN. Cubism. (Translated). 133 p. ill. London, Leipzig, T. Fisher Unwin, 1913.

*B 9 GLEIZES, ALBERT. Kubismus. 101 p. incl. 47 ill. München, Albert Langen, 1928. *(Bauhausbücher 13)*.

B 10 JANNEAU, GUILLAUME. L'Art cubiste: Théories et Réalisations, Étude critique. 111p. ill. Paris, Moreau, 1929.

B 11 KAHNWEILER, DANIEL-HENRY. The Rise of Cubism. 35 p. ill. New York, Wittenborn, Schultz, 1949. *Published 1920 as* Der Weg zum Kubismus *by Daniel Henry.*

B 12 DAS KUNSTWERK (Periodical). Abstrakte Kunst: Theorien und Tendenzen. 132 p. ill. Baden-Baden, Klein, 1951. *Reissue of no. 8–9 1950.*

B 13 KÜPPERS, PAUL ERICH. Der Kubismus, ein künstlerisches Formproblem unserer Zeit. 62 p. plus 40 ill. Leipzig, Klinkhardt & Biermann, 1920.

*B 14 NEW YORK, MUSEUM OF MODERN ART. Cubism and Abstract Art. 249 p. ill. New York, Museum of Modern Art, 1936. *Historical survey of abstract and cubist art in Europe for exhibition organized by Alfred H. Barr, Jr. "Cubist sculpture", p. 103–115. Includes valuable chronologies, extensive catalog and bibliography.*

B 15 PARIS. MUSÉE NATIONAL D'ART MODERNE. Le Cubisme (1907—1914), 30 Janvier — 9 Avril. 63 p. plus 48 pl. Paris, Ed. des Musées Nationaux, 1953.

B 16 SEUPHOR, MICHEL, ed. L'Art abstrait: ses Origines, ses premiers Maîtres. 322 p. ill. Paris, Maeght, 1949. *Includes "témoignages" and "texts". Biographical and bibliographical notes.*

Constructivism and Concrete Art

C 1 ART CONCRET. Numéro d'introduction du Groupe et de la revue "Art concret". 16 p. ill. Paris, 1930.

C 2 BASEL. KUNSTHALLE. Konkrete Kunst. 64 p. ill. 1944. *Exhibition, held Mar. 18—Apr. 16, included "Oeuvre-Gruppen" (Arp, Bill, Bodmer, Taeuber-Arp, Vantongerloo).*

C 3 Bibliografico dell'arte astratta e concreta. *Spazio* 2 no. 2: 53—54, Jan.—Feb. 1951. *Abstract — concrete number, with articles by Argan, Dégand, Seuphor, etc.*

C 4 BIEDERMAN, CHARLES. Art as the Evolution of Visual Knowledge. 696 p. ill. Red Wing, Minn., Biederman, 1948. *Bibliography.*

C 5 BILL, MAX. Von der abstrakten zur konkreten Kunst: eine Einführung in Probleme der zeitgenössischen Kunst. *Amphioxus* 2 no. 3: 5—8, 1946.

C 6 CIRCLE. International Survey of Constructive Art. Editors: J. L. Martin, Ben Nicholson, N. Gabo. 292 p. ill. London, Faber & Faber, 1937.

C 7 DROUIN, RENÉ, GALLERY. Art Concret. [16] p. plus 12 pl. Paris, 1945. *Exhibit held June—July, including Arp, Freundlich, Pevsner, Taeuber-Arp, Van Doesburg.*

C 8 GEGENSTAND. Internationale Rundschau der Kunst der Gegenwart, no. 1—2. Berlin, 1922. *Edited by El Lissitzky and Ilya Ehrenburg in German, French ("Objet") and Russian ("Vesch") text.*

C 9 HARTLAUB, G. F. Rückblick auf den Konstruktivismus. *Das Kunstblatt* 10 no. 7: 253–263, 1927.

C 10 KÁLLAI, ERNST. Konstruktivismus. *Jahrbuch der Jungen Kunst* 5: 374–84 ill. 1924.

De Stijl and Neoplasticism

D 1 AMSTERDAM. STEDELIJK MUSEUM. De Stijl. 120 p. ill. 1951. *Catalog 81, for exhibition held July 6 — Sept. 25. Articles in original language; parts translated into English and French.*

*D 2 MONDRIAN, PIET. Neue Gestaltung, Neoplastizismus, Nieuwe Beelding. 66 p. ill. München, Langen, 1925. *Bauhausbücher 5. Incorporates 1920 text.*

D 3 MONDRIAN, PIET. Plastic Art and Pure Plastic Art, 1937; and other Essays, 1941—1943. 63 p. ill. New York, Wittenborn, Schultz, *third printing 1951; first edition, 1945. Bibliographical note.*

D 4 NEW YORK. MUSEUM OF MODERN ART. De Stijl. 13 p. ill. 1952. *The museum Bulletin, v. 20 no. 2, Winter 1952/53, issued for the exhibition also shown at Amsterdam and the Biennale, Venice.*

D 5 SEUPHOR, MICHEL. Piet Mondrian et les origines du néo-plasticisme. *Art d'Aujourdhui* no. 5: [8–9] ill. Dec. 1949. *This number contains a sequence of articles: Piet Mondrian [Texte manuscrit], p. [6–7]; Le home, la rue, la cité, p. [10–11]. Del Marle, Influence de Mondrian, p. [12–13].*

D 6 ZEVI, BRUNO. Poetica dell'Architettura neoplastica. 178 p. ill. Milano, Tamburini, 1953. *Bibliography, p. 157–162, largely on Van Doesburg. Text covers Van Doesburg, De Stijl, Mondrian and neoplasticism.*

D 7 VORDEMBERGE-GILDEWART, F. Zur Geschichte der "Stijl"-Bewegung. *Werk* 38 no. 11: 349–355 ill. Nov. 1951.

The Bauhaus

D 8 ARGAN, GUILIO CARLO. Walter Gropius e la Bauhaus. 202 p. Torino, Einaudi, 1951. *Bibliography on Gropius and the Bauhaus, p. 169–172.*

D 9 BAUHAUS. Zeitschrift für Gestaltung. Dessau, 1926—1931. *Quarterly: 1926—1929, 1931. Editors: Gropius, Moholy-Nagy (1926—1928); Meyer, Kállai (1929); Hilbersheimer, Albers, Kandinsky (1931).*

a

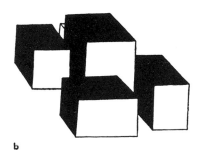

b

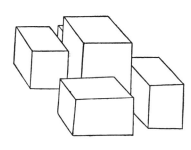

c

Plate 1 Theo van Doesburg:
a) Basic Composition in Painting
b) Basic Composition in Sculpture
c) Basic Composition in Architecture   *From bibl. D 4.*

D 10   MÜNCHEN. HAUS DER KUNST. Die Maler am Bauhaus. 65 p. ill. München, Prestel, 1950. *Exhibition catalog, May—June. Biographical notes.*

D 11   NEW YORK. MUSEUM OF MODERN ART. Bauhaus, 1919—1928. Edited by Herbert Bayer, Walter Gropius, Ise Gropius. 224 p. ill. 1938. *Issued on the occasion of exhibition organized and installed by Herbert Bayer. Bibliography. Second printing: Boston, Branford, 1952, retains the "bibliography of Bauhaus publications". German edition issued 1955 by Gerd Hatje, Stuttgart.*

D 12   STAATLICHES BAUHAUS, WEIMAR, 1919—1923. 226 p. ill. Weimar—München, Bauhaus-Verlag, 1923.

D 13   THWAITES, J. A. The Bauhaus painters and the new style-epoch. *Art Quarterly* 14 no. 1: 19—32 ill. 1951. *Bibliography.*

Expressionism and Blaue Retter

E 1   APOLLONIO, UMBRO. "Die Brücke" e la Cultura dell'Espressionismo. 102 p. ill. Venezia, Alfieri, 1952. *Note bio-bibliografiche, p. 43–59.*

E 2   BERN. KUNSTHALLE. Brücke [3. Juli bis 15. August]. 32 p. ill. 1948. *Texts by Kirchner, Rüdlinger, Arntz. Bibliographies, p. 15–22.*

E 3   BOLLIGER, HANS. Special-Bibliographie der Expressionisten. p. 150–153. *In* Geschichte der modernen Malerei: Matisse, Munch, Rouault: Fauvismus und Expressionismus. [v. 2] Genève, Skira, 1950. *Appears only in German edition of Skira's tri-lingual* History of Modern Painting.

E 4   CHENEY, SHELDON. Expressionism in Art. 415 p. ill. New York, Tudor, 1948 (c. 1934).

*E 5   FECHTER, PAUL. Der Expressionismus. 55 p. ill. München, Piper, 1914. *Third edition, 1919.*

E 6   HODIN, J. P. Expressionism. *Horizon* 19 no. 109: 38–53 ill. Jan. 1949.

*E 7   KANDINSKY, WASSILY. Über das Geistige in der Kunst. München, Piper, 1912. *Several editions and translations include authorized edition:* Concerning the Spiritual in Art, and Painting in Particular, 1912. *93 p. ill. New York, Wittenborn, Schultz, 1947. Other works by Kandinsky include:* Klänge *(München, Piper, 1912) and* Der Blaue Reiter *(München, Piper, 1912). Edited in association with Franz Marc; second edition, 1914.*

E 8   MÜNCHEN. HAUS DER KUNST. Der Blaue Reiter: München und die Kunst des 20. Jahrhunderts, 1908—1914. 45 p. ill. München-Pasing, Filser, 1949. *Shown at Kunsthalle, Basel, 1950. Text by L. Grote. Extracts from writings by Kandinsky, Klee, Marc.*

E 9   READ, HERBERT. Art Now. p. 76–87 ill. London, Faber & Faber, 1948; New York, Putnam, 1949. *"Expressionism: the theory of subjective integrity".*

E 10   SAMUEL, RICHARD & THOMAS, R. HINTON. Expressionism in German Life, Literature and the Theatre (1910—1924). 196 p. ill. Cambridge, Heffer, 1939. *Bibliography, p. 192–196.*

Futurism

E 11   BENET, RAFAEL. El Futurismo comparado, el Movimiento dada. 77 p. ill. Barcelona, Omega, 1949.

E 12   CLOUGH, ROSA TRILLO. Looking back at futurism. 207 p. New York, Cocce Press, 1942. *Doctoral thesis on the writings of the futurists. Bibliography, p. 205–207.*

E 13   CURJEL, HANS. Bemerkungen zum Futurismus. *Das Kunstwerk* 5 no. 3: 5–13 ill. 1951.

E 14   GIEDION-WELCKER, CAROLA. Vergängliches und Zukünftiges im Futurismus. *Werk* 37 no. 11: 345–353 ill. Nov. 1950.

E 15   LACERBA (Firenze). Directore: Giovanni Papini. no. 1 1913 — no. 22 1915. *A futurist journal. Manifestoes, writings and reproductions, e. g. Ugo Tommei "Scultura futurista" 2: 136–141 1914, etc.*

E 16   MARINETTI, FILIPPO TOMMASO. Le futurisme. 238 p. Paris, Sansot [1911]. *"Manifestes et proclamations futuristes." p. 137–238.*

E 17   DER STURM (GALLERY). Zweite Ausstellung: Die Futuristen. 2. Aufl. ill. Berlin, 1912. *"Manifest des Futurismus", p. 3–9. Texts, illustrations, and manifestoes appeared frequently in the 1912—1913 pages of Der Sturm, magazine edited by H. Walden, director of the gallery.*

E 18   VERGNET—RUIZ. Notice historique sur le Futurisme. *In* Huyghe, René. Histoire de l'Art contemporain. p. 479–480 Paris, Alcan, 1935. *Bibliography on Italian paintings, p. 479. — Futurist exhibitions, books, periodicals, "notices", p. 480–482.*

Fantasy, Dada and Surrealism

F 1   BASEL.KUNSTHALLE. Phantastische Kunst des XX. Jahrhunderts, 30. August bis 12. Oktober. 38 p. plus pl. 1952. *Biographical notes.*

F 1a   BAZIN, GERMAIN. Notice historique sur Dada et le Surréalisme. *In* Huyghe, René, ed. Histoire de l'Art contemporain. p. 340–342 Paris, Alcan, 1935.

F 2   BO, CARLO. Antologia del Surrealismo. 315 p. ill. Milano, Edizione di Uomo, 1944.

F 3   BOSQUET, ALAIN. Surrealismus, 1924—1949: Texte und Kritik. 192 p. Berlin, Henssel, 1950. *Biographical and bibliographical notes, p. 185–192.*

*F 4   BRETON, ANDRÉ. Les Manifestes du Surréalisme. 211 p. Paris, Ed. du Sagittaire, 1946. *Texts dated 1924—1942.*

F 5   BUFFET-PICABIA, GABRIELLE. Matières plastiques. *XXe Siècle* no. 2: 31–35 ill. May 1938.

Installation View, Bauhaus Show, New York, 1938. See bibl. D 11.

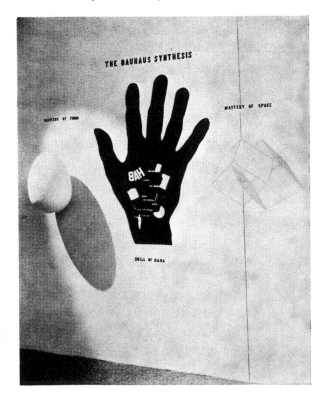

EXPRESSIONNISME ALLEMAND

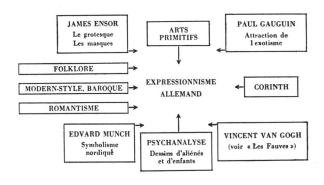

Expressionist Synthesis. Diagram from bibl. A 55a.

*F 6   HUELSENBECK, RICHARD. En avant Dada; eine Geschichte des Dadaismus. 44 p. Hannover, Leipzig, Wien, Zürich: Steegemann, 1920. *(Die Silbergäule, 50-51).*

F 7   MATARASSO, H. Surréalisme: Poésie et Art contemporains. Catalogue à prix marques. [108] p. ill. Paris, Matarasso, 1949.

F 8   MOTHERWELL, ROBERT, ed. The Dada Painters and Poets: an Anthology. 388 p. ill. New York, Wittenborn, Schultz, 1951. *Extensive bibliography by B. Karpel, p. 318–377.*

F 9   NADEAU, MAURICE. Histoire du Surréalisme. 2 vol. Paris, Editions du Seuil, 1945. *Vol. 1, Histoire. — Vol. 2: Documents surréalistes. Bibliographies.*

F 10   NEW YORK, MUSEUM OF MODERN ART. Fantastic art, dada, surrealism. Edited by Alfred H. Barr, Jr.; essays by Georges Hugnet. 3 ed. New York, Museum of Modern Art, distributed by Simon and Schuster, 1947. *Revision of 1936 catalog. Bibliography.*

F 11   PARIS. GALERIE MAEGHT. Le Surréalisme en 1947. 139 p. ill. Paris, Pierre à Feu (Maeght), 1947. *"Exposition internationale du surréalisme présenté par André Breton et Marcel Duchamp". Also an edition de luxe, with supplementary material.*

F 12   RAYMOND, MARCEL. From Baudelaire to Surrealism. 428 p. New York, Wittenborn, Schultz, 1950. *Translation of Corti edition (Paris, 1947). Bibliography by B. Karpel, p. 366–412.*

F 13 READ, HERBERT, ed. Surrealism. 251 p. ill. London, Faber & Faber, 1936.

*F 14 TZARA, TRISTAN. Sept Manifestes Dada. 97 p. Paris, Editions du Diorama, Jean Budry, [1924]. *Texts dated 1916—1920. Translated in bibl. F 8.*

F 15 WYSS, DIETER. Der Surrealismus: Eine Einführung und Deutung surrealistischer Literatur und Malerei. 88 p. ill. Heidelberg, Schneider, 1950. *"Quellenverzeichnis", p. 87–88.*

General Periodicals

While the asterisk (*) indicates inclusion in the 1937 bibliography of this text, some additions have been made, sometimes by indexing relevant contents in the appropriate sections of this bibliography. An excellent international list of significant magazines in art and literature was compiled by Konrad Farner for the Lucerne catalog *Thèse, Antithèse, Synthèse* p. 22–23 1935 (bibl. A 51). Inadequate in some details, and now in need of revision, it is the most convenient starting point as well as a startling summary of the experimental ferment that characterized its generation.

*G 1 *Abstraction, Création, Art Non Figuratif* (Paris) no. 1—5 1932—1936.
       Issued by the Association Abstraction-Création, established Feb. 15 1931. Occasional English texts. Spirit of the group revived by *Réalités Nouvelles.*

G 2 *"A C". Documentos de Actividad Contemporanea.* (Barcelona, Madrid). no. 1 1930—1936?

G 3 *Art d'Aujourd'hui.* (Boulogne, Seine). Editor: André Bloc. 1949—current.
       Special numbers include "Cinquante années de sculpture" (1951), "Art et cubisme" (1953). Excellent review of current art in Paris as well as the international avantgarde in Germany, Great Britain, Italy, etc.

G 4 *Axis. A Quarterly Review of Contemporary "Abstract" Painting & Sculpture.* (London). Editor: Myfanwy Evans. no. 1—8 1935—1937.

*G 5 *Bauhaus.* (Dessau). See bibl. D 9.

G 6 *Cahiers d'Art.* (Paris). Edited by Christian Zervos. 1926—current.
       "A major archive on modern art, which in its early years rallied to cubism and such artists as Braque, Gris, Picasso. The editor has also issued separate monographs based on material published in this encyclopaedic periodical, as well as a pictorial anthology."

*G 7 *Dada.* (Zürich, Paris). Edited by Tristan Tzara. 1917—1920.
       No. 1—5 printed by J. Heuberger, Zürich. No. 4—5 issued in variant German edition. Dada 4—5: cover-title, "Anthologie Dada" May 15 1919, Zürich. — Dada 6: cover-title "Bulletin Dada", Feb. 5 1920. — Dada 7: cover-title "Dadaphone", Mar. 1920, Paris. No. 6 has lettered on cover: "Programme de la matinée du mouvement Dada le 5 Février 1920." Sometimes *Dada Au Grand Air* is cited as a final number, continued in *Cannibale.*

*G 8 *Documents.* (Paris). "Sécrétaire général: Georges Bataille. Comité de rédaction: J. Babeln, G. Contenau, C. Einstein," etc. Vol. 1—2 1929—1933.

G 9 *L'Esprit Nouveau.* (Paris). Edited by Le Corbusier and A. Ozenfant. 1920—1925.
       Material published here subsequently incorporated in bibl. A 30, A 31.

*G 10 *"G".* (Berlin). Material zur elementaren Gestaltung. Hrsg.: Hans Richter. Redaktion: W. Gräff, El Lissitzky, H. Richter. no. 1—5/6 1923—[1926].
       Nos. 1, 2 in newspaper format; nos. 3, 4, 5/6 issued in standard format. No. 4 Mar. 1926; no. 5/6 not dated.

*G 11 *Gaceta de Arte.* (Tenerife). Editor: E. Westerdahl. 1932—1936?

*G 12 *"i 10".* (Amsterdam). Edited by Arthur Müller-Lehning. 1927—1928.

*G 13 *Merz.* (Hannover). Edited by Kurt Schwitters. 1923—1932.
       Special numbers on "Holland-dada", "Arpaden", prints and texts by Schwitters etc. Collaborative work with Doesburg, El Lissitzky etc.

*G 14 *Minotaure.* (Paris). Directeur: E. Tériade. Editeur: A. Skira. no. 1—13 1933—1939.
       Numerous contributions by writers and artists of the surrealist movement.

G 15 *Plastique.* (Paris, Meudon, New York). Editor: S. H. Taeuber-Arp. no. 1—5 1937—1939.
       "Avec la collaboration de A. E. Gallatin, G. L. K. Morris et H. Arp."

*G 16 *Quadrante.* (Roma). Editors: P. Bardi, M. Bontempelli. no. 1—34 1932—1936.

G 17 *Réalités Nouvelles.* (Paris). 1947—current.
       See bibl. K 20. The annual catalog of the association of the same name, issued serially as a record of painting and sculpture in the non-objective tradition.

*G 18 *La Révolution Surréaliste.* (Paris). Editors: Pierre Naville, Benjamin Péret. no. 1—12 1924—1929.
       Continued as *Le Surréalisme au Service de la Révolution.* Editor: André Breton. no. 1—5/6 1930—1933.

G 19 *De Stijl.* (Leiden, Clamart, Meudon). Maandblad voor Nieuwe Kunst, Wetenschap en Kultur. Editor: Theo van Doesburg, 1917—1931. no. 1—[90]. 1917—1932.
       No. 79—84: "Jubileum Serie (XIV) 1927, 10 Jahren Stijl 1917—1928." — no. 87—89: "Aubette Nummer (XV) 1928." — "Dernier numéro", Jan. 1932, is not numbered.

*G 20 *Der Sturm.* (Berlin). Editor: Herwarth Walden. V. 1—21 1910—1932.
       A magazine of futurism and expressionism as well as modern art in Germany, especially the pioneer gallery of the same name, directed by Herwarth Walden.

*G 21 *Transition.* (Paris, Haag, New York). Editor: Eugen Jolas; Associate Editor: J. J. Sweeney. no. 1—27 1927—1938.

*G 22 *Valori Plastici.* (Roma). Direttore: Mario Broglio. no. 1 1918 — no. 5 1921.
       Primarily a document on the metaphysical group in Italy.

G 23   *XXe Siècle.* (Paris). Editor: G. di San Lazzaro. 6 nos. 1938—1939.

> No. 4 (Christmas 1938), no. 5—6 (1939), and 2 no. 1 (supplement to no. 5—6) also issued in English text as *Twentieth Century.* No. 1—3 includes Pierre Guégen's "Esthétique de l'identité" on sculpture.

G 24   *XXe Siècle, Nouvelle Série.* (Paris). Editor: G. di San Lazzaro. 1951—current.

> Already issued: no. 1 (June 1951), "Nouveaux destins de l'art." — no. 2 (Jan. 1952), "Nouvelles conceptions de l'espace." — no. 3 (June 1952), "Art et poésie depuis Apollinaire." No. 1 includes "Message de la sculpture". p. 59–70.

Special Numbers on Sculpture

H 1   *L'Architecture d'Aujourd'hui.* (I) Apr. 1946. — (II) Mar. 1949.

> (I). "Art, numéro hors-série." Texts and plates, p. 50–85, titled "La sculpture." M. Raynal: "La sculpture devant l'architecture." — Paul Herbé: "Visite à Brancusi." — A. Marchand: "Les 'mobiles' de Jean Peyrissac." Other sections include material on Le Corbusier. — (II). "2e numéro hors-série ... consacré aux arts plastiques." Edited by A. Bloc. Artistes chez eux, vus par Maywald, p. 3–43. —L'Atelier, par F. Ponge, p. 44–46. — Art abstrait et architecture (p. 72—79).

H 2   *Art d'Aujourd'hui.* Jan. 1951.

> Ser. 2 no. 3: 1–27, titled "Cinquante années de sculpture". Brief, illustrated articles from Rodin to 1950. *Important sculptural references in special numbers May-June 1953 ("Synthèse des Arts") and May-June 1954 ("Le Cubisme"), etc.*

H 3   *Axis.* no. 3 July 1935.

> Contemporary sculpture issue devoted to Brancusi, Calder, Hepworth, Moore. Additional sculpture plates in other numbers, no. 1—8 1935—1937.

H 4   *Cahiers d'Art.* no. 1—3 June 1936.

> Special illustrated issue on "L'Objet: objets mathématiques, naturels, sauvages, trouvés, irrationnels, ready made, interprétés, incorporés, mobiles." Articles include "Mathématiques et art abstrait" (11 no. 1—3: 4—20 1936).

H 5   *Formes et Couleurs.* no. 2 1943.

> "Sculpture", 5e année, no. 2, unpaged. Includes R. Claude: "Aristide Maillol à l'Acropole" (12 p.). — R. Cogniat: "Sculptures de peintres" (7 p.). — C. Reymond: "Sculpture".

H 6   *Le Point.* no. 12 1937.

> "La Sculpture", v. 2 no. 6: 223–260 Dec. 1937. Articles by G. Besson, A.-H. Martinie, J. Cladel, C. Roger-Marx. Excellent illustrations.

H 7   *The Tiger's Eye.* no. 4 1948.

> Special section: "The ides of art; 14 sculptors write", no. 4: 73–107 June 1948. Statement by Arp, Calder, Callery, Giacometti, Hare, Lippold, Noguchi, Phillips, Smith. Plates, p. 85–106.

H 8   *XXe Siècle.* no. 1 1939.

> English edition: *XXth Century,* "IInd year, 1939, Sculpture, supplement to no. 5/6." Contents:

P. Courthion: Look out for sculpture. — H. Read: Three English sculptors. — P. Fierens: Marino Marini. — M. Bill: The mastery of space. Numerous plates. Important material in other issues (no. 1—5/6).

International Sculpture: History and Technique

I 1   ADRIANI, BRUNO. Problems of the Sculptor. 99 p. New York, Nierendorf Gallery, 1943.

I 2   AUERBACH, ARNOLD. Sculpture, a History in Brief. 111 p. ill. London, Elek, 1952.

I 3   BRUMMÉ, C. LUDWIG. [Bibliography of] Contemporary American and European Monographs and Autobiographies. *In his* Contemporary American Sculpture. p. 150–156, New York, Crown, 1948.

I 4   CLARIS, EDMOND. De l'Impressionisme en Sculpture: Lettres et Opinions de Rodin, Rosso. 132 p. ill. Paris, La Nouvelle Revue, 1902.

I 5   FEGDAL, CHARLES. Ateliers d'Artistes. 322 p. ill. Paris, Stock, 1925.

*I 6   FIERENS, PAUL. Sculpteurs d'Aujourdhui. 22 p. plus 53 pl. Paris, Chroniques du jour; London, Zwemmer, 1933.

I 7   GERTZ, ULRICH. Plastik der Gegenwart. 224 p. ill. Berlin, Rembrandt, 1953. *Text, p. 5–40. Plates, p. 41–216. Biographies, p. 219–224.*

I 8   GIEDION-WELCKER, CAROLA. Moderne Plastik: Elemente der Wirklichkeit, Masse und Auflockerung. Zürich, Girsberger, 1937. *Translated as:* Modern Plastic Art: Elements of Reality, Volume and Disintegration. *161 p. ill. 1937. Biographical appendix, bibliography. Revised edition, 1955.*

I 9   HEILMEYER, ALEXANDER. La Escultura moderna y contemporanea. p. 159–280 ill. Barcelona, Buenos Aires, Poseidon, 1928.

I 10   HUDNUT, JOSEPH. Modern Sculpture. 90 p. New York, Norton, 1929.

*I 11   KUHN, ALFRED. Die neuere Plastik, von Achtzehnhundert bis zur Gegenwart. 2. Aufl. 128 p. 77 pl. München, Delphin, 1922.

I 12   NEW YORK. MUSEUM OF MODERN ART. Modern Sculpture. 4 leaves plus 40 plates (boxed) 1949. *Teaching portfolio no. 1. Bibliography.*

I 13   RAMSDEN, E. H. Sculpture: Theme and Variations. 56 p. plus 103 ill. London, Lund Humphries, 1953.

I 14   RAMSDEN, E. H. Twentieth Century Sculpture. 42 p. plus 63 pl. London, Pleiades, 1949.

I 15   RICH, JACK C. The Materials and Methods of Sculpture. 416 p. ill. New York, Oxford University Press, 1947. *Includes glossary and extensive bibliography.*

I 16   RINDGE, AGNES M. Sculpture. 186 p. plus 40 pl. New York, Payson & Clarke, 1929.

I 17   RITCHIE, ANDREW C. Sculpture of the Twentieth Century. 238 p. ill. New York, Museum of Modern Art, 1953. *Plates p. 48–224. Bibliography by B. Karpel.*

I 18   ROTHSCHILD, LINCOLN. Sculpture through the Ages. p. 208–250 ill. New York, McGraw Hill, 1942.

I 19   SCHEFFLER, KARL. Geschichte der europäischen Plastik im neunzehnten und zwanzigsten Jahrhundert. p. 225–338 ill. Berlin, Cassirer, 1927.

I 20 SEYMOUR, CHARLES. Tradition and Experiment in modern Sculpture. 86 p. ill. Washington, D. C., American University Press, 1949. *Fine critique.*

I 21 STRUPPECK, JULES. The Creation of Sculpture 260 p. ill. New York, Holt, 1952. *Bibliography.*

I 22 VALENTINER, WILHELM R. Origins of modern Sculpture. 180 p. ill. New York, Wittenborn, 1946.

*I 23 WILENSKI, REGINALD H. The Meaning of modern Sculpture. p. 83–164 ill. New York, Stokes, 1935.

Selected Articles

J 1 BENSON, EMANUEL M. Seven sculptors. *Magazine of Art* 28: 454–469 Aug. 1935.

J 2 BILL, MAX. De la surface à l'espace. *XXe Siècle* (n.s.) no. 2: 59–65 ill. Jan. 1952.

J 3 BILL, MAX. Die mathematische Denkweise in der Kunst unserer Zeit. *Werk* 36 no. 3: 86–91 ill. Mar. 1949.

J 4 BLANC, PETER. The artist and the atom. *Magazine of Art* 44 no. 4: 145–152 ill. Apr. 1951.

J 5 BRUMMÉ, C. LUDWIG. Contemporary sculpture, a renaissance. *Magazine of Art* 42 no. 6: 212–217 ill. Oct. 1949.

J 6 CURJEL, HANS. Bemerkungen zum Thema "Skulptur". *Werk* 37 no. 10: 313–319 Oct. 1950. *French resumé inserted.*

J 7 DEGAND, LÉON. L'Espace des arts plastiques. *Art d'Aujourd'hui* 2 no. 5: 2–5 ill. Apr.—May 1951.

J 8 DEWASNE, JEAN. Espaces mathématiques et art abstrait. *XXe Siècle* (n. s.) no. 2: 49–58 ill. Jan. 1952.

J 9 Enquete sur la sculpture. *Cahiers d'Art* 3 no. 9: 382–387 ill. 1928. — 3 no. 10: 370–378 ill. 1928. — 4 no. 4: 143–148 ill. 1929.

J 10 FLORISOONE, MICHEL. La sculpture moderne et l'espace. *L'Amour de l'Art* 27 no. 5: 219–224 ill. 1947.

J 11 FREY, ERWIN F. Humanist sculpture or meaningless decoration? *College Art Journal* 11 no. 2: 66–74 Winter 1951/52.

*J 12 GIEDION, SIEGFRIED. Construction and aesthetics. *Transition* no. 25: 181–201 Fall 1936.

*J 13 GIEDION-WELCKER, CAROLA. New roads in modern sculpture. *Transition* no. 23: 198–201 July 1935.

J 14 GREENBERG, CLEMENT. Cross-breeding of modern sculpture. *Art News* 51 no. 4: 74–77, 123–124 ill. June—Aug. 1952.

J 15 GREENBERG, CLEMENT. The new sculpture. *Partisan Review* 16 no. 6: 637–642 June 1949.

16 GUÉGUEN, PIERRE. Existe-t-il un expressionisme dans la sculpture contemporaine? *Art Présent* no. 1: [54–59] ill. 1945. *English summary.*

J 17 GUÉGUEN, PIERRE. La sculpture cubiste. *Art d'Aujourd'hui* 4 no. 3—4: 50–58 May—June 1953.

J 18 HESS, THOMAS B. Many-sided look at modern sculpture. *Art News* 51 no. 6: 16–21 ill. Oct. 1952. *Review of "Sculpture of the 20th Century", bibl. K 21.*

J 19 JANIS, HARRIET. Mobiles. *Arts and Architecture* ill. 65 no. 2: 26–28, 56–59 Feb. 1948.

J 20 KAHNWEILER, DANIEL HENRY. Negro art and cubism. *Horizon* 18 no. 108: 412–420 ill. Dec. 1948.

J 21 LIPTON, SEYMOUR A. Experience and sculptural form. *College Art Journal* 9 no. 1: 52–54 1949.

J 21 a MARTINELLI, VALENTINO. Sculture moderne all'aperto. *Commentari* 4 no. 4: 306–317 ill. Oct.—Dec. 1953. *Footnotes refer to the following exhibitions: Battersea Park (London, 1948, 1951), Kelvingrove Park (Glasgow, 1949), Villa Mirabello (Varese, 1949, 1953), Middelheimpark (Antwerp, 1950, 1953), Arnheim (Sonsbeck, 1952), Alstervorland (Hamburg, 1953).*

J 22 MORRIS, GEORGE L. K. Relations of painting and sculpture. *Partisan Review* 1 no. 1: 63–71 ill. Jan.—Feb. 1943.

J 23 OESTREICH, DIETER. Formtendenzen unserer Zeit. *Werk* 40 no. 6: 194–199 ill. 1953.

J 23 a PIPER, JOHN. Reassessment: Stonehenge. *Architectural Review* no. 633: 177–182 ill. Sept. 1949.

J 24 RAYNAL, MAURICE. Dieu — table — cuvette. *Minotaure* no. 3—4: 39–53 ill. 1933.

J 25 ROSZAK, THEODORE J. Some problems of modern sculpture. *Magazine of Art* 42: 53–56 ill. Feb. 1949.

J 26 SCHACK, WILLIAM. On abstract sculpture. *Magazine of Art* 27: 580–588 ill. Nov. 1934.

J 27 SECKLER, DOROTHY. This march of the sculptors. *Art News* 49 no. 1: 28–29, 66–67 ill. Mar. 1950.

J 28 SWEENEY, JAMES J. Eleven Europeans in America. *Museum of Modern Art Bulletin (New York)* 13 no. 4—5; 2–39 ill. 1946.

J 29 SWEENEY, JAMES J. Sculpture today and tomorrow. *In* Byrdcliffe Afternoons. p. 65–73 Woodstock, N. Y., Overlook Press, 1940.

J 30 TÉRIADE, E. Aspects actuels de l'expression plastique. *Minotaure* no. 5: 33–44 incl. ill. 1934.

J 31 UEBERWASSER, WALTER. Zur Entwicklung der Draht-Plastik. *Werk* 35 no. 4: 118–122 ill. Apr. 1948.

J 32 VALENTINER, WILHELM R. The simile in sculptural composition. *Art Quarterly* 10 no. 4: 262–277 ill. Autumn 1947.

J 33 WESTHEIM, PAUL. Vom Wesen des plastischen Gestaltens. *Das Kunstblatt* no. 7: 193–208 ill. July 1917.

J 34 ZERVOS, CHRISTIAN. Notes sur la sculpture contemporaine. *Cahiers d'Art* 4: 465–473 ill. 1929.

J 35 ZERVOS, CHRISTIAN. Sculptures des peintres d'aujourd'hui. *Cahiers d'Art* 3: 276–289 ill. 1928.

Collections and Exhibitions

K 1 AMSTERDAM. STEDELIJK MUSEUM. 13 Beeldhouwers uit Paris. [48]p. ill. Amsterdam, 1948. *Biographical notes; portraits; studio views.*

K 2 AVIGNON. PALAIS DES PAPES. Exposition de Peintures et Sculptures contemporaines 92 p. ill. 1953. *Biographical notes; preface by C. Zervos.*

K 3 BERN. KUNSTHALLE. Sculpteurs contemporains de l'École de Paris. 18 p. ill. 1948. *Biographical and bibliographical notes.*

K 4 CHICAGO. ART INSTITUTE. 20th Century Art from the Louise and Walter Arensberg Collection. 104 p. ill. 1949. *A pioneer collection now in the Philadelphia Museum of Art.*

K 5   HAMBURG. ALSTERPARK. Plastik im Freien, hrsg. von Carl Georg Heise. 64 p. ill. München, Prestel, 1953. *Catalog and biographical notes, p. 11–16. Also supplementary exhibition catalog, 30 p., with preface by W. Haftmann.*

K 6   HANNOVER. KESTNER GESELLSCHAFT. [Exhibition Catalogs]. ill. 1916-current. *Numerous collective and individual shows, e. g. no. 37, Lehmbruck (1920); no. 108, Gabo (1930). Recent shows have included:* Deutsche Bildhauer der Gegenwart *(1951),* Plastik im Garten und am Bau *(1951),* Marino *(winter 1951—52),* Henry Moore *(1953). Notes by A. Hentzen and others.*

K 7   LONDON. COUNTY COUNCIL. Sculpture, an open air Exhibition at Battersea Park, May to September 1951. [10]p. plus 85 ill. London [Lund Humphries] 1951. *"In association with the Arts Council of Great Britain". Essay by Nikolaus Pevsner. First Battersea catalog issued 1948.*

K 7 a   LONDON. COUNTY COUNCIL. Sculpture in the open air. [14] p. ill. 1954. *"Third international exhibition of sculpture, Holland Park, May to September." Preface by Sir Kenneth Clark. Note Martinelli's review of open air shows, bibl. J 21 a.*

K 8   LONDON. TATE GALLERY. The Unknown Political Prisoner, International Sculpture Competition sponsored by the Institute of Contemporary Arts. [24] p. plus insert ill. London [Lund Humphries] 1953. *Illustrations and biographical notes on major winners: Butler, Basaldella, Hepworth, Pevsner, Gabo, Chadwick, Adam, Calder, Hinder, Bill, Lippold, Minguzzi.*

K 9   LUCERNE. KUNSTMUSEUM. Thèse, Antithèse, Synthèse. 47 p. ill. 1935. *Catalog for Feb.-Mar. show of 22 artists. Bibliography by K. Farner, p. 18–38.*

K 10   MINNEAPOLIS. WALKER ART CENTER. The Classic Tradition in Contemporary Art. 56 p. ill. 1953. *Apr.-June exhibition; biographical and bibliographical notes.*

K 11   NEW HAVEN. YALE UNIVERSITY. ART GALLERY. Collection of the Société Anonyme: Museum of Modern Art 1920. 223 p. ill. 1950. *Collection presented by Katherine S. Dreier and Marcel Duchamp, trustees. Catalog edited by G. H. Hamilton, Curator. Numerous biographical and bibliographical notes.*

K 12   NEW YORK. ART OF THIS CENTURY [GALLERY]. Art of This Century ...1910 to 1942, ed. by Peggy Guggenheim. 156 p. ill. 1942. *A personal "anthology of non-realistic art". Also exhibited as "La Collezione Guggenheim", with minor catalogs and modifications, at Venice (1948), Florence and Milan (1949), and at Zurich (1951).*

K 13   NEW YORK. ASSOCIATION OF AMERICAN PAINTERS AND SCULPTORS. Catalogue of International Exhibition of Modern Art. 105 p. 1913. *Variant catalogs for Chicago and Boston. Best known as the "Armory" show.*

K 14   NEW YORK. BUCHHOLZ GALLERY. Catalogues. 4 vols. ill. New York, Curt Valentin, 1948—1954. *A partial record, bound by exhibition seasons, of a distinguished series of sculpture exhibitions dating from the early forties, in which almost every artist of international significance has been represented. Illustrations, biographical notes, texts and statements, occasional bibliographies.*

K 15   NEW YORK. MUSEUM OF MODERN ART. Modern Art in Your Life, by R. Goldwater in collaboration with R. d'Harnoncourt. 48 p. ill. 1949. *The influence of new plastic forms on modern design and living. Catalog issued as museum Bulletin, v. 17, no. 1, 1949.*

K 16   NEW YORK. MUSEUM OF MODERN ART. Painting and Sculpture in the Museum of Modern Art, edited by Alfred H. Barr, Jr. [2. ed.] 327 p. ill. New York, Museum of Modern Art, distributed by Simon and Schuster, 1948. *"Sculpture", p. 237–249. ff. Supplemented by the Bulletin of the Museum, 17 no. 2–3 1950, 20 no. 3–4 1953.*

K 16 a   NEW YORK. MUSEUM OF MODERN ART. Masters of Modern Art, edited by Alfred H. Barr, Jr. 239 p. ill. 1954. *The most important publication issued by the Museum, on the occasion of its 25th anniversary, to accompany its showing of major works in the collection. Other language editions in preparation in Europe and elsewhere. Sections on sculpture in the most important public collections of its kind.*

K 17   NEW YORK UNIVERSITY. MUSEUM OF LIVING ART. A. E. Gallatin Collection. [40] p. plus 48 pl. 1936. *Catalogs issued 1930, 1933, 1937. Collection began 1927, now in the Philadelphia Museum of Art. Texts by Gallatin, Hélion, Sweeney; notes by G. L. K. Morris.*

K 18   OSLO. KUNSTNERFORBUNDET. International Nutidskunst: Konstruktivisme, Neo-Plasticisme, Abstrakt Kunst, Surrealisme. [24] p. ill. 1938. *Organized by Arp, Bjerke-Petersen, Taeuber-Arp.*

*K 19   PARIS. GALERIE GOEMANS. La Peinture au Défi: Exposition de Collages. 32 p. plus 23 ill. 1930. *March exhibition, with text by Louis Aragon.*

K 20   PARIS. SALON DES RÉALITÉS NOUVELLES. Réalités Nouvelles. 6 parts ill. 1947—current. *Annual catalog, no. 1 (1947) — no. 6 (1952). Président-fondateur: A. Frédo Sides. Catalog of French and international abstract painting and sculpture.*

K 21   PHILADELPHIA. MUSEUM OF ART. Sculpture of the Twentieth Century. 47 p. ill. New York, Museum of Modern Art, distributed by Simon and Schuster, 1952. *Exhibition shown successively at the Philadelphia Museum of Art (1952), the Art Institute of Chicago (1953), and at the Museum of Modern Art, New York (1953). Brief introduction by A. C. Ritchie, director of the exhibition and author of its major text (bibl. I 17).*

K 22   VENICE. PALAZZO VENIER DEI LEONE. Mostra di Scultura Contemporanea, Presentata da Peggy Guggenheim. 34 p. ill. Venezia, [Carlo Ferrari], 1949. *September show at the Giardino del Palazzo, with preface by G. Marchiori.*

K 22 a   YVERDON. HOTEL DE VILLE. Sept pionniers de la sculpture moderne. [40] p. ill. 1954. *Exhibit, held July 18—Sept. 28, of Laurens, Duchamp-Villon, Brancusi, Arp, Chauvin, Pevsner, Gonzalez. Introduction and editing of artists' texts by Michel Seuphor. M. Hagenbach annotates the 31 works by Arp. Show reviewed by C. Giedion-Welcker in Werk no. 9: 209–210 Sept. 1954. For variant exhibition and catalog see bibl. N 10.*

View of Armory Show, New York, 1913. From bibl. L 6a.

National Groups: American

L 1   AMERICAN ABSTRACT ARTISTS. [68] p. ill. New York, Ram Press (printers), Wittenborn, Schultz (distributors), 1946.

L 2   BRUMMÉ, C. LUDWIG. Contemporary American Sculpture. 156 p. incl. 130 pl. New York, Crown, 1948. *Foreword by William Zorach. Biographical notes; bibliography. A picture book.*

L 3   GREENBERG, CLEMENT. The present prospects of American painting and sculpture. *Horizon* 16 no. 93—94: 20–30 Oct. 1947.

L 4   GREENBERG, CLEMENT. The new sculpture. *Partisan Review* 16 no. 6: 637–642 June 1949.

L 5   MODERN ARTISTS IN AMERICA. Editors: R. Motherwell, A. Reinhardt, B. Karpel. p. 9–22 ill. New York, Wittenborn, Schultz [1951]. *"Artists' Sessions at Studio 35" reports conversations in which Lippold, Hare, Ferber, Lassaw and other American artists participated.*

L 6   MORRIS, GEORGE L. K. La sculpture abstraite aux U. S. A. *Art d'Aujourd'hui* 4 no. 1: 3–8 ill. Jan. 1953.

L 6 a   LARKIN, OLIVER W. Art and Life in America. 574 p. ill. New York, Rinehart, 1949. *Bibliography.*

L 7   NEW YORK. MUSEUM OF MODERN ART. Abstract Painting and Sculpture in America, by Andrew C. Ritchie. 159 p. ill. 1951. *Bibliography by B. Karpel, p. 156–159.*

L 8   PARIS, MUSÉE NATIONAL D'ART MODERNE. 12 Peintres et Sculpteurs américains contemporains. [26] p. ill. 1953. *Includes statements by Calder, Roszak, Smith. Exhibited July—August at the Kunsthaus Zürich.*

L 9   SCHNIER, JACQUES. Sculpture in modern America. 224 p. ill. Berkeley & Los Angeles, University of California, 1948. *Largely plates.*

L 10   UNIVERSITY OF ILLINOIS. Contemporary American Painting and Sculpture. 236 p. ill. Urbana, ill., 1953. *Catalog for spring show with preface by A. S. Weller. Notes and quotes on Hare, Lassaw, Roszak, Smith, etc.*

National Groups: English

L 11   ALLOWAY, L. Britain's new iron age. *Art News* 52: 18–20, 68–70 ill. June 1953.

L 11 a ALLOWAY, LAWRENCE. Non-figurative art in England 1953. *Arti Visive* no. 6–7: [14–17] ill. 1954. *Also Italian summary.*

L 12   AXIS. A Quarterly Review of Contemporary "Abstract" Painting and Sculpture. London, 1935—1937.

L 13   CASSON, HUGH. South Bank sculpture. *Image* no. 7: 48–60 ill. Spring 1952.

L 14   DEGAND, LEON. . . . La sculpture d'aujourd'hui en Grande-Bretagne. *Art d'Aujourd'hui* no. 2: 16–17 Mar. 1953.

L 15   English sculptors at Venice. *Architectural Review* 112: 129–130 ill. Aug. 1952.

L 15 a HODIN, J. P. Testimonianza sulla sculptura inglese attuale. *Sele Arte* 2 no. 9: 57–64 Nov.—Dec. 1953.

L 16   MacEWEN, FRANK. Regate France Angleterre. *XXe Siècle* no. 1: 76–77 ill. 1951.

L 17   MIDDLETON, MICHAEL. Huit sculpteurs britanniques. *Art d'Aujourd'hui* no. 2: 6, 18 Mar. 1953.

L 18   NEWTON, ERIC. British Sculpture. 1944—1946. 22 p. plus 64 pl. London, Tiranti, 1947.

L 19   READ, HERBERT. Bildhauerkunst in England. *Das Kunstblatt* 15: 167–170 ill. June 1931.

L 20   READ, HERBERT. Three English sculptors. *XXe Siècle* 2 no. 1: 45 ill. 1939.

L 21   READ, HERBERT, ed. Unit 1: The modern Movement in English Architecture, Painting and Sculpture. 124 p. ill. London, Cassell, 1934.

L 22   THWAITES, JOHN A. Notes on some young English sculptors. *Art Quarterly* 15 no. 3: 234–241 ill. 1952.

L 23   WALDBERG, ISABELLE. Essor de la sculpture anglaise. *Numero* (Firenze) 5 no. 1—2: 12 Jan. — Mar. 1953.

Installation View of Gabo Exhibition, Pierre Matisse Gallery, New York, 1953. See bibl. M 159.

National Groups: French

L 24   AMSTERDAM. STEDELIJK MUSEUM. Rondom Rodin: Tentoonstelling hondred Jaar fransche Sculptuur. [150] pl. plus ill. 1939.

L 25   BASLER, ADOLPHE. Die neue Plastik in Frankreich. *Jahrbuch der Jungen Kunst* 3: 211–216 ill. 1922.

*L 26   BASLER, ADOLPHE. La Sculpture moderne en France. 169 p. incl. 76 ill. Paris, Crès, 1928.

L 27   BLOC, ANDRÉ. La sculpture abstraite en France. *Spazio* 3 no. 6: 13–20 ill. Dec. 1951—Apr. 1952.

L 28   CASSON, STANLEY. XXth Century Sculpture. 130 p. ill. London, Oxford, 1930.

L 29   COQUIOT, GUSTAVE. Cubistes, Futuristes, Passéistes: Essai sur la jeune Peinture et la jeune Sculpture. 230 p. ill. Paris, Ollendorf [1923]. *First edition, 1914.*

L 29 a   ESPACE (ASSOCIATION). Catalogue de l'exposition organisée à Biot par le groupe Espace. Paris, Architecture d'Aujourd'hui, 1954. *Reviewed by P. Guéguen in L'Art d'Aujourd'hui 5 no. 6: 18–21 ill. Sept. 1954.*

L 30   GEORGES-MICHEL, MICHEL. Peintres et Sculpteurs que j'ai connus, 1900—1942. p. 261–284 ill. New York, Brentano [1942].

L 31   GISCHIA, LEON & VÉDRÈS, N. La Sculpture en France depuis Rodin. 182 p. ill. Paris, Éd. du Seuil, 1945.

L 32   THE HAGUE. GEMEENTEMUSEUM. Franse Beeldhouw Kunst: Rodin, Bourdelle, Maillol, Despiau, 30 Juni—4 September. [56] p. ill. 1950.

L 33   HAMBURG. KUNSTHALLE. Junge französische Plastik. 54 p. ill. 1953. *Exhibit of July—August, organized by Le Service des Relations Artistiques; texts by J. Mougin, R. Cogniat, C. Goldscheider in French and German.*

L 34   LE POINT. Les Maîtres de l'Art indépendant, 1895—1925: Portraits d'artistes. p. [133–143] ill. Colmar, 1937. *Vol. 2, no. 3 of "Le Point".*

L 35   LE POINT. La Sculpture. [p. 223–260] ill. Colmar, 1937. *Vol. 2, no. 12 of "Le Point".*

L 36   ROSTRUP, HAAVARD. Franske Billedhuggere fra det 19. og 20. Aarhundrede. 80 p. incl. 61 pl. Copenhagen, Levin & Munksgaard, 1938.

L 37   SALMON, ANDRÉ. La jeune Sculpture française. Paris, Société des Trente (Messein), 1919.

L 37 a   SALON DE LA JEUNE SCULPTURE. La jeune sculpture. n. p. ill. Paris, Gizard [1954]. *Prefaces by M. Aubert, D. Chevalier; biographical notes.*

L 38   SALON DES RÉALITÉS NOUVELLES. Paris, 1947—current. *See bibl. K 20.*

L 39   STAHLY, FRANÇOIS. Die junge französische Plastik. *Werk* 39 no. 11: 369–376 ill. Nov. 1952.

National Groups: German

L 40   L'Art abstrait en Allemagne. *Art d'Aujourd'hui* 4 no. 6: [1–32] ill. Aug. 1953.

L 41   BIERMANN, GEORG. Enquête sur la sculpture en Allemagne et en France. *Cahiers d'Art* 3 no. 9: 382–387 ill. 1928. *Continued by W. Grohmann in no. 10 1928 and P. Westheim in no. 4 1929.*

L 42   DOCUMENTS (Periodical). L'Art allemand contemporain. p. 50–59 ill. Offenbourg en Bade, Bureau international de Liaison et de Documentation, 1951. *Also English edition, with text by Alfred Hentzen on sculpture.*

L 43   HENTZEN, ALFRED. Deutsche Bildhauer der Gegenwart. 126 p. ill. Berlin, Rembrandt [1934]. *Biographical notes, p. 113–119. Brought up to date by his catalog Deutsche Bildhauer der Gegenwart [26] p. ill. Hannover, Kestner-Gesellschaft, 1951.*

L 43 a   HILDEBRANDT, H. Deutsche Plastik der Gegenwart. *Werk* 39: 265–272 ill. Aug. 1952.

L 44   LUCERNE, KUNSTMUSEUM, Deutsche Kunst: Meisterwerke des 20. Jahrhunderts. 64 p. plus 56 pl. 1953.

L 45   NEMITZ, FRITZ. Junge Bildhauer. 79 p. ill. Berlin, Rembrandt-Verlag, 1939.

L 46   NEW YORK. MUSEUM OF MODERN ART. German painting and sculpture. Mar. 13 – Apr. 26 1931. 43 p. ill. 1931. *Biographical notes. Preface by A. H. Barr also published in Omnibus 1932.*

National Groups: Italian

L 47   ART D'AUJOURD'HUI (Periodical). Italie. 1951. *Special number, v. 3 no. 2, Jan. 1951, on "L'art d'avant-garde en Italie".*

L 48   CAIROLA, STEFANO, ed. Arte italiana del nostro Tempo . . . Saggi critici. [130] p. plus 104 pl. Bergamo, Istituto italiano d'Arte grafiche, 1946. *Anthology of painters and sculptors; biographical sections include photograph of the artist; text accompanies each plate.*

L 49   CARRIERI, RAFFAELE. Pittura, Scultura d'Avanguardia in Italia (1890—1950). [345] p. ill. Milano, Conchiglia, 1950. *Extensive bibliography.*

L 50   COSTANTINI, VINCENZO. Scultura e Pittura italiana contemporanea (1880—1926). 502 p. ill. Milano, Hoepli, 1940. *Supplemented by his L'Arte italiana moderna. 350 p. ill. Milano, Ceschinia, 1951.*

L 51   MARCHIORI, GIUSEPPE. Scultura italiana moderna. 48 p. plus 36 pl. Venezia, Alfieri, 1953. *Plates annotated; bibliography. English summary inserted.*

L 52   NEW YORK. MUSEUM OF MODERN ART. Twentieth-Century Italian Art, by James T. Soby and Alfred H. Barr, Jr. 144 p. ill. 1949. *Bibliography by B. Karpel, p. 136–144.*

L 53   SAPORI, FRANCESCO. Scultura italiana moderna. 508 p. incl. 600 ill. Roma, Libreria dello Stato, 1949. *English edition 1950; Spanish edition 1951.*

L 54   ZERVOS, CHRISTIAN, ed. Un Demi-Siècle d'Art italien. 276 p. ill. Paris, Cahiers d'Art, 1950. *Special number, Cahiers d'Art, 25e année, tome 1. Bibliography.*

National Groups: Russian

L 55   DIEMEN, GALERIE Van. Erste russische Kunstausstellung. 31 p. plus pl. Berlin, 1922. *Reviewed in Das Kunstblatt, bibl. L 64.*

L 56   EHRENBOURG, ELIE. L'Art russe d'aujourd'hui. *L'Amour de l'Art* 2 no. 11: 367–370 ill. November 1921.

L 57   FREEMAN, J., KUNITZ, J. & LOZOWICK, L. Voices of October: Art and Literature in Soviet Russia. p. 265–291 ill. New York, Vanguard, 1930.

L 58   GABO, NAUM. The concepts of Russian art. *World Review* (London) p. 48–53 June 1942.

L 59   KARPFEN, FRITZ. Gegenwartskunst: I. Russland. 42 p. plus 21 pl. Wien, Literaria, 1921.

L 60   LOZOWICK, LOUIS. Modern Russian Art. 60 p. ill. New York, Museum of Modern Art, Société Anonyme, 1925.

L 61   NEW YORK. MUSEUM OF MODERN ART. Cubism and abstract Art. 249 p. ill. 1936. *In addition to text passim, the bibliography refers to numerous, although inaccessible, Russian references.*

L 62   SALMON, ANDRE. Art russe moderne. Paris, Laville, 1928.

L 63   STEPUN, FEDOR. Das Schicksal der abstrakten Kunst in Russland. *Das Kunstwerk* 4 no. 8—9: 61–62 1950.

L 64   STERENBERG, D. Die künstlerische Situation in Russland. *Das Kunstblatt* 6 no. 11: 484–492 ill. 1922. *Review of van Diemen exhibit (bibl. L 55) followed, p. 493–498, by additional comment by P. W. (Paul Westheim).*

L 65   UMANSKIJ, KONSTANTIN. Neue Kunst in Russland, 1914—1919. Potsdam, Kiepenheuer; München, H. Goltz, 1920. *Bibliography. Supplemented by his "Die neue Monumentalskulptur in Russland". Der Ararat no. 5—6: 29–33 Mar. 1920.*

L 66   WASHBURN, GORDON. Isms in Art since 1800. p. 64–68 [Providence, R. I., The Author] 1949. *Suprematism, non-objectivism and constructivism: Malevich, Rodchenko, Kandinsky, Lissitzky, Pevsner.*

Sculpture: Swiss

L 66 a   GIEDION-WELCKER, CAROLA. Wettbewerb für ein Denkmal des unbekannten politischen Gefangenen; die deutschen und schweizerischen Einsendungen. *Werk* 40, sup. 65–66 ill. Apr. 1953.

L 67   LEONHARD, KURT. Züricher konkrete Kunst. *Das Kunstwerk* 3 no. 4: 41–42 1949.

L 68   SCHMIDT, GEORG. Abstrakte und surrealistische Kunst in der Schweiz. *Werk* 30 no. 2: 41–45 ill. Feb. 1943.

L 69   ZÜRICH. KUNSTHAUS. Zeitprobleme in der Schweizer Malerei und Plastik. 42 p. ill. 1936. *Exhibit held June—July. Texts by Bill, Le Corbusier and Giedion.*

Readings on Swiss sculpture should be supplemented by *general* reference, e. g. C 2, N 10, etc., as well as individual references on Bill, Bodmer, Burckhardt, Giacometti, etc.

Modern Sculptors

At this point, attention should be directed to the numerous references in the preceding material which add significantly to the following lists. Calder's article in Evans (bibl. A 13), for example, is not repeated below. Similarly, no complete analysis has been attempted for such entries as bibl. H 7. It is presumed the initiative of the reader will replace the requirements of a detailed cross-index.

Adam

M 1   ADAM. [Message de la sculpture]. *XXe Siècle* (n. s.) no. 1: 61–62, 64 ill. 1951.

M 2   ADAM. [Statement]. *In* Premier Bilan de l'Art actuel. p. 276 1953. *(See bibl. A 24). Portrait, biographical note.*

M 3   DEGAND, LÉON. Adam. *Art d'Aujourd'hui* no. 5: [4] ill. Dec. 1949.

M 4   DERRIÈRE LE MIROIR. Adam [8] p. ill. Paris, Maeght, 1949. *Special number 24, Dec. 1949. Includes catalog of Maeght show ; texts by Marchiori, Elgar, Cassou, Badouin.*

Archipenko

M 5   ARCHIPENKO, ALEXANDER. The spirit of music in sculpture. *Europa* no. 1: 32–35 ill. May—July 1933.

M 6   ARCHIPENKO, ALEXANDER. Nature and the point of departure. *The Arts* 5: 31–36 ill. Jan. 1924.

M 7   ANDERSON GALLERIES. Archipenko: Catalogue of Exhibition and Description of Archipentura. 20 p. ill. New York, 1928. *Archipentura, p. 3–5, 8. Catalog (99 works, 17 drawings). List of exhibitions ; extracts from reviews. Literature, p. 20.*

M 8   COLLEGE ART ASSOCIATION. Index of Twentieth-Century Artists, v. 3, no. 6. New York, 1934. *"Alexander Archipenko — Sculptor", a bibliography in its issue of Mar. 1934, p. 249–252. Includes preface, collections, exhibitions, reproductions, books, articles.*

M 9   DÄUBLER, THEODOR. Archipenko-Album: 32 Abbildungen. Einführungen von Theodor Däubler und Ivan Goll. Gedicht von Blaise Cendrars. [16] plus ill. Potsdam, Kiepenheuer, 1921.

M 10   HILDEBRANDT, HANS. Alexandre Archipenko, son Oeuvre. 65 p. ill. Berlin, Ukrainske Slowo, 1923. *Text in French, German, English, Ukrainian. Spanish edition issued 1924 by Editora Internacional (Buenos Aires).*

M 11   RAYNAL, MAURICE. A. Archipenko. 14 p. ill. Roma, Valori Plastici, 1923. *Previously published: Die Skulptomalerei Alexander Archipenkos. "Der Ararat" no. 5—6: 33–34 Mar. 1920.*

M 11 a   SCHACHT, ROLAND. Alexander Archipenko. Berlin, Verlag Der Sturm, 1924. *Sturmbilderbuch II.*

M 12   SOFFICI, ARDENGO. Alessandro Archipenko. *In his* Trenta Artisti moderna. p. 305–308 Firenze, Valecchi, 1950.

M 13   WIESE, ERICH. Alexander Archipenko. 9 p. plus 32 ill. Leipzig, Klinkhardt & Biermann, 1923 (Junge Kunst, Bd. 40).

FORMES

Poem by Arp. From bibl. M 16, no. 11–12, 1950.

LES FORMES QUE J'AI CREEES DANS LES ANNEES 1927 A 1948 ET QUE J'AI NOMMEES

DES FORMES COSMIQUES,

ETAIENT DES FORMES VASTES,

QUI DEVAIENT ENGLOBER UNE MULTITUDE DE FORMES, TELLES PAR EXEMPLE : L'ŒUF,

L'ORBITE PLANETAIRE,

LE COURS DES PLANETES,

LE BOURGEON,

LA TETE HUMAINE,

LES SEINS,

LA COQUILLE,

LES ONDES,

LA CLOCHE.

JE CONSTELLAIS CES FORMES

« SELON LES LOIS DU HASARD ».

J'OBEISSAIS INCONSCIEMMENT A UNE LOI QUI AUJOURD'HUI EST DEVENUE UNE LOI SUPREME.

JE DONNAIS CE NOM « SELON LES LOIS DU HASARD »

NAIVEMENT, SANS SAVOIR QUE C'ETAIT UNE LOI QUI ENGLOBAIT LA LOI DE CAUSE ET EFFET SELON PLANCK.

CES FORMES COSMIQUES SEMBLAIENT MUETTES

PARCE QUE LEUR LANGAGE DEPASSE LES ONDES PERCEPTIBLES POUR L'HOMME.

EN VISITANT LA CATHEDRALE DE CHARTRES, EN 1948,

LA PLENITUDE, L'AUGUSTE GRANDEUR ET LA PERFECTION DES VITRAUX

QU'AUCUN ART NE POURRA JAMAIS DEPASSER,

M'ENGAGEAIENT A REFLECHIR SUR LES LIMITES DE NOS FORCES ET A REDUIRE

LE REGNE DE NOTRE DEPLOIEMENT.

JE CHOISISSAIS DONC A PARTIR DE LA, DES FORMES PLUS PRIMITIVES,

DES FORMES PARTIELLEMENT RECTILIGNES,

QUI PERMETTAIENT D'ATTIRER, D'INTERCEPTER, D'INCLURE DES MOUVEMENTS ET DES IDEES SE RAPPROCHANT DE

L'IMAGE HUMAINE.

JEAN ARP.
1950

Armitage

M 13 a Exhibition at Gimpel Fils. *Architectural Review* 113: 133 ill. Feb. 1953.

M 13 b SCHAEFER, BERTHA, GALLERY. Kenneth Armitage: First American showing, Mar. 22—Apr. 15. New York, 1954. *Illustrated checklist with biographical release. Reviewed Art Digest 28: 18 Mar. 15 1954, Art News 53: 47 Apr. 1954.*

M 13 c YALE UNIVERSITY. ART GALLERY. Object and image in modern art and poetry. [36] p. ill. 1954. *Preface by G. H. Hamilton for Apr.—June collective show on "aspects of the poetic principle". Includes Armitage and others.*

Arp

M 14 ARP, JEAN. Notes from a diary. *Transition* no. 21: 190–194 Mar. 1932.

M 15 ARP, JEAN. On my Way: Poetry and Essays 1912 . . . 1947. 147 p. ill. New York, Wittenborn, Schultz, 1948. *Preface by R. Motherwell, editor. Extensive bibliography by B. Karpel. Documents of Modern Art, 6.*

M 16 [Arp]. *Art d'Aujourd'hui* no. 10—11: [34–41] ill. May—June 1950. *Includes illustrations, portrait, texts by Arp, article by C. Estienne and M. Seuphor.*

M 17 Arp, poète et sculpteur. *Cahiers d'Art* 28: 76–81 ill. 1953.

Manifesto by Boccioni
From bibl. L 49.

Manifesto della Scultura futurista —

(handwritten draft manuscript, largely illegible)

M 18 BILLE, EJLER. Hans Arp; Udtaleser af Hans Arp. *In his* Picasso, Surrealisme, Abstrakt Kunst. p. 169–175 ill. Copenhagen, Helios, 1945.

M 19 CROXLEŸ, HUBERT. Quelques considerations sur le problème plastique tel qu'il se pose pour Hans Arp. *Centaure* 3: 36–38 ill. 1928. *Also another article in "Cahiers d'Art" 3 no. 5—6: 229–230 1928.*

M 20 EINSTEIN, CARL. L'enfance néolithique. *Documents* 2 no. 8: 35–43 ill. 1930.

M 21 GIEDION-WELCKER, CAROLA. Contemporary sculptors, IV: Jean Arp. *Horizon* 14 no. 82: 232–239 ill. Oct. 1946.

M 21a GIEDION-WELCKER, CAROLA. Urelement und Gegenwart in der Kunst Hans Arps. *Werk* 39: 164–172 ill. May 1952.

M 21b HUELSENBECK, Richard. Die Arbeiten von Hans Arp. *Dada* 3: 7 Dec. 1918. *A signed English translation is deposited in the Museum of Modern Art Library, N.Y.*

Baldessari

M 22 Breda, an experiment in exhibition design. *Graphis* 7 no. 37: 368–371 ill. 1951. *With German and French texts by C. Bianconi.*

M 22a Design for industry: architecture as sculpture. *Architectural Record* 112: 18 ill. Oct. 1952. *Luciano Baldessari and Mariello Grisotti on the La Breda company's building at the 1952 fair at Milan.*

M 23   Pavillons de la Société Breda à la foire de Milan. *Architecture d'Aujourd'hui* 24: 74–77 ill. July 1953.

Beothy

M 23a BÉOTHY, ÉTIENNE. L'abstraction et la qualité spécifique de l'homme. *Abstraction Création, Art Non Figuratif* no. 4: 4 ill. 1935. *Additional statements: no. 1: 4 1932, no. 2: 3 1933, no. 3: 4 1934, no. 5: 3 1936.*

M 23b BÉOTHY, ÉTIENNE. La conquête de la réalité. *Réalités Nouvelles* no. 1: 12 ill. 1947. *Additional statements: "Rythme-plastique". no. 4: 5 ill. 1950; also no. 5: 5 ill. 1951.*

M 23c BÉOTHY, ÉTIENNE. L'espace-temps. *Art d'Aujourd'hui* 2 no. 5: 10 ill. Apr.—May 1951.

M 23d BÉOTHY, ÉTIENNE. Fonctionnalisme et eurythmie. *Formes et Vie* no. 1: 14–17 1951. *English translation p. 17.*

M 23e DEGAND, LÉON. Les rythmes plastiques de Béothy. *Art et Décoration* 10: 37–40 ill. 1948.

M 23f GINDERTAEL, R. V. E. Béothy. *In* Témoignages pour l'Art Abstrait. p. 22–27 ill. Paris, Art d'Aujourd' hui, 1952.

Bill

M 24   BILL, MAX. La costruzione concreta e il dominio della spazio. *Domus* no. 210: 18–21 ill. June 1946.

M 25   BILL, MAX. The mastery of space. *XXe Siècle* 2 no. 1: [51–54] ill. 1939.

M 26   BILL, MAX. Über konkrete Kunst. *Das Werk* 25: 250–254 Aug. 1938.

M 27   d'AGUINO, FLAVIO. Max Bill, o inteligente iconoclasta. *Habitat* 3 no. 12: 34–35 ill. Sept. 1953. *With complete English translation.*

M 28   FREIBURG IM BREISGAU. KUNSTVEREIN. Max Bill, Julius Bissier, G. Vantongerloo. p. [1–5] ill. 1951.

M 29   KAISER, HANS. "Continuita" di Max Bill. *Domus* no. 223—225: 40–43 ill. Oct.—Dec. 1947.

M 30   KÁLLAI, E. Zu den Arbeiten von Max Bill. *Plastique* no. 5: 13–15 ill. 1939.

M 31   ROGERS, ERNESTO. Max Bill. *Magazine of Art* 46: 226–230 ill. May 1953.

M 32   SCHMIDT, GEORG. Max Bill. *XXe Siècle* (n. s.) no. 1: 73–74 June 1951.

M 33   SCHMIDT, GEORG. Max Bill's "Kontinuität". *Das Werk* 35 no. 3: 76–77 ill. Mar. 1948.

Bloc

M 34   ALVARD, JULIEN. André Bloc. *In* Témoignages pour l'Art Abstrait 1952. p. 28–35 ill. Paris, Art d'Aujourd'hui, 1952.

M 35   DEGAND, LÉON. A. Bloc. *Art d'Aujourd'hui* 3 no. 1: 4 ill. Dec. 1951. *Another article, no. 5: 21 Dec. 1949.*

M 36   DEGAND, LÉON. Antologia di Spazio: André Bloc. *Spazio* no. 7: 47–48 ill. Dec. 1952—Apr. 1953.

M 37   DELAHAUT & SEAUY, J. Exposition André Bloc à Bruxelles. *Art d'Aujourd'hui* 4 no. 1: 25 ill. Jan. 1953.

M 37a GUÉGUEN, PIERRE. André Bloc. [48] p. ill. Boulogne, Seine, Collection Espace, 1954.

Boccioni

M 38   BOCCIONI, UMBERTO. Estetica e Arte futuriste. 193 p. Milano, Il Balcone, 1946. *Reprints main text of bibl. M 41.*

*M 39 BOCCIONI, UMBERTO. Manifeste technique de la sculpture futuriste, 11 avril 1912. *Cahiers d'Art* 25: 50–61 1950.

M 40   BOCCIONI, UMBERTO. Opera Completa. Foligno, Campitelli, 1927.

*M 41 BOCCIONI, UMBERTO. Pittura, Scultura futuriste (Dinamismo plastico). 469 p. plus 51 pl. Milano, Ed. Futuriste di "Poesia", 1914.

M 42   ARGAN, GIULIO CARLO. Umberto Boccioni. Scelta degli Scritti, Regestri, Bibliografia e Catalogo delle Opere a cura di Maurizio Calvesi. 77 p. plus 80 ill. Roma, DeLuca, 1953.

M 43   COQUIOT, GUSTAVE. Boccioni. *In* his Cubistes, Futuristes, Passéistes. p. 205–237 ill. Paris, Ollendorf, 1914 (also 1923).

M 44   PASTONCHI, FRANCESCO. Boccioni. *Cahiers d'Art* 25 no. 1: 33–44 ill. 1950.

M 45   SARFATTI, MARGHERITA G. Umberto Boccioni. *Vita d'Arte* 16: 41–69 ill. 1917.

M 46   VALSECCI, MARCO. Umberto Boccioni. 8 p. plus 12 pl. Venezia, Cavallino, 1950.

Bodmer

M 47   BODMER, WALTER. [Statement]. *In* Premier Bilan de l'Art actuel. p. 282 Paris, 1953. *Biographical notes, portrait (bibl. A 24).*

M 48   BERN. KUNSTHALLE. Calder, Léger, Bodmer, Leuppi. p. 6–7 ill. 1947. *Preface by W. Rüdlinger for May exhibit; biographical statement.*

M 49   NETTER, M. Bilder und Drahtplastiken. *Werk* no. 36: 195–199 ill. June 1949.

M 50   SCHMIDT, GEORG. Walter Bodmer. *Plastique* no. 5: 20–21 ill. 1939.

Bourdelle

M 51   BOURDELLE, ÉMILE-ANTOINE. La Matière et l'Esprit dans l'Art. 90 p. Paris, Presses Litteraires de France, 1952.

M 52   BOURDELLE, ÉMILE-ANTOINE. L'Oeuvre d'Antoine Bourdelle, avec un Commentaire technique par l'Artiste et une Autobiographie. 6 fascicules ill. Paris, Librairie de France, n. d. [193?]. *Includes 43 p. of texts, 16 colorplates, numerous plates.*

M 53   BOURDELLE, ÉMILE-ANTOINE. La Sculpture et Rodin. 236 p. ill. Paris, Émile-Paul, 1937.

M 54 BASEL. KUNSTHALLE. Antoine Bourdelle, 1861–1929; Giovanni Giacometti, 1868–1933. 32 p. ill. 1952. *Bibliography, p. 26.*

M 55 DROUIN, RENÉ, GALLERY. Antoine Bourdelle. [8] p. ill. Paris, 1942. *Lists 37 sculptures, 25 "objets de vitrine". Introduction by Maurice Denis.*

M 56 FONTAINAS, ANDRÉ. Bourdelle. 64 p. ill. Paris, Rieder, 1930.

M 57 LORENZ, PAUL. Bourdelle, Sculptures et Dessins. ill. Paris, Rombaldi, 1947.

M 58 READ, HELEN A. Emile Antoine Bourdelle. *The Arts* 8: 184–205 ill. Oct. 1925.

M 59 RONNEBECK, ARNOLD. Bourdelle speaks for himself. *The Arts* 8: 206–222 ill. Oct. 1924.

M 59a VARENNE, GASTON. Bourdelle par Lui-Même. Paris, Fasquelle, 1937.

Bourgeois

M 60 BOURGEOIS, LOUISE. Natural History. *In* Porter, David, ed. Personal Statement: Painting Prophecy 1950. p. [9] [Washington, D. C., David Porter Gallery] 1945.

M 60a BOURGEOIS, LOUISE. [Statement]. *Design Quarterly* (Minneapolis) no. 30: 18 ill. 1954. *Also biographical note.*

M 61 Artist's Sessions at Studio 35 (1950). *In* Modern Artists in America; First Series. p. 12, 17. New York, Wittenborn, Schultz [1951].

M 61a BEWLEY, MARIUS. An introduction to Louise Bourgeois. *Tiger's Eye* no. 7: 89–92 ill. Mar. 1949.

M 62 BOURGEOIS, LOUISE. *Magazine of Art* 41: 307 ill. Dec. 1948.

Brancusi

M 63 BRANCUSI, CONSTANTIN. [Texts]. *This Quarter* no. 1: 235–237 plus 44 ill. 1925. *Special Brancusi section of the "Art Supplement". Extracts frequently reprinted.*

M 64 BRUMMER GALLERY. Brancusi Exhibition, Nov. 17–Dec. 15. [46] p. ill. New York, 1926.

M 65 DREYFUS, A. Constantin Brancusi. *Cahiers d'Art* 2: 69–74 ill. 1927.

M 66 GIEDION-WELCKER, CAROLA. Constantin Brancusi. *Horizon* 19 no. 11: 193–202 Mar. 1949.

M 67 GIEDION-WELCKER, CAROLA. Brancusi. *Magazine of Art* 42: 290–295 ill. 1949.

M 68 GIEDION-WELCKER, CAROLA. Constantin Brancusis Weg. *Das Werk* 35: 321–331 ill. Oct. 1948.

M 69 M......., M....... Constantin Brancusi, a summary of many conversations. *The Arts* 4: 15–17 ill. July 1923. *A resumé of "ideas suggested". Plates, p. 18–29.*

M 70 PALEOLOG, V. G. C. Brancusi. Bucharest, 1947.

M 71 POUND, EZRA. Brancusi. *The Little Review* Autumn Number p. 3–7 plus 24 pl. 1921.

M 72 RICH, DANIEL. Constantin Brancusi. *In* Chicago. Art Institute. 20th Century Art, from the Louise and Walter Arensberg Collection. p. 19–23, 25, 34–42 ill. 1949.

M 73 VITRAC, ROGER. Constantin Brancusi. *Cahiers d'Art* 4: 382–396 ill. 1929.

M 74 ZORACH, WILLIAM. The sculpture of Constantin Brancusi. *The Arts* 9: 143–150 ill. Mar. 1926.

Braque

M 75 BRAQUE, GEORGES. Propos de Georges Braque. *Verve* 7 no. 27–28: 71–82 ill. 1952.

M 76 FUMET, STANISLAS. Sculptures de Braque. 14 p. plus 35 pl. Paris, Damase, 1951.

M 77 GALLATIN, ALBERT E. Georges Braque, Essay and Bibliography. 26 p. plus 12 pl. New York, Wittenborn, 1943.

M 78 NEW YORK. MUSEUM OF MODERN ART. Georges Braque, by Henry R. Hope. 170 p. ill. 1949. *Exhibition monograph "in collaboration with the Cleveland Museum of Art". Preface by J. Cassou. Bibliography by H. B. Muller includes extensive list of catalogs.*

M 79 ZERVOS, CHRISTIAN. Georges Braque et le développement du cubisme. *Cahiers d'Art* 7 no. 1–2: 13–27 ill. 1932. *Also special Braque number, v. 8 no. 1–2, 1933.*

Burckhardt

M 79a BURCKHARDT, CARL. Rodin und das plastische Problem. 98 p. ill. Paris, 1937.

M 80 BARTH, W. Carl Burckhardt, der Bildhauer und Maler. Zürich, Füssli, 1936.

M 80a SCHMIDT, GEORG. Carl Burckhardt und Albert Müller. *Werk* 41 no. 2: 61–68 ill. Feb. 1954.

M 80b VOLLMER, HANS. Allgemeines Lexikon der bildenden Künstler des XX. Jahrhunderts. V. 1, p. 352–353. Leipzig, Seemann, 1953. *Bibliography.*

Butler

M 81 BUTLER, REG. [Statement]. In Premier Bilan de l'Art actuel. p. 284. 1953. *Biographical note; portrait. (See bibl. A 24).*

M 82 BUTLER, REG. & HEPWORTH, BARBARA. [Broadcast, Artists on Art, 3d programme, Aug. 26, 1952.] [London, BBC 1952?] *Probably available only as script.*

M 83 GASSER, HANS. Der englische Plastiker Reg Butler. *Werk* 38 no. 6: 189–192 ill. June 1951.

M 84 LONDON. TATE GALLERY. The Unknown Political Prisoner; International Sculpture Competition sponsored by the Institute of Contemporary Arts [24] p. ill. London, 1953. *Insert includes text by Butler on his prize-winning work.*

M 85 MELVILLE, R. Personages in iron: work of Reg Butler. *Architectural Review* 108: 147–151 ill. Sept. 1950.

M 86 SYLVESTER, A. D. B. El joven escultor ingles: Cotterell Butler. *Espacio* (Lima) no. 4: 12 ill. Apr. 1950. *Modified text, with added illustrations, in "Espacios" (Mexico) no. 4 Jan. 1950.*

Calder

M 87 CALDER, ALEXANDER. [Statement]. *Tiger's Eye* no. 4: 74 June 1948. *For a series "The ides of art — 14 sculptors write".*

M 88 CALDER, ALEXANDER. What abstract art means to me. *Museum of Modern Art Bulletin (New York)* 18 no. 3: 8 Spring 1951.

M 89 BUFFET-PICABIA, GABRIELLE. Sandy Calder, forgeron lunaire. *Cahiers d'Art* 20—21: 324–333 ill. 1946. *Supplemented by p. 334–335: L'objet de Calder, par Georges Mounin.*

M 90 CARRÉ, LOUIS, GALLERY. Alexander Calder: Mobiles, Stabiles, Constellations. [44] p. ill. Paris, 1946. *Major exhibition, Oct. 25—Nov. 16. Extracts from Sweeney monograph (1943). Essay by J.-P. Sartre "Les mobiles de Calder", p. 8–19, frequently reprinted.*

M 91 CLAPP, TALCOTT. Calder. *Art d'Aujourd'hui* no. 11—25: [2–11] ill. June 1950. *Supplemented by p. 12: "Notes sur Calder", par Léon Degand.*

M 92 COAN, ELLEN S. The mobiles of Alexander Calder. *Vassar Journal of Undergraduate Studies.* 15: 1–18 ill. May 1944.

M 93 SARTRE, JEAN-PAUL. Existentialist on mobilist; Calder's newest works judged by France's newest philosopher. *Art News* 46 no. 10: 22–23, 55–56 ill. Dec. 1947.

M 94 SCHILLER, RONALD. Calder. *In* Portfolio, the Annual of the Graphic Arts. [16] p. ill. Cincinnati, Zebra Press; New York, Duell, Sloane & Pearce, 1951.

M 95 SCHNEIDER-LENGYEL, I. Alexander Calder, der Ingenieur-Bildhauer. *Prisma* 1 no. 6: 14–15 ill. Apr. 1947.

M 96 SWEENEY, JAMES J. Alexander Calder. 2. ed. rev. 80 p. ill. New York, Museum of Modern Art, 1951. *First edition issued 1943 as exhibition catalog. Bibliography by B. Karpel.*

M 97 SZITTYA, EMIL. Alexander Calder. *Kunstblatt* 13: 185–186 June 1929.

Callery

M 98 BUCHHOLZ GALLERY. Mary Callery [exhibitions]. 4 catalogs New York, Curt Valentin, 1944—1952. *Shows held Oct. 9—28 1944, Apr. 29—May 24 1947, Mar. 14—Apr. 2 1950, Oct. 21—Nov. 15 1952. Zervos article from "Cahiers d'Art" partially translated in 1950 catalog; Henry McBride preface in 1952 catalog.*

M 99 GINDERTAEL, R.V. Mary Callery. *Art d'Aujourd'hui* no. 4: 4 ill. Nov. 1949. *Review of Galerie Mai exhibition.*

M 100 MILLER COMPANY (Meriden, Conn.). The Miller Company Collection of Abstract Art: Painting toward Architecture. Text by Henry-Russell Hitchcock. p. 114–116 ill. New York, Duell, Sloane & Pearce, 1948.

M 101 Nouvelles Sculptures de Mary Callery. *Cahiers d'Art* v. 20–21: 303–306 1945–46. *Illustrations only.*

Chadwick

M 101a ALLOWAY, L. Britain's new iron age. *Art News* 52: 68 ill. June 1953.

M 102 Painting and sculpture collections, July 1, 1951 to May 31, 1953. *Museum of Modern Art Bulletin (New York)* 20 no. 3—4: 5, 40, 42 ill. Summer 1953.

M 102a SORRELL, M. Mobiles of Lynn Chadwick. *Studio* 144: 76–79 ill. Sept. 1952.

M 103 THWAITES, JOHN A. Notes on some young English sculptors. *Art Quarterly* 15 no. 3: 234–241 ill. Autumn 1952.

Daumier

M 104 BERLIN. DEUTSCHE AKADEMIE DER KÜNSTE. Honoré Daumier: Die Parlamentarier, Die Büsten der Deputierten der Juli-Monarchie. Ausstellung. 28 p. plus 47 pl. 1952. *Konrad Kaiser: Honoré Daumiers Büsten, p. 7–18.*

M 105 BOUVY, EUGÈNE. Trente-Six Bustes de H. Daumier. ill. Paris, Le Garrec, 1932.

M 106 GOBIN, MAURICE. Daumier, Sculpteur, 1808—1879. Avec un Catalogue raisonné et illustré de l'Oeuvre sculpté. 336 p. pl. Genève, Cailler, 1952. *Illustrations, p. 165–328. Numerous footnotes.*

M 107 GOBIN, MAURICE. Daumier, sculpteur. *Art — Documents* no. 28: 14–15 ill. Jan. 1953.

M 108 SCHEIWILLER, GIOVANNI. Honoré Daumier. 35 p. ill. Milano, Hoepli, 1936. *Bibliography, p. 22–35.*

Degas

*M 109 DEGAS, HILAIRE. Letters, ed. by Marcel Guérin. London, Oxford (& Cassirer), 1947. *Also Grasset edition (Paris, 1931).*

M 110 BERN. KUNSTMUSEUM. Degas, 25. November 1951 bis 13. Januar 1952. [36] p. ill. 1952. *252 works. Texts by Huggler, Valéry, Schmalenbach.*

M 111 BOREL, PIERRE. Les Sculptures Inédites de Degas. 12 p. plus pl. Genève, Cailler, 1949.

M 112 HAUSENSTEIN, W. Degas der Plastiker. *Ganymed* 4. 273–276 plus 6 pl. 1922. *Also article in "Kunst für Alle", Jan. 1925.*

M 113 OSTY, LEIF. Omkring Degas' Skulpturer. *Kunst og Kultur* 32 no. 2: 95–106 ill. 1949.

M 114 REWALD, JOHN, ed. Works in Sculpture, a complete Catalogue. 124 p. 112 pl. New York, Pantheon, 1944. *Plates, p. 33–144. Bibliography lists sculpture exhibitions, 1921—1945.*

M 115 RIVIÈRE, GEORGES. Mr. Degas, Bourgeois de Paris, ill. Paris, Floury, 1935.

M 115a VOLLMER, HANS. Allgemeines Lexikon der bildenden Künstler des XX. Jahrhunderts. V. 1, p. 531–532. Leipzig, Seemann, 1953. *Extensive bibliography.*

M 116 ZORACH, WILLIAM. The sculpture of Edgar Degas. *The Arts* 8: 263–265 Nov. 1925.

Doesburg

M 117 DOESBURG, THÉO Van. [About the art of sculpture.] *De Eenheid* [no. ?] 1916. *Dutch article in Mrs. Van Doesburg's archives at Meudon.*

M 118 DOESBURG, THÉO Van. Classique — Baroque — Moderne. 31 p. plus 17 pl. Anvers, De Sikkel; Paris, Rosenberg, 1921. *Translation of 1920 De Sikkel edition.*

M 119 DOESBURG, THÉO Van. The end of art. *De Stijl* 7 no. 73—74: 29–30 1926.

*M 120 DOESBURG, THÉO Van. Grundbegriffe der neuen gestaltenden Kunst. 40 p. plus 32 ill. München, Bauhaus Verlag, 1925. *Translated from Dutch edition of 1919.*

M 121 DOESBURG, THÉO Van. The progress of the modern movement in Holland. *Ray* no. 2: [11–13] ill. 1927.

M 122 DOESBURG, THÉO Van. Zur elementaren Gestaltung. *G* (Berlin) no. 1: 1–2 ill. July 1921.

M 123 NEW YORK. MUSEUM OF MODERN ART LIBRARY [Van Doesburgs Records, 1922—1949]. Unpaged [1950]. *Includes unique documentation assembled through the cooperation of Mrs. van Doesburg, plus checklist for dissertation by Mr. Scollar (Columbia Univ., N.Y.). Typescripts include: Quelques notices biographiques sur le peintre et architecte Théo van Doesburg [4 p.]. — Van Doesburg material, 1922—1931, in the library of Mrs. Theo van Doesburg, Meudon, Paris [4 p.]. — Bibliography of published writings of Theo van Doesburg by Irwin Scollar, New York, 1949 [11 p.], presumably a complete listing up to Apr. 1, 1949.*

M 124 PRISMA DER KUNSTEN. Théo van Doesburg. [32] p. ill. Zeist, Holland, De Torentrans, 1936. *Special memorial issue, May 1936, p. 85–116. Article by P. Citroën, Doesburg's "Manifeste sur l'art Concrete" and extracts (1912—1929); catalog of Stedelijk Museum exhibit, May 2—31, 1936, at Amsterdam. Biographical and bibliographical note.*

M 125 SCHWITTERS, KURT. Théo Van Doesburg and Dada (1931). *In* The Dada Painters and Poets. p. 275–276 New York, Wittenborn, Schultz, 1951. *From the German, "De Stijl", Jan. 1932. Bibliography on Doesburg, p. 354–356.*

M 126 WICHMAN, ERICH. Monsieur Théo van Doesburg et son Style. *In his* Erich Wichman tot 1920. p. 201-206. Amsterdam, Broekmans, 1920.

Duchamp

M 127 DUCHAMP, MARCEL. Boîte-en-Valise . . . 69 principals Oeuvres de Marcel Duchamp. New York, 1941—1942. *Reproductions in miniature; limited edition in leather case.*

M 128 DUCHAMP, MARCEL. A complete reversal of art opinions by Marcel Duchamp iconoclast. *Arts and Decoration* 5 no. 11: 427–428, 442 Sept. 1915.

M 129 CHICAGO. ART INSTITUTE. 20th Century Art from the Louise and Walter Arensberg Collection. p. 11–18 ill. 1949. *Article by Katherine Kuh.*

M 129a KRASNE, BELLE. A Marcel Duchamp profile. *Art Digest* 26 no. 8: 11, 24 ill. Jan. 15, 1952.

M 130 LEIRIS, MICHEL. Arts et métiers de Marcel Duchamp. *Fontaine* no. 54: 188–193 ill. 1946.

M 131 MOTHERWELL, ROBERT, ed. The Dada Painters and Poets. p. 136–140, 185–186, 207–211, 255–263, 306–315, 356–357 et passim ill. New York, Wittenborn, Schultz, 1951. *Bibliography. Includes articles by Janis and others from View Magazine.*

M 132 VIEW. [Marcel Duchamp Number.] 54 p. ill. New York, 1945. *No. 1, Series 5, Mar. 1945, also issued in special autographed edition.*

M 133 YALE UNIVERSITY. ART GALLERY. Collection of the Societé Anonyme. p. 148–150 ill. New Haven, Conn., 1950. *Text by K. S. Dreier. Biography, exhibition list, bibliography.*

Duchamp-Villon

M 133a DUCHAMP-VILLON, RAYMOND. Variations de la connaissance pendant le travail de l'art. *[Unpublished manuscript, n. d.].*

*M 134 DUCHAMP-VILLON, RAYMOND. Raymond Duchamp-Villon, Sculpteur. 85 p. ill. Paris, Povolozsky, 1924. *A book of reproductions; preface by Walter Pach, p. 11.*

M 135 APOLLINAIRE, GUILLAUME. Duchamp-Villon. *In his* The Cubist Painters, Aesthetic Meditations 1913. p. 48-50. New York, Wittenborn, Schultz, 1949.

M 136 DORIVAL, B. Raymond Duchamp-Villon au Musée d'Art moderne. *Musées de France* no. 3: 64–68 ill. Apr. 1949.

M 137 HAMILTON, GEORGE H. Duchamp, Duchamp-Villon, Villon. *Bulletin of the Associates in Fine Arts at Yale University* 13 no. 2: 1–4 Mar. 1945. *Introduction to joint exhibition. Bibliography.*

M 138 McBRIDE, H. Duchamps du monde, family exhibition at Rose Fried Gallery. *Art News* 51: 33–35 ill. Mar. 1952.

M 139 PACH, WALTER. A Sculptor's Architecture. New York, Association of American Painters and Sculptors, 1913. *An Armory show pamphlet.*

M 140 PACH, WALTER. Duchamp-Villon. *Formes* no. 15: 84–85 May 1931.

*M 141 PIERRE, GALERIE. Sculptures de Duchamp-Villon, 1876—1918. Paris, 1931. *June exhibition; preface by A. Salmon.*

Ernst

M 142 BOSQUET, JOE & TAPIÉ, MICHEL. Max Ernst. 61 p. ill. Paris, Drouin, 1950.

M 143 CAHIERS D'ART. Max Ernst: Oeuvres de 1919 à 1936. [110] p. ill. Paris, Cahiers d'Art, 1937. *An anthology of numerous articles and plates from the magazine.*

M 144 ERNST, MAX. Beyond Painting, and other Writings by the Artist and his Friends. 204 p. ill. New York, Wittenborn, Schultz, 1948. *Preface by R. Motherwell. Bibliography by B. Karpel, p. 197–204.*

M 145 House at St. Martin d'Ardeche rebuilt and decorated by Max Ernst. *London Bulletin* no. 18—20: 23 June 1940. *Also illustrated in "Cahiers d'Art" 1939.*

M 146 HUGNET, GEORGES. Max Ernst. *Cahiers d'Art* no. 5—10: 140–145 ill. 1939. *A poem, supplemented by 10 illustrations of sculpture, p. 141–145.*

M 147 VIEW (MAGAZINE). Max Ernst. ill. New York, 1942. *Special number, v. 2 no. 1, Apr. 1942. Includes catalog of Valentine gallery show; bibliography.*

Giacometti Manuscript.
From bibl. G 24, no. 3, 1952.

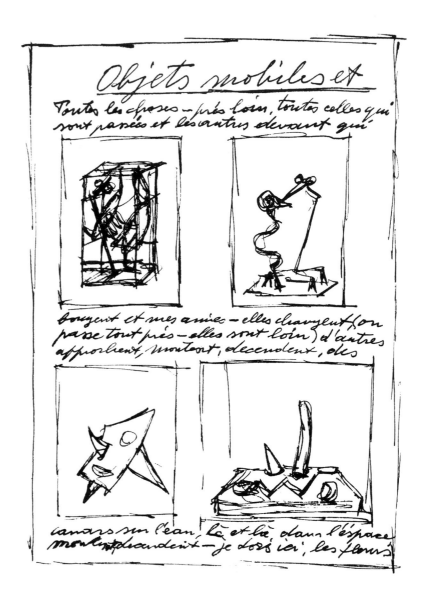

Ferber

M 147a FERBER, HERBERT. On sculpture and painting. *Tiger's Eye* no. 4: 75–76 June 1948. *See also no. 2: 44 1947.*

M 147b FITZSIMMONS, J. Artists put faith in new ecclesiastical art. *Art Digest* 26: 15, 23 ill. Oct. 15, 1951. *Ferber also reviewed in 22: 19 Jan. 1, 1948; 24: 14 Mar. 15 1950; 27: 16 May 1 1953.*

M 147c GOODNOUGH, R. Ferber makes a sculpture: "And the bush was not consumed". *Art News* 51: 40–43, 66 ill. Nov. 1952.

M 147d NEW YORK. MUSEUM OF MODERN ART. 15 Americans; ed. by D. C. Miller, with statement by the artists. p. 10, 11, 46 ill. 1952. *Also exhibited in their "Abstract Painting and Sculpture in America" p. 124, 150 ill. 1951.*

Freundlich

M 148 FREUNDLICH, OTTO. [Statement]. *Abstraction, Création, Art Non Figuratif* no. 2: 12 ill. 1933. *Also briefly in no 1: 13 1932.*

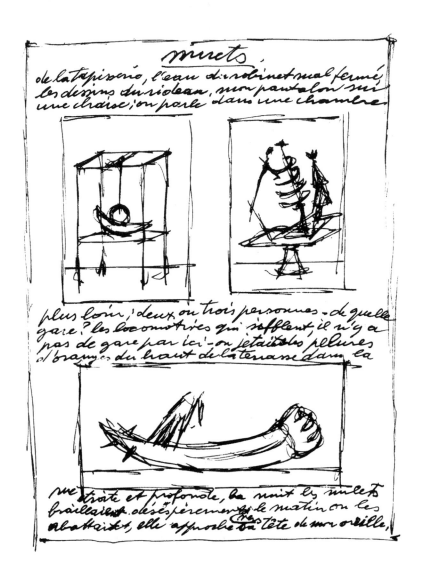

M 149 GINDERTAEL, R. V. Freundlich. *Art d'Aujourd'hui* 3 no. 7—8: 59–60 ill. Oct. 1952.

M 150 SEUPHOR, MICHEL. Otto Freundlich. *In his* L'Art Abstrait. p. 292–293 et passim ill. Paris, Maeght, 1949.

Gabo

M 151 GABO, NAUM. The Constructive Idea in Art. *In* Circle, International Survey of Constructive Art. Editors: J. L. Martin, Ben Nicholson, N. Gabo. p. 1–10 ill. London, Faber & Faber, 1937.

M 152 GABO, NAUM. L'Idée du Réalisme constructif. *In* Témoignages pour l'Art abstrait. p. 115-122. Paris, Art d'Aujourd'hui, 1952. *"Extraits d'une conférence faite à Yale University . . . 1948." Full text below.*

M 153 GABO, NAUM. A Retrospective View of Constructive Art. *In* Three Lectures on Modern Art. p. 65–87. New York, Philosophical Library, 1949. *So listed on title-page; chapter-title is "On Constructive Realism".*

M 154 GABO, NAUM. Toward a unity of the constructive arts. *Plus* no. 1: 3–6 ill. 1938. *Same as "Architectural Forum" 69: 455–458 Dec. 1938.*

M 155 GABO, NAUM & PEVSNER, ANTOINE. Auszug aus einem Brief. *Das Werk* 25 no. 8: 255 ill. Aug. 1938. *Similar formulation in "Réalités Nouvelles", no. 1, 1947.*

M 156 GABO, NAUM & READ, HERBERT. Constructive art, an exchange of letters. *Horizon* 10 no. 55: 57–65 ill. July 1944. *Also published in his* The Philosophy of Modern Art *(bibl. A 35).*

M 157 GOLDWATER, ROBERT & TREVES, MARCO. Artists on Art. p. 454-455. New York, Pantheon, 1945. *Extracts from "Realistic Manifesto" (1920); frequently printed in extracts.*

M 158 KÁLLAI, ERNST. Der Plastiker Gabo. *i10 (Internationale Revue)* 1 no. 7: 245–249 ill. 1927. *Supplemented by his* Der Raumplastiker Gabo. "*Das Neue Frankfurt*" 4 no. 1: 17–19 ill. 1930.

M 159 MATISSE, PIERRE, GALLERY. Gabo: Space and Kinetic Constructions, Apr. 21—May 16. [8] p. ill. 1953. *Introduction by G. H. Hamilton.*

M 160 NEW YORK. MUSEUM OF MODERN ART. Naum Gabo, Antoine Pevsner. Introduction by Herbert Read. Text by Ruth Olson and Abraham Chanin. 83 p. ill. 1948. "*Constructivism: The art of Naum Gabo and Antoine Pevsner*", *p. 7–13, also published in Read's* The Philosophy of Modern Art *(bibl. A 35). Detailed bibliography by H. B. Muller.*

M 161 SWEENEY, JAMES J. Construction unconstructible? Projects of N. Gabo. *Art News* 50: 34-35, 61–62 ill. Mar. 1951.

Giacometti

M 162 GIACOMETTI, ALBERTO. Mai 1920. *Verve* 7 no. 27—28: 33–34 ill. Dec. 1952.

M 163 GIACOMETTI, ALBERTO. Objets, mobiles et muets. *Le Surréalisme au Service de la Révolution* no. 3: 18–19 Dec. 1931. *Other articles and illustrations: no. 3: 18–19 1931, no. 5: 15, 44–45 May 1933.*

M 164 GIACOMETTI, ALBERTO. $1 + 1 = 3 \ldots$ [and] A letter from Giacometti. *Trans/formation* (N.Y.) 1 no. 3: 165–167 1953. *Letter reprinted from Matisse catalog (1948).*

M 165 GIACOMETTI, ALBERTO. Le rêve, le sphinx, et la mort de T. *Labyrinthe* no. 22—23: 12–13 ill. Dec. 1946.

M 166 BASEL, KUNSTHALLE. André Masson, Alberto Giacometti, 6. Mai bis 11. Juni. p. 18–20 1950.

M 167 BILLE, EJLER. Alberto Giacometti; "Palaeet" af Alberto Giacometti. *In his* Picasso, Surrealisme, Abstrakt Kunst. p. 176–184 ill. Copenhagen, Helios, 1945.

M 168 LEIRIS, MICHEL. Alberto Giacometti. *Documents* 1 no. 4: 209-214 ill. Sept. 1929.

M 169 LEIRIS, MICHEL. Thoughts around Alberto Giacometti. *Horizon* 19 no. 114: 111–117 ill. June, 1949. *Revised preface for Maeght exhibition (1951).*

M 170 LIMBOUR, GEORGES. Giacometti. *Magazine of Art* 41: 253–255 ill. Nov. 1948.

M 171 MATISSE, PIERRE, GALLERY. Alberto Giacometti, Exhibition of Sculptures, Paintings, Drawings (Jan. 19—Feb. 14). 47 p. ill. New York, 1948. *Preface by Sartre (bibl. M 173).*

M 172 PONGE, FRANCIS. Réflexions sur les statuettes, figures & peintures d'AlbertoGiacometti.*Cahiers d'Art* 26: 74–90 ill. 1951.

M 173 SARTRE, JEAN-PAUL. La recherche de l'absolu. *Les Temps Modernes* no. 28: 1153–1163 ill. Jan. 1948.

M 174 STAHLY, F. Der Bildhauer Alberto Giacometti. *Werk* 37: 181–185 June 1950.

M 175 VERONESI, GIULIA. Alberto Giacometti. *Emporium* 57 no. 7: 36–37 ill. July 1951.

M 176 WESCHER, HERTA. Giacometti: a profile. *Art Digest* 28 no. 5: 17, 28–29 ill. Dec. 1 1953.

M 177 ZERVOS, CHRISTIAN. Quelques notes sur les sculptures de Giacometti. *Cahiers d'Art* 7 no. 8—10: 337–342 ill. 1932.

Gilioli

M 177a BORDIER, R. La progressivité chez Gilioli. *Art d'Aujourd'hui* 5 no. 1: 23–24 ill. Feb. 1954. *Also p. 32 by H. Wescher.*

M 178 CHEVALIER, DENYS. Emile Gilioli. *Arts* no. 291: 5 ill. Dec. 29 1950.

M 179 GINDERTAEL, R. V. Emile Gilioli. *In* Témoignages pour l'Art abstrait. p. 130–136 ill. Paris. Art d'Aujourd'hui, 1952.

M 180 GINDERTAEL, R. V. Gilioli. *Art d'Aujourd'hui* no. 1: 14–15 Nov. 1953. *Biographical note, portrait.*

M 180 GOLDSCHEIDER, CÉCILIE. Gilioli. *In* Hamburg. Kunsthalle. Junge französische Plastik. p. 11, 38 1953.

M 181 S——, A——. Gilioli: [Monument aux déportés de l'Isère]. *Art d'Aujoud'hui* 1 no. 10—11: [25] ill. May—June 1950. *Also illustrated in "Architecture d'Aujourd'hui" 20: XXXI July 1950.*

Gonzalez

M 182 BRUGIÈRE, P.-G. Julio Gonzalez, les étapes de l'oeuvre. *Cahiers d'Art* 27 no. 1: 19–31 ill. July 1952.

M 183 DEGAND, LÉON. Julio Gonzalez, 1876—1942. *Art d'Aujourd'hui* no. 6: [16–20] ill. Jan. 1950.

M 184 FERNÁNDEZ, LUIS. El escultor Gonzalez. *A. C.* 2 no. 5: 30–31 ill. 1932.

M 185 JAKOVSKI, ANATOLE. Julio Gonzalez. *D'Aci d'Alla* 22 no. 179: 53 ill. Dec. 1934.

M 186 PARIS. MUSÉE NATIONAL D'ART MODERNE. Julio Gonzalez, Sculptures. 23 p. ill. Paris, Éd. des Musées nationaux, 1952.

M 187 PÉREZ ALFONSECA, RICARDO. Julio Gonzalez. Madrid. 1934. *Review by Pedro Garcia Cabrera in "Gaceta de Arte" no. 30 1934.*

M 188 RITCHIE, ANDREW C. Sculpture of the Twentieth Century. p. 29–30, 104–105, 164–167, 228 ill. New York, Museum of Modern Art, 1952.

Gris

M 189 KAHNWEILER, DANIEL-HENRY. Juan Gris, his Life and Work. 178 p. plus 113 pl. New York, Curt Valentin, 1947. *Translation of* Juan Gris, sa Vie, son

Oeuvre, ses Écrits. *(Paris, Gallimard, 1946). Chap. X: Sculptures, Drawings and Engravings. Detailed bibliography by H. B. Muller.*

M 190 YALE UNIVERSITY. ART GALLERY. Collection of the Société Anonyme. p. 59–60 New Haven, 1950. *Comment by M. Duchamp and G. Stein; biographical and bibliographical notes.*

Hajdu

M 190a SEUPHOR, MICHEL. Etienne Hajdu. ill. Paris, Presses Litteraires de France, 1950. *Collection Artistes de ce Temps.*

M 190b ZERVOS, CHRISTIAN. Note sur Etienne Hajdu. *Cahiers d' Art* 28 no. 1: 100–106 ill. June 1953.

Hare

M 191 HARE, DAVID. The spaces of the mind. *Magazine of Art* 43:48—53 ill. Feb. 1950.

M 192 KOOTZ, SAMUEL M., GALLERY. Women, a Collaboration of Artists and Writers. p. [33–35] ill. New York, Kootz Editions, 1948. *Portfolio, with Sartre essay: N-Dimensional Sculpture. The gallery also issued an illustrated checklist of 15 new sculptures from Cannes (Mar. 1952).*

M 193 MODERN ARTISTS IN AMERICA: First Series. p. 10, 12, 14, 16. New York, Wittenborn, Schultz [1951]. *Quotations from "Artist's Sessions at Studio 35".*

M 194 NEW YORK, MUSEUM OF MODERN ART. Fourteen Americans, ed. by Dorothy C. Miller. p. 24–27, 77 ill. 1946.

M 195 SARTRE, JEAN-PAUL. Sculptures à N dimensions. *Arts* no. 144 : 1 Dec. 12, 1947. *Part of text for Hare exhibit at Galerie Maeght (Paris).*

Hartung

M 196 HARTUNG, KARL. [Statement]. *In* Premier Bilan de l'Art actuel. p. 298. Paris, Le Soleil Noir, 1953. *Biographical note; portrait.*

M 197 BERLIN. HAUS AM WALDSEE. Karl Hartung, Ausstellung. 22 p. ill. 1952. *Preface by K. L. Skutsch.*

M 198 KESTNER-GESELLSCHAFT. Karl Hartung [14] p. ill. Hannover, 1953. *Text by A. Hentzen for May 28—June 28 show.*

M 199 ROSEN, GERD, GALLERY. Karl Hartung, Plastik und Graphik. n. p. Berlin, 1946—1948. *Exhibit pamphlets: Apr. 1946, signed H. H.; Mar. 1948, signed C. L.*

M 200 THWAITES, J. A. Karl Hartung. *Art d'Aujourd'hui* 4 no. 6: [10] ill. Aug. 1953.

Hausmann

M 201 HAUSMANN, RAOUL, ed. Der Dada. Nos. 1—3 Berlin, 1919—1920. *No. 1—2 edited solely by Hausmann, including many illustrations by him. No. 3 issued with imprint of Der Malik Verlag.*

M 202 HUELSENBECK, RICHARD. En avant Dada; eine Geschichte des Dadaismus 44 p. Hannover, etc., Steegemann, 1920. *Translated in bibl. M 205.*

M 203 HUGNET, GEORGES. L'Esprit dada dans la peinture. *Cahiers d'Art* 7 no. 6—7 : 281–285 1932. *"Part II: Berlin (1918—1922)." Translated in bibl. M 205.*

M 204 JANIS, SIDNEY, GALLERY. Dada, 1916—1923... April 15 to May 9. [1 sheet] New York, 1953. *Catalog lists nos. 113—122 by Raoul Hausmann, including sculpture.*

M 205 MOTHERWELL, ROBERT, ed. The Dada Painters and Poets. p. XXIV–XXV, 41–42, 45–46, 144–152, 254, 316, 361–362 et passim ill. New York, Wittenborn, Schultz, 1951. *Bibliography.*

Hepworth

M 206 HEPWORTH, BARBARA. [Statement]. *Abstraction, Création, Art Non Figuratif* no. 2: 6 ill. 1933. *Similar statements recorded in her monograph below, bibl. M 207.*

M 207 HEPWORTH, BARBARA. Barbara Hepworth, Carvings and Drawings. With an Introduction by Herbert Read. [30] p. plus [165] pl. London, Lund Humphries, 1952. *Bibliography, p. XII–XV, notes numerous statements, e. g. The Studio no. 12 1932, no. 643 1946; Unit One (London, 1934); Circle (London, 1937).*

M 208 HEPWORTH, BARBARA. [Sculpture, an Album of Photographs] [74] p. incl. 49 pl. 1940. *Unique album of original photographs, compiled and arranged by the artist. Bibliography. (Folio in the Museum of Modern Art Library, New York).*

M 209 BROWSE, LILLIAN, ed. Barbara Hepworth, Sculptress. 65 p. ill. London. Published for the Shenval Press by Faber & Faber, 1946. *Preface by W. Gibson; bibliography.*

M 210 FLEIG, HANS. Barbara Hepworth. *Schweizer Journal (Zürich)* 16 no. 9—10 ill. Sept.—Oct. 1950.

M 211 HODIN, J. P. Les oeuvres récentes de Barbara Hepworth. *Les Arts Plastiques* no. 5—6: 245–246 ill. 1948. *One of a series of articles, supplemented by "Werk" Apr. 1949; "Kroniek van Kunst en Kultuur" Apr. 1950; "Les Arts Plastiques" July—Aug. 1950; "Espacios" no. 7 1951, etc.*

M 212 LEWIS, DAVID. The sculptures of Barbara Hepworth. *Eidos* no. 2: 25–31 ill. Sept.—Oct. 1950.

M 213 RAMSDEN, E. H. The sculpture of Barbara Hepworth. *Polemic* no. 5: 33–34 ill. Sept.—Oct. 1946. *Supplemented by another article in "Horizon" 10 no. 42: 418–422 June 1943.*

M 213a WHITECHAPEL ART GALLERY, LONDON. Barbara Hepworth. 31 p. ill. 1954. *Carvings and drawings, 1927–1954; exhibited Apr. 8—June 6. Texts by the artist, B. Robertson, D. Baxandall.*

Jacobsen

M 214 JACOBSEN, ROBERT. [Statement]. *In* Premier Bilan de l'Art actuel. p. 300. Paris, Le Soleil Noir, 1953. *Biographical note; portrait.*

M 215 ALVARD, JULIEN. Robert Jacobsen. *In* Témoignages pour l'Art abstrait. p. 158–165 ill. Paris, Art d'Aujourd'hui, 1952.

M 216 DEGAND, LÉON. R. Jacobsen. *Art d'Aujourd'hui* 3 no. 1: 12 ill. Dec. 1951. *Also review in 4 no. 1: 26 Jan. 1953.*

M 217 DEWASNE, J. Jacobsen. *Art d'Aujourd'hui* no. 6: 23 ill. Jan. 1950. *Also "XXe Siècle" no. 4:78—79 Jan. 1954.*

M 217a DEWASNE, JEAN. Le Sculpteur: Robert Jacobsen. [46] p. ill. Copenhague, Galerie Denise René, 1951. *Bilingual edition: Billedhuggeren Robert Jacobsen, et Udvalg af hans seneste Arbejder. Collection Scripta no. 8.*

M 218 HULTEN, KARL G. Jacobsen. *Art d'Aujourd'hui* 4 no. 7: 23 ill. Oct.—Nov. 1953.

Lardera

M 219 LARDERA, BERTO. [Statement]. *In* Premier Bilan de l'Art actuel. p. 304. Paris, Le Soleil Noir, 1953. *Biographical note, portrait.*

M 220 COURTHION, PIERRE. Berto Lardera — ou la sculpture par plans. *Art d'Aujourd'hui* 5 no. 2–3: 60 ill. Mar.—Apr. 1954.

M 221 GINDERTAEL, R. V. Berto Lardera. *In* Témoignages pour l'Art abstrait. p. 174–181 ill. Paris, Art d'Aujourd'hui, 1952.

M 222 Sculptures à la Galerie Denise René. *Arts (Paris)* p. 4 Mar. 12 1948.

M 223 Scultura all'aperto. *Domus* no. 287: 38–39 ill. Oct.1953.

M 224 SEUPHOR, MICHEL. Lardera. [7] p. plus [31] ill. Milano, La Bibliofilia, 1953.

Lassaw

M 225 LASSAW, IBRAM. On inventing our own art. *In* American Abstract Artists, part VIII. New York, [The A. A. A. Association] 1938. *Biographical note.*

M 226 LASSAW, IBRAM. [Statement]. *Réalités Nouvelles* no. 4: 45 ill. 1950.

M 227 CAMPBELL, L. Lassaw makes a sculpture: clouds of magellan. *Art News* 53: 24–27, 66–67 mar. 1954.

M 227a KERN, WALTER. Ibram Lassaw. *Werk* 41 no. 8: 335 ill. Aug. 1954.

M 227b KOOTZ, SAMUEL M., GALLERY. Lassaw, new sculpture. [4] p. ill. New York, 1954. *Shown Oct. 23—Nov. 13; biographical notes; preface by J. Fitzsimmons.*

M 228 MODERN ARTISTS IN AMERICA: First Series. p. 11–12, 17 ill. New York, Wittenborn, Schultz [1951].

M 229 NEW YORK. MUSEUM OF MODERN ART. Abstract Painting and Sculpture in America, by A. C. Ritchie. p. 123, 131, 152 ill. New York, The Museum and Simon & Schuster, 1951.

Laurens

M 230 LAURENS, HENRI. [Témoignage: L'espace]. *XXe Siècle* (n. s.) no. 2: 73–74 ill. Jan. 1952.

M 231 BRUSSELS. PALAIS DES BEAUX ARTS. Henri Laurens. 29 p. ill. Bruxelles, Éd. de la Connaissance, 1949. *Preface by D.-H. Kahnweiler.*

M 232 GEORGE, WALDEMAR. Laurens et la pérennité des rythmes français. *Art et Industrie* 28 no. 26: 30–31 ill. 1953.

M 233 GIACOMETTI, ALBERTO. Henri Laurens. *Verve* 7 no. 27—28: 22 Dec. 1952. *Plates, p. 23–27.*

M 234 KOCHNITZKY, LÉON. Henri Laurens. *Horizon* 15 no. 85: 15–24 ill. Jan. 1947.

M 235 PARIS. MUSÉE NATIONAL D'ART MODERNE. Henri Laurens, 9 Mai—17 Juin. 14 p. ill. Paris, Ed. des Musées nationaux, 1951. *Text by Jean Cassou. Reviewed by L. Degand in "Art d'Aujourd'hui" June 1951, and C. Zervos in "Cahiers d'Art" v. 26 1951.*

M 236 LE POINT. Henri Laurens. 48 p. ill. Lanzac, 1946. *Special no. 33, July 1946; six essays by Raynal and others.*

M 237 RAYNAL, MAURICE. Laurens. *L'Esprit Nouveau* 1: 1152–1164 ill. 1920.

M 238 TAILLAUDIER, Y. Laurens talar om konst. *Konstrevy* 28 no. 1: 1–8 1952.

M 239 VERONESI, GIULIA. Henri Laurens e la restaurazione della forma. *Emporum* 57 no. 7: 2–8 ill. July 1951.

Le Corbusier

M 240 LE CORBUSIER. New World of Space. 128 p. ill. New York, Reynal & Hitchcock; Boston, Institute of Contemporary Art, 1948. *Includes previously published material. Foreword by F. S. Wight.*

M 241 LE CORBUSIER. Recherches pour conduire à une sculpture destinée à l'architecture. *Art d'Aujourd'hui* no. 2: 10–11 ill. July—Dec. 1949. *The Marseille façade in construction.*

M 242 LE CORBUSIER & JEANNERET, PIERRE. Oeuvre Complète. 5 vol. ill. Zürich, Girsberger, 1930—1953, New York, Wittenborn, 1953. *Texts in English, French, German. Vol.5, p. 225–230: "Art et poétique (art as architecture)".*

M 243 ARCHITECTURE D'AUJOURD'HUI. Le Corbusier, Numéro hors Série. 116 p. ill. Boulogne (Seine), 1948. *"19e année, avril 1948." Bibliography, p. 115.*

M 244 GAUTHIER, MAXIMILIEN. Le Corbusier. 286 p. Paris, Denoël, 1944. *"Catalogue sommaire", p. 275–283, lists exhibitions (1918—1938).*

M 245 PAPADAKI, STAMO, ed. Le Corbusier: Architect, Painter, Writer. 152 p. ill. New York, Macmillan, 1948. *Includes translations. Biographical and bibliographical notes, p. 149–152.*

Lehmbruck

M 246 HOFF, AUGUST. Wilhelm Lehmbruck, Seine Sendung und sein Werk. 117 p. 90 ill. Berlin, Rembrandt, 1936. *"Kurzes Werkverzeichnis", p. 115–117.*

M 247 MANNHEIM. STÄDTISCHE KUNSTHALLE. Wilhelm Lehmbruck, April—Mai. 34 p. ill. 1949. *Also shown at Düsseldorf, Stuttgart, etc. Lists 184 works; texts by W. Passarge & J. Meier-Graefe. Extensive bibliography.*

M 247a NEW YORK. MUSEUM OF MODERN ART. Sculpture [by] Wilhelm Lehmbruck [and] Aristide Maillol. 10 p. plus 12 pl. 1930. *Introduction by J(ere) A(bbott)*.

M 248 VALENTINER, W. R. The simile in sculptural composition. *Art Quarterly* 10 no. 4: 264 ill. Autumn 1947. *Comment on "The Kneeling Woman"*.

M 249 WESTHEIM, PAUL. Wilhelm Lehmbruck. 65 p. plus pl. Potsdam-Berlin, Kiepenheuer, 1919. *"Meditationen", p. 55–62. "Das Werk Lehmbrucks", p. 63–65. Second edition, 1922*.

Lipchitz

M 250 LIPCHITZ, JACQUES. The story of my Prometheus. *Art In Australia* 4 no. 6: 28–35 ill. June—Aug. 1942.

M 251 LIPCHITZ, JACQUES. The Drawings of Jacques Lipchitz. 3 p. plus 20 pl. New York, Buchholz Gallery, Curt Valentin, 1944.

M 252 LIPCHITZ, JACQUES. Twelve Bronzes by Jacques Lipchitz. 16 collotype plates with introductory note. New York, Curt Valentin, 1943.

M 253 BARON, JACQUES. Jacques Lipchitz. *Documents* 2 no. 1: 17–24 ill. 1930.

M 254 CASSOU, JEAN. Lipchitz. *Horizon* 14 no. 84: 367–370 ill. Dec. 1946.

M 255 GEORGE, WALDEMAR. Jacques Lipchitz. *Das Kunstblatt* 6: 58–64 ill. 1922.

M 256 GUÉGUEN, PIERRE. Jacques Lipchitz, ou l'histoire naturelle magique. *Cahiers d'Art* 7 no. 6—7: 252–258 ill. 1932.

M 257 PORTLAND. ART MUSEUM. Jacques Lipchitz, an Exhibition of his Sculpture and Drawings, 1914—1950. [32] p. ill. 1950. *Organized by Portland; exhibited later at San Francisco and Cincinnati. Text by A. C. Ritchie; statements by the artist; bibliography by H. B. Muller*.

M 258 RAYNAL, MAURICE. Jacques Lipchitz. 17 p. plus 72 pl. Paris, Bucher, 1947.

M 259 SCHWARTZBERG, MIRIAM B. The Sculpture of Jacques Lipchitz, a Dissertation. 136 p. plus 56 pl. New York [New York University] 1941. *Unpublished typescript; copy in Library of Museum of Modern Art, New York. Extensive bibliography, p. 105–132*.

Lippold

M 260 LIPPOLD, RICHARD. i to eye. *Tiger's Eye* no. 4: 79–80 June 1948.

M 261 LIPPOLD, RICHARD. Sculpture? *Magazine of Art* 44: 315–319 ill. Dec. 1951.

M 262 LIPPOLD, RICHARD. [Statement]. *In* Premier Bilan de l'Art actuel. p. 305. Paris, Le Soleil Noir, 1953. *Biographical note; portrait*.

M 263 LIPPOLD, RICHARD. Variation number seven: Full moon. *Arts & Architecture* 67: 22–23, 50 May 1950. *Another personal statement in Aug. 1947 number*.

M 264 BREUNING, MARGARET. Lippold's lunar magic. *Art Digest* 24 no. 12: 14 Mar. 15 1950.

M 265 Designing in space. *Craft Horizons* 12 no. 3: 34–36 ill. May—June 1952.

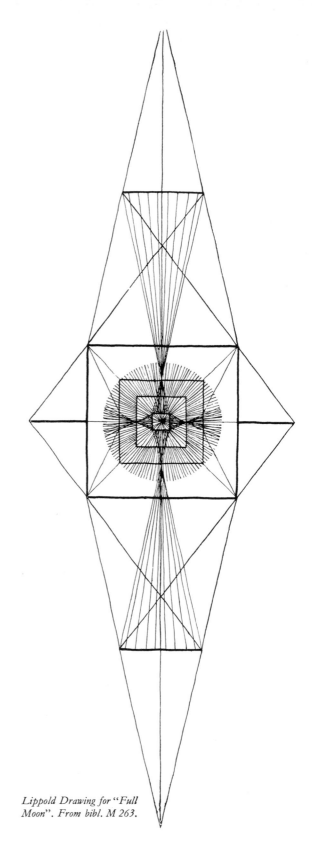

Lippold Drawing for "Full Moon". From bibl. M 263.

M 266 LONDON. INSTITUTE OF CONTEMPORARY ARTS. International sculpture competition: The Unknown Political Prisoner. insert and ill. 1953. *Exhibited at Tate Gallery. Special insert includes comment by Lippold on his winning design.*

M 267 NEW YORK. MUSEUM OF MODERN ART. 15 Americans, ed. by D. C. Miller. p. 27–29 ill. 1952. *Biographical note; personal statement.*

Maillol

M 268 ALBRIGHT ART GALLERY. Aristide Maillol . . . ed. by Andrew C. Ritchie. 128 p. ill. Buffalo, 1945. *Translations from "Sayings of Maillol". Bibliography by John Rewald.*

M 269 CLADEL, JUDITH. Aristide Maillol: sa Vie, son Oeuvre, ses Idées. [182] p. ill. Paris, 1937. *Bibliography, p. [177].*

M 270 DENIS, MAURICE. A Maillol. 42 p. plus 42 pl. Paris, Crès, 1925.

M 271 GEORGE, WALDEMAR. Aristide Maillol. *The Arts* 5 no. 2: 84–109 Feb. 1924.

M 272 KUHN, ALFRED. Aristide Maillol: Landschaft, Werke, Gespräche. 24 p. plus 43 pl. Leipzig, Seemann, 1925.

M 273 LE POINT. Les Ateliers de Maillol. [44] p. ill. Colmar, 1938. *Text by John Rewald. Special number 3 no. 17: 199–240 Nov. 1938.*

M 274 REWALD, JOHN. Maillol. 167 p. ill. London, Paris, New York, Hyperion, 1939. *Extensive bibliography, p. 29–30.*

M 275 RONNEBECK, ARNOLD. The teachings of Maillol. *The Arts* 8 no. 1: 38–40 ill. July 1925. *Preceded by "Maillol speaks", p. 35–37.*

M 276 TERNOVETZ, BORIS. Aristide Maillol. 30 p. plus 30 ill. Milano, Hoepli, 1950. *Bibliography, p. 25–30.*

M 277 WEBER, HUGO. Erinnerungen an Aristide Maillol. *Werk* 31 no. 12: 365–370 ill. Dec. 1944.

Malevich

M 278 MALEVICH, KASIMIR. Die gegenstandslose Welt: Begründung und Erklärung des russischen Suprematismus. 104 p. ill. München, Langen, 1927. *Bauhausbücher 11.*

M 279 MALEVICH, KASIMIR. Suprematismus. Aus den Schriften, 1915—1920. *Plastique* no. 1: 3 ill. Printemps, 1937.

M 280 MALEVICH, KASIMIR. Suprematism: the non-objective world. *In* Goldwater, R. & Treves, M. Artists on Art. p. 452–453 New York, Pantheon, 1945.

M 281 ALVARD, JULIEN. Les idées de Malevich. *Art d'Aujourd'hui* 4 no. 5: 16–21 ill. July 1953. *Additional Malevich material in Jan. 1951 and June 1952 numbers.*

M 282 KÁLLAI, ERNST. Kasimir Malewitsch. *Das Kunstblatt* 10 no. 7: 264–266 ill. 1927.

M 283 NEW YORK. MUSEUM OF MODERN ART. Cubism and Abstract Art, by Alfred H. Barr, Jr. p. 120–128, 215–216, 241–246 ill. 1936.

M 284 WESCHER, H. Hommage à Malewitsch, Malewitsch in memoriam. *Plastique* no. 1: 5–10 ill. Printemps, 1937

Marini

M 285 APOLLONIO, UMBRO. Marino Marini. 40 p. plus 116 pl. Milan, Edizione del Milione, 1953. *Lists of works and exhibitions; bibliography.*

M 286 CARLI, ENZO. Marino Marini. 27 p. plus 36 pl. Milano, Hoepli, 1950. *Bibliography, p. 22–27.*

M 287 CARRIERI, RAFFAELE. Marino Marini, Scultore. 36 p. plus 90 pl. Milano, Il Milione, 1948. *Extensive bibliography, p. 26–33.*

M 288 HAFTMANN, WERNER. Marino Marini. *Das Kunstwerk* 6 no. 4: 3–16 ill. 1952. *Followed, p. 17–18, by Conrad Westphal "Plastik als Raumwesen: Über Marini".*

M 289 HJERN, KJELL. Marino Marini. *Konstrevy* 29 no. 1: 20–28 ill. 1953.

M 290 KESTNER-GESELLSCHAFT. Marino Marini, erste Ausstellung in Deutschland, 1951—1952. [15] p.ill. Hannover. 1951. *"Veranstaltet von der Kestner-Gesellschaft . . . und dem Kunstverein in Hamburg."*

M 290a TRIER, EDUARD. Marino Marini. Köln, Galerie der Spiegel, 1954. *First German monograph, with English and French translation. Bibliography.*

M 291 VITALI, LAMBERTO. Marino Marini. *Horizon* 18 no. 105: 203–207 ill. Sept. 1948.

M 292 VITALI, LAMBERTO. Marino Marini. 25 p. plus 33 pl. Milano, Hoepli, 1937. *Bibliography, p. 21–25. Another monograph, subtitled "Maturità di Marini", issued by Edizione U, Firenze, 1946 (37 p. plus 64 pl.).*

Martins

M 293 BRETON, ANDRÉ. Les Statues Magiques de Maria présentées par André Breton et Michel Tapié. [23] p ill. Paris, Drouin, 1948. *"Presentation par André Breton de l'exposition de Maria à Julien Levy Gallery à New York en 1947."*

M 293a GEORGE, WALDEMAR. Maria, sculpteur des tropiques. *Art et Industrie* no. 16: 18–20 ill. 1949.

M 294 LEVY, JULIEN, GALLERY. Maria, recent Sculptures. Introduction by André Breton. [12] p. ill. 1947.

M 295 MINNIGERODE, C. POWELL. Sculptures by Maria Martins. *Pan American Union Bulletin* 75 no. 12: 682–685 ill. Dec. 1941. *Early work in the naturalistic tradition.*

M 296 TAPIÉ, MICHEL. 3 Artistes d'Amérique latine. *XXe Siècle* no. 1: 78 ill. 1951.

M 297 VALENTIN, CURT, GALLERY. Amazonia by Maria. [13] p. plus 15 pl. New York, 1943. *Issued in association with exhibition; at head of title: March 22 1943. Foreword by Jorge Zarur.*

M 297a ZERVOS, CHRISTIAN. La vision imaginative de Maria. *Cahiers d'Art* 24: 139–143 ill. 1949.

Matare

M 298 KÁLLAI, ERNST. Der Plastiker Mataré. *Das Kunstblatt.* 11: 67–68 ill. 1927.

M 299 SCHEFFLER, K. Mataré, Ausstellung bei Flecht-heim. *Kunst und Künstler* 32:152 Apr. 1933.
M 300 SCHÖN, GERHARD. Die Kuh des Mataré. *Das Kunstwerk* 2 no. 8: 33–34 ill. 1948.
M 301 SCHOPPA, HELMUT. Mataré: 8 Keramiken. 1 leaf plus 8 pl. Wiesbaden [195?] *(Saaten-Kunstmappe.)*
M 302 SVENSK-FRANSKA KONSTGALLERIET. Ewald Mataré, Skulpturer, Träsnitt, 1921–1953. [12] p. ill. Stockholm, 1954. *Preface by H.-E. Haack. 91 sculptures shown Jan. 1954.*
M 303 VELLINGHAUSEN, ALBERT S. Ewald Mataré. *Werk* 34 no. 10: 337–340 ill. Oct. 1947.

Matisse

M 304 MATISSE, HENRI. Notes d'un peintre sur son dessin. ill. *Le Point* 4 no. 3: 8–15 July 1939.
M 305 MATISSE, HENRI. [Témoignage: L'espace]. *XXe Siècle* (n. s.) no. 2: 66–67 Jan. 1952.
M 306 ARTS COUNCIL OF GREAT BRITAIN. An Ex-hibition of the Sculpture of Matisse ... [10] p. ill. London, 1953. *At the Tate Gallery, Jan. 9—Feb. 22. Texts by P. James and J. Cassou.*
M 307 BARR, ALFRED H., JR. Matisse: His Art and his Public. 591 p. ill. New York, Museum of Modern Art, 1951. *Issued in association with Matisse retrospective at Philadelphia, New York and Cleveland. Bibliography by B. Karpel, p. 564—574.*
M 308 GRÜNEWALD, ISAAC. Matisse och Expressio-nismen. p. 167-170. Stockholm, Wahlström & Wid-strand, 1944.
M 309 GUÉGUEN, PIERRE. The sculpture of a great painter: Henri Matisse. *Twentieth Century* no. 4: 3–13 Dec. 1938. *Also French edition, "XXe Siècle".*
M 310 PHOTO-SECESSION GALLERY. An Exhibition of Sculpture — the first in America — and recent Drawings by Henri Matisse ... Mar. 14—Apr. 6. New York, 1912. *Announcement and checklist of 24 works, including 12 sculptures, at the "291" gallery of Alfred Stieglitz. Reviews published in "CameraWork" no. 38 1912.*
M 311 POULAIN, GASTON. Sculptures by Henri Matisse. *Formes* no. 9: 9–10 plus 6 pl. Nov. 1930.
M 312 SALLES, G. A visit to Matisse. *Art News* 50 no. 7: part 2 Nov. 1951. *Art News annual 1952, special Matisse number, which also includes "Matisse speaks" by E. Tériade.*
M 313 SWANE, LEO. Henri Matisse. 165 p. ill. Stockholm, Nordstedt, 1944. *"Matisse som tecknare. Matisse som skulptör", p. 116–131. "Litteratur", p. 155–164.*
M 314 SYLVESTER, DAVID. The sculpture of Matisse. *The Listener (London)* 49 no. 1248: 190–191 Jan. 29 1953.
M 315 ZERVOS, CHRISTIAN, ed. Henri Matisse. 96 p. ill. Paris, Cahiers d'Art; New York, E. Weyhe, 1931. *Modified Matisse number of Cahiers d'Art 6 no. 5—6: 229–316 1931.*

Meduniezky

M 316 DIEMEN, GALERIE Van. Erste russische Kunst-ausstellung. 31 p. ill. Berlin, 1922.

M 317 DREIER, KATHERINE. Kasimir Meduniezky. *In* Yale University Art Gallery. The Collection of the Société Anonyme. p. 119–120 ill. New Haven, 1950. *Bibliography.*
M 318 STERENBERG, D. Die künstlerische Situation in Russland. *Das Kunstblatt* 6 no. 11: 484–492 ill. 1922. *Review of Diemen exhibition, followed, p. 493–498, by Paul Westheim: Die Ausstellung der Russen.*

Minguzzi

M 318a JAHIER, P. Minguzzi Scultore. 24 p. plus 24 ill. Bologna, Orsa, 1946.
M 318b TATE GALLERY, LONDON. The Unknown political prisoner: international sculpture compe-tition. [24] p. ill. 1953. *Insert includes biographical note on Minguzzi, a prizewinner.*
M 318c Exposition à l'Athénée, Genève. *Werk* 36: 112 (suppl.) Aug. 1949.
M 318d RITCHIE, ANDREW C., ed. The New Decade: 22 European Painters and Sculptors. p. 90–93 ill. New York, Museum of Modern Art, 1955. *Includes statement by the artist and biographical note. Also Mirko, p. 94–97.*

Mirko (Basaldella)

M 319 APOLLONIO, UMBRO. Mirko Basaldella. *In* Cairola, Stefano, ed. Arte italiano del nostro Tempo. p. 4–5, plate 11, 12 port. Bergamo, 1946.
M 320 CARRIERI, R. Pittura, Scultura d'Avanguardia in Italia (1890—1950). p. 278–282 ill. Milano, Conchiglia, 1950.
M 321 MARCHIORI, GUISEPPE. Scultura italiano mo-derna. p. 42–43, 47; plate 35. Venezia, Alfieri, 1953. *Bibliography.*
M 322 Mirko [exhibition reviews]. *Le Arti* 1: 291–293 Feb. 1939; 2: 196–197 Feb. 1940.
M 323 PADOVANO, ETTORE. Dizionario degli Artisti contemporanei. p. 19. Milano, Istituto Tipografico, 1951.
M 324 ROME. GALLERIA DELL'OBELISCO. Mirko. [4] p. 1952. *Catalog of May show, with detailed bio-graphical note. Other catalogs: Cometa Gallery, N.Y., Apr. 1938; Knoedler & Co. N. Y., 1947; Viviano Gallery, N. Y., Apr. – May 1950. Also see bibl. M 318 d.*

Miro

M 325 CAHIERS D'ART. L'Oeuvre de Joan Miro de 1917 à 1933. Paris, 1934. *Special number, 9 no. 1—4. Also note 24 no. 1(1949) passim for later work.*
M 326 CIRICI-PELLICER, A. Miro y la Imaginacion. 41 p. ill. Barcelona, Omega, 1949.
M 327 CIRLOT, J.-E. Joan Miro. 52 p. ill. Barcelona, Cobalto, 1949. *"Exposiciones", p. 49–50.*
M 328 DERRIÈRE LE MIROIR. [Joan Miro]. 2 parts ill. Paris, 1948—1950. *Special exhibition numbers for the Galerie Maeght, no. 14—15 1948, no. 29—30 1950.*

Some Notes on **SPACE. AND FORM** *in Sculpture*

One distorts the forms in order to create space....
If space is a willed, a wished-for element in the sculpture, then some
distortion of the form — to ally itself to the space — is necessary

At one time the holes in my sculpture were
made for their own sakes. Because I was
trying to become conscious of space in the sculpture —
I made the hole have a shape in its own right,
the solid body was encroached upon, eaten into, +
sometimes the form was only the shell holding
the hole. Recently I have attempted to
make the forms + the spaces (not holes!)
inseparable, neither being more important
than the other. In the last bronze Reclining
Figure I think I have in some measure succeeded
in this aim. What I mean is perhaps most obvious
if the figure is looked at lengthwise from the Head
end through to the foot end + the arms
body, legs, elbows etc are seen as forms
inhabiting a tunnel, in recession.
Seen in plan the figure has 'pools' of space.

Facsimile Notes on Sculpture by Moore. From bibl. M 352a.

M 329 Exposition Miro de sculptures — objets. *Cahiers d'Art* 6 no. 9—10: 431 ill. 1931. *At the Galerie Pierre.*

M 330 GASSIER, PIERRE. Miro et Artigas. *Labyrinthe* no. 22—23: 10—11 ill. Dec. 1946.

M 331 GREENBERG, CLEMENT. Joan Miro. 133 p. ill. New York, Quadrangle, 1948. *Bibliography by H. B. Muller, p. 123–128.*

M 332 Joan Miro's sculptures. *Formes* no. 21: 210 ill. Jan. 1932.

M 333 NEW YORK. MUSEUM OF MODERN ART. Joan Miro, by James Johnson Sweeney. 87 p. ill. 1941. *Catalog for major exhibition. Bibliography, p. 85–87.*

Modigliani

M 334 FRANCHI, RAFFAELO. Modigliani. 3. ed. 44 p. plus 52 pl. Firenze, Arnaud, 1946. *Bibliography, p. 35–42.*

M 335 GRAMANTIERI, TULLIO. Amedeo Modigliano e la scultura negra. *Anteprima (Rome)* Nov. 1948.

M 335a JEDLICKA, GOTTHARD. Modigliani als Plastiker. *Neue Züricher Zeitung* Aug. 18 1931.

M 335b JEDLICKA, GOTTHARD. Amedeo Modigliani. Zürich-Erlenbach, Eugen-Rentsch-Verlag, 1953.

M 336 LIPCHITZ, JACQUES. I remember Modigliani. *Art News* 49 no. 10: 26—29, 64—65 ill. Feb. 1951.

M 337 NEW YORK. MUSEUM OF MODERN ART. Modigliani: Paintings, Drawings, Sculpture; with introduction by James Thrall Soby. 55 p. ill. New York, 1951. *"In collaboration with the Cleveland Museum of Art". Bibliography by H. B. Muller.*

M 338 PFANNSTIEL, ARTHUR. Modigliani. Préface de Louis Latourettes. 199 p. 142 pl. Paris, Seheur, 1929. *"Catalogue presumé", p. 1–[61]. Bibliography, p. 131–135.*

M 339 SCHEIWILLER, GIOVANNI. Amedeo Modigliani. 5. ed. 24 p. plus 40 pl. Milano, Hoepli, 1950. *Bibliogr. p. 14–24. First edition 1927, variant French edition 1928.*

Moholy-Nagy

M 340 MOHOLY-NAGY, LÁSZLÓ. The New Vision, 1928. (fourth revised edition 1947); and Abstract of an Artist. 92 p. ill. New York, Wittenborn, Schultz, 1949. *"Volume: Sculpture", p. 41–45. Translation of*

FORM FROM THE INSIDE OUTWARDS.

Tension + inner force of forms.

Force, Power, is made by forms straining or pressing from inside.

Knees, elbows, foreheads, knuckles, all seek to press outwards.

Hardness, projection outwards, gives tension, force + vitality.

~~a~~ clenched fist ~~is the natural~~ symbol of power — of force.

Although carved sculpture is approached from the outside, yet ends by seeming to be sliced or scooped into its shape out of a larger mass, it will not have its maximum sense of bigness

SCULPTURE in the open air looks smaller than when seen in the enclosed space of indoors.

Landscape, clouds, the sky, impinge on the sculpture + reduce its bulk — then linear forms tend to get lost. —

It seems that in the open air a certain minimum bulk is needed, to contrast with the great space of the sky + large distances.

SPACE in sculpture should not become such a fetish that the form is weak + impoverished

Von Material zu Architektur, *1929 (based on the Bauhaus lectures), later published as* The New Vision: From Material to Architecture *(N. Y., Brewer, Warren & Putnam, 1930, second edition 1938) and issued by Wittenborn as a "third revised edition, 1946". Bibliography.*

M 341 MOHOLY-NAGY, LÁSZLÓ. Vision in Motion. 371 p. ill. Chicago, Theobald, 1947. *"Sculpture", p. 216–243, "is a revised version of the chapter on 'volume' from* The New Vision *and contains examples of student work . . ." Extraits published, in French, in "Art d'Aujourd'hui" 2 no. 5: 6–8 ill. Apr.—May 1951.*

M 342 CHICAGO. INSTITUTE OF DESIGN. Paintings, Sculptures, Photograms and Photographs. 14 p. ill. [1945 ?]. *Exhibition catalog, with text by S. Giedion from "Telehor". Memorial catalogs also were published by Art Institute, Chicago, Sept. 18—Oct. 26, 1947 (texts by Kuh and Schniewind); by the New York Museum of Non-Objective Painting (text by Rebay with biographical and bibliographical notes, 1947); by the Fogg Art Museum, Feb. 6—27 1950, etc.*

M 343 GIEDION, SIEGFRIED. Notes on the Life and Work of L. Moholy-Nagy, Painter Universalist. *In* Architects' Year Book. No. 3, p. 32–35 ill. London, 1949.

M 344 MOHOLY-NAGY, SIBYL. Moholy-Nagy, Experiment in Totality. 253 p. ill. New York, Harper, 1950.

*M 345 TELEHOR. I: Moholy-Nagy. 136 p. ill. Brno, 1936. *Special number, I. 1—2: 1–136 (28. II. 1936), ed. by Fr. Kalivoda. Texts by the artist, S. Giedion, and the editor, in French, English, Czech, German.*

Moore

M 346 MOORE, HENRY. Notes on Sculpture. *In* Ghiselin, Brewster. The Creative Process. p. 68–73. Berkeley and Los Angeles, Univ. of California, 1952. *Frequently published, e. g. bibl. A 13, M 356.*

M 347 MOORE, HENRY. Sculptor in modern society. *Art News* 51 no. 6: 24–25, 64–65 ill. Nov. 1952.

M 348 MOORE, HENRY. The sculptor speaks. *The Listener* 18 no. 449: 338–340 Aug. 18 1937. *Frequently reprinted.*

M 349 ARGAN, GUILIO CARLO. Henry Moore. 26 p. plus 32 pl. Torino, Francesco De Silva, 1948.

M 350 ARNHEIM, RUDOLF. The holes of Henry Moore: on the function of space in sculpture. *Journal of Aesthetics and Art Criticism* 7: 29–38 ill. Sept. 1948.

M 351 CLARK, KENNETH. Henry Moore's metal sculpture. *Magazine of Art* 44: 171–174 ill. May 1951.

M 352 HENDY, PHILIP. Henry Moore. *Art d'Aujourd'hui* no. 4: [8–12] ill. Nov. 1949. *Also "Henry Moore" par Léon Degand, p. (13—15).*

M 352a MAN, FELIX, ed. Eight European Artists. [Chapter 6] ill. London, Heinemann, 1954. *Text in English, French, German.*

M 353 NEW YORK. MUSEUM OF MODERN ART. Henry Moore, by James Johnson Sweeney. 95 p. ill. 1946. *Exhibition monograph, "in collaboration with the Art Institute of Chicago, the San Francisco Museum of Art". Bibliography by H. B. Muller.*

M 354 RAMSDEN, E. H. Der Bildhauer Henry Moore. *Werk* 34 no. 4: 129–135 ill. Apr. 1947.

*M 355 READ, HERBERT. Henry Moore. London, Zwemmer, 1934.

M 356 READ, HERBERT. Henry Moore, Sculpture and Drawings. 3. rev. and enl. ed. 350 p. ill. New York, Curt Valentin, 1949. *"Copyright 1949 by Percy Lund, Humphries & Co., London". Bibliography by H. B. Muller. First edition, 1944.*

*M 357 RICHARDS, J. M. Henry Moore, sculptor. *Architectural Review* 76: 90–91 ill. Sept. 1934.

M 358 SYLVESTER, A. D. B. Evolution of Henry Moore's sculpture. *Burlington Magazine* 90: 158–165, 189–195 ill. June—July 1948.

M 359 VRINAT, ROBERT. L'évolution de la figure couchée dans l'oeuvre de Henry Moore. *L'Age Nouveau* [insert, 16 p.] ill. Nov. 1949. *Bibliography.*

Muller (Erich)

M 359a *Werk* no. 6, 1952, p. 83.

M 359b *Werk* no. 7, 1954, p. 298.

M 359c GIEDION-WELCKER, CAROLA. Contemporary Sculpture. p. 239 ill. Stuttgart, Hatje; New York, Wittenborn, 1955. *Biographical notes.*

Nivola

M 360 GUEFT, O. Sardinia and an artist: Nivola's sand sculpture. *Interiors* 113: 86–93 ill. June 1954. *Additional material in Jan. 1948 (Nightclub murals), Aug. 1948 (Biographical sketch), Jan. 1953 (Pergola village), Olivetti shop (Nov. 1954).*

M 360a HUXTABLE, ADA L. Olivetti's lavish shop in New York. *Art Digest* 28:15 July 1954. *Also review of Peridot Gallery show in May 1, 1954 (Olivetti mural).*

M 360b KRAUS, H. F. Costantino Nivola at work in the U.S.A. *Art & Industry* 33:42–46 ill. Aug. 1942.

M 360c Nouveau magasin Olivetti à New York . . . Relief de Nivola. *Architecture d'Aujourd'hui* 26 no. 58:58–59 ill. Feb. 1955.

M 360d Scultura dipinta all'aperto. *Domus* no. 274:46–49 ill. Oct. 1952.

Noguchi

M 361 NOGUCHI, ISAMU. Isamu Noguchi defines the nature and enormous potential importance of sculpture — "the art of spaces". *Interiors* 108 no. 8: [118–123] Mar. 1949. *"Quotations from a speech at Yale University and from his outline for a proposed book The Environment of Leisure."*

M 361a NOGUCHI, ISAMU. Meanings in modern sculpture. *Art News* 48 no. 1: 12–15, 55–56 ill. Mar. 1949.

M 362 NOGUCHI, ISAMU. [Statement: Work in Japan] *Arts & Architecture* 67 no. 11: 24, 27 ill. Nov. 1950.

M 363 NOGUCHI, ISAMU. Toward a reintegration of the arts. *College Art Journal* 9 no. 1: 59–60 1949.

M 364 D[REXLER], A[RTHUR]. Noguchi in Japan. *Interiors* 110 no. 9: 140–145 ill. Apr. 1951.

M 365 HESS, THOMAS B. Isamu Noguchi, '46. *Art News* 45: 34–38, 47, 50–51 ill. Sept. 1946.

M 366 LEVY, JULIEN. Isamu Noguchi. *Creative Art* 12 no. 1: 29–35 ill. Jan. 1933.

Sketch by Pevsner. Fontaine imaginée au centre d'une ville moderne. 1929. (model page 186) Coll. E. Hoffmann, Basel.

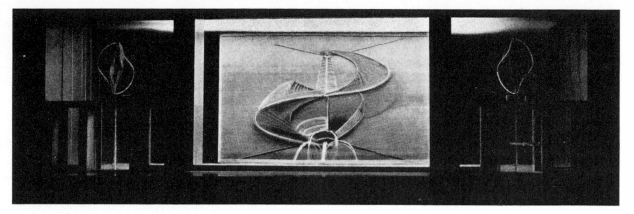

Model of Project for Front of Esso Building by Gabo. From bibl. K 16, 1953.

M 367 NEW YORK. MUSEUM OF MODERN ART. Fourteen Americans, ed. by Dorothy C. Miller. p. 39, 40–43, 78 ill. 1946. *Includes personal statement.*

M 367a PORTFOLIO, The Annual of the Graphic Arts, ed. by G. S. Rosenthal & F. Zachary. [8] p. ill. Cincinnati, Zebra Press; New York, Duell, Sloan & Pearce, 1951. *Insert of unnumbered pages titled "Astronomical City". Photographs by Noguchi of structures at Jaipur, India with quotations.*

M 368 TAKIGUCHI, SHUZO (AND OTHERS). Noguchi. 100 p. ill. Tokyo, Bijutsu Shuppan-Sha, 1953. *Text in Japanese and English.*

Obrist

M 368a OBRIST, HERMANN. Neue Möglichkeiten in der bildenden Kunst. *Kunstwart* 16 pt. 2: 21 1903.

M 368b OBRIST, HERMANN. Neue Möglichkeiten in der bildenden Kunst: Aufsätze von 1896–1900. 170 p. ill. Leipzig, Diedrichs, 1903.

M 368c BRATTSKOVEN, O. Hermann Obrist. *In* THIEME, U. & BECKER, F. Allgemeines Lexikon der bildenden Künstler. v. 25, p. 552 Leipzig, Seemann, 1931. *Biography and bibliography.*

M 368d CURJEL, H. Konfrontationen. *Werk* 39: 382–384 ill. Dec. 1952. *"Formensprache um 1900 . . ." Also note p. 392: "Worte und bauten der pioniere".*

M 368e GRADY, JAMES. A Bibliography of the Art Nouveau. [68] p. unpublished mss. [195?] *Compiled by a faculty member of the School of Architecture, Institute of Technology, Atlanta, Ga. Commentary on and extensive summary of the movement, with special section on Obrist. p. [45].*

M 368f PEVSNER, NIKOLAUS. Pioneers of Modern Design. 2. rev. ed. p. 16, 63–67, 118, 137 ill. New York, Museum of Modern Art, 1949.

M 368g SCHEFFLER, KARL. Hermann Obrist. *Kunst und Künstler* 8: 555–559 Jan. 8 1910.

Paolozzi

M 368h ALLOWAY, L. Britain's new iron age. *Art News* 52: 68 ill. June 1953.

M 368i THWAITES, J. A. Notes on some young English sculptors. *Art Quarterly* 15 no. 3: 236–237 ill. 1952. *Also note bibl. L 11–23 passim.*

Pevsner

M 369 PEVSNER, ANTOINE. Espaces. *Réalités Nouvelles* no. 4: 12 ill. 1950. *Also no. 6 1952.*

M 370 PEVSNER, ANTOINE. [Statement]. *Abstraction, Création, Art Non Figuratif* no. 2: 35 ill. 1933.

M 371 PEVSNER, ANTOINE. [Témoignage: L'espace]. *XXe Siècle* no. 2: 78–80 ill. 1952.

M 372 PEVSNER, A. [Propos]. *In* Témoignages pour l'Art abstrait. p. 213–214 ill. Paris, Art d'Aujourd'hui, 1951.

M 373 BILL, MAX. Anton Pevsner zum 60. Geburtstag. *Werk* 34 no. 1: 3–4 (suppl.) Jan. 1947.

M 374 DROUIN, RENÉ, GALERIE. Antoine Pevsner. [10] p. plus 24 pl. Paris, 1947. *Texts by Duchamp, Le Corbusier, Giedion-Welcker and others.*

M 374a GUÉGUEN, PIERRE. Pevsner, et la conquête plastique de l'espace. Art d'Aujourd'hui 5 no. 1: 6–9 ill. Feb. 1954.

M 375 MASSAT, RENÉ. Antoine Pevsner. *Cahiers d'Art* 25, part 2: 349–364 ill. 1950.

M 376 NEW YORK. MUSEUM OF MODERN ART. Naum Gabo — Antoine Pevsner. Introduction by Herbert Read; text by Ruth Olson and Abraham Chanin. p. 50–83 ill. 1948. *Bibliography by H. B. Muller.*

M 377 SOTTSASS, ETTORE, Jr. Antoine Pevsner. *Domus* no. 281: 27–29 ill. Apr. 1953.

M 378 ZÜRICH. KUNSTHAUS. Antoine Pevsner, Georges Vantongerloo, Max Bill. [30] p. ill. 1949. *Preface by W. Wartmann; texts by the artists. Reviewed by C. Giedion-Welcker in "Werk" 36 no. 12: 167–168 Dec. 1949.*

Phillips

M 378a Young Americans: Helen Phillips. *American Magazine of Art* 29: 532–533 ill. Aug. 1936.

M 378b HUGO GALLERY, NEW YORK. Bloodflames 1947. p. 14 ill. 1947. *Collective show, including Phillips, with text by N. Calas.*

M 378c LA HUNE GALERIE, PARIS. Cuivres gravés et sculptures par Helen Phillips. [1 sheet] 1954. *Folded announcement for July exhibition. Sculptures: no. 25–34; biographical note; preface by Max Clarac-Serou.*

Picasso

M 379 PICASSO, PABLO. 2 Statements. 62 p. port. New York, Los Angeles, Armitage, 1936. *Texts were published in "The Arts" May 1923 and "Creative Art" June 1930. Comment by Merle Armitage, p. 51–60.*

M 380 ARGAN, GIULIO CARLO. Scultura di Picasso. [36] p. plus 48 ill. Venezia, Alfieri, 1953. *English translation, p. 23–34.*

M 381 BARR, ALFRED H., Jr. Picasso: Fifty Years of his Art. 314 p. ill. New York, Museum of Modern Art, 1946. *Bibliography, p. 286–306.*

M 382 BRETON, ANDRÉ. Picasso dans son élément. *Minotaure* no. 1: 4–37 ill. 1933. *Includes "L'atelier de Picasso" with photographs by Brassaï.*

M 382a GONZALEZ, JULIO. Picasso sculpteur; exposition de sculptures récentes de Picasso. *Cahiers d'Art* ill. 11 no. 6—7: 189–191 1936.

M 383 GIEURE, MAURICE. Initiation à l'Oeuvre de Picasso. 337 p. plus 142 ill. Paris, Deux Mondes, 1951.

M 384 KAHNWEILER, DANIEL HENRY. The Sculptures of Picasso. Photographs by Brassaï. [8] p. plus [218] pl. London, Rodney Phillips, 1949. *Translated from the edition by Du Chêne (Paris, 1948).*

M 385 PRAMPOLINI, ENRICO. Picasso, Scultore. 31 ill. ill. Rome, Bocca, 1943.

M 385a RUSSOLI, FRANCO. Pablo Picasso, Settembre-Novembre, Palazzo Reale, Milano. [Introduzione e Catalogo di Franco Russoli]. 116 p. plus 236 ill. Milano, Amilcare Pizzi, 1953. *329 works dated 1901–1953; chronology; bibliography.*

M 386 SWEENEY, JAMES JOHNSON. Picasso and Iberian sculpture. *Art Bulletin* 23 no. 3: 191–198 ill. Sept. 1941.

M 387 VENTURI, LIONELLO. Mostra di Pablo Picasso; Catalogo Ufficiale. 69 p. plus 171 pl. Roma, De Luca, 1953. *"Sculture (1931—1953)", nos. 136—167, all illustrated. Biographical and bibliographical notes, p. 63–69.*

M 388 VERONESI, GIULIA. Scultura di Picasso. *Emporium* 57 no. 4: 146–153 ill. Apr. 1951. *Review of show at Maison de la Pensée, Paris.*

M 389 ZERVOS, CHRISTIAN. Pablo Picasso. 4. ed. 38 p. plus 37 ill. Milano, Hoepli, 1946. *Bibliography by G. Scheiwiller, p. 20–38. Text by editor of "Cahiers d'Art" which published numerous Picasso articles, and also issued definitive Picasso catalogs (Paris, 1932—date).*

Richier

M 390 DERRIÈRE LE MIROIR. Germaine Richier. [7] p. ill. Paris, 1948. *Special number 15 of magazine issued by Galerie Maeght, with list of "sculptures exposées". Includes texts by Ponge, Limbour, de Solier.*

M 391 GASSER, MANUEL. Germaine Richier. *Werk* 33 no. 3: 69–77 ill. Mar. 1946.

M 392 Germaine Richier. *Biennale* (Venice). no. 7: 35–39 ill. Jan. 1952.

M 393 JACOMETTI, NESTO. Femmes-artistes d'aujourd' hui. *Vie, Art, Cité* (Lausanne) no. 3: [26–28] ill. May—June 1946.

M 394 LIMBOUR, GEORGES. Visite à un sculpteur: Germaine Richier. *Arts de France* no. 17—18: 51–58 ill. 1947.

M 395 SOLIER, RENÉ DE. Germaine Richier. *Cahiers d'Art* 28: 123–129 ill. 1953.

Rodchenko

M 396 LOZOWICK, LOUIS. Modern Russian Art. 60 p. ill. New York, Museum of Modern Art, Société Anonyme. 1925. *"The suprematists", p. 18–27; "The constructivists", p. 29–45.*

M 397 NEW YORK. MUSEUM OF MODERN ART. Cubism and Abstract Art, by Alfred H. Barr, Jr. passim ill. 1936. *Material on Russian movements and personalities. Bibliography by Newhall mentions numerous titles in Russian, including sculpture, e. g. nos. 38, 64–72, 120–124, 148, 172, 201, 209–213, 358–360, 439–441.*

M 398 UMANSKI, KONSTANTIN. Die neue Monumentalskulptur in Russland. *Der Ararat* no. 5—6: 29–33 Mar. 1920. *Also his Neue Kunst in Russland, 1914–1919. Potsdam und München, 1920.*

M 399 WASHBURN, GORDON. Isms in Art since 1800. p. 65 [Providence, R. I., The Author, 1949]. *An exhibition at the Providence Museum of Art. The Russians, p. 64–68.*

Rodin

M 400 RODIN, AUGUSTE. L'Art. Entretiens réunis par Paul Gsell. 318 p. ill. Paris, Grasset, 1911. *English editions: Boston, Small, Maynard, 1912; New York, Dodd, 1916, 1928. German edition: Wien, Leipzig, 1947, etc.*

M 401 AUBERT, MARCEL. Rodin Sculptures. Photographies de Sougez et de Marc Foucault. 62 p. pl. Paris, Éditions Tel, 1952.

M 402 BOURDELLE, ÉMILE ANTOINE. La Sculpture et Rodin. 236 p. ill. Paris, Émile-Paul, 1937.

M 403 BURCKHARDT, CARL. Rodin und das Plastische Problem. 98 p. plus 48 ill. Basel, Schwabe, 1921.

M 404 CLADEL, JUDITH. Rodin: the Man and his Art. Translated by S. K. Star. New York, Century, 1917. *Translated from the French (Bruxelles, Van Oest, 1908).*

M 405 ELSEN, A. Genesis of Rodin's "Gates of Hell". *Magazine of Art* 45: 110–119 ill. Mar. 1952.

M 406 EMDE, URSULA. Rilke und Rodin. 116 p. ill. Marburg-Lahn, Verlag des Kunstgeschichtlichen Seminars, 1949. *Anmerkungen —Schrifttum, p. 103–116.*

M 407 GOLDSCHEIDER, C. La genèse d'une oeuvre: le "Balzac" de Rodin. *Revue des Arts* 2: 37–44 ill. Mar. 1952. *Bibliography.*

*M 408 GRAUTOFF, OTTO. Auguste Rodin. Leipzig, 1908.

*M 409 MAUCLAIR, CAMILLE. Auguste Rodin. Paris, La Renaissance du Livre, 1918. *Earlier edition issued in translation by C. Black: London, Duckworth, 1909. Includes chronology and bibliography, p. 124–135.*

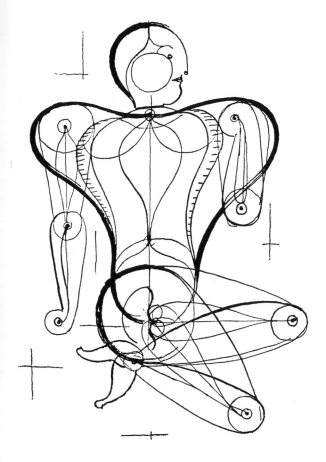

Drawing by Schlemmer. From bibl. M 427.

M 410 GRAPPE, GEORGES. Catalogue au Musée Rodin. I. Hotel Biron. Essai de classement chronologique des oeuvres d'Auguste Rodin. 159 p. ill. Paris, 1944. *Bibliography.*

M 410a ROH, FRANZ. Rodin. Bern, A. Scherz, 1949.

M 411 STORY, SOMMERVILLE. Rodin. London, Oxford University Press, 1951 (cop. 1939). *Sculptures from the Rodin Museum in a Phaidon picture book, published in several languages and many editions.*

Rosso

M 411a BARBANTINI. NINO. Medardo Rosso. Venezia, Neri Pozza, 1950.

M 411b BORGHI, NINO. Medardo Rosso. Milano, Ed. del Milione, 1950.

M 412 CARRIERI, RAFFAELE. Rivoluzione Plastica di Medardo Rosso. *In his* Pittura, Scultura d'Avanguardia. p. 1–15 Milano, Conchiglia, 1950. *Bibliography, p. 341.*

M 413 FLES, ETHA. Medardo Rosso, der Mensch und der Künstler. Freiburg i. B., 1922.

M 413a GIEDION-WELCKER, CAROLA. Sublimierung und Vergeistigung der plastischen Form bei Medardo Rosso. *Werk* 41 no. 8: 329–334 ill. Aug. 1954. *English summary.*

M 414 Medardo Rosso, 1858–1928. *Burlington Magazine* 92: 277–279 ill. Oct. 1950. *Bibliography.*

M 415 MEIER-GRAEFE, JULIUS. Modern Art. v. 2, p. 31–36. New York, Putnam; London, Heinemann, 1908. *Translated from the German. Essays on "Medardo Rosso" and "Impressionism in Sculpture".*

M 416 PAPINI, GIOVANNI. Medardo Rosso. 2. ed. 41 p. ill. Milano, Hoepli, 1945. *Bibliography by G. Scheiwiller, p. 21–41.*

M 417 SOFFICI, ARDENGO. Medardo Rosso. 206 p. ill. Vallecchi, 1929. *"Pensieri e sentenze di Medardo Rosso", p. 199–206. A chapter on Rosso also included in his* Trenta Artisti Moderni *(Firenze, Vallecchi, 1950).*

M 418 VIANELLO-CHIDDO, MARIO. Ricordo di Medardo Rosso. *La Biennale* (Venice) no. 3: 27–28 ill. Jan. 1951.

Roszak

M 419 ROSZAK, THEODORE J. Some problems of modern sculpture. *Magazine of Art* 42: 53–56 ill. Feb. 1949.

M 420 KRASNE, BELLE. A Theodore Roszak profile. *Art Digest* 27 no. 2: 9–18 ill. Oct. 15 1952. *Extensive quotations from the artist, including extracts from sculpture symposium at the Museum of Modern Art.*

M 421 NEW YORK. MUSEUM OF MODERN ART. Fourteen Americans, ed. by Dorothy Miller p. 58–61, 79 ill. 1949. *Exhibition catalog includes personal statement.*

M 422 PARIS. MUSÉE D'ART MODERNE. 12 Peintres et Sculpteurs américains contemporains. [26] p. ill. 1953. *The three chosen sculptors: Calder, Roszak, Smith. Later shown at Zurich.*

M 423 RITCHIE, ANDREW C. Sculpture of the Twentieth Century, p. 37, 46–47, 222, 232 ill. New York, Museum of Modern Art [1953]. *Quotes from sculpture symposium.*

Schlemmer

M 424 SCHLEMMER, OSKAR, ed. Die Bühne im Bauhaus. 87 p. ill. München, Langen, 1925. *Bauhausbücher 4. Includes material by Moholy-Nagy, Molnar, Breuer, Schmidt, etc.*

M 425 BÖHME, FRITZ. Konstruktivistische und choreographische Tänze. *In his* Der Tanz der Zukunft. p. 20–34 ill. München, Delphin, 1926.

M 426 HILDEBRANDT, HANS. Oskar Schlemmer. Magazine of Art 43: 23–28 Jan. 1950. *Also essays published in "Prisma" no. 10 Aug. 1947, "Aussaat" no. 10—11 1947, "Das Kunstwerk" no. 8—9 1946—1947, "Werk" no. 1 Jan. 1948.*

M 427 HILDEBRANDT, HANS. Oskar Schlemmer. 152 p. ill. München, Prestel, 1952. *Catalog of works, p. 133–149. Bibliography by Frau Schlemmer, p. 150–152.*

M 428 SCHMIDT, PAUL F. Oskar Schlemmer. *Jahrbuch der Jungen Kunst* 2: 269–280 ill. 1921. *Supplemented by a recent essay in "Prisma" no. 10: 33–34 Aug. 1947.*

SCULPTURE IS

The goddess Sephet, Hapi and Neith

The bright face of Shamash illuminated by the sun and the moon

Gilgamish wrestling the lion

Eabani tossing the bull

Isthar of Ninevah standing on a gryphon

the carrying mud of bricks by yoke and cord

the bald headed harpist in Thebian tomb plucking the strings of the goddess body

the dialectic of survival

everything I sought

everything I seek

what I will die not finding

Statement by David Smith. From bibl. M 447, 1947

Schnabel

M 428a BRANDT GALLERY, NEW YORK. Day N. Schnabel, May 7 to May 25. 4 p. ill. [1946]. *Biographical note; figurative work of the last five years. Reviewed Art Digest 20: 8 May 15 1946; Art News 45: 64 May 1946.*

M 428b Exhibition of non-objective sculpture at Parsons gallery. *Art Digest* 25: 20 ill. Mar. 15 1951. *Also reviewed Art News 50: 45 Mar. 1951. Current work also illustrated in Werk 39: 119 (suppl.), 372 1952.*

M 428c TÉMOIGNAGES POUR L'ART ABSTRAIT 1952. p. 256–263 ill. Paris, Art d'Aujourd'hui, 1952. "*Propos recueillis par R. V. Gindertael". Biographical notes; exhibitions.*

Schwitters

M 429 SCHWITTERS, KURT. *Merz.* Hannover, 1923—1932. *Magazine edited by the artist, with numerous illustrations and contributions.*

M 430 SCHWITTERS, KURT. Les Merztableaux. *Abstraction, Création, Art Non Figuratif* no. 1: 33 1932. *Additional text and illustration in no. 2: 41 1933.*

M 430a BERGGRUEN, HEINZ, GALERIE. Kurt Schwitters: Collages. Paris, 1954. *Illustrated catalog, with important chronology by Hans Bolliger.*

M 431 GIEDION-WELCKER, CAROLA. Schwitters; or the allusions of the imagination. *Magazine of Art* 41: 218–221 ill. Oct. 1948.

M 432 JANIS, SIDNEY, GALLERY. Schwitters: Merzbild, Merzrelief, Merzkonstruktion. [8] p. ill. 1952. *Catalog of 70 works and documents. Preface, "Kurt Schwitters 1887—1948", by Tristan Tzara.*

M 433 HANNOVER. MERZAUSSTELLUNG. Kurt Schwitters Katalog. ill. 1927. *Merz no. 20: 98–105, with factual introduction by Schwitters, and catalog of 150 works (1913—1926).*

M 434 MOTHERWELL, ROBERT. The Dada Painters and Poets. p. XXI–XXIV, 162–164, 275–276, 368–372. New York, Wittenborn, Schultz, 1951. *Bibliography. Includes translation of "Merz" from "Der Ararat" 2: 3–10 1921.*

M 435 NEBEL, OTTO. Kurt Schwitters. [32] p. ill. Berlin, Der Sturm, n. d. *Sturm Bilderbücher, possibly 1923.*

M 436 SEUPHOR, MICHEL. L'Art Abstrait. p. 61, 180, 311–312 ill. Paris, Maeght, 1949. *Essay by Edith Thomas; bibliography.*

M 437 VORDEMBERGE-GILDEWART, F. Kurt Schwitters (1887—1948). *Forum* 3 no. 12: 356–362 ill. 1948.

M 438 YALE UNIVERSITY. ART GALLERY. Collection of the Société Anonyme. p. 89–90 ill. New Haven, Conn. 1950. *Biographical notes, exhibitions list, bibliography by K. S. Dreier.*

Smith

M 439 SMITH, DAVID. Art forms in architecture. *Architectural Record* 88: 77–80 ill. Oct. 1940.

M 440 SMITH, DAVID. I never looked at a landscape. — Sculpture. *Possibilities* (N.Y.) no. 1: 24–26, 30, 33, 37 ill. Winter 1947/1948.

M 441 SMITH, DAVID. The language is image. *Arts & Architecture* 69 no. 2: 20–21, 33–34 ill. Feb. 1952.

M 442 SMITH, DAVID. A Statement: Who is the artist? How does he act? *Numero* (Firenze) 5 no. 3: 21 May—June 1953. "*Comment by Herman Cherry*", p. 21.

M 443 DE KOONING, E. David Smith makes a sculpture. *Art News* 50: 38–41, 50–51 ill. Sept. 1951:

M 444 KRASNE, BELLE. A David Smith profile. *Art Digest* 26 no. 13: 12–13, 26, 29 ill. Apr. 1 1952.

M 445 MELTZOFF, STANLEY. David Smith and social realism. *Magazine of Art* ill. 39: 98–101 Mar. 1946.

M 446 VALENTINER, W. R. Sculpture by David Smith. *Arts & Architecture* 65: 22–23, 52 ill. Aug. 1948.

M 447 WILLARD GALLERY. Medals for Dishonor by David Smith. Foreword by William Blake and Christiana Stead. [16] p. ill. New York, 1940. *Includes symbolic commentary. This November 1940 catalog also supplemented by texts for Jan. 1946 show (W. R. Valentiner) and Apr.— May 1950 exhibition (R. Motherwell). Apr. 1947 catalog prints Smith's statement on "Sculpture Is".*

Stahly

M 448 STAHLY, FRANÇOIS. Die junge französische Plastik. *Werk* 39 no. 11: 369–376 ill. Nov. 1952.

M 449 STAHLY, FRANÇOIS. [Statement]. *Réalités Nouvelles* no. 1: 78 ill. 1947.

M 450 STAHLY, FRANÇOIS. [Statement]. *In* Premier Bilan de l'Art actuel. p. 321 Paris, Le Soleil Noir, 1953. *Biographical note; portrait.*

M 451 ARP, JEAN & ROCHÉ, H. François Stahly. 12 pl. Paris, Facchetti [1953].

M 452 GOLDSCHEIDER, CÉCILIE. Stahly. *In* Hamburg. Kunsthalle. Junge französische Plastik. p. 24, 50 ill. 1953.

Taeuber-Arp

M 453 TAEUBER-ARP, SOPHIE, ed. Plastique (Revue internationale). 5 nos. ill. Paris, New York, 1937—1939. *Edited in association with H. Arp, A. E. Gallatin, G. L. K. Morris.*

M 454 BILL, MAX. Sophie Täuber-Arp. *Werk* no. 6: 167–171 ill. 1943. *Also issued as reprint.*

M 455 JAKOWSKI, ANATOLE. S. H. Taeuber-Arp. *In his* Hans Erni p. 42–53 ill. Paris, Abstraction, Création, 1934.

M 456 KANDINSKY, WASSILY. Les "reliefs colorés" de Sophie Taeuber-Arp. 1943. *Essay printed in Schmidt, p. 88 (below), dated "Paris, June 1943".*

M 457 SCHMIDT, GEORG. Sophie Taeuber-Arp. 152 p. ill. Basel, Holbein, 1948. *Catalog by Weber. Texts by H. Arp, H. Ball, Ball-Hennings, Bryen, Buffet-Picabia, Kandinsky, Schlegel-Taeuber. Bibliography, p. 150–151.*

M 458 SEUPHOR, MICHEL. Sophie Taeuber-Arp, Jean Arp. *Art d'Aujourd'hui* no. 10—11: [28–36] ill. May—June 1950. *Additional text in "Abstraction, Création, Art Non Figuratif" no. 1 1936, and his L'Art Abstrait p. 109–111 (Paris, Maeght, 1949).*

Tatlin

M 459 NEW YORK. Cubism and Abstract Art, by Alfred H. Barr, Jr. passim ill. 1936. *Includes material on Russian art and personalities. Tatlin bibliography notes references below.*

M 460 PUNIN, N. Tatlin — Protiv Kubizma. 25 p. plus pl. St. Petersburg, Gosudartsvennoe Izdatelistvo, 1921.

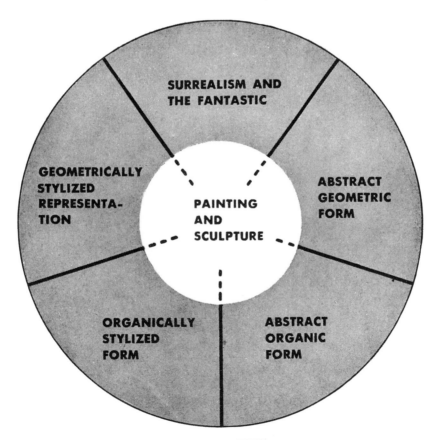

Component Elements of the Modern Style. From bibl. K 15.

☐ CENTRAL GALLERY OF PAINTING AND SCULPTURE

■ GALLERIES OF APPLIED ART

M 461 PUNIN, N. Pamiatnik III internationala. Petersburg, Izdonie Otela Izobratzitelnavo Isskusstva, 1920.

M 462 Vladimir Evgrafovich Tatlin. [1915]. *Reprinted from "Novago Jurnala Dlia Vsekh"*.

Thommesen

M 463 THOMMESEN, ERIK. Le fond et la forme. *Cobra* 2 no. 10: 2 ill. Automne 1951.

M 464 BILLE, EJLER. Erik Thommesen. *Konstrevy* 28 no. 4—5: 221–223 ill. 1952. *English summary*.

Turnbull

M 465 ALLOWAY, L. Britain's new iron age. *Art News* 52: 18–20 ill. June 1953.

M 466 MIDDLETON, MICHAEL. Huit sculpteurs britanniques. *Art d'Aujourd'hui* no. 2: 6, 18 Mar. 1953.

M 467 WALDBERG, ISABELLE. Essor de la sculpture anglaise. *Numero* 5 no. 1—2: 12 Jan.—Mar. 1953.

Uhlmann

M 467a BREMER GALERIE, BERLIN. Hans Uhlmann: Zeichnungen—Plastik. [1 sheet] 1953. *Announcement of February show; biographical note*.

M 467b SEEL, EBERHARD. Hans Uhlmann. *Das Kunstwerk* 4 no. 8–9: 81–82 ill. 1950. *Also in special number "Abstrakte Kunst" (Kunstwerk-Schriften, Bd. 19–20)*.

M 467c RITCHIE, ANDREW C. The New Decade. p. 44–47 ill. New York, Museum of Modern Art, 1955.

Vantongerloo

*M 468 VANTONGERLOO, GEORGES. L'Art et Son Avenir. [58] p. plus 27 ill. Anvers, De Sikkel; Santpoort, Mees, 1924. *Texts dated 1919—1921. Part I: L'Évolution de l'Art Sculptural (1919)*.

M 469 VANTONGERLOO, GEORGES. Paintings, Sculptures, Reflections. 48 p. plus 49 ill. New York, Wittenborn, Schultz, 1948. *Essays written over a period of thirty years, with biographical and bibliographical note by the artist, including exhibitions list. Preface by Max Bill*.

M 470 VANTONGERLOO, GEORGES. [Statements]. *Abstraction, Création, Art Non Figuratif* ill. 1932–1936. *In no. 1: 40–41 1932, no. 2: 43–46 1933, no. 4: 30–32 1935, no. 5: 27–28 1936*.

M 471 BILL, MAX. Georges Vantongerloo zum 60. Geburtstag. *Werk* 33 no. 11: 136–137 ill. Nov. 1946.

M 472 FREIBURG. KUNSTVEREIN. Max Bill, Julius Bissier, Georges Vantongerloo. p. [10–16] ill. 1951. *With statement by the artist*.

M 473 HUBERMAN, BEATRIZ. Georges Vantongerloo. *Ver y Estimar* (Buenos Aires) 5 no. 17: 30–36 May 1950. *Also note "Opina Vantongerloo" in June 1949 issue (3 no. 11—12: 81–83)*.

M 474 Vantongerloo. *Arti Visive* (Rome) no. 4—5: 3 ill. May 1953.

Viani

M 475 APOLLONIO, UMBRO. Alberto Viani. *Magazine of Art* 45: 203–208 ill. May 1952.

M 476 EICHMANN, INGEBORG. Letter from Italy: the Fronte nuove. *Magazine of Art* 42 no. 2: 68–71 ill. Feb. 1949.

M 477 MARCHIORI, GIUSEPPE. Viani. 24 p. plus pl. Paris, P. L. F., 1950.

M 478 NEW YORK. MUSEUM OF MODERN ART. Twentieth-Century Italien Art, by J. T. Soby and A. H. Barr, Jr. p. 32, 124, 135 ill. 1949.

M 479 SCULTURE DI ALBERTO VIANI. 29 p. plus 10 pl. Milano, Spiga, 1946. *"Testimonianze di Anceschi, Apollonio, Bettini, Birolli, Emanuelli, Guidi, Marchiori, Martini, Pallucchini, Valsecchi."*

Addenda: Books and Catalogs

N 1 BASEL. KUNSTHALLE. Ausstellung Henry Moore, Oskar Schlemmer, 12. Jan.—13. Feb. 29 p. ill. 1954. *Texts and biographical notes*.

N 2 GROHMANN, WILL. Bildende Kunst und Architektur: Zwischen den beiden Kriegen III. p. 231-272. Berlin, Suhrkamp, 1953.

N 3 HAMMACHER, A. M., ed. Europäische Bildhauer. [Series] Amsterdam, Lange, 1954; Cologne-Marienburg, Kiepenheuer & Witsch, 1955. *Bilingual series in progress, including booklets on Lipchitz (R. Goldwater), Marini (E. Langui), etc.*

N 4 HUMBERT, AGNES. La Sculpture contemporaine au Musée d'Art moderne. 14 p. plus 32 ill. Paris, Morancé, 1954. *French and English text*.

N 5 PHILADELPHIA. MUSEUM OF ART. The Louise and Walter Arensberg Collection: 20th Century Section. [20] p. plus 200 ill. Philadelphia, 1954. *Text by Fiske Kimball and Henry Clifford. Catalogue compiled by Marianne Winter-Martin*.

N 6 RAGON, MICHEL. Expression et Non-Figuration. p. 21-24. Paris, La Revue Neuf, 1951. *"Problèmes et tendances de l'art d'aujourd'hui"*.

N 7 RICHMAN, ROBERT, ed. The Arts at Mid-Century. p. 269-282 New York, Horizon Press, 1954. *From a contribution to the "New Republic" titled: American painting and sculpture*.

N 8 TRIER, EDUARD. Moderne Plastik. 104 p. plus 96 ill. Berlin, Gebr. Mann Verlag, 1954.

N 9 VALENTIN, CURT, GALLERY. Reg Butler, Jan. 11—Feb. 5. 16 p. ill. New York, 1955. *Recent works; preface by Roland Penrose*.

N 10 ZÜRICH. KUNSTHAUS. Begründer der modernen Plastik. [44] p. plus 16 ill. 1954. *Exhibit of Arp, Brancusi, Chauvin, Duchamp-Villon, Gonzalez, Laurens, Lipchitz, Pevsner, from Nov. 27–Dec. Includes quotations, biographical notes. Notes on Arp by M. Hagenbach also in Yverdon catalog, bibl. K 22a. Catalog and important bibliography by Hans Bolliger, p. 19–27, includes many recent and unpublicized European citations*.

Photo Credits

Aeschbacher Hans, Zürich 243
Antoine, Paris 192, 193
Archivio fotografico del Comune di Milano 87
ATP Bilderdienst, Zürich 322 (Bill)

Ruth Baehnisch, Düsseldorf-Oberkassel 222, 338 (Kricke)
Oliver Baker, New York 245, 313
Berezov (Kootz Gallery), New York 338 (Lassaw)
Galerie Claude Bernard, Paris 328 (D'Haese), 340 (Penalba)
Dr. H. A. Bernatzik, Wien 138
Betting, Kobenhavn 284 (below), 348 (Thommesen)
La Biennale di Venezia, Rivista Illustrata 191
Paul Bijtebier, Brussels 120
Binia Bill, Zürich 216
Kurt Blum, Bern 303, 315
Grace Borgenicht Gallery, New York 221
Borroni, Legnano 251
Tet Borsig, New York 327 (Callery)
Constantin Brancusi, 40, 66, 124-133, 135-137, 139, 142, 284
  (above), 318
Brassaï, Paris 20 (above right), 214
Brenwasser, New York 262
J. E. Bulloz, Paris 29, 41, 143
Rudolph Burckhardt, New York 182, 183, 249, 273, 274, 275
Jo. Butler, Hatfield, Herts. 327 (Butler)
Reg Butler, Hatfield, Herts. 212, 213

Cahiers d'Art, Paris 65 (below), 85 (below), 91 (below left), 195,
  297, 301
Pierre Cailler, Genève 2, 3
Carjat, Paris 327 (Daumier)
Alfred Carlebach 340 (Moore)
Galerie Louis Carré, Paris 20 (above left), 76 (below)
Leo Castelli Gallery, New York 244
Yvonne Chevalier, Paris 73
Chevojon, Paris 93
A. Cintract, Paris 108
Denise Colombe, Paris 218, 322 (Adam)
Conzett & Huber, Zürich 211
J. Custer-Cornut, Zürich 113

Toso Dabac, Zagreb 247, 281, 322 (Bakic)
Robert Decharnes, Paris 339 (Martin)
Domon-Iken, Tokyo 340 (Noguchi)
Walter Dräyer, Zürich 32
Galerie Druet, Paris 9

Atelier Eidenbenz, Basel 322 (Bodmer)
Hugo Erfurth, Dresden 339 (Moholy-Nagy)

Paul Facchetti, Paris 289
F. Fäh, Gstaad 279
David Farrell, Gloucester 215, 248
Felbermeyer, München 339 (Mataré)
Ferruzi, Venezia 13, 17, 85 (above), 280, 294
Film Publishers Inc., New York 338 (Laurens)
Semo Flechine, Paris 186
Adrienne Füssiner, New York 244, 338 (Kohn)

Naum Gabo, Woodbury, Conn. 168, 169, 179, 180, 181
A. E. Gallatin, Paris 347 (Picasso)
Giacomelli, Venezia 307
C. Giedion-Welcker, Zürich 8, 70 (above), 94, 95, 101 (right),
  322 (Arp)
Giraudon, Paris 49
Ewald Gnilka, Berlin-Charlottenburg 219, 267, 348 (Uhlmann)
Grand Central Moderns, New York 340 (Nevelson)
Marius Gravot, Paris 196 (below left)
René Groebli, Zürich 328 (Ernst)
Solomon R. Guggenheim Museum, New York 51

Ernst Hahn, Kunstgewerbemuseum Zürich 164
Hansa Gallery, New York 264
Härtnagel & Weider, Zürich 256
A. Hébrard, Paris 5, 7 (below)
Peter Heman, Basel 217, 259
Nigel Henderson, London 260
Henrot 230
Hugo P. Herdeg, Zürich 283
Lucien Hervé, Paris 231 (above), 233
Yves Hervochon, Paris 196 (above), 242, 310, 338 (Lipsi)
Hesse, Bern 7 (above)
Friedrich Hewicker, Kaltenkirchen, Holstein 36
Martha Holmes, New York 340 (Nevelson)

Leni Iselin, Paris 348 (Stahly)
Jacques, Paris 43
Luc Joubert, Paris 234, 309, 340 (Robert Müller)
Peter A. Juley & Son, New York 23

Karquel, Aulnay-s/s-Bois (S-et-O) 270
Berni Kaufmann, New York 285 (above left)
Ida Kaw, Camera Press, London 327 (Chadwick)

F. L. Kenett, London 235, 257
Kootz Gallery, New York 225, 261, 249
Kunstmuseum Winterthur 46

Mme. Henri Laurens, Paris 77
Galerie Louise Leiris, Paris 18 (below), 44, 45, 50, 64, 71, 88, 304
Alexander Liberman, New York 328 (Derain)
Walter Lichtenstein, Studio Limot, Paris 338 (Le Corbusier)
Lidbrooke, London 210
Herbert List, München 16 (above)

Peter Löffler, Zürich 70 (right)

Mandello, Paris 308
Mme. H. de Mandrot, Le Pradet 58
Herbert Matter. New York 205, 207, 209, 327 (Calder)
Jean Michalon, Paris 347 (Signori)
Frits Monshouwer, Rotterdam 184
Henry Moore, Hoglands, Much Hadham, Herts. 144 (below), 145, 148
Museé Bourdelle, Paris 30, 31, 327 (Bourdelle)
Museé de Paléonthologie, Paris 109
Museés Nationaux, Paris 25. 86
Museum of Fine Arts, Boston, Mass. 38, 293
Museum of Modern Art, New York 89, 165, 199, 206, 272, 328
  (Ferber), 339 (Miro)
Hans Namuth, New York 246, 338 (Lippold), 340 (Nivola)
O. E. Nelson, New York 286
Lennart Olson, Enskede 337 (Jacobsen)
Cas Oorthuys, Amsterdam 185
Pierre Olry, Paris 268, 347 (Poncet)

Betty Parsons Gallery, New York 313
Perls Gallery, New York 84 (above right)
Moris Perriti, Milano 42
Pérusset, Yverdon 200
H. B. Pflaum, Gebhard, Wien 269
Philadelphia Museum of Art 132
Picardy, Grenoble 140, 141
Porta, Milano 57, 266
Praesens Group, Warsaw 163 (above)
Prodi, Varese 241 (below)

Man Ray, Paris 99, 339 (Matisse)
REP, Paris 19 (left)
Riess, Berlin 322 (Archipenko)
Claire Roessiger, Basel 28
Galerie Rosengart, Luzern 47
M. Routhier, Paris 295
Le Rouzic, Carnac 316, 317

Dr. Salchow, Köln 84
André Sas, Paris 327 (César)
Ernest Scheidegger, Zürich 100, 101, 103, 105, 107, 208, 227, 299,
  337 (Giacometti)
Giovanni Scheiwiller, Milano 16 (below)
Schuh, Davos 328 (van Doesburg)
Schweizer Landesmuseum (Zürich 98 (above)
Ernst Schwitters 228 (right), 347 (Schwitters)
Aaron Siskind, New York 288
R. Spreng, Basel 33
Stable Gallery, New York 273
Hans Stebler, Bern 21
Stichting Museum Boymans, Rotterdam 4
Ezra Stoller, New York 314 (above left)
Studio St. Ives Ltd., St. Ives, Cornwall 152 (below), 153, 155
Adolph Studly, New York 61
Soichi Sunami, New York 89, 206, 298, 339 (Miro)

Tate Gallery, London 10, 39 (right)
Rolf Tietgens, Basel 114, 115
Trewyn Studio, St. Ives, Cornwall 337 (Hepworth)

Curt Valentin Gallery, New York 14
Serge Vandercam, Paris 322 (Bloc)
Marc Vaux, Paris 62, 91 (above right), 240, 277, 285 (below), 291
Jan Versnel, Amsterdam 263
Jacques Villon, Puteaux/Paris 76 (above), 77 79, 81
The Virginia Museum of Fine Arts, (Photo Whitaker), Richmond,
  Virginia 204 (below right)
Catherine Viviano Gallery, New York 312, 347 (Rosenthal)
Vizzavona, Paris 65 (above)

Hugo van Wadenoyen, Cheltenham 327 (Chadwick)
Hugo Weber, Basel 339 (Maillol)
Etienne Bertrand Weill, Paris 118, 119, 121, 238
Hermann Weishaupt, Stuttgart 35, 37, 106
Sabine Weiss, Paris 146
Dietrich Widmer, Basel 271
Willard Gallery, New York 224, 253, 254, 305 (left)
Ruth A. Wuest, Zürich 322 (Aeschbacher)

Yale University Art Gallery, New Haven 56 (right) 78

Books, Prints, Art Magazines published or distributed by George Wittenborn, Inc.

1018 Madison Avenue New York 21, N.Y.

Abstract Artists (ed.) *The World of Abstract Art.* 162 ill. 1957 $8.50
Albers (Josef) *Poems and Drawings.* 21 ill. 1960 $7.50
Alvard (Julien) and S. Lupasco. *Benrath.* 10 ill. 1959 $2.50
American Abstract Artists, Essays by J. Albers, A. E. Gallatin, K. Knaths, F. Leger, L. Moholy-Nagy, P. Mondrian, G. L. K. Morris. Ill. 1946. $2.50
Arango & Martinez, *Arquitectura en Colombia.* 150 ill. 1951. $4.50
Architecture: forms & functions. Vol. 6. 300 ill. 1959 $5.00
Architecture: forms & functions. Vol. 7. 500 ill. 1960 $5.00 (paper) $7.50 (cloth)
Arp (Jean) *Three original wood engravings.* Set $75.00, single $30.00
Art de France. Ed. by P. Beres & Andre Chastel. Vol. 1. 510 ill. color. 1960. $12.50
Atelier 17. Texts by H. Read, J. J. Sweeney, H. Mayor, C. Zigrosser, S. W. Hayter. Ill. 1949. $2.50

Beaudin (A.) *Peintures.* 58 ill. 1957 $2.00
Braque (Georges) *Still Life, 1913,* color silk-screen repr. 1943. $15.00
Brenson (Theodore) *Light into Color, Light into Space.* 22 ill. 1959. $2.50
Bufano (Benjamino) *American Sculptor.* Vol. 1. 122 ill. 1957. $17.50

Calder (Alexander) *The Big "I",* etching 1944. $100.00
Callery (Mary) *Sculpture.* 135 ill. 1960. $10.00
Campigli (Massimo) *Scrupules.* 117 ill. 1957 $5.00
Ceroni (Ambrogio) *Amadeo Modigliani, Peintre.* With English translation. 164 ill. 1958. $15.00
Cuevas (J.) *The Worlds of Kafka and Cuevas.* 20 ill. 1959. $25.00

Debord (Guy-Ernest) *Memoires.* ill. 1959. $10.00
Degas (Edgar) *Huit Sonnets.* Ill. 1946. $4.00
Delacroix (Eugene) *On Art Criticism.* Engl. Tr. 1946. $0.50
Denby (Edwin) *Mediterranean Cities.* 30 ill. 1956. $4.50
Dereux (Philippe) *Raymond Grandjean.* 10 ill. 1959. $2.50
Deroudille (Rene) *Laubiès.* 10 ill. 1957. $3.00
Dey (Mukul) *Birbum Terracottas.* 45 ill. 1959. $3.25
Documenti d'Arte d'Oggi. Details on request
Ditzel (Nanna & Jorgen) *Danish Chairs.* 90 ill., 1954. $6.00

The Documents of Modern Art. Dir.: Robert Motherwell.

d.m.a. 1. G. Apollinaire, *The Cubist Painters,* 12 ill., $2.00
d.m.a. 2. P. Mondrian, *Plastic Art.* 26 ill., 2 in color. Out-of-print
d.m.a. 3. L. Moholy-Nagy, *The New Vision* 84 ill, $2.50
d.m.a. 4. L. H. Sullivan, *Kindergarten Chats.* 18 ill., $4.50
d.m.a. 5. W Kandinsky, *Concerning the Spiritual in Art* $2.50
d.m.a. 6. Jean (Hans) Arp, *On My Way.* 50 ill., 2 color woodcuts. $3.00
d.m.a. 7. Max Ernst, *Beyond Painting.* 140 ill., $3.00
d.m.a. 8. *The Dada Painters and Poets* Edited by Robert Motherwell. 480 p., 180 ill., cloth, $15.00
d.m.a. 9. H. D. Kahnweiler, *The Rise of Cubism* 23 ill., $2.00
d.m.a. 10. M. Raymond, *From Baudelaire to Surrealism* $2.50, cloth ed., $5.00
d.m.a. 11. G. Duthuit, *The Fauvist Painters.* 16 in color. $4.50
d.m.a. 12. C. Giedion-Welcker, *Contemporary Sculpture,* 371 ill., rev. ed., 1960. $16.50
d.m.a. 13. B. Karpel, *Arts of the Twentieth Century.* A selective guide to the literature of the Modern Arts, 1900-1950, 800 pages, 12,000 references, 200 pages of ill., documents, intr. and captions in English, French and German. In preparation.
d.m.a. 14. M. Duchamp, *The Green Box,* 130 ill., 1960. $6.00

Duthuit (Georges) *Le Serpent dans la Galere.* 34 drawings by André Masson. 425 copies. 1945. $10.00

Ernst (Max) *La Femme 100 Tetes.* 149 ill. 1956. $12.50

Far Eastern Antiquities Museum, Stockholm: Bulletin. Details on request
Focillon (Henri) *The Life of Forms in Art.* Ill. 1948. $2.50
Fuller (Sue) *Cock,* color engraving. 1944. $75.00

Gallatin (A. E.) *Paintings.* Ill., 1948. $2.00
Gangoly (O. C.) *Indian Terracotta Art.* 50 ill. 1959. $9.00
George (W.) *Hilaire Hiler and Structuralism.* 8 ill. 1958. $5.00, cloth $7.50
Goswami (A.), ed. *Art of the Pallavas.* 46 ill. 1957. $8.50
Gaswami (A.), ed. *Art of the Rashtrakutas.* 40 ill. 1958 $8.50
Gleizes (Albert) *Le Cubisme 1908-1914.* Cahiers. Vol. 1, Ill. 1957 $3.00
Golding (J.) *Cubism, A History of the Movement 1907-1914.* 127 ill. 1959. $11.50
Great Master Drawings of 7 Centuries. Ed. J. S. Held. 80 ill. 1959. $4.50
Gris (Juan) *Peintures de 1926 et 1927.* 22 Ill. 1958. $2.00

398

Books, Prints, Art Magazines published or distributed by George Wittenborn, Inc.

1018 Madison Avenue New York 21, N. Y.

Haab (Armin) *Mexican Printmakers.* 90 ill. 1957 $8.00
Haas (Terry) and M. Ferrand *Germinal.* Poem. 6 ill. 1958. $35.00
Hammer (Victor) *Memory and Her Nine Daughters.* 1957. $9.50
Hammer (Victor) *On Architecture.* Ill. 250 copies. 1952. $6.00
Hayter (Stanley William) *Flight,* engraving 1944. $100.00
Honegger (Gottfried) *Transmissions: seven original lithographs.* 1954. $75.00
Honegger (Gottfried) *Fiktion und Realität.* 5 color litho. 1956. $25.00
Hostettler (R.) *Technical Terms of the Printing Industry.* 1959. $3.50
Howarth (T.) *Charles Rennie Mackintosh and the Modern Movement.* 250 ill. 1952. $10.00

Idea: International Design Annual, vol. 2, 1953-1954. $8.50
Ioannou (A. S.) *Byzantine Frescoes of Euboea.* 103 ill. 1959. $10.00

Janco (M.) *Dada, Monograph of a Movement.* 300 ill. 1957. $10.00
Jonsdottir (S.) *11th Cent. Byzantine Last Judgment in Iceland.* 66 ill. $8.50

Kahnweiler (D.-H.) *50 Ans d'Edition de D.-H. Kahnweiler.* Intr. & Catalogue par J. Hugues, 30 ill., color. 1959. $2.00
Kent (Adaline) *Autobiography.* 78 ill. 1958 $5.00
Kermadec (E. de) *Peinture 1927-1957.* 60 ill. 1958 $2.00
Klee (Paul) *The Thinking Eye.* 1200 ill. 1961 $25.00

Lascaux (Elie) *Peintures 1921-59.* 63 ill. 1959. $2.00
Laurens (Henri) Intr. by A. Giacometti. 40 ill. 1960. $4.00
Laurens (Henri) *Sculpteurs en Pierre 1919-1943.* 28 ill. 1959 $2.00
LeCorbusier *Antonio Gaudi.* 61 ill. 1958 $6.50
Le Corbusier *Complete Works, 1910-1960.* 800 ill. 1960. $15.00
Le Corbusier, *Oeuvre Complete,* vol. 5, 1946-52, 700 ill. 1953. $13.50
LeCorbusier *Complete Works, Vol.* 6 1952-57. 500 ill. 1957 $13.50
Leger (Fernand) *Dessins et gouaches 1909-1955.* 87 ill. 1958 $2.00
Lewis (David) *Constantin Brancusi.* 65 ill. 1958. $3.50
Lewis (David) *Mondrian: His Paintings.* 10 ill. 1957 $2.50
18 Litografias de Artistas Argentinos: Badii, Fernandez, Muro, Sarah Grilo, Hlito, Lanus, Ocampo, Presas, Ideal Sanchez, Torres Aguero. 9 color and 9 black and white lithographs, each signed in stone by the artist. 19 by 14 inches, pulled 500 copies, 1955. $30.00

Mac Agy (Douglas) *James Boynton. American Painter.* 14 ill. 1959. $3.95
Madsen (St. T.) *Art Nouveau (Sources, History).* 263 ill. wrappers. 1956 $18.50
Magalhaes (A.) and E. Feldman *Doorway to Portuguese.* 12 ill. 1957. $7.50
Magalhaes (A.) and E. Feldman *Doorway to Brasilia.* 15 ill. 1959. $12.50
Maldonado (T.) *Max Bill.* 84 ill. 1956. $7.50
Marchal (G. L.) *Zadkine, His Life and Work.* 11 ill. 1956. $4.50
Masson (Andre) *Peintures.* 63 ill. 1957. $2.00
Masson (Andre) *Mythology of Being.* Ill. 1942. $10.00, ed. with original etching $75.00
Mathieu (Georges) *From the Abstract to the Possible.* ill. 1960. $3.50
mETRO. Ed. by Bruno Alfieri. Review of contemporary Art. Details on request
Mocsanyi (Paul) *Karl Knaths.* 60 ill. 1958. $5.00
Modern Artists in America: 1st. Series: A Biennial of Art in America. Ed. by Robert Motherwell, Ad Reinhardt, Bernard Karpel. 150 ill. $6.50
Muehsam (Alice) *German Readings: A Brief Survey.* 1959. $3.50
Munari (Bruno) *The Discovery of the Square.* 120 ill. 1960. $3.60

New Furniture, vol. 4. 1956-57. Edited by Gerd Hatje. ill. $9.00
New Graphic Design. Ed. by R. Lohse, et al. Details on request
Noguchi (Isamu) *His Sculptures:* Japan 1931 and 1950-52. ill. 1954. $9.50

Palencia (C.) *Leonardo Nierman.* 24 ill. 1958. $3.00
Picasso (Pablo) *Peintures 1955-56.* 50 ill. 1957. $3.00
Picasso (Pablo) *Les Menines.* 57 ill. 1959, $2.50
Picasso (Pablo) *45 Gravures sur Linoléum, 1958-60.* $2.00
Picasso (Pablo) *Dessins, 1959-60. Romancero du Picador.* ill. 1960. $2.00
Picasso (Pablo) *Lithographs 1945-1948.* Intr. by B. Geiser, 67 ill. 1948. $3.00

Problems of Contemporary Art

p.c.a. 2. H. Read, *The Grass Roots of Art.* Ill. $2.50
p.c.a. 4. *Possibilities,* vol 1. An occasional Review, ed. by John Cage (music), Pierre Chareau (architecture), Robert Motherwell (art), Harold Rosenberg (writing). Ill. $2.50
p.c.a. 5. G. Vantongerloo, *Paintings, Sculptures, Reflections.* Ill. 1948. $3.00
p.c.a. 7. R. Sowers, *The Lost Art;* a survey of 1000 years of stained glass. 75 ill., 4 in color. 1954. $5.00

Books, Prints, Art Magazines published or distributed by George Wittenborn, Inc.

1018 Madison Avenue New York 21, N. Y.

Quadrum—A Semi-Annual Report on Modern Art. Ed. W. Grohmann, Georges Salles, Herbert Read, Robert Goldwater. Details on request

Rand (Paul) *Trademarks*. 28 color ill. 425 copies. 1960. $7.50
Rand (Paul) *Thoughts on Design*. Ill. rev. ed. 1951. $10.00
Read (H.) *Wassily Kandinsky, Paintings & Watercolors*. 16 ill. 1959 $2.50
Rety (Louis) *Fely Mouttet, Peintre*. 12 ill. 1958. $2.00
Rilke (Rainer Maria) *The Sonnets of Orpheus*. With nine engravings by Kurt Roesch. 1944. $120.00
Ring des Arts. Ed. by Cercle d'Art Contemporain, Brussels, Paris, Zurich. Details on request
Rodin (Auguste) *A la Venus de Milo*. Ill. 1946. $4.00
Roger (Suzanne) *Peinture 1923-58*. Int. by G. Limbour. 65 ill. 1958. $2.00

Samstag (N.) *Kay-Kay comes Home*. 23 drawings by Ben Shahn. 1952. $1.00
Sandström (Sven) *Le Monde Imaginaire d'Odilon Redon*. 136 ill. 1955. $7.50
Saraswati (S. K.) *Glimpses of Mughal Architecture*. 60 ill. 1953. $23.60
Schanker (Louis) *Line, Form, Color*. Five color prints. $150.00
Schweizer Grafiker-Graphistes Suisses. Directory of 137 members of the VSG. 800 ill. 1960. $13.50
Seuphor (Michel) *Lee Hersch, Abstract Artist*. 12 ill. 1954. $2.50
Seuphor (Michel) *Berto Lardera, his Sculptures, Drawings*. $2.50
Shorr (Dorothy C.) *The Christ Child in Devotional Images in Italy during the XIV century*. 450 ill., 1953. $6.50
Stokes (Adrian) *Claude Monet Portfolio*. 8 ill. 1958. $2.50
Structure Series. Ed. by Joost Baljeu. Details on request
Structurist (The) Ed. by Eli Bornstein, vol. 1, 51 ill. color. 1960-61. $2.50
Sweeney (J. J.) *The Miro Atmosphere*. 93 ill. 1959. $7.50

Tapie (M.) *Claire Falkenstein*. 19 ill. 1959. $4.50
Tapie (M.) *Antonio Tapies*. 46 ill. 1959. $7.50
Tapie (M.) *Observations*. Ed. by P. & E. Jenkins. ill. 1956. $3.50
Teshigahara (Sofu) *Portfolio*. 31 ill. $9.00
Teshigahara (Sofu) *Sculpture 1957-58*. 37 ill. $6.00
trans/formation: arts, communication, environment. A world review. Ed. by Harry Holtzmann and Martin James. Vol. 1, no. 1. 1950. $2.50

Vokolo (Helen) *Contemporary Greek Painters*. 110 ill. color. 1961. $15.00
Vingtieme Siecle (XX Century). Details on request

Wilke (Ulfert) *One, Two and More*. Portfolio of 23 calligraphic Sumi Paintings. 300 copies. 1960. $20.00
Wilke (Ulfert) *Fragments from Nowhere*. 19 ill. 1959. $16.00

Yale University School of Design. *Portfolio of Student Work*. 37 ill. 1954. $1.00

Zodiac. A Semi-Annual Report on Internat'l Contemp. Architecture. Details on request